Planning for Rites and Rituals

A Resource for Episcopal Worship, Year B, 2017–2018

Planning for Rites and Rituals

A Resource for Episcopal Worship, Year B, 2017–2018

Church Publishing
NEW YORK

Church Publishing Incorporated
Editorial Offices
19 East 34th Street
New York, NY 10016

Cover design by: Jennifer Kopec, 2 Pug Design
Typeset by: Progressive Publishing Services

Printed in the United States of America

A record of this book is available from the Library of Congress.

ISBN: 978-0-89869-180-1

Contents

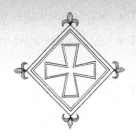

Lent

Holy Week

Easter

Pentecost

WELCOME

Welcome to the inaugural edition of *Planning for Rites and Rituals*. All of us at Church Publishing are pleased to bring you this new resource for liturgical planning.

The editorial team (Nancy Bryan, Sharon Ely Pearson, and Milton Brasher-Cunningham) tasked with creating this volume worked with some amazing folks to bring you a wide range of thought-provoking, creative options for Sundays and holy days throughout the liturgical year. Looking for ways to engage a range of ages? It's here. Looking for help "seeing" the images in each week's scripture? We've got that. Want hymns keyed to the lectionary or brief introductions to the scriptures? It's all here, in a single resource.

You will find this resource offers two areas for engaging in planning, grouped by liturgical season and date. Each season begins with a "Preparing for . . . " section designed to get you thinking and your creative juices flowing. "Seasonal Rites" follows, offering expansive ideas for worship within or outside the primary Sunday service. Following these two overview documents, every Sunday's set of resources offers all you need for putting together a Sunday (or holy day) service as well as other ideas for formation and community engagement within and beyond your church doors.

Dozens of individuals were part of the creation of this all-in-one volume. Priests, educators, musicians, members of Altar Guilds, and many others are featured within these pages. Our intention is to provide a similar mix of established writers, new voices—those working in small parishes and those in larger ones, those in rural locales and those in cities, clergy and lay—in each new volume of this resource over the years to come.

Here is a description of the areas to deepen themes of each Sunday and holy day, along with those who have contributed their creative ideas this year:

Engaging all ages offers ideas for deepening all ages in their engagement with worship (children, youth, and adults). They include thoughts for the congregation to take home and discuss, things to notice or highlight during worship (colors, senses, symbols, gestures), and ideas for action. Contributors for these portions are: Roger Hutchison, Director of Christian Formation and Parish Life at Palmer Memorial Church in Houston; Wendy Claire Barrie, Program Manager of Children and Youth at Trinity Wall Street; and Elizabeth Hammond, retired Christian educator of St. Paul's Episcopal Church in Greenville, South Carolina.

Prayers of intercession are the offerings of Lowell Grisham, priest at St. Paul's Episcopal Church in Fayetteville Arkansas.

Ideas for the day offers thoughts for approaching the day and its text in preaching and worship, including contemporary issues, movies, technology and social media, literature, historical events, and figures related to the Sunday lections and season. Contributing these ideas are: Linda Nichols, a Christian educator in Gadsen, Alabama; Jake Owensby is the fourth bishop of the Episcopal Diocese of Western Louisiana; Valerie Bailey Fischer, adjunct lecturer at Bexley Hall Seabury Western Theological Federation; Miguelina Espinal-Howell, dean of Christ Church Cathedral, Hartford, Connecticut; Emily Slichter Given, director of parish participation at Saint Thomas Church, Whitemarsh, Pennsylvania; Ernesto Medina, rector of St. Martha's Episcopal Church in Papillion, Nebraska; Mike Angell, rector of the Episcopal Church of the Resurrection in St. Louis; Jay Fluellen, composer, organist, and choir director of the African American Episcopal Church of St. Thomas in Philadelphia; and Sharon Ely Pearson, Christian educator from Norwalk, Connecticut.

Making connections offers insights into connecting our Episcopal tradition to each Sunday. This may take the form of referencing other areas of the Book of Common Prayer, our Baptismal Covenant, or faith in daily life. Contributors here are: Mark Bozzuti-Jones, priest for pastoral care at Trinity Wall Street; Demi Prentiss, small

Welcome

congregation lay leader and ministry developer from Fort Worth; and Megan Castellan, associate rector and day school chaplain at St. Paul's Episcopal Church in Kansas City, Missouri.

Images in the reading taps into the metaphors, names, history, and theology that are found in the day's lections. Gail Ramshaw, well-known author and speaker, provides these rich resources.

Hymn suggestions are drawn from Carl Daw Jr. and Thomas Pavlechko's *Liturgical Music for the Revised Common Lectionary, Year B* (Church Publishing Incorporated, 2008). These compliment the theme and readings of the day and come from *Hymnal 1982, Lift Every Voice and Sing II,* and *Wonder, Love, and Praise*

Your feedback and perspective, of course, are also critical to these efforts. Let us hear from you—what would you appreciate seeing? What was most helpful? Who are the writers you would recommend to us for future editions?

Thank you for the trust you put in Church Publishing Incorporated to provide liturgical planning tools for your parish use. We value our partnership on the journey and are grateful for the many ways in which you care for the church's worship.

YEAR B: THE YEAR OF MARK AND JOHN

The design of the Revised Common Lectionary Year B follows Mark's gospel and is supplemented by readings from the Gospel of John in Advent, Christmas, Epiphany, Lent, and Easter; and in the time after Pentecost, five Sundays of readings from John 6.

The Gospel of Mark

Not only is Mark the earliest of the four canonical gospels, but it is the first piece of literature to which we have given the name *gospel*, a word that describes both the book's genre and its subject: the gospel, *evangelion*, "good news." The first line of Mark announces itself as "The beginning of the good news of Jesus Christ, the Son of God." The "beginning" speaks of both the beginning of the book and the origin of the good news that the narrative itself proclaims. The Gospel of Mark tells the story of Jesus without reference to its author (cf. John 19:35; 21:24) or the circumstances of its writing (cf. Luke 1:1-2). The omniscient narrator tells the story with absolute authority from the citation of the prophet Isaiah in 1:2-3 to the silent flight from the tomb in 16:8. The narrator relates the story of Jesus in the language and imagery of the scriptures of Israel, creating a rich texture of allusions to exodus, exile, prophets, law, and covenant. The style is fast-paced, lacking smooth transitions between episodes. Its spare narrative casts specific details in high relief.

The World Behind the Text

Written around 70 CE during the violence of the Jewish war with Rome or after the destruction of the temple, the gospel presents traditions about Jesus' teaching and healing ministry, words and deeds, and an extended narrative of the events of his passion and death. Scholars have placed the gospel in Rome, Syria, or another part of the Roman Empire. The social setting of Mark's community is one of suffering and marginalization in Roman occupied Palestine. In its depiction of the scribes and Pharisees as opponents of Jesus and in details of the trial, it reflects early stages in the mutual self-definition between the early Christian assembly and the Jewish community from which it came. The gospel shows Jesus reinforcing the teaching of Torah and emphasizing its true intention (Mark 7:9-23; 10:1-12; 12:28-34). Mark is the primary literary source for the composition of the Gospels of Matthew and Luke and a strong influence on John. The depiction of women as exemplars of faith and of the values taught by Jesus (1:30-31; 5:25-34; 7:24-30; 12:41-44; 14:1-9; 15:40-41; 16:1-8) may indicate the prominence of women as leaders in the ministry of Jesus and in the community of Mark's gospel.

The World in Front of the Text

Church historian Eusebius cites Papias's testimony that the gospel was written by Mark, who interpreted Peter's experience. Christian leaders in the second century thought it important to link the inherited gospels to apostles who knew Jesus. Sometime in the process of transmission, the shorter ending (16:8b) and the longer ending (16:9-20) were added to the original gospel, perhaps to resolve the mysterious ending and to make it resemble the pattern of the other gospels that report appearances of the risen Jesus.

How the Gospel "Works"

Literary critical scholarship on Mark has explored Mark as story, and studies of orality in the early Christian context have given renewed attention to how the story of Mark would have been heard. Contemporary performance of Mark displays how the drama plays out, creating suspense, surprise, irony, and paradox. Individual episodes refer backward and forward with repeated key words, summoning the entire good news. To preach one episode of healing or teaching in Mark, reading it in the larger context of the whole story, is most powerful.

As a rhetorical work, the Gospel of Mark does something to those who hear it. The good news provokes emotion and motivates to action. Older scholarship spoke of the outline or structure of Mark as a passion narrative with an extended introduction, noting that Mark 1–8 showed Jesus as a divine man doing deeds of power, then seeming to reverse or correct that picture with a narrative of arrest, humiliation, and death. Literary criticism explicated the plot of Mark in which the identity of Jesus as Messiah was both revealed and concealed as the story progressed. Understanding Mark as rhetorical performance highlights how the reader/hearer experiences the story: you know the end, and it is still a shock; you experience the shift from power to powerlessness; you are propelled from the tomb to speak or not and to meet Jesus in Galilee "just as he told you" (16:7). Some interpreters have read Mark's gospel as itself an ordeal or baptism into death as a kind of literary-liturgical journey.

The World of the Text: Narrative Arc and Peak Events

The citation of the prophet Isaiah in Mark 1:2-3 (actually, Malachi *and* Isaiah), followed by John baptizing in the wilderness, summons up the setting of the Exile and prophetic vision of redemption. Readers are propelled into Galilee, where God and Satan are at war for control of the cosmos, the society, and the human individual. Jesus' exorcisms demonstrate that he casts evil spirits from unwilling human hosts as he casts out a legion of demons into the countryside (5:1-20); the strong man is bound in order to plunder his house (3:23-27). Controversy ensues as conflict with the religious authorities escalates, and the disciples, despite being given the secret of the kingdom of God (4:11), misunderstand and misinterpret Jesus' teaching and the significance of his deeds of power. Jesus' family attempts to restrain him (3:21). At the same time, many without privilege exhibit confidence in Jesus' power to heal, those who are in desperate need of healing for themselves or someone close to them: a leper (1:40), friends of the paralyzed man (2:3-4), Jairus (5:22-23), a bleeding woman (5:25), and a Syro-phoenician woman (7:25). Readers/hearers of Mark are caught up in the ironic dynamic that those on the inside misunderstand while those on the outside or at the edge respond with faith: "your faith has made you well" ("saved you") (5:34; 10:52).

Readers, like the characters in Mark, are confronted with how to comprehend Jesus' teaching that the Son of Man must be killed and rise again, announced three times with intensifying detail (8:31; 9:31; 10:33-34). Will they seek positions of glory as James and John and the Gentiles (10:42) or be those who lose their lives for "my sake, and for the sake of the gospel" (8:35)? Jesus' teaching in Mark

8:27—10:45 is bracketed by two stories of Jesus healing a blind man, one at Bethsaida, where Jesus gives sight in two stages (8:22-26), and another outside of Jericho, where Bartimaeus asks for and receives his sight, then follows Jesus "on the way" (10:46-52). In the oral performance of the gospel, these two stories evoke the reality of partial sight/knowledge and the difficulty and remarkable gift of complete sight.

The climactic episode in the drama of knowing/not knowing, saving and losing, opens the passion narrative. At Bethany, a woman breaks open a jar of costly ointment and pours it on Jesus' head while he sits at the table. Her prophetic action of anointing Jesus' head and Jesus' acknowledgment that she has "anointed my body beforehand for its burial" (14:8) reveal the paradoxical truth that the anointed one is also the one who will die. Rather than being wasteful, her pouring out all the ointment is the epitome of the way of life that Jesus teaches: losing life to save it. For this reason, her "good service" will be told wherever the gospel is proclaimed "in remembrance of her" (14:9).

The passion narrative recounts Jesus' betrayal and arrest, desertion by his followers, trial, torture, and execution by his enemies. Having exhibited extraordinary power in Galilee, Jesus becomes seemingly powerless and mostly silent, the one able to save others but unable to save himself (15:31). Jesus' cry from the cross, "My God, my God, why have you forsaken me?" expresses abandonment and despair, a realistic depiction of human loneliness and death.

Three critical moments of the naming of Jesus as Son punctuate the gospel. The first is at his baptism, when a voice from heaven says, "You are my Son, the Beloved; with you I am well pleased" (1:11). The second is at his transfiguration, when a voice from the cloud says, "This is my Son, the Beloved; listen to him!" (9:7). The third is after his death, when a centurion says, "Truly this man was God's Son!" (15:39). These three voices resonate within the hearers of the gospel, setting up an implicit but unexplained relationship between baptism, transfiguration, and crucifixion.

Mary Magdalene, Mary the mother of James, and Salome's arrival at the tomb culminates the theme of women following and serving Jesus (1:30-31; 15:40-41) and recalls the anointing at the table at Bethany (14:3-9). The young man announces "He has been raised" and commissions the women to tell the others that "he is going ahead of you to Galilee; there you will see him" (16:6, 7). The ambiguous conclusion—that the women flee in silence and fear—has often been interpreted as failure and lack of faith. However, other heroes in the biblical tradition (Daniel, John,

Ezekiel, Isaiah) are overcome by fear and struck dumb by extraordinary revelation. When they behold Jesus' resurrection, the faithful women fear, tremble, and are amazed. The gospel ends in the moments before their speech, anticipating reunion with Jesus in Galilee and ongoing ministry to restore the world.

Mark in Year B

The pattern of the Revised Common Lectionary, built around themes of the liturgical season, governs the placement of readings from Mark: in Advent, Jesus' apocalyptic speech (13:24-37) and the appearance of John baptizing (1:1-8); in the time after Epiphany, controversies and healings (Mark 1) and transfiguration (9:2-10); in Lent, Jesus' temptation and first passion prediction; and in the time after Pentecost, passages from Mark 3–13. The Markan passion narrative is assigned for the Sunday of the Passion, and the story of the sending out from the empty tomb, on Easter Sunday. Notable omissions from the RCL are the parable of the sower and teaching about parables (4:1-25), the exorcism of the Gerasene demoniac (5:1-20), and the two-stage healing of the blind man at Bethsaida (8:22-26). Readings from the Gospel of John in each season interrupt the connected narrative of Mark.

Within the liturgical year, the preacher can exploit the dramatic arc of Mark by drawing on the whole gospel when preaching on one episode. The paradox of seeing/not seeing, saving/losing, being served/serving, and power/weakness run throughout the gospel. Resurrection happens in Galilee when Peter's mother-in-law rises to serve and when Jesus tells the one who is paralyzed and the one whose hand is withered to rise (2:11; 3:3). The exorcism of Legion from the man in the tombs, the healing of the bleeding woman, and the raising of Jairus's daughter are all stories of resurrection that amplify the significance of Jesus' teaching and his death. Other key words such as *bread*, *serve*, *clothes*, and *save* set up resonances that reward spiritual and homiletical reflection.

The Gospel of John in Year B

The Gospel of John has its own narrative and symbolic integrity. Using a style and sensibility very different than Mark, John portrays Jesus as the preexistent Word who descends to "his own" and ascends at the time of his exaltation. The fourth gospel interprets the crucifixion as Jesus' being lifted up (John 3:14; 8:28; 12:32, 34). The motif of Jesus' "hour," summarizing the paschal mystery, runs through the entire gospel. Readings from John in year B are concentrated in Lent (3, 4, 5) and Easter (2, 4, 5, 6, 7). John's narration of events shapes the liturgies of Holy Week. Five Sundays in the time after Pentecost explore Jesus' bread of life discourse in John 6. Lenten readings from John use distinctive Johannine images: destroying and raising the temple, lifting up the Son of Man, dying and bearing much fruit to anticipate the resurrection. Readings in the Easter season recount the appearances to the disciples and Thomas, Jesus as good shepherd and true vine, and the prayer for the disciples from his farewell discourse. With John, as with Mark, effective preaching connects an individual passage in John with its role in the imaginative world of the whole gospel.

The Very Reverend Cynthia Briggs Kittredge
Dean and president, Seminary of the Southwest, Austin, Texas

Advent

Preparing for Advent

Overview

"O Come, O Come, Emmanuel." (Hymn 56, *Hymnal 1982*)

"Come, Thou Long-Expected Jesus, born to set thy people free. . . ." (Hymn 66, *Hymnal 1982*)

"Lo! he comes with clouds descending, once for our salvation slain. . . ." (Hymn 57/58, *Hymnal 1982*)

Ending and Beginning.
Darkness. Light. Hoping. Watching. Waiting.

The word Advent, of course, is from the Latin for "coming". The hymns reference above make that clear. But for whom, or for what, are we waiting? Advent is often described as a season of preparation for Christmas. Yes, of course it is. But it is so much more than that. We wait for a baby to be born in Bethlehem two thousand years ago, as we depict in our Christmas pageants each year. But, equally importantly, we rejoice in the presence of our Lord Jesus with us now, every day and in every person. We look for (with both longing and holy fear) Christ's Second Coming as the consummation of all things, when "we will see face to face" (1 Corinthians 13:12 NRSV). We are looking for "God's coming in every way and time possible."[1] William Petersen says that Advent is about, above all, "the manifestation of God's reign"[2]

While the program year in many of our parishes begins in September, Advent is the beginning of the liturgical year in the western church. It is the dawn of the Paschal Mystery in which we participate through baptism and Eucharist. (While the Paschal Mystery is commonly thought of as Christ's death and resurrection, in the early church it was often understood to encompass all of Christ's work, from Incarnation to Second Coming.) In Advent, we look toward Nativity, Incarnation, Epiphany, Passion, Resurrection, Ascension, Second Coming, and the Reign of God in its fullness. And while Advent has some parallels with Lent, it is, more than anything else, a season of faithful, expectant, joyful, watchful waiting.

Advent can be a challenge. Society at large tends to start celebrating Christmas in October or November, and we may feel the temptation to rush to Christmas, too. Perhaps we, too, can't wait, or we feel that it is fruitless to try and observe Advent in the midst of a society that has been in Christmas mode for weeks already. However, a well-thought-out Advent, fully and intentionally celebrated, provides needed preparation and a needed setting for a full and rich Christmas season.

Environment

- Advent is an ideal time to assess your worship space. Is it being used as fully and creatively as possible? Are font, altar/table, and place where the Word of God is proclaimed equally accessible (both visually and aurally) and given equal dignity?
- If your space permits, create a path or walkway that emphasizes that Advent is a journey.

    This is especially appropriate if you have candidates who are preparing for baptism on the feast of the Baptism of our Lord in January (one of the recommended baptismal days in the 1979 Book of Common Prayer)[3] This can work for Lent as well,

---

[1] *Sundays and Seasons Year C* 2016 (Minneapolis: Augsburg Fortress, 2015), 23.
[2] http://theadventproject.org/Documents/rationale.pdf; accessed October 25, 2016.

[3] Advent is an ideal season for baptismal preparation, even if it is rarely used that way. *The Book of Occasional Services* (BOS) provides a form for the enrollment of candidates for baptism, and the rubrics note that candidates are enrolled at the beginning of Advent for baptism on the feast of the Baptism of Our Lord; *The Book of Occasional Services* (New York: Church Publishing, 2003), 116. How would our understanding of Advent change if we saw it as a time for baptismal preparation in addition to its other emphases?

Advent

especially if your parish has candidates who will be baptized at Easter.

♦ Think about how to decorate the worship space for Advent. Schedule an intergenerational event two or three weeks before Advent begins. At this, an Advent wreath for the parish, and Advent wreaths for the home, can be made. An Advent banner and/or stars for the worship space (referencing, perhaps, the Advent hymn "Creator of the Stars of Night") are other possibilities.

♦ Think about ways to use a good quantity of blue or purple cloth in your worship space.

Liturgy

Think about where seasonal elements would be appropriate:

♦ The Advent wreath. Make sure that it is an appropriate size for the space and that it is visually significant. The *Book of Occasional Services* recommends that the lighting of the wreath be done without "special prayers or ceremonial elaboration" (30). However, if your parish wishes to do more around the lighting, look at suggestions of The Advent Project (http://theadventproject.org/Documents/AdventWreathLighting.pdf; accessed November 12, 2016) and the resources in *Evangelical Lutheran Worship* (*ELW*) (Leaders Desk Edition, 60-63), *Sundays and Seasons* (*S & S*) ("Seasonal Rites"), and the *Book of Common Worship* of the Presbyterian Church (U.S.A.) (*BCW*) (165-167).[4]

♦ Opening Acclamation. Seasonal options are found in *Enriching Our Worship 1* (*EOW 1*) (50).[5]

♦ The *Gloria* is not sung during Advent. The *Trisagion* or *Kyrie* may be sung instead. Or, because "some other song of praise" is permitted in place of the *Gloria* (1979 *BCP*, 356), consider canticles such as "The Song of Mary" (15), "The Song of Zechariah" (16), "The First Song of Isaiah" (9), and "The Song of the Redeemed" (19). Possible canticles are found in the 1979 BCP (85-96) and *EOW 1* (25-41).

♦ Prayers of the People. Consider using a different format for each season, and craft the petitions

with the season in mind. Look at the guidelines and suggestions in the 1979 BCP (383) and *EOW 1* (54-55). "Maranatha!" or "Come, Lord Jesus!" are possible congregational responses to the petitions during this season. Be creative in the choice of a closing collect (see guidelines and provided collects in the 1979 *BCP* [394-395] and *EOW 1* [54-55]). Look at the seasonal resources in *ELW* (60-63, 138-139), *S & S* ("Seasonal Rites") the Church of England's *Common Worship: Times and Seasons* (*CW*) (36-37),[6] and *A New Zealand Prayer Book* (*NZPB*) as well (525-526).[7] *BCW* contains fine seasonal resources, too (165-177), including a Litany for Advent, based on the O Antiphons (166-167), which could be used to structure the various categories for which we are called to pray. Consider another prayer from *BCW* to conclude the Prayers of the People: "Strengthen us, O God, in the power of your Spirit, to bring good news to the poor, and lift blind eyes to sight, to loose the chains that bind, and claim your blessing for all people. Keep us faithful in your service until Christ comes in final victory, and we shall feast with all your saints in the joy of your eternal realm. Through Christ . . ." (171).

♦ The eucharistic prayer. Think about the different emphases of the available Eucharistic prayers. Eucharistic Prayer B (1979 BCP, 367-369) and Eucharistic Prayer 3 (*EOW 1*, 62-65) would be especially appropriate for Advent.

♦ Fraction Anthem. See the options in *EOW 1* (69).

♦ Postcommunion Prayer. *EOW 1* provides an alternative (69).

♦ Blessing. This is required in Rite I and optional in Rite II. See the options in *BOS* (22-23), *EOW 1* (70-71), *CW* (41), and *NZPB* (526).

♦ Think about using "An Order of Worship for the Evening," one of the underused gems of this prayer book. A version including Advent elements is available on The Advent Project's website: http://theadventproject.org/Documents/Practica.pdf, 12-15; accessed November 13, 2016. It may be used on its own or may replace the entrance rite of the Eucharist (1979 BCP, 112).

♦ Think about ways to use the O Antiphons; e.g., at the lighting of the Advent wreath, as responses

---

[4] *Sundays and Seasons 2016* (Minneapolis: 1517 Media).
[5] Standing Liturgical Commission, *Enriching Our Worship: Supplemental Liturgical Materials* (New York: Church Publishing Incorporated, 1998).

[6] *Common Worship: Times and Seasons.* Church House Publishing ©The Archbishop's Council 2006.
[7] *A New Zealand Prayer Book.* Collins Liturgical Publications ©1989 The Church of the Province of New Zealand.

during the Liturgy of the Word, at the offertory, or during communion.

In every season, think about how to include children and teens whenever possible.

Laurence Hull Stookey reminds us that "worship during Advent should ever clearly and forcefully proclaim the fullness of the coming of Christ into our midst—future, past, and present."[8]

Lectionary

In Year B, key themes are longing for divine intervention; hope in, and watchfulness for, Jesus' second coming; faithfulness in working and waiting; repentance (especially in the message of John the Baptist); the revelation of the mystery of God in Emmanuel, "God with us"; and rejoicing in that revelation.

Music

+ *Hymnal 1982*, and many other resources, contain wonderful Advent hymns and songs. These tend to get overlooked if we rush to start singing Christmas carols too soon. Think outside the box. "Joy to the World," for example, is as appropriate for Advent as it is for Christmas. Think about songs of light (e.g., "I Want to Walk as a Child of the Light"), songs of waiting and hope ("Wait for the Lord" [Taize] and "O God Our Help in Ages Past"), and songs that look toward the Reign of God ("Jesus Shall Reign" and "O Day of Peace"). Consider options in the hymnal under "The Kingdom of God" and "Christian Responsibility." *Lift Every Voice and Sing* is a rich resource, as are *Wonder, Love, and Praise* and *Voices Found*.
+ Consider Advent hymn texts that have been set to Christmas tunes. The United Methodist Church has compiled a helpful list: http://www.umcdiscipleship.org/resources/advent-hymns-set-to-christmas-tunes; accessed December 3, 2016.
+ A service of Advent Lessons and Carols is not only a beautiful service for the season but a great opportunity to sing old favorites and classics and introduce new songs. See the options in *BOS* (31-34) and *CW* (44-49).
+ Remember the importance of silence. Advent is an ideal time to begin practicing and becoming comfortable with silence in worship.

[8] Laurence Hull Stookey, *Calendar: Christ's Time for the Church* (Nashville: Abingdon Press, 1996), 131.

Formation/Activities

+ Consider holding intergenerational events (one just before each season, perhaps). These can provide an organizing structure for the season ahead and reinforce the unity of the community. They also provide an opportunity for ongoing—*lifelong*—formation and learning. A pre-Advent event can be a time to make Advent wreaths and other decorations for both church and home, and to talk about the Advent season and how to embrace it fully.
+ Organize a season-long study session around the O Antiphons.

Through the Eyes of a Child

During Advent, we, along with our families and all who are the church, wait for the birth of the baby Jesus, who is a gift God gave to us and to all people because God loves us so much and has made us one big family. It is a time we prepare for when Jesus will come again to earth, and God will be in all and make all things new. During this season, we ask what we can give to others to celebrate the fact that in Jesus, God loves us so much his promise to be with us always is complete. In Advent, we tell stories of hope and promise and wonder how the light breaks through the darkness. The Advent wreath helps us to count the days and weeks toward Christmas, a circle of evergreen shows us that God's love never ends, and we light candles (one for each Sunday of Advent) to help us remember that Jesus brings the light into the world.

Through the Eyes of Youth

In Advent we advertise that we have faith in the birth of Jesus as well as faith that Christ will come again. We in the church prepare for the birth of Christ by giving the gift of ourselves as we wait in joy. It is a time of action: Hold onto the promise that Christ will come again by hosting an "alternative gift fair" such as an angel tree in which members of your community can provide gifts to those in your community who are in need. Pray, ask, and respond: Who are the people in our world who need the message of God's love? What are our hopes for how people today can receive the message of God's love? How do we help others know God's love?

Advent

Through the Eyes of Daily Life

Advent is a time of preparation, of patience, of remembering what grounds and sustains us. The function of Advent is to remind us who God is and who we are meant to be, as well. Advent is about the riches of emptiness. God coming as an infant without retinue or riches is the metaphor of a humility that requires us to remember how really small we are in the universe. In our secular culture, a tone of wanting more, spending more, and accumulating riches on earth surround us. As Christians, we long for our society to live up to God's vision, for the kingdom to come in its fullness outside of materialism. The cry of Advent, "Wake up! Be alert! Watch for his coming" is difficult amidst the busyness of the season. We can practice some simple, but not easy, disciplines. We can fast from the media to become more alert to the still small voice of God. We can focus on the giving of ourselves to God. Plan to spend time apart from the busyness of the season each day so you can be alert to God in the silent, the small, and the simple.

Through the Eyes of the Global Community

Advent is a time of concern for God's judgment, particularly in reference to the coming kingdom. The power of this theme of judgment brings about a realization of the sinfulness of the present age. As Christians, we believe it is Jesus who bears this judgment through his life, death, and resurrection, revealing the reign of God to the church in every generation. Our Eucharistic Prayer reminds us that Christ will come again. This is the hope for Advent, and this is the hope we find in the Lord's Prayer in "thy will be done" and "thy Kingdom come." These familiar words call us into a reality of the real presence of Christ in our lives as we look at our own response to today's world. The Collects of Advent remind us how we are living in the reality of Christ's presence that allows us to approach ethical, social justice, and global issues.

Seasonal Checklist

+ Think about how to celebrate a rich Advent and Christmas without scheduling so much that people are overwhelmed. Often less is more.
+ Consider holding the annual pageant on the Second Sunday after Christmas (or at some point during the Christmas season) instead of on the Fourth Sunday of Advent or on Christmas Eve. This has several advantages. The integrity of Advent is maintained. The parish is not trying to cram too much into Christmas Eve, when children are already excited and parents frazzled. It is more likely that a full cast will be available, too, since Mary and Joseph, shepherds and angels, will be back from their Christmas visits with the grandparents!
+ Think about outreach projects for each season. For Advent—perhaps in cooperation with other churches or community groups—sponsor or participate in a toy or clothing drive (especially coats and sweaters and warm baby clothes, for those in colder climates) or a food drive. Plan an ingathering for the Third Sunday of Advent, with a special coffee hour after to prepare and box the donations.
+ Advent Lessons and Carols
+ Greening of the Church/Preparation of Nativity Scene

The Advent Project

What Are We Waiting For?

Is it possible to observe Advent meaningfully in our culture, when Christmas decorations begin appearing in stores in late August and then take center stage once Halloween décor is removed on November 1? The months of November and December have become an extended period of holiday advertisements, parties, shopping, and concerts. With an accelerated and extended Christmas season, many churches succumb by putting up trees and decorations and begin singing carols at the beginning of Advent. Though Advent is recognized as preparation for the celebration of the nativity, within our cultural context the two seasons often fuse into in a four-week focus on the babe in the manger, angels, shepherds, and, since they make appearances in crèches and carols, the magi.

The problem with the above scenario is that the essence of Advent is eschatological. Advent invites us to prepare for the coming of Christ at the end of time even as we welcome his appearance in our weekly assembly and in the world to which we are sent. Not until the fourth Sunday of Advent do the readings turn to texts we associate with the nativity. The spiritually rich themes of Advent are difficult to accentuate when our culture is fixated on merriment, not to mention crazed schedules and demands.

In response to the above challenges, the Advent Project[1] proposes a seven-week Advent to afford an earlier and longer opportunity to glean the riches of the season's themes of waiting, expectation, preparation, and hope. Arguing that most churches are already on the way to Bethlehem at the beginning of December, their proposal argues that the primary focus of Advent is the full manifestation of the reign of God. If the culture of Christmas is in full swing by early December, perhaps we can begin to catch the attention of folks with some early weeks of eschatological (i.e., Advent) themes in November. The proposal does not suggest that December become a month to celebrate Christmas; rather, it provides an extended period to mine the riches of the Advent season.

The Advent Project began in 2006 as a continuing seminar of the North American Academy of Liturgy. Since then, a number of congregations—mostly Episcopal and Methodist—have experimented with a seven-week Advent. A website (theadventproject.org) provides background and resources. In October 2017, Church Publishing produced *What Are We Waiting For? Reclaiming Advent for Time to Come* by Bill Petersen as a further help for those considering the renewal of this ancient practice.

The Ecumenical Question

The Advent Project notes that the season of Advent has not always been four weeks and that Orthodox Christians still observe a longer Advent. Should a congregation experiment with the proposal, they would find themselves slightly out of sync with the common Western liturgical calendar. To many, it would seem quite strange to announce that the first week of Advent in early November, when most churches would be waiting three weeks to begin the season.

However, there is one essential and intriguing element to the proposal: *it retains the current cycle of readings in the Revised Common Lectionary.* Since the majority of the readings in November already have an eschatological focus, the final three Sundays of the church year are simply given an Advent overlay. In an expanded Advent, the first Sunday of the season would occur between November 5 and 12. Occasionally, this would overlap with All Saints Sunday and create a juxtaposition either difficult or ripe with creative possibilities, depending on one's perspective

On one hand, the question of catholicity seems integral to this proposal. When are we free to veer away from what we hold in common with others in our denomination or in the Western church? On the other hand, students of liturgical history note that in the early church there was much diversity in regard to rites and calendars, and local churches were not always in sync with one another.

---

[1] http://www.theadventproject.org/

Advent

Hybrid Option

An option to a full-blown, extended Advent is to link the seven Sundays together yet still retain the season of Advent in common with the Western catholic church. Here are a number of practical suggestions:

1. In the same way that some communities mark liturgical seasons with a change in musical settings and seasonal texts, link the seven weeks together. One musical option is Richard Proulx's *Missa Emmanuel*, which uses the chant melody from "O come, O come, Emmanuel" (available to those with a subscription to OneLicense.net). Throughout the seven weeks, the assembly response to the intercessions could be "Come, Lord Jesus," and this well-known table prayer could serve as an offering prayer or an invitation to communion:

> Come, Lord Jesus, be our guest.
> Let these gifts to us be blessed.
> Blessed be God who is our bread.
> May all the world be clothed and fed.

2. The Advent Project suggests linking each of the seven Sundays with one of the O Antiphons. One of the antiphons—or the appropriate stanza of "O come, O come, Emmanuel"—could be sung at the beginning of the liturgy, perhaps connected to confession and forgiveness. *Music Sourcebook for All Saints through Transfiguration* (Augsburg Fortress, 2013) notes this option of tying the seven weeks together this way and provides several settings of the O Antiphons (see the notes, pp. 67–68). In order to connect the O Antiphon related to "king" to what is commonly called Christ the King Sunday, the Advent Project slightly rearranges the traditional order:

> Advent 1 (or third last Sunday): *O Sapientia* (Wisdom)
> Advent 2 (or second last Sunday): *O Adonai* (Lord)
> Advent 3 (or Christ the King): *O Rex Gentium* (King/Ruler of nations)
> Advent 4 (or Advent 1): *O Radix Jesse* (Root/ Branch of Jesse)
> Advent 5 (or Advent 2): *O Clavis David* (Key of David)
> Advent 6 (or Advent 3): *O Oriens* (Morning Star/ Dayspring)
> Advent 7 (or Advent 4): *O Emmanuel*

3. With so many fine Advent hymns, it is difficult to get them all scheduled during Advent. Be creative and think outside the box. Consider "The King shall come when morning dawns" and "Blest be the King whose coming" on Christ the King Sunday. Hymns such as the Taize chant "Wait for the Lord," or "Blessed be the God of Israel" work equally well in November. There are many others, considered appropriate for Advent but not in the Advent sections in *The Hymnal 1982, Wonder, Love and Praise,* and *Lift Every Voice and Sing II*, that work well in November. Take a look at the Topical Index of Hymns under the categories of Advent, End Time, and Judgment.

4. Two practical concerns arise: color and wreath. If a full seven-week Advent is observed, it would be natural to use the color blue for the entire season, and to consider using a wreath with seven candles. The Advent Project website contains resources for the wreath lighting, but you would need to devise your own way to display seven candles. If a hybrid approach is employed, it would seem logical to use green for the first three weeks and blue during Advent, and to retain the traditional wreath with four candles.

What About Christ the King?

What shall we do with the Christ the King Sunday? Often preachers and hymn selectors fixate on the word "king"—either positively or negatively—and miss the many other themes related to eschatology or consummation on this day. The festival of Christ the King is a very late addition to the calendar, and various denominations have taken different approaches to the naming of the last Sunday of the church year. Examples include "The Reign of Christ" or "The Last Sunday after Pentecost." This is all to say that in an extended seven-week November/Advent, one option is to not make the last Sunday after Pentecost a festival, retain green as the liturgical color, and use Last Sunday of the Year or something similar to name the day.

November 2018

How might the concept of an expanded Advent work this year? In 2018, the final Sundays of year B include an assortment of eschatological texts that resonate with Advent themes. In particular, the gospels include:

> November 11: Mark 12:38-44 *Judgment on hypocrisy and the rich (the poor widow)*
> November 18: Mark 13:1-8 *Birth pangs, signs of consummation*
> November 25: John 18:33-37 *Pilate and the kingship of Jesus*

The gospel on November 25 may seem most difficult to connect, particularly for those who have relied on images of kingship on this day. However, the first two readings include explicit references to the one coming with the clouds of heaven. Rather than dwelling solely on the image of Christ as king, consider themes of consummation and the kingdom that is not of this world.

If your congregation experiments with a seven-week Advent, a hybrid approach as suggested above, or something similar, consider sending feedback to the Advent Project via their website.

May the observance of Advent lead not simply to a meaningful celebration of Christmas, but to a deeper reflection on the coming of Christ to our world both today and at the end of time.

Craig M. Mueller
Holy Trinity Lutheran Church, Chicago

The Advent Wreath

The Advent wreath is a visual symbol marking the progress of the season of Advent. When it is used in the church, no special prayers or ceremonial elaboration beyond what is described in the Prayer Book is desirable. At morning services, the appropriate number of candles is lighted before the service begins.

When used in private homes, the Advent Wreath provides a convenient focus for devotions at the time of the evening meal. Here we offer the Prayer for Light as well as prayers for using an Advent wreath in the home.

Prayer for Light

Grant us, Lord, the lamp of charity which never fails, that it may burn in us and shed its light on those around us, and that by its brightness we may have a vision of that holy City, where dwells the true and never-failing Light, Jesus Christ our Lord. *Amen.*

Prayers for the Advent Wreath at Home[1]

First Week in Advent

Leader: Almighty God, give us grace to cast away the works of darkness.

And put on the armor of light,

Leader: Now in the time of this mortal life in which your Son Jesus Christ came to visit us in great humility; that in the last day, when he shall come again in his glorious majesty to judge both the living and the dead, we may rise to the life immortal; through him who lives and reigns with you and the Holy Spirit, one God, now and for ever. *Amen.*

Second Week in Advent

Leader: Merciful God, who sent your messengers the prophets to preach repentance,

And prepare the way for our salvation,

_____

[1] Anne E. Kitch. *The Anglican Family Prayer Book* (Harrisburg, PA: Morehouse Publishing, 2004), 115-121.

Leader: Give us grace to heed their warnings and forsake our sins, that we may greet with joy the coming of Jesus Christ our Redeemer: who lives and reigns with you and the Holy Spirit, one God, now and for ever. *Amen.*

Third Week in Advent

Leader: Stir up your power, O Lord.

And with great might come among us;

Leader: And, because we are sorely hindered by our sins, let your bountiful grace and mercy speedily help and deliver us; through Jesus Christ our Lord, to whom with you and the Holy Spirit, be honor and glory, now and for ever. *Amen.*

Fourth Week in Advent

Leader: Purify our conscience, Almighty God,

by your daily visitation,

Leader: That your Son Jesus Christ, at his coming, may find in us a mansion prepared for himself; who lives and reigns with you, in the unity of the Holy Spirit, one God, now and for ever. *Amen.*

Advent Blessing

The following blessing may be used by a bishop or priest whenever a blessing is appropriate. It is a three-fold form, with an Amen at the end of each sentence, leading into a Trinitarian blessing.

May Almighty God, by whose providence our Savior Christ came among us in great humility, sanctify you with the light of his blessing and set you free from all sin. *Amen.*

May he whose second Coming in power and great glory we await, make you steadfast in faith, joyful in hope, and constant in love. *Amen.*

May you, who rejoice in the first Advent of our Redeemer, at his second Advent be rewarded with unending life. *Amen.*

And the blessing of God Almighty, the Father, the Son, and the Holy Spirit, be upon you and remain with you for ever. *Amen.*

Advent Festival of Lessons & Hymns

Nine lessons are customarily selected (but fewer may be used), interspersed with appropriate Advent hymns, canticles, and anthems. When possible, each Lesson should be read by a different lector, preferably voices of male and female readers as well as a variety of ages. The Lesson from the third chapter of Genesis is never omitted.

Genesis 2:4b-9, 15-25
Genesis 3:1-22 *or* 3:1-15
Isaiah 40:1-11
Jeremiah 31:31-34
Isaiah 64:1-9a
Isaiah 6:1-11
Isaiah 35:1-10
Baruch 4:36—5:9
Isaiah 7:10-15
Micah 5:2-4
Isaiah 11:1-9
Zephaniah 3:14-18
Isaiah 65:17-25
Luke 1:5-25 *or* Luke 1:26-38 *or* Luke 1:26-56

The Celebration of our Lady of Guadalupe

The Feast of Our Lady of Guadalupe (Dia de Nuestra Señora de Guadalupe) is a celebration of the appearance of the Virgin Mary to an Aztec peasant during the first years of Spanish rule. Today it is both a national and religious holiday in Mexico. The festival begins on the eve of December 12, when concero dancers gather in the atrium of the church.

In the Roman Catholic tradition, the liturgy includes a celebration of the Eucharist followed by a festive meal.

Readings

Zechariah 2:10-13 *or* Revelation 11:19a; 12:1-6a, 10
Luke 1:26-38 *or* Luke 1:39-47

O God of power and mercy, you blessed the Americas at Tepeyac with the presence of the Virgin Mary of Guadalupe. May her prayers help all men and women to accept each other as brothers and sisters. Through Your justice present in our hearts, may your peace reign in the world. We ask this through our Lord Jesus Christ, Your Son, who lives and reigns with you and the Holy Spirit, One God, forever and ever. *Amen.*

The Angelus (English)

Leader: The Angel of the Lord declared unto Mary

And she conceived by the Holy Ghost.

Leader: Hail Mary, full of grace: The Lord is with thee. Blessed art thou among women and blessed is the fruit of thy womb, Jesus. Holy Mary, Mother of God: Pray for us sinners now and at the hour of our death. *Amen.*

Leader: Behold, the handmaid of the Lord.

Be it done unto me according to thy word.

Leader: Hail Mary . . .

Holy Mary . . .

Leader: And the Word was made flesh

And dwelt among us.

Leader: Hail Mary . . .

Holy Mary . . .

Leader: Pray for us, O holy Mother of God,

That we may be made worthy of the promises of Christ.

Leader: Let us pray.

Pour forth, we beseech thee, O Lord, thy grace unto our hearts, that we, to whom the Incarnation of Christ, thy Son, was made known by the message of an Angel, may by His Passion and Cross be brought to the glory of His Resurrection, through the same Christ, our Lord, Amen.

El Angelus (Español)

Líder: El Angel del Señor anunció a María.

Y concibió por obra del Espíritu Santo.

Líder: Dios te salve, María. Llena eres de gracia: El Señor es contigo. Bendita tú eres entre todas las mujeres. Y bendito es el fruto de tu vientre: Jesús.

Santa María, Madre de Dios, ruega por nosotros pecadores, ahora y en la hora de nuestra muerte. Amén.

Líder: He aqui la esclava del Señor.

Hagase en mi segun Tu palabra.

Líder: Dios te salve María . . . .

> *Santa María . . . .*

Líder: Y el Verbo se hizo carne.

> *Y habito entre nosotros.*

Líder: Dios te salve María . . . .

> *Santa María . . . .*

Líder: Ruega por nosotros, Santa Madre de Dios.

> *Para que seamos dignos de alcanzar las promesas de Jesucristo.*

> *Todos:* *Derrama, Señor, Tu gracia en nuestros corazones; que habiendo conocido la Encarnación de Cristo, Tu Hijo, por la voz del Angel, por los meritos de Su Pasión y cruz seamos llevados a la gloria de la Resurrección. Por el mismo Cristo, Nuestro Señor. Amén.*

Las Posadas

Las Posadas (Spanish for "the inn" or "lodgings") is a traditional Mexican festival which re-enacts Joseph's search for room at the inn. Beginning on December 16 and continuing for nine days leading up to Christmas Eve worship, a procession carrying a doll representing the Christ Child and images of Joseph and Mary riding a burro walks through the community streets. The processional stops at a previously selected home and asks for lodging for the night. People are invited in to read scriptures and sing Christmas carols. Refreshments are provided by the hosts. The doll is left at the chosen home and picked up the next night when the procession begins again.

Elements for the Procession

Invite participants to sing together a beloved Christmas carol. "O Little Town of Bethlehem" or the traditional Mexican song "Los Peregrinos" ("The Pilgrims").

The Collect

O God, you have caused this holy night to shine with brightness of the true Light: Grant that we, who have known the mystery of that Light on earth, may also enjoy him perfectly in heaven; where with you and the Holy Spirit he lives and reigns, one God, in glory everlasting. *Amen.*

The Phos Hilaron

O gracious Light,
pure brightness of the everlasting Father in heaven,
O Jesus Christ, holy and blessed!

Now as we come to the setting of the sun,
and our eyes behold the vesper light,
we sing your praises, O God: Father, Son, and Holy Spirit.

You are worthy at al times to be praised by happy voices,
O Son of God, O Giver of life,

And to be glorified through all the worlds.

The Song of Mary, the *Magnificat,* Luke 1:46-55

And Mary said, "My soul magnifies the Lord, and my spirit rejoices in God my Savior, for he has looked with favor on the lowliness of his servant. Surely, from now on all generations will call me blessed; for the Mighty One has done great things for me, and holy is his name. His mercy is for those who fear him from generation to generation. He has shown strength with his arm; he has scattered the proud in the thoughts of their hearts. He has brought down the powerful from their thrones, and lifted up the lowly; he has filled the hungry with good things, and sent the rich away empty. He has helped his servant Israel, in remembrance of his mercy, according to the promise he made to our ancestors, to Abraham and to his descendants forever."

An Advent Bidding Prayer for an End to Global Poverty and Instability[2]

This is a litany prepared by the Office of Government Relations. It is based on the Millennium Development Goals and can be used in place of the Prayers of the People.

Leader: Brothers and sisters in Christ: As we await the great festival of Christmas, let us prepare hearts so that we may be shown its true meaning. Let us pray for the world that God so loves; for peace and unity all over the earth; for the poor, the hungry, the cold, the helpless, and the oppressed; the sick and those who mourn; the aged and the little children; and all who

---

[2] www.episcopalchurch.org/library/article/advent-bidding-prayer-end-global-poverty-and-instability; accessed August 14, 2017.

rejoice with us but on another shore and in a greater light, that multitude which none can number, whose hope was in the Word Made Flesh, and with whom, in our Lord Jesus Christ, we forever more are one.

Silence

Stir up our hearts, O Lord, to prepare the way for your only Son: By his coming, give us grace to cast away the works of darkness and put on the armor of light, that our feet may be strengthened for your service, and our path may be brightened for the work of justice and reconciliation in our broken world.

God of love, in your mercy,

Hear our prayer.

Let us pray for the poor, hungry, and neglected all over the world, that their cries for daily bread may inspire works of compassion and mercy among those to whom much has been given

Silence

Almighty and most merciful God, you took on human flesh not in the palace of a king but in the throes of poverty and need: Grant that your holy and life-giving Spirit may so move every human heart; that, following in the steps of your blessed Son, we may give of ourselves in the service of others until poverty and hunger cease in all the world, and all things are reconciled in the reign of Christ.

God of love, in your mercy,

Hear our prayer.

Let us pray for schools and centers of learning throughout the world, for those who lack access to basic education, and for the light of knowledge to blossom and shine in the lives of all God's people.

Silence

Eternal God, the author and source of all knowledge and Truth: bless all who seek to learn and those who teach them, and inspire us to break down barriers that withhold education from your children; that, enlightened with the bright beams of Wisdom, all may be equipped to seek the blessings of liberty, justice, and peace.

God of love, in your mercy,

Hear our prayer.

Let us pray for an end to the divisions and inequalities that scar God's creation, particularly the barriers to freedom faced by God's children throughout the world because of gender; that all who have been formed in God's image might have equality in pursuit of the blessings of creation.

Silence

O God, in whom there is neither male nor female, Jew nor Gentile, slave nor free: Unite the wills of all people, that the walls which divide us and limit equality among your children may crumble, suspicions disappear, and hatreds cease; so that all may live together in justice, harmony, and peace.

God of love, in your mercy,

Hear our prayer.

Let us pray for the health of women, children and families around the world, especially for an end to maternal and child mortality, that in building healthy families, all God's people may be empowered to strengthen their communities and repair the breaches which divide nations and peoples.

Silence

Almighty and ever-living God, you were born into human flesh and sanctify all families: Protect the health and safety of all women in childbirth and the children whom they bear, and inspire your people to build strong and healthy families and communities, where all may be strengthened to do your will on earth until the day when you gather us into one heavenly family.

God of love, in your mercy,

Hear our prayer.

Let us pray for an end to pandemic disease throughout the world, particularly the scourges of HIV/AIDS, malaria, and tuberculosis; that plagues of death may no longer fuel poverty, destabilize nations, and inhibit reconciliation and restoration throughout the world.

Silence

O God, the strength of the weak and the comfort of all who suffer: Grant your saving health to all who are afflicted by disease throughout the world. Bless the labors of all who minister to the sick, and unite the wills of nations and peoples in seeking an end to the pandemics of our age; that sickness may be turned to health, sorrow turned to joy, and mourning turned to praise of your Holy Name.

God of love, in your mercy,

Hear our prayer.

Let us pray for an end to the waste and desecration of God's creation, for access to the fruits of creation to be shared equally among all people, and for communities and nations to find sustenance in the fruits of the earth and the water God has given us.

Silence

Almighty God, you created the world and gave it into our care so that, in obedience to you, we might serve all people: Inspire us to use the riches of creation with wisdom, and to ensure that their blessings are shared by all; that, trusting in your bounty, all people may be empowered to seek freedom from poverty, famine, and oppression.

God of love, in your mercy,

Hear our prayer.

Let us pray for all nations and people who already enjoy the abundance of creation and the blessings of prosperity, that their hearts may be lifted up to the needs of the poor and afflicted, and partnerships between rich and poor for the reconciliation of the world may flourish and grow.

Silence

Merciful God, you have bestowed upon us gifts beyond our imagining and have reminded us that all that we have belongs to you alone and is merely held in trust by human hands: we give you thanks for those moments of reconciliation and grace we see in our world, of wrongs that are made right, knowing that in your love all things are possible. Inspire in our nation, its leaders and people a spirit of greater sacrifice and devotion in the use of our treasures for the reconciliation of your world; that, in forsaking wealth and giving up ourselves to walk in the way of the Cross, we may find it to be none other than the way of life and peace.

God of love, in your mercy,

Hear our prayer.

Let us pray for the departed, particularly those who have died as a result of poverty, hunger, disease, violence, or hardness of the human heart;

Silence

Almighty God, whose blessed Son Jesus Christ was born into human flesh to live and die as one of us and destroy forever the bondage of sin and death: We commend to your mercy all your departed servants, particularly those who have died as a result of the brokenness of our world; and we pray that we, too, may share with the Blessed Virgin Mary, [_____ and] all the saints in the joy of your heavenly reign.

God of love, in your mercy,

Hear our prayer.

The Celebrant adds a concluding Collect:

Eternal God, in whose perfect kingdom no sword is drawn but the sword of righteousness, no strength known but the strength of love: So mightily spread abroad your Spirit, that all peoples may be gathered together and reconciled under the banner of the Prince of Peace, as children of one Father; to whom be dominion and glory, now and forever. **Amen.**

An Advent Litany of Darkness and Light[3]

Voice 1: We wait in the darkness, expectantly, longingly, anxiously, thoughtfully.

Voice 2: The darkness is our friend. In the darkness of the womb, we have all been nurtured and protected. In the darkness of the womb, the Christ-child was made ready for the journey into light.

You are with us, O God,
in darkness and in light.

Voice 1: It is only in the darkness that we can see the splendor of the universe—blankets of stars, the solitary glowings of distant planets.

---

[3] "An Advent Litany of Darkness and Light," in *The Wideness of God's Mercy: Litanies to Enlarge Our Prayers* Jeffrey W. Rowthorn, editor (New York: Church Publishing, 2007), 65-66.

Advent

Voice 2: It was the darkness that allowed the magi to find the star that guided them to where the Christ-child lay.

You are with us, O God,
in darkness and in light.

Voice 1: In the darkness of the night, desert people find relief from the cruel relentless heat of the sun.

Voice 2: In the blessed darkness, Mary and Joseph were able to flee with the infant Jesus to safety in Egypt.

You are with us, O God,
in darkness and in light.

Voice 1: In the darkness of sleep, we are soothed and restored, healed and renewed.

Voice 2: In the darkness of sleep, dreams rise up. God spoke to Jacob and Joseph through dreams. God is speaking still.

You are with us, O God,
in darkness and in light.

Voice 1: In the solitude of darkness, we sometimes remember those who need God's presence in a special way—the sick, the unemployed, the bereaved, the persecuted, the homeless; those who are demoralized and discouraged, those whose fear has turned to cynicism, those whose vulnerability has become bitterness.

Voice 2: Sometimes in the darkness, we remember those who are near to our hearts—colleagues, partners, parents, children, neighbors, friends. We thank God for their presence and ask God to bless and protect them in all that they do—at home, at school, as they travel, as they work, as they play.

You are with us, O God,
in darkness and in light.

Voice 1: Sometimes, in the solitude of darkness, our fears and concerns, our hopes and our visions rise to the surface. We come face to face with ourselves and with the road that lies ahead of us. And in that same darkness, we find companionship for the journey.

Voice 2: In that same darkness, we sometimes allow ourselves to wonder and worry whether the human race is going to make it at all.

We know you are with us, O God, yet we still
await your coming. In the darkness that contains
both our hopelessness and our expectancy, we
watch for a sign of God's Hope. Amen.

First Sunday of Advent

December 3, 2017

The day will come when God's wisdom and patience will be fully revealed. It will be a time of both tremendous hope and promise, but it will also be a time of judgment. God's people must live in readiness for that great day to come.

Color   Violet or Blue

Preface   Advent

Collect

Almighty God, give us grace to cast away the works of darkness, and put on the armor of light, now in the time of this mortal life in which your Son Jesus Christ came to visit us in great humility; that in the last day, when he shall come again in his glorious majesty to judge both the living and the dead, we may rise to the life immortal; through him who lives and reigns with you and the Holy Spirit, one God, now and for ever. Amen.

Readings and Psalm

Isaiah 64:1-9

The Hebrew Bible lesson presents a contrite plea to God for merciful justice. The prophet recalls earlier times when the Lord's presence made the very mountains quake.Now the people have sinned grievously and are suffering for their wrongs. They can only pray that the Lord will remember them as God's children, God's creatures, and temper divine anger.

Psalm 80:1-7, 16-18

A lament and a plea to the Lord, the shepherd of Israel, that God will turn away divine anger and restore the people.

1 Corinthians 1:3-9

In this reading Paul greets the new disciples in Corinth, telling them of his gratitude to God on their behalf and offering comfort and assurance. Because they are sanctified in Christ, these converts, together with those everywhere who call upon Jesus, have a vocation as saints. They are rich in spiritual gifts. Trusting in a faithful God, they wait for the great revelation of the Lord Jesus Christ.

Mark 13:24-37

In this gospel lesson, Jesus presents his disciples with a vision of the end of human history and repeatedly urges them to be on watch. The universe itself will reflect this transformation as the Son ofMan comes. That time is near, but no one knows it exactly. Disciples must live expectantly and be on the alert for their Lord's coming.

Prayers of the People

Presider: *Faithful God, stir up your strength and come to help us as we look for the revealing of our Lord Jesus Christ; hear our prayers and strengthen us to the end as we pray: Restore us, O God of hosts; show us the light of your countenance, and we shall be saved.*

Litanist: We give thanks to you, our Loving God, for the grace you have given to us in Christ Jesus: Enrich your Church in speech and knowledge of every kind that she may not be lacking in any spiritual gift and may be awake, alert, and blameless.

Restore us, O God of hosts;

> *show us the light of your countenance, and we shall be saved.*

Make your name known, Almighty One, so that the nations might tremble at your presence: Gather the elect from the ends of the earth to the ends of heaven, that all humanity may know that we are the work of your hand and the sheep of your flock.

Restore us, O God of hosts;

> *show us the light of your countenance, and we shall be saved.*

Come among us with great power and glory, O Shepherd of your people, shine forth and give to all the earth the light of your presence.

Restore us, O God of hosts;

> *show us the light of your countenance,*
> *and we shall be saved.*

Be near to this community, at our very gates and within our hearts, and do not hide your face from us, that we may know your glory in the evening and at midnight and at cockcrow and at dawn, and not be found asleep at the day of your coming.

Restore us, O God of hosts;

> *show us the light of your countenance,*
> *and we shall be saved.*

Compassionate One, open the heavens and come down with your healing grace for those for whom we pray, especially ___.

We give thanks for the grace and peace that come from God our Father and the Lord Jesus Christ, offering our special gratitude for ___.

May your angels gather your beloved into the day of your triumph as we remember those who have died, especially ___.

Restore us, O God of hosts;

> *show us the light of your countenance,*
> *and we shall be saved.*

Presider: *No one has heard, no ear has perceived, no eye has seen any God besides you, O Holy One; you are the potter and we are the clay, the work of your hand: Shine forth upon your creation, stir up your strength, and come to help us, as we put our trust in you, O Father, through our Savior Jesus Christ in the power of your Holy Spirit, one God, forever and ever.* Amen.

Images in the Readings

The four gospels repeatedly refer to the Jewish apocalyptic figure called the Son of Man, a mysterious human-like judge who as part of the cosmic upset at the end of time will appear in the sky to represent God to the people and the people to God. The term does not mean that Jesus was the human son of Mary. Today's several readings describe the end of the world with the arrival of the Son of Man in both frightening and comforting language. As Mark says it, the sun will be darkened, yet summer buds promise new life.

There are many biblical references to the fig tree. An image in ancient myth and literature for male fertility, the fig tree provided both food and shade for Israelites, and even clothing in the story of the fall. Thus in Mark 13, the fig tree is a positive image for the arrival of God. What is now in bud will see its fruition.

God is like a potter, shaping us who are made of clay. Not only did God create the universe, but also forms us daily in the grace given us in Christ Jesus.

God will assemble us from the ends of the earth. The author imagines earth as a flat four-cornered plain, edged with mountains. The evangelist, only three decades after the ministry of Jesus, anticipates that the elect will come from all corners of the earth.

Ideas for the Day

♦ For some, the Second Coming inspires a misplaced fear of wrathful judgment. Today's popular culture gives us the *Left Behind* books and movies. Hieronymus Bosch's "The Garden of Earthly Delights" comes to us from the sixteenth century. By contrast, this gospel encourages hope. God's grace is at work in even our most trying moments. The film *The Shawshank Redemption* uses a cruel prison setting to illustrate the power of hope. The falsely convicted Andy refuses to allow his unjust imprisonment, the prison's dismal conditions, and the guards' inhumane treatment to erase his own and his fellow inmates' dignity and worth.

♦ Be watchful. Advent is a time of preparation, anticipation, and expectation (not penance.) The modern color is blue, originally for Mary, as we celebrate (re)birth. We know for whom we wait, the question is: How are we waiting? View a slideshow from Mumford & Sons on YouTube: Advent 'Waiting for Jesus' https://youtu.be/UMJO-f3FqS4 (accessed August 14, 2017).

♦ Advent themes are traditionally hope, peace, joy, and love—all gifts from God to the earth. Can these gifts be prioritized? Illuminated? What would the world be like if we focused on gifts from God? In this 'season for giving.' Consider an "Alternative Christmas" with a focus on others. Choose a reputable organization such as www.episcopalrelief.org to support. Discuss: what is the difference between giving and outreach?

♦ Christians are called out to be the watchmen for an ever-evolving new age in which the world and presence of God can be actualized in the lives of people. Martin Luther King Jr. (*Lesser Feasts and Fasts*, April 4) is a classic example of a dreamer who took the Advent readings seriously and moved to seek fulfillment of the word in his own life and in the lives of others.

Making Connections

God seeks to come to us. God also desires us. Human beings contain an intrinsic desire to seek and find God. However, seeking God requires that we make choices. In the Book of Common Prayer, we pray on this First Sunday of Advent: Almighty God, give us grace to cast away the works of darkness, and put on the armor of light, now in the time of this mortal life in which your Son Jesus Christ came to visit us in great humility. Advent reminds us that God imitates human life in the mystery of Advent, Christmas, and the Incarnation. We are called to imitate Christ Jesus, as the BCP reminds us, in "great humility." May we seek each other and God in great humility.

Engaging all Ages

Walking into the church you are reminded that something special is afoot. Your senses awake with the fragrance of evergreen boughs circling a ring of candles. Only one candle burns—a tiny but deter-mined flicker of light. You notice that the inside of the church is dressed differently. Purples and blues adorn the worship space. The music is ripe with expectancy and the clergy and worship ministers move down the aisle with palpable anticipation. It is the First Sunday of Advent. Our journey towards Christmas begins. It's time to begin to prepare the manger of your heart. Jesus is coming.

Hymns for the Day

The Hymnal 1982
Blest be the King whose coming 74
Hark! a thrilling voice is sounding 59
The King shall come when morning dawns 73
Before the Lord's eternal throne 391
Immortal, invisible, God only wise 423
Judge eternal, throned in splendor 596
O day of God, draw nigh 600, 601
How firm a foundation 636, 637
O Jesus, I have promised 655
Strengthen for service, Lord, the hands 312
"Sleepers, wake!" A voice astounds us 61, 62
Lo! he comes, with clouds descending 57, 58

Wonder, Love, and Praise
God the sculptor of the mountains 746, 747
Signs of endings all around us 721

Lift Every Voice and Sing II
Have thine own way, Lord 145
Better be ready 4
My Lord, what a morning 13

Weekday Commemorations

Monday, December 4
John of Damachscus, Priest, c. 760
John succeeded his father, a tax collector for the Mohammedan Caliph of Damascus. About 715, John entered St. Sabas monastery near Jerusalem, where he lived ascetically, studying the Fathers. He was ordained a priest in 726, the year the Byzantine Emperor Leo the Isaurian inveighed against Holy Images, beginning the iconoclastic controversy. About 720, John wrote three treatises against the Iconoclasts, arguing that they were not idols but saints and distinguishing between veneration and worship. True worship, he wrote, was due to God alone. John also synthesized theology in *The Fount of Knowledge*. To Anglicans, he is known for his Easter hymns, including "Come, ye faithful, raise the strain."

Tuesday, December 5
Clement of Alexandria, Priest, c. 210
Clement's liberal approach to secular knowledge laid the foundations of Christian humanism. Born mid-second-century, Clement was a cultured Greek philosopher: he sought truth widely until he met Pan-taenus, founder of the Christian Catechetical School at Alexandria. In 190, Clement succeeded Pantaenus as headmaster; Origen was Clement's most eminent pupil. Clement's learning and allegorical exegeses helped commend Christianity to intellectual circles of Alexandria during an age of Gnosticism. Clement dissented from the negative Gnostic view of the world, which denied free will. In *What Rich Man Will Be Saved?*, Clement sanctioned the "right use" of wealth and goods. Among his writings is the hymn "Master of eager youth." The time and place of his death are unknown.

Wednesday, December 6
Nicholas, Bishop of Myra, c. 342
Nicholas is the traditional patron saint of seafarers and sailors, archers, repentant thieves, brewers, pawn brokers, and, most important, of children. He bore gifts to children. His name, Sinterklaas, was brought to America by Dutch colonists in New York, and from there, Saint Nicholas became known as Santa Claus.

Advent

Because of many miracles attributed to his intercessions, Nicholas is also called the Wonderworker. Born in Patara, Lycia in Asia Minor (now Turkey) in 270, he traveled to Egypt and around Palestine, and became the bishop of Myra. He was tortured and imprisoned during the persecution of Diocletian. After his release, he was possibly present at the First Ecumenical Council of Nicea in 325.

Thursday, December 7
Ambrose, Bishop of Milan, 397
Ambrose was hastily baptized so he could become a bishop on December 7, 373, after the Milanese people demanded his election. He had been brought up in a Christian family; in 373, he succeeded his father as governor in Upper Italy. As bishop and a statesman of the Church, he soon won renown defending orthodoxy against Arianism. He was a skilled hymnodist, introducing antiphonal chanting to enrich liturgical texture; among hymns attributed to him is a series for the Little Hours. Ambrose, who was a fine educator in matters of doctrine, persuaded Augustine of Hippo to convert. He feared not to rebuke emperors, including the rageful Theodosius, made to perform public penance for slaughtering thousands of citizens.

Second Sunday of Advent

December 10, 2017

John the Baptist announces the coming of the long expected day pointed to in the Hebrew scriptures. The "good tidings" of Isaiah 40 become the "good news" announced in the opening words of the gospel according to Mark. Repentance is a part of accepting the good news

Color   Violet or Blue

Preface   Advent

Collect

Merciful God, who sent your messengers the prophets to preach repentance and prepare the way for our salvation: Give us grace to heed their warnings and forsake our sins, that we may greet with joy the coming of Jesus Christ our Redeemer; who lives and reigns with you and the Holy Spirit, one God, now and for ever. Amen.

Readings and Psalm

Isaiah 40:1-11

The first reading is a message of comfort and new hope to God's people. The time of exile in Babylon is coming to an end. A new way is made through the desert, and the mighty Lord comes, bringing peace and pardon to Jerusalem. Though all human powers fail, the Lord's word will stand. Like a shepherd, God will care for the people.

Psalm 85:1-2, 8-13

The psalm both celebrates and prays for the Lord's gracious favor, for God's forgiveness, deliverance, and justice.

2 Peter 3:8-15a

This lesson is a reminder that the divine perspective on time can be very different from that of human beings. Many wonder why the Lord seems so slow to fulfill the promises of salvation and judgment. God, however, is patient and has divine purposes. Still, the day of the Lord will come suddenly, bringing a new heaven and earth. Christians must live both in patience and with a zeal for righteousness and peace in readiness for that judgment.

Mark 1:1-8

The Gospel of Mark begins with the ministry of John the Baptist. He is the messenger spoken of in the scriptures, the voice that cries aloud in the wilderness. He is sent to prepare the way of the Lord through his call for repentance and baptism in water for the forgiveness of sins. The people flock to him, but he tells of a mightier one still to come who will baptize with the Holy Spirit.

Prayers of the People

Presider: *Gracious God, through your messengers the prophets you have called your people to prepare the way of the Lord and to welcome the good news of Jesus Christ, the Son of God: Speak tenderly to your people that we may wait for and hasten the coming day, saying: Mercy and truth have met together; righteousness and peace have kissed each other.*

Litanist: Indwelling God, you have baptized your Church with the Holy Spirit: Inspire us to lead lives of holiness and godliness as we prepare for new heavens and a new earth, that as Christ comes he finds us to be a people of peace and justice.

Mercy and truth have met together;

righteousness and peace have kissed each other.

Holy and Mighty God, open the ears and eyes of the leaders of all the nations that they may listen to what the Lord God is saying, for you are speaking peace to your faithful people and to those who turn their hearts to you.

Mercy and truth have met together;

righteousness and peace have kissed each other.

Advent

Advent

Compassionate God, look upon the needs of all humanity: Feed your flock like a shepherd; gather the lambs in your arms and carry them in your bosom, gently leading the mother sheep, that all may know the comfort of your strength.

Mercy and truth have met together;

righteousness and peace have kissed each other.

Ever-present God, lift up your voice with power to herald good tidings to the people of this community to cast out all fear as we listen for the happy cry of your coming salvation.

Mercy and truth have met together;

righteousness and peace have kissed each other.

Glorious God, come with might in your divine recompense to reveal your glory to all who look to you in hope, as we pray especially for ___.

Accept our glad tidings for those who offer you their gracious thanksgivings, especially for ___.

Bring into your everlasting reign those who have died, especially ___.

Mercy and truth have met together;

righteousness and peace have kissed each other.

Presider: *Look upon your creation and comfort your people, O Holy One: Let every valley be lifted up and every mountain and hill be made low; let the uneven ground become level and the rough places a plain, that all people may see the revelation of the glory of God, in the power of the Holy Spirit, through Jesus Christ our Savior.* **Amen.**

Images in the Readings

The first reading and the gospel refer to the wilderness, an inhospitable terrain symbolic of much human life. Yet in such a barren place we hear God's promise. It is best if your sanctuary is not yet decorated for Christmas: we are still in the desert. The wilderness is an honest image, and it is good to let it speak.

Yet, paradoxically, Mark situates the Jordan River in the wilderness, as if the years of nomadic wanderings were also the time that the Israelites crossed the water into the Promised Land. Led by Jesus, who bears the same name as Joshua, who entered the wilderness of our lives, Christians, too, cross a river in baptism, and so enter into the kingdom of God. Law, gospel: wilderness, river.

In the ancient Near East and the Roman Empire, highways were constructed by conquering monarchs to facilitate the movement of troops and celebratory parades, and paths in the wilderness must be marked out by those who have gone before us. But on this highway Jesus walks toward the cross, and on this pathway walked the fascinating crew of saints we commemorate in December: Francis Xavier, John of Damascus (*ELW* 361), Nicholas ("Santa Claus"), Ambrose (*ELW* 263, 559, 571), Lucy (think of candles in a young girl's hair), John of the Cross, and Katherine von Bora Luther, to name a few. We join them, walking to God, and meeting Christ on the way.

Ideas for the Day

- The origin of the word "gospel" comes from the Isaiah text and from Mark's opening words. "Gospel" means "good news." Today's beautiful text from Isaiah may also be familiar from Handel's "Messiah."

- What voices do we listen to today to prepare a highway for our God? Where do we need forgiven? Where do we need to forgive, keeping in mind we are to forgive as we are forgiven. What does that look like? How do we seek peace and pursue it? Are we gentle and respectful toward others? How do we demonstrate harmony, sympathy, love, compassion, and humility? How do these characteristics interact? Is one more important? The Psalm mentions love and faithfulness meet together, and righteousness and peace kiss. Does this ever happen? Where?

- John the Baptist preaches a baptism of *metanoia*. Translators render the Greek word as "repentance." While *metanoia* may include the remorse and amendment of life signified by repentance, it refers to the radical transformation of heart, mind, and soul. For example, Benedictine monks vow to commit themselves to lifelong conversion, that is, they promise to submit to the changes that God will bring about in them over time. The film *The Curious Case Benjamin Button* offers an illustration of lifelong conversion. Born old, the character grows younger throughout the film. In the end, he is a newborn.

- How is Advent revolutionary from the lens of Isaiah and John the Baptist? Listen to the Rt. Rev. Robert Barron discuss the "Advent Revolution" on YouTube: https://youtu.be/jz-l8rEIdEc (accessed August 14, 2017).

Making Connections

Our baptism names and claims us as children of God. When we hear this message of John the Baptist in Advent, we remember that through our baptism we are invited into a life that proclaims God's life to the world. Every Sunday of Advent might be well spent recording our Baptismal Covenant. Which baptismal vow or promise comes most easily for us? Which baptismal vow or promise gives us the greatest challenge? This season of Advent may we seek to love God more dearly and follow Jesus more nearly by living more deeply into our Baptismal Covenant. Maybe we could pray on each baptismal vow or promise this week.

Engaging all Ages

It is the Second Sunday of Advent. Two candles are burning now. The one flame from the First Sunday of Advent now has a companion, and the flames dance with spiritual fervor. Two candles around the Advent Wreath remain dark. Their dance will come. When the time comes for the Peace, the Celebrant calls out "The peace of the Lord be with you!" and you respond "And also with you!" Look into the eyes of your neighbor this day. The world calls out for peace. It is the Second Sunday of Advent and you are called to be a peacemaker.

Hymns for the Day

The Hymnal 1982
Blessed be the God of Israel 444
Redeemer of the nations, come 55
Savior of the nations, come 54
Comfort, comfort ye my people 67
O heavenly Word, eternal Light 63, 64
Once he came in blessing 53
Songs of praise the angels sang 426
The Lord will come and not be slow 462
O day of God, draw nigh 600, 601
Hark! a thrilling voice is sounding 59
Herald, sound the note of judgment 70
On Jordan's bank the Baptist's cry 76
Prepare the way, O Zion 65
There's a voice in the wilderness crying 75
What is the crying at Jordan? 69

Wonder, Love, and Praise
Blessed be the God of Israel 889

Lift Every Voice and Sing II
Prepare ye the way of the Lord 11
Christ is coming 6

Weekday Commemorations

Monday, December 13
Lucy
Lucy stands for "light," the meaning of her name. Born of a noble family about 283 in Syracuse, Sicily, She was denounced as Christian during the Diocletian persecution, and she died by a sword run through her throat in 303. Lucy was said to be so beautiful as to have attracted the unwanted attention of a pagan suitor. To discourage him, Lucy reportedly gouged out her eyes; therefore, in religious art, she often appears with her eyes in a dish, and she is the patron saint of those suffering from eye diseases. Her day in Italy is celebrated with torchlight processions; in Sweden, Santa Lucia is haloed with light in a crown of lit candles.

Advent

Third Sunday of Advent

December 17, 2017

The promised day of God is dawning. John is the herald of that day.

Color Violet, Blue, or Rose

Preface Advent

Collect

Stir up your power, O Lord, and with great might come among us; and, because we are sorely hindered by our sins, let your bountiful grace and mercy speedily help and deliver us; through Jesus Christ our Lord, to whom, with you and the Holy Spirit, be honor and glory, now and for ever. Amen.

Readings and Psalm

Isaiah 61:1-4, 8-11

The principle of justice is to guide the nation of Israel, and they are to understand that it is none other than God who is an advocate for the poor, the oppressed, the downtrodden, and the brokenhearted. Written in the second half of the sixth century before Christ, Second Isaiah (as Isaiah 40–66 is known) envisions God's formation of a faithful Servant of the Lord, sometimes seen as a repentant Israel and sometimes as a great prophet yet to arise, as in today's lesson. The servant will bring Israel to a fulfillment of her original promise and potential, and to a time of joy and celebration. Christians perceive a foretelling of Christ's ministry in these passages.

Psalm 126 or . . .

A psalm of joy and hope sung to the Lord, who restores the fortunes of the people.

Canticle   Luke 1:47-55 (Magnificat)

Mary offers a song of praise to God who has looked with favor on her and who has lifted up the lowly and brought down the powerful.

1 Thessalonians 5:16-24

As he concludes his letter to the church in Thessalonica, Paul exhorts the new converts to live joyfully and prayerfully in readiness for the Lord's coming. Although they are to test what they hear, the disciples are to expect to discover the Spirit in prophecy. Trusting in a faithful God, the followers of Jesus are to seek to avoid all forms of evil and to become holy in every way.

John 1:6-8, 19-28

In the opening passages of his gospel, the fourth evangelist firmly characterizes the mission of John the Baptist: he is the forerunner and witness to the Christ. He bears testimony to the one who is the light of all human life. John is not the Christ or a figure for Elijah or one of the other prophets. He prepares the Lord's way and baptizes, while even now the one whom John is unworthy to serve stands unknown in their midst.

Prayers of the People

Presider: Holy God, you have spoken through your prophets and called us to make straight the way of the Lord: Visit us with your grace to cause righteousness and praise to spring up before all the nations, as we pray: God has done great things for us, and we are glad indeed.

Litanist: O God of peace, you have called your people to rejoice always and to pray without ceasing, giving thanks in all circumstances: Sanctify your Church and her members that our spirit and soul and body may be kept sound and blameless at the coming of our Lord Jesus Christ.

God has done great things for us,

and we are glad indeed.

God of Justice and Mercy, you love justice and hate wrongdoing: Guide our leaders and all in authority, that they may bring good news to the oppressed, bind up the brokenhearted, proclaim liberty to the captives, repair the ruined cities and cause righteousness and praise to spring up before all the nations.

God has done great things for us,

and we are glad indeed.

God of Compassion, look upon the needs of the world: Proclaim the year of your favor, and clothe your children with the garments of salvation and the robe of righteousness.

God has done great things for us,

and we are glad indeed.

God of Grace, be among us in this community that we may be a people whom you have sanctified to testify to the light and to become oaks of righteousness.

God has done great things for us,

and we are glad indeed.

Receive our prayers for those for whom we pray in intercession, especially ___.

Hear our gratitude as we offer our thanksgivings, especially for ___.

Comfort all who mourn, giving them a garland instead of ashes, the oil of gladness instead of mourning, the mantle of praise instead of a faint spirit, as we remember before you those who have died, especially ___.

God has done great things for us,

and we are glad indeed.

Presider: *Loving God, your Advent people look expectantly for the coming of Christ: As the earth brings forth its shoots, and as a garden causes what is sown in it to spring up, nurture our prayers and the thoughts of our hearts, that we may receive with joy the goodness of your strength and live in the power of the Holy Spirit, through Jesus Christ our Savior.* **Amen.**

Images in the Readings

The light begins to shine in our texts, illumines Christmas Day with the full poem from John 1, and culminates in Epiphany and Transfiguration. The fourth-century Western Christians who standardized a commemoration of the birth of Jesus chose the cultural celebration of the winter solstice, with its focus on the sun, and biblical texts that speak of Christ as the light of the world became connected with the Christmas celebration. Our perpetual electric lighting obscures nature's turn toward darkness. Perhaps the church can find ways to help us realize the truth of darkness.

The Isaian oracle is filled with lively images: garlands and garments, oaks and gardens, repaired cities and wedding celebrations. Medieval celibate Christians delighted especially in the marriage imagery: refraining from regular marriage, monks and nuns wrote poetically of their union with Christ as like a marriage. Today's poem is particularly appropriate for our time, with the bride and the bridegroom equally described.

In one of his sermons, Gregory the Great (d. 604) said that since sandals are made from the skins of dead animals, a reference to Jesus' sandals tells us that he donned the mortality of our humanity. Gregory's use of biblical images exemplifies the way patristic preaching was focused not on literal biblical history, but rather on metaphoric appropriation of the Bible for contemporary theological meaning.

Ideas for the Day

- Paintings of John the Baptist often feature what some people call the "John gesture." With his right index figure the Baptist points away from himself. Leonardo da Vinci's work may be the most famous. A robust, smiling prophet looks directly at the observer and gestures heavenward. In his book, *The Da Vinci Code*, Dan Brown imagined that symbols like this hinted at ecclesiastical conspiracies. Art historians do not know definitively what the "John gesture" means, but many agree that it derives from John's role of pointing beyond himself to the Messiah. That is what all the baptized do.
- Today is about joy! Have you ever been so full of joy that you had to sing? What would that song sound like? Mary's song, known as the *Magnificat* (BCP, p. 50, 91), glorifies God. What would be the normal response of someone in this peculiar situation? Dissect her words and see how it resonates with you.
- Compare today's Isaiah passage to Luke 4:16-19. Is this Jesus' mission statement? What is the mission statement of your church? How do we bring healing and hope to a broken world? How does the church rebuild, restore, renew?
- The tradition of lighting Advent candles comes from references to the light and to the dawning of a new day expressed in this Sunday's gospel reading. Light the pink candle if you use purple/pink colors on your Advent wreath. The third Sunday of Advent is called Gaudete Sunday in the Roman

Catholic calendar of the church year. The term is derived from the Latin opening words of the introit antiphon, "Rejoice (Gaudete) in the Lord always." The theme of the day expresses the joy of anticipation at the approach of the Christmas celebration, as this was the mid-point of Advent when the season had been six weeks long. Also known as "Rose Sunday," in Episcopal churches that observe a traditional Anglo-catholic piety, vestments worn may also be rose-colored.

Making Connections

Luke 1:46-55 recounts the words of Mary's glorious hymn, the *Magnificat*. Sometimes the temptation is to view Mary as docile and submissive; but to do that is to miss an important lesson about Mary. Mary challenges us to interpret Scripture and to see God as one who challenges us to imagine new possibilities in the world. We get to a place of seeing new possibilities by allowing the Holy Spirit to overshadow all our thoughts, words, and actions. A wonderful exercise this week would be to read the entire first chapter of Luke and pay special attention to Mary's hymn. How is this hymn inviting us to view the world differently? How is this hymn inviting us to relate to the poor, the least, and the lost in different ways?

Engaging all Ages

Three candles around the Advent Wreath now shine with an anticipatory glow. Winter light pours in through the windows. Christmas will soon be here and the Christ-child's first cry will fill our hurting world with a holy joy. Notice the children around you—their sparkling eyes, happy smiles, and curious questions. Tell them good morning and give a smile of encouragement and support to their parents or caretakers. Children worship with their entire bodies . . . they sing, talk, dance, play, color . . . and often disturb us. *Good for them*. May we be disturbed and changed by the tiny infant who will soon cry out from the manger.

Hymns for the Day

The Hymnal 1982
Blessed be the God of Israel 444
Tell out, my soul, the greatness of the Lord 437, 438
Watchman, tell us of the night 640
Blest be the King whose coming 74
Hail to the Lord's Anointed 616
Hark! the glad sound! the Savior comes 71, 72
O day of God, draw nigh 600, 601
If thou but trust in God to guide thee 635
O heavenly Word, eternal Light 63, 64
Rejoice, the Lord is King! 481
Herald, sound the note of judgment 70
On Jordan's bank the Baptist's cry 76
Prepare the way, O Zion 65
There's a voice in the wilderness crying 75

Wonder, Love, and Praise
Gracious Spirit, give your servants 782
Blessed be the God of Israel 889

Lift Every Voice and Sing II
Prepare ye the way of the Lord 11

Weekday Commemorations

Thursday, December 21
Saint Thomas the Apostle
John's Gospel narrates incidents in Thomas' life. He was with Jesus when he went to Judea to visit friends at Bethany. At the Last Supper, Thomas questioned our Lord: "Lord, we do not know where you are going; how can we know the way?" Thomas questioned Christ's resurrection until Jesus himself showed Thomas his wounds. Thomas, a staunch friend, was skeptical but did not deserve to be reduced to "doubting Thomas": he did not dare believe; also, a doubter was needed for contrast in the story, and Thomas became the protagonist. According to tradition, Thomas evangelized Parthians, Syrian Christians, and Indians in Kerala. The Gospel of Thomas, an apocryphal writing, is attributed to Saint Thomas the Apostle.

Fourth Sunday of Advent

December 24, 2017

God's promise of favor to the house of David and to the people is fulfilled in Jesus. A mystery is revealed. The promise now includes the Gentiles.

Color Violet or Blue

Preface Advent

Collect

Purify our conscience, Almighty God, by your daily visitation, that your Son Jesus Christ, at his coming, amy find in us a mansion prepared for himself; who lives and reigns with you, in the unity of the Holy Spirit, one God, now and for ever. Amen.

Readings and Psalm

2 Samuel 7:1-11, 16

In our Hebrew scriptures, the enemies of David have been subdued and David turns his thoughts to building a temple to the Lord. Through the prophet Nathan, God declares to David that the construction of an earthly temple is not among the purposes for which God has anointed David. God has chosen David from among the lowly, a mere shepherd boy, and given him victory over his enemies. Now God will make of David a great house, securing the hopes of the people of Israel. David's throne shall be established forever, the prophet Nathan declares.

Canticle   Luke 1:47-55 (Magnificat) *or . . .*

Mary offers a song of praise to God, who has looked with favor on her and who has lifted up the lowly and brought down the powerful.

Psalm 89:1-4, 19-26

The Lord is praised for faithful love and mighty justice. As a Father, God promises to the anointed servant David an everlasting kingdom.

Romans 16:25-27

In words that close his long letter to the community in Rome, Paul reminds the new Christians of the mystery now disclosed to all nations, bringing them to faith and obedience. Although the secret had long been kept in silence, the promise of the eternal God has been revealed and is made known through the prophetic scriptures. Glory to God who enables disciples to stand firm in the good news of Jesus!

Luke 1:26-38

Our gospel relates the story of the visit to Mary by an angel: Gabriel tells her that she is to bear Jesus, who will be called the Son of God. This happens during the sixth month of the pregnancy of Elizabeth, a kinswoman of Mary, who will soon give birth to John the Baptist. Mary is assured of God's favor and that this is the work of the Holy Spirit in fulfillment of the prophecy to David of an eternal kingdom. The narrative points to the transcendent origin of this child born into history.

Prayers of the People

Presider: *Extend your greeting to your favored ones, O God, and let your Holy Spirit overshadow us, that we may proclaim your love to our generation, as we await the coming of Christ, saying: Let your faithfulness and love be with us; for your love is established for ever.*

Litanist: Make of your Church, O Holy One, a house that shall be made sure forever before you, that we, like Mary, may respond in faithfulness and be bearers of the Christ Child to all the world.

Let your faithfulness and love be with us;

for your love is established for ever.

Raise up just leaders, Almighty One, and guide the nations of the world, that all people may live in their own place, and be disturbed no more; and that evildoers shall afflict them no more.

Let your faithfulness and love be with us;

for your love is established for ever.

Compassionate One, let the prophetic writings be made known to all the nations to bring release and comfort to all who are oppressed, to lift up the lowly and fill the hungry with good things.

Let your faithfulness and love be with us;

for your love is established for ever.

Loving God, empower your Holy Spirit to come upon this community that we may be the servants of the Lord and live graciously according to your word.

Let your faithfulness and love be with us;

for your love is established for ever.

Gracious One, visit all for whom we pray with your mysterious love, and honor the intercessions of your people as we pray for ___.

Hear our glad tidings as we offer you our praise and thanksgiving, especially for ___.

Raise up into your glorious eternal presence those who have died, especially ___.

Let your faithfulness and love be with us;

for your love is established for ever.

Presider: *Holy One, cast out all fear by your Word of perfect love, the revelation of the mystery that was kept secret for long ages but is now disclosed, that we may joyfully bring about the obedience of faith to the only wise God, through Jesus Christ, to whom be the glory forever.* **Amen.**

Images in the Readings

In Luke's narratives, angels appear in the stories of Jesus' birth and resurrection. In our society, many depictions of angels are, unfortunately, quite cutesy, rather unhelpful as images of the might of God who strike fear in one's heart. The angel is the divine messenger, the extension of the power and mercy of God, and Gabriel comes to announce the eschatological arrival of God.

The pregnant woman can be a symbol of the life that comes from God. In the Bible, many women, from Eve in Genesis 4:1 on, conceive and bear children with the help of God. When we acclaim God as creator, we attest that God is continually creating life on this earth.

In Ancient Near Eastern religious practice, a king maintained a temple as a house of God. Most of these temples housed a huge statue of the god or goddess: think of the Lincoln Memorial. Because of the proscription against sculpting images of God, Israel's temple housed the Ark of the Covenant, that sacred chest containing artifacts of the history of the relationship between God and the people. Christian churches are both like and unlike houses of God. In today's readings, Mary becomes the house of God, and in our baptism, so do we all. We marvel not so much at parthenogenesis, as at the presence of God's Holy Spirit in each one of us.

That Mary conceives while a virgin has birthed endless Christian imaginings, some of which Protestants, especially, have judged to be an ill-considered debasing of sexual intercourse. Greco-Roman religion included tales of virgin births. Luke did not know how sperm and eggs function: thus we have here no gynecological report, but a theological statement told in narrative, similar to that told in the poetry of John's Prologue, that Jesus comes from God.

Ideas for the Day

♦ Thy kingdom come, thy will be done. Where is the kingdom of God? Will it ever end? Do we believe that? What does it look like when we live like we believe that? "For nothing is impossible with God," said Mary. What if that was our creed? Could our actions reflect that? What do we tell the next generation? What is our covenant with God? Are God's promises the same as a covenant? By what name do we address God? Father? Rock? Savior? How does the name we use influence our expectations and/or our response to God?

♦ Luke's account of the Annunciation provides the biblical source for the first portion of the prayer commonly called the Hail Mary. "Hail Mary, full of grace, the Lord is with thee, blessed art thou amongst women." Elizabeth's words to Mary at the Visitation appear in the next phrase: "and blessed is the fruit of thy womb (Jesus)." (Luke 1:42) The prayer concludes with a petition to Mary for her prayers. Our prayers join with the prayers of those who have entered eternal life. The Hail Mary reminds us that we are always surrounded by a cloud of witnesses.

♦ The references in the liturgy of the church to the House of David and the honor given to King David find their significance in today's lections. The tradition of constructing a "Jesse Tree" filled with ornaments depicting Old Testament stories is a fun activity (see www.buildfaith.org/jesse-tree-advent-service/). "A shoot shall come out from the stock of Jesse, and a branch shall grow out of his roots."

Making Connections

What does it mean to be the servant of the Lord? What does it mean to serve God in all we do? One way of deepening our desire to serve God is to recite the Collect from this Sunday's service every day this week:

Purify our conscience, Almighty God, by your daily visitation, that your Son Jesus Christ, at his coming, may find in us a mansion prepared for himself; who lives and reigns with you, in the unity of the Holy Spirit, one God, now and for ever. *Amen.*

It is said that the best way of serving God is through prayer. We can make our daily living a prayer to God. One way of making our life a prayer to God is by actually praying. As we approach Christmas, what if we took time this week and prayed the Offices of Morning Prayer, Noonday Prayer, Evening Prayer, and/or Compline?

Engaging all Ages

It is the Fourth Sunday of Advent, and the light of a quartet of candles circles the evergreen wreath. Advent has provided us the opportunity to prepare the manger of our hearts. We've done so—but not with soft hay or strips of fabric. We have prepared the manger of our hearts with peace, joy, love, and anticipation. The closer we get, the brighter the Light shines. It's time to let our lights shine! Jesus is coming . . . for all of us . . . not just those who look like us or love like us. Jesus is coming for all of us! Listen closely . . . the time is near.

Hymns for the Day

The Hymnal 1982
God himself is with us 475
Tell out, my soul, the greatness of the Lord 437, 438
Blessed be the God of Israel 444
Sing we of the blessed Mother 278
The angel Gabriel from heaven came 265
The Word whom earth and sea and sky 263, 264
Virgin-born, we bow before thee 258

O come, O come, Emmanuel 56
Come, thou long-expected Jesus 66
To the Name of our salvation 248, 249
Creator of the stars of night 60
Gabriel's message does away 270
Nova, nova 266
Praise we the Lord this day 267
Ye who claim the faith of Jesus 268, 269

Wonder, Love, and Praise
Blessed be the God of Israel 889

Lift Every Voice and Sing II
Salamu Maria / Hail Mary, O Mother 51

Weekday Commemorations

Tuesday, December 26
Saint Stephen, Deacon and Martyr
Stephen became the first deacon by his appointment to assist the apostles. He was one of the "seven men of good repute, full of the Spirit and of wisdom," chosen by the apostles to help them serve at tables and care for widows. Stephen served beyond tables, for the Acts of the Apostles describes him preaching and performing miracles. These activities pushed him to confront Jews, who accused him of blasphemy and brought him before the Sanhedrin; his powerful sermon before the Council is recorded in Acts 7. Enraged, councilmen dragged him out of the city to stone him to death. In fear, the Christian community scattered and, thus, spread the Word.

Wednesday, December 27
Saint John, Apostle and Evangelist
John and James, sons of Zebedee, were fishers who became "fishers of men" as disciples. With Peter and James, John became one with the "inner circle" whom Jesus chose to witness his raising of Jairus' daughter, his Transfiguration, and his praying in the garden of Gethsemane. John and James were such angry males that Jesus called them "sons of thunder." Ambitious, they sought to sit next to Jesus at table; willing companions, they shared the communal cup of wine, little knowing the cost. Possibly, John held a special relationship as the "disciple whom Jesus loved," the one asked to care for His mother. It is said that John, alone of the Twelve lived long—no martyr he.

Thursday, December 28
The Holy Innocents
The Holy Innocents were the baby boys ordered killed by Herod. Herod the Great, ruler of the Jews,

was described by the historian Josephus as "a man of great barbarity towards everyone." Appointed by the Romans in 40 BCE, Herod kept peace in Palestine for 37 years. Ruthless yet able, this Idumaean was married to the daughter of Hyrcanus, the last legal Hasmonean ruler, so Herod always feared losing his throne. According to the story, the magi report of the birth of a King of the Jews scared him: He ordered the slaughter of all male children under two in Bethlehem. Although not recorded in secular history, the massacre of the Innocents keeps to Herod's character.

Christmas

Preparing for Christmas

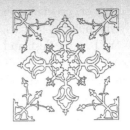

Overview

Almighty God, you have poured upon us the new light of your incarnate Word: Grant that this light, enkindled in our hearts, may shine forth in our lives. (Collect for the First Sunday after Christmas Day, BCP)

Birth. Emmanuel: God with us.
The inbreaking of the reign of God. Joy.

The world begins to celebrate Christmas just after Halloween, often, and then Christmas is over at the end of Christmas Day. (These days, after-Christmas sales start on Christmas Day in some stores!) For Christians, however, Christmas is a glorious twelve-day festival, beginning on Christmas Eve and ending with the Feast of the Epiphany on January 6th. During these twelve days we celebrate Nativity, Incarnation, and Epiphany. (While the Book of Common Prayer does give Epiphany its own season, Christmas and Epiphany are inextricably linked.)

It is tempting to slack off after Christmas Eve and do only the bare minimum for the rest of the season (clergy and lay leaders alike are tired), but there is opportunity to make this a rich season, even in parishes with limited resources, and even if what your parish does is simple. "Planning and enacting robust liturgies throughout the twelve days of Christmas can reinvigorate congregational life and feed a spiritual hunger among the people in our assemblies who have only been beaten up or abused this season" (*Sundays and Season*, 48).

Environment

Think about how and when you will green the church for Christmas, and how you will transition your space from Advent to Christmas.

Think about creating different atmospheres for Christmas Eve (focusing on Nativity) and Christmas Day (focusing on Incarnation). While this is desirable, it may be logistically difficult in many parishes.

Liturgy

Incorporate seasonal elements:
- "Other song of praise." Consider Canticles 11 or 17 or "Angels we have heard on high," *The Hymnal 1982* (96).
- Prayers of the People. Consider the seasonal options in *Common Worship* (67-71, 81-82, 124-125, 164) (the form on p. 71 is especially appropriate at Eucharists that include children), *Book of Common Worship* (Litany for Christmas B, 179-180), and *Sundays & Seasons* ("Seasonal Rites").
- Eucharistic Prayer. Think about B, D, and Prayer 2 from *Enriching Our Worship I*.
- Fraction Anthem. See the options in *Enriching Our Worship 1* (69), *The Hymnal 1982* (S167-S172), *Common Worship* (85, 167), and *Book of Common Worship* (182-183).
- Postcommunion Prayer. *Enriching Our Worship 1* provides an alternative (69).
- Blessing. See the options in *Book of Occasional Services* (23), *Enriching Our Worship 1* (70-71), *Common Worship* (73-74, 101, 135-136, 169), and *New Zealand Prayer Book* (528).

Lectionary

The lessons for the Christmas season are the same in all three years. Each gospel focuses on a different aspect of the story. Luke tells of Joseph and Mary journeying to Bethlehem, where Mary gives birth to Jesus and lays "him in a manger, because there was no place for them in the inn;" of shepherds, to whom this good news of Jesus is proclaimed first: "I am bringing you good news of great joy for all the people: to you is born this day in the city of David a Savior, who is the Messiah, the Lord." John (the principal gospel reading, traditionally read at the midnight

Christmas

Eucharist) proclaims that "the Word became flesh and lived among us" (or, as *The Message* puts it: "The Word became flesh and blood, and moved into the neighborhood"[1]). The story continues on the Sundays after Christmas with the visit of the magi (Matthew), the flight to Egypt (Matthew), and the boy Jesus in the Temple (Luke).

Music

+ Consider putting together an intergenerational "pickup choir" for services and events when the regular choir may be away.
+ If you have a children's choir, perhaps they could lead the singing at an early Christmas Eve service.
+ Plan for old favorites, but introduce some new hymns/songs, too; Christmas Lessons and Carols is an ideal way to provide for both. See the options in *Book of Occasional Services* (38-41) and *Common Worship* (88-91).
+ Go caroling in your area, maybe with neighboring churches. Remember especially to reach out to shut-ins and people going through a difficult time.

Through the Eyes of a Child

At Christmas, we who are the church welcome Jesus and joyfully celebrate his birth. The church is often filled with greens and trees and lights. Something wonderful has happened and it is time to celebrate. We give thanks for God's greatest gift of love to us, the Son, Jesus Christ. We give to others in response to the gift that has been given to us. This is the time to blend family traditions—meals, visits, and activities—with an awareness of the birth of Jesus. The traditional crèche and manger need to have a prominent place for children to touch and re-enact the story of the birth of Jesus. Child-friendly pageants and Christmas plays that invite the children into telling and being a part of the story are critical, as well as doing something as a family, such as gathering up clothes that no longer fit to give to those in need, to teach and demonstrate ways to bring the light of Christ into the darkness. Music is also important; singing the beloved Christmas carols that announce the birth of Christ will offer the child a way to proclaim how the love of God breaks into the world in the birth of Jesus.

---

[1] Eugene H. Peterson, *The Message: The New Testament, Psalms and Proverbs* (Colorado Springs: Navpress, 1996), 188.

Through the Eyes of Youth

The Church is called to demonstrate how the birth of Jesus changes the whole world. This is the time for families to talk about God, for parents to share their faith with their teens, and particularly talk about their faith in regard to family traditions, which show [or "embody"] Christ's presence through the way the family marks the change in seasons. To welcome all to the joy of the birth of Christ, encourage youth to invite friends to attend worship services, to sit at dinner table, and to gather for sharing of gifts at the tree. Some of the sharing of gifts could include special reflections on gifts of faith, gifts of courage, gifts of sports, or intellectual gifts. Invite youth into the question, "Where is there need for peace in our country? In our world? What can one do? Jesus came to offer peace to all people, how can each one of us make a difference?" Choose a particular project to complete during the Christmas and Epiphany seasons.

Through the Eyes of Daily Life

Christmas is to be celebrated for twelve days. Reflect on how we can live the joy of Jesus' birth this and every day, knowing that the Spirit of Christ dwells in us and guides us so that we may be his witnesses in all that we say and do. How do you live your life, knowing that God's Word lives among us?

Through the Eyes of the Global Community

Christmas is the perfect time to offer opportunities for seeing the season of Christmas from the perspective of children from around the world. While the tradition of the 1979 Prayer Book centers us on the incarnation, it is vitally important that we look at the state of children from a global perspective. Holy Innocents (December 28th) is often overlooked; this is a time to learn of those places were children are persecuted and the places where children have no hope. Expand the vision of mission during Christmas to respond to those who are most vulnerable, which includes the children of our world. The United Nations and the Children's Defense Fund offer current statistics and initiatives that a congregation can learn from and discuss as a way to discern possible mission initiatives for the New Year.

Seasonal Checklist

- Be creative and intentional about publicity around Christmas services and events: signboards, newspaper, website, Facebook.
- As mentioned in the section on Advent, consider holding the pageant at some point during the twelve days of Christmas, instead of on the Fourth Sunday of Advent or Christmas Eve.
- Christmas Lessons and Carols

Christmas

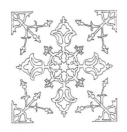

Seasonal Rites for Christmas

The Christmas Crèche[1]

At their entry into the church for the celebration of the Holy Eucharist, the Celebrant (and other ministers) may make a station at a Christmas Crèche. The figure of the Christ Child may be carried in the procession and placed in the Crèche. Other figures may also be brought in if desired.

A versicle may be said, followed by a prayer.

V. The word was made flesh and dwelt among us.
R. And we beheld his glory.

Most merciful and loving God, you have made this day holy by the incarnation of your Son Jesus Christ, and by the child-bearing of the Blessed Virgin Mary: Grant that we your people may enter with joy into the celebration of this day, and may also rejoice for ever as your adopted sons and daughters; through Jesus Christ our Lord. *Amen.*

Christmas Blessing[2]

The following blessing may be used by a bishop or priest whenever a blessing is appropriate. It is a three-fold form, with an Amen at the end of each sentence, leading into a Trinitarian blessing.

May Almighty God, who sent his Son to take our nature upon him, bless you in this holy season, scatter the darkness of sin, and brighten your heart with the light of his holiness. *Amen.*

May God, who sent his angels to proclaim the glad news of the Savior's birth, fill you will joy, and make you heralds of the gospel. *Amen.*

May God, who in the Word made flesh joined heaven to earth and earth to heaven, give you his peace and favor. *Amen.*

And the blessing of God Almighty, the Father, the Son, and the Holy Spirit, be upon you and remain with you for ever. *Amen.*

Blessing of a Christmas Tree

The Christmas tree stems from an ancient tradition of bringing evergreens into the home during the winter months as a hopeful reminder that spring would come. It has now become a familiar symbol of the Christian holiday in homes and in many churches.

Most Holy and Blessed One, you sent your beloved Son into the world to show us the path to true life. May the green of this tree remind us of the everlasting life you offer. May the boughs of this tree remind us that we are the living branches of your love. May the life of this tree remind us of the cross on which your Son gave his life. May the lights of this tree remind us that Christ is the light of the world. As we gather round this tree, we gather in your name, and in your light, and in your love. *Amen.*[3]

Christmas Festival of Lessons & Music

Nine Lessons are customarily selected (but fewer may be used), interspersed with appropriate carols, hymns, canticles, and anthems during this service, which can take place within the twelve days of Christmas. When possible, each Lesson should be read by a different lector, preferably voices of male and female readers as well as a variety of ages. The Lesson from the third chapter of Genesis is never omitted.

Genesis 2:4b-9, 15-25
Genesis 3:1-23 *or* 3:1-5
Isaiah 40:1-11
Isaiah 35:1-10
Isaiah 7:10-15
Luke 1:5-25
Luke 1:26-58
Luke 1:39-46 *or* 1:39-56
Luke 1:57-80
Luke 2:1-20
Luke 2:21-36
Hebrews 1:1-12
John 1:1-18

---

[1] *Book of Occasional Services*, 36.
[2] Ibid, 23.

[3] Anne E. Kitch. *The Anglican Family Prayer Book* (Harrisburg, PA: Morehouse Publishing, 2004), 125–126.

A Children's Christmas Presentation

While not a traditional "pageant," this presentation invites children to create a simple tableau without much rehearsal. It can occur during the sermon or at the end of a service, or can stand alone as a gathering of families for the telling of the birth of Christ with community singing.

Children assemble and put on simple costumes. Mary, Joseph, a donkey, and cows are seated beside a manger. Angels are behind and "above" them.

Mary, Joseph, and the Animals:
This Christmas time we worship
As we gather here tonight
To welcome Baby Jesus
Who came to bring us light.

All sing: Away in a Manger (v. 1)
Shepherds enter with sheep and gather around the manger.

Shepherds and Sheep:
We worship as the shepherds
Who came from hills so far.
They brought the little lambs
To see the baby lying there.

All sing: Rise Up, Shepherd and Follow

Angels:
We worship as the angels
Who sang the first Noel.
God had sent His only Son—
Glad tidings did they tell!

All sing: Angels We Have Heard on High (v. 3)

The Community Gathered:
To Jesus, Lord and Savior,
We bring ourselves this night.
We worship and adore Him
Who brought us peace and light.

All sing: Joy to the World
Candles can be distributed and lit as lights are turned down.

All sing: Silent Night

Feast of the Holy Innocents[4]

Psalm 124 is appointed for this day. Different individuals can read each portion a refrain offered by all.

If you had not been on our side
when destructive powers rose up and barred our path,
if you had not been committed to our good,
like monsters they would have swallowed us alive.
Refrain: Praise to the God who is for us, and for all that is being created.

Their anger was kindled against us,
like the sweep of the forest fire.
Their fury bore down upon us,
like the raging torrent in flood,
the waters of chaos that know no limits,
trespassers that are hard to forgive. *Refrain.*

Thanks be to you, our deliverer,
you have not given us as prey to their teeth.
We escaped like a bird from the snare of the fowler:
the frame snapped and we have flown free. *Refrain.*

In the joy of deliverance we praise you, O God.
Our hearts expand in a new generosity:
we embody love with which you create.
Even the powers you do not destroy:
you redeem all our failures to live,
you are strong to bring good out of evil.
Refrain.

Service for New Year's Eve[5]

During the evening of December 31, which is the eve of the Feast of the Holy Name and also the eve of the civil New Year, this service begins with the Service of Light (BCP, 109) and continues with readings, silence, and prayer.

The Hebrew Year
Exodus 23:9-16, 20-21
Psalm 111 *or* Psalm 119:1-8

O God our Creator, you have divided our life into days and seasons, and called us to acknowledge your providence year after year: Accept your people who come to offer their praises, and, in your mercy, receive their prayers; through Jesus Christ our Lord. *Amen.*

The Promised Land
Deuternomony 11:8-12, 26-28
Psalm 36:5-10 *or* Psalm 89, Part I

---

[4] Jim Cotter. *Psalms for a Pilgrim People.* (Harrisburg, PA: Morehouse Publishing, 1998), 282

[5] Ibid, 43-45.

Almighty God, the source of all life, giver of all blessing, and savior of all who turn to you: Have mercy upon this nation; deliver us from falsehood, malice, and disobedience; turn our feet into your paths; and grant that we may serve you in peace; through Jesus Christ our Lord. *Amen.*

A Season for All Things
Ecclesiastes 3:1-15
Psalm 90

In your wisdom, O Lord our God, you have made all things, and have allotted to each of us the days of our life: Grant that we may live in your presence, be guided by your Holy Spirit, and offer all our works to your honor and glory; through Jesus Christ our Lord. *Amen.*

Remember your Creator
Ecclesiastes 12:1-8
Psalm 130

Immortal Lord God, you inhabit eternity, and have brought us your unworthy servants to the close of another year: Pardon, we entreat you, our transgressions of the past, and graciously abide with us all the days of our life; through Jesus Christ our Lord. *Amen.*

Marking the Times, and Winter
Ecclesiasticus 43:1-22
Psalm 19 *or* Psalm 148 *or* Psalm 74:11-22

Almighty Father, you give the sun for a light by day, and the moon and the starts by night: Graciously receive us, this night and always, into your favor and protection, defending us from all harm and governing us with your Holy Spirit, that every shadow of ignorance, every failure of faith or weakness of heart, every evil or wrong desire may be removed far from us; so that we, being justified in our Lord Jesus Christ,

may be sanctified by your Spirit, and glorified by your infinite mercies in the day of the glorious appearing of our Lord and Savior Jesus Christ. *Amen.*

The Acceptable Time
2 Corinthians 5:17—6:2
Psalm 63:1-8 *or* Canticle 5 *or* Canticle 17

Most gracious and merciful God, you have reconciled us to yourself through Jesus Christ your Son, and called us to new life in him: Grant that we, who begin this year in his Name, may complete it to his honor and glory; who lives and reigns now and for ever. *Amen.*

While it is Called Today
Hebrews 3:1-15 (16—4:13)
Psalm 95

O God, through your Son you have taught us to be watchful, and to await the sudden day of judgment: Strengthern us against Satan and his forces of wickedness, the evil powers of this world, and the sinful desires within us; and grant that, having served you all the days of our life, we may finally come to the dwelling place your Son has prepared for us; who lives and reigns for ever and ever. *Amen.*

New Heavens and New Earth
Revelation 21:1-14, 22-24
Canticle 19

Almighty and merciful God, through your well beloved Son Jesus Christ, the King of kings and Lord of lords, you have willed to make all things new: Grant that we may be renewed by your Holy Spirit, and may come at last to that heavenly country where your people hunger and thirst no more, and the tears are wiped away from every eye; through Jesus Christ our Lord. *Amen.*

Christmas

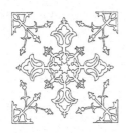

Christmas Eve

December 24, 2017

God came in Jesus of Nazareth to reveal the power of God's love and healing. In the birth of Jesus we realize that God shares life with us intimately. We meet God "in the flesh" of human struggle and most especially in the midst of human love. Christmas celebrates the incarnation of God; God "in the flesh of" human life. (Carne comes from the Latin for meat or flesh.)

Color   White

Preface   Of the Incarnation

Collect

O God, you have caused this holy night to shine with the brightness of the true Light: Grant that we, who have known the mystery of that Light on earth, may also enjoy him perfectly in heaven; where with you and the Holy Spirit he lives and reigns, one God, in glory everlasting. Amen.

Readings and Psalm

Isaiah 9:2-7

From the Hebrew Bible, we hear a hymn of thanksgiving and hope offered at the birth of a new king in Jerusalem. The prophet hails the one born to be the ruler of his people. His reign will end oppression and bring justice, righteousness, and a lasting peace. Christians see these words coming to fulfillment in Jesus.

Psalm 96

A song of praise to the Lord, in which the whole heavens and earth are invited to join.

Titus 2:11-14

This New Testament reading speaks of the two comings of Christ: first in his sacrificial ministry for all people and then in glory. He has enabled his disciples to free themselves from ways of evil. Disciplined and eager to do good, they look forward to the fulfillment of the hope God has given to the world in Jesus.

Luke 2:1-14(15-20)

The gospel presents the story of the birth of Jesus. He is born amid very humble human circumstances. A government registration program requires Joseph and Mary to go to Bethlehem, the city of David. Because there was no other place for them to stay, Mary lays her new son in a stable manger.

An angel then appears to shepherds and announces the joyful news of the Savior's birth.

If the longer version is used, the last sentence may read:

An angel announces the joyful news of the Savior's birth to shepherds who come to Bethlehem and report the angelic vision.

Prayers of the People

Presider: *Gracious and Loving God, in Jesus you have filled all humanity with your divine life: Hear our prayers of joy and thanksgiving as we offer our supplications to you, saying: Glory to God in the highest heaven, and peace to God's people on earth.*

Litanist: You have entrusted the Church with good news of great joy for all people: Inspire our witness that we may spread the light of Jesus' love to all humanity.

Glory to God in the highest heaven,

> ***and peace to God's people on earth.***

Let your power and compassion guide those who exercise authority on earth, that they may be servants of peace, bringing comfort and security to all who are vulnerable.

Glory to God in the highest heaven,

> ***and peace to God's people on earth.***

Embrace with your eternal protection all who are poor: refugees and the displaced, those threatened by violence, and families with no place to call their home.

Glory to God in the highest heaven,

> *and peace to God's people on earth.*

Fill this community with hospitality and generosity, that we may care for one another and celebrate the joy of your presence in our humanity.

Glory to God in the highest heaven,

> *and peace to God's people on earth.*

We entrust to your divine grace all for whom we pray, especially ___.

We give thanks for shepherds and all the vigilant who work while others sleep. Hear our grateful thanksgiving for all the gifts and blessings in our lives, especially ___.

We entrust into your eternal arms those who have died, especially ___.

Presider: *Loving God, the joyful message of the angels fills us with gladness as we celebrate the coming of the Christ child to live among us in vulnerable humility: Let your divine light so dwell within us, that we may treasure your words, ponder them in our hearts, and continue the work of Christ's incarnation in our day, through Jesus our Savior, to whom with you and the Holy Spirit be honor and glory, now and for ever.* Amen.

Images in the Readings

Luke's gospel presents images of the poor: those oppressed by Roman government, a woman giving birth in a place that houses both people and barn animals, a newborn wrapped only in strips of cloth, the socially despised and religiously unclean shepherds. In our society where Christmas suggests unrestricted spending and continual feasting, Luke's image of the poor is striking.

Both the gospel and the first reading suggest the image of the mother bearing new life. Often in the Bible, childbirth is credited to God's power. All Christians are now Mary, bearing Christ for the world.

The Hebrew word *Bethlehem* means "house of bread." From this historic city, famous for its connection to King David, comes the one who will feed the people forever. In the liturgy, we enter that house of bread and eat.

Ideas for the Day

- Through the centuries, saints and mystics have reported visions and encounters with the infant Jesus. For example, tradition tells us that, as Teresa of Avila (also known as Teresa of Jesus) was descending the steps of her convent, she saw a beautiful young boy. He asked her who she was. She answered, "I am Teresa of Jesus." The boy then responded, "I am Jesus of Teresa." People will gather for worship on Christmas Eve for a variety of reasons. Even the most world weary and cynical hope, however slightly, to encounter a living God who yearns for intimate connection.

- This is the time to sing! The People of God waited a long time for a savior. What makes you so full of joy you cannot contain yourself? What are the songs of your heart? The angels sang, "Glory to God in the highest and peace to humankind." Peace is certainly worth singing about, or shouting from the mountaintops. What does good will look like? Is it different or the same as peace? How do we continue to spread the joy of Christmas after Christmas? What if patience and kindness were in the air all year?

- In the birth of Jesus, God gave us the greatest gift by becoming a human being and dwelling among us. Jesus is truly God and truly human—the Incarnation is God's plan for reconciling and redeeming God's people. In Christ we, who are made in the image of God, behold the dignity of our human nature. Because Christ came to bring salvation (healing, "salving"), we have hope and assurance of sharing his life both now and always.

Making Connections

Christmas Eve gets the most attention in many of our churches and oftentimes Christmas Day services find the church empty. We live in a society where it is so easy to get distracted. Increasingly stores put up Christmas decorations at the beginning of November and then strip the malls of anything Christmas related. How can we encourage each other and those around us on Christmas Eve to continue the welcoming of Christ into our lives tomorrow and in the days to come?

Christmas Eve, with all its drama, seeks to remind us who we are and whose we are. God has given us everything in Christ Jesus. How have we given ourselves to God? How have we been the incarnate presence of Jesus Christ in our world? How have we lived the Good News?

Christmas

Christmas

Engaging all Ages

In the darkness of night, a sharp cry shatters the silence and our world will never be the same. Today we gather on Christmas Eve and listen with our ears . . . and our hearts . . . , to the ancient story of Christ's birth. In the midst of all of our Christmas finery, family gatherings, festive worship, gift giving, gloriously decorated churches, and bustling shopping centers, may we stop and catch our breath. May we listen to Mary as she holds Jesus in her arms and sings him to sleep. The manger is full. Our hearts are full. Blessings to you on this beautiful Christmas Eve.

Hymns for the Day

The Hymnal 1982
Hark! the herald angels sing 87
It came upon the midnight clear 89, 90
Sing, O sing, this blessed morn 88
The people who in darkness walked 125, 126
Unto us a boy is born! 98
Joy to the world! The Lord is come 100
A child is born in Bethlehem 103
A stable lamp is lighted 104

Angels we have heard on high 96
Away in a manger 101
Go, tell it on the mountain 21
From heaven above to earth I come 80
God rest you merry, gentlemen 105
In the bleak midwinter 112
It came upon the midnight clear 89
Lo, how a Rose e'er blooming 81
O come, all ye faithful 83
O little town of Bethlehem 78, 79
Once in royal David's city 102
Silent night, holy night 111
The first Nowell the angel did say 109
The snow lay on the ground 110

Wonder, Love, and Praise
Shengye qing, shengye jing/
Holy night, blessed night 725

Lift Every Voice and Sing II
Away in a manger 27
Go, tell it on the mountain 21
Mary borned a baby 22
That boy-child of Mary was born in a stable 25
Silent night, holy night 26

The Nativity of Our Lord Jesus Christ
Christmas Day

December 25, 2017

God came in Jesus of Nazareth to reveal the power of God's love and healing. In the birth of Jesus, we realize that God shares life with us intimately. We meet God "in the flesh" of human struggle and most especially in the midst of human love. Christmas celebrates the incarnation of God; God "in the flesh of" human life. (Carne comes from the Latin for meat or flesh.)

Color   White

Preface   Of the Incarnation

Collect

Almighty God, you have given your only-begotten Son to take our nature upon him, and to be born this day of a pure virgin: Grant that we, who have been born again and made your children by adoption and grace, may daily be renewed by your Holy Spirit; through our Lord Jesus Christ, to whom with you and the same Spirit be honor and glory, now and for ever. Amen.

Readings and Psalm

Isaiah 52:7-10

The Hebrew scripture lection heralds a time of great joy as the Lord saves the people and brings deliverance to Jerusalem. The long exile is at an end. The messenger proclaims the good news, "The Lord reigns." The watchmen of the city respond with shouts of triumph to see God's salvation.

Psalm 98

A song of thanksgiving and praise to the victorious Lord, who has made righteousness known and shown faithfulness to God's people.

Hebrews 1:1-4 (5-12)

In this lesson, the Letter to the Hebrews begins with a declaration of Jesus' sonship. He is far above all angels at the right hand of God. Previously God had spoken through the prophets, but now the will of God is expressed in the Son, through whom the world was created and who bears the stamp of divine being. After making purification for sins, he has taken his seat of greatest honor.

If using Hebrews 1:1-12, this concluding sentence may be added:

A series of quotations from the Hebrew Bible is used to show the Son's superiority to the angels, who are the highest order of created beings.

John 1:1-14

The gospel opens with a hymn to the expression of God's very being, God's Word, who has now become flesh and lived among us. Through the Word all things have their life. The Word is the light of all humankind, and was witnessed to by John the Baptist. Although the world made by the Word did not recognize the Word, those who believe in the Word have been given the right to become children of God.

Prayers of the People

Presider: *In Christ God's Word has become flesh, dwelling among us, full of grace and truth. Let us pray to the true light which enlightens the world, asking all creation may receive grace upon grace from the fullness of God, saying: What has come into being in Christ was life, and the life was the light of all people.*

Litanist: You have given the Church the call to witness to the light which enlightens everyone: Empower our testimony that all persons may know themselves to be children of God and share in gospel of the Word made flesh.

What has come into being in Christ was life,

> ***and the life was the light of all people.***

Inspire the leaders of our nation and all in authority in the ways of grace and truth, that we may no longer be

Christmas

a people enslaved under the law, and know ourselves to be heirs, adopted as God's children.

What has come into being in Christ was life,

> *and the life was the light of all people.*

Be light in the darkness for all the world, that the fullness of Christ's heart may be made known for the healing of the earth.

What has come into being in Christ was life,

> *and the life was the light of all people.*

Live among us, O Word made flesh, and reconcile this community to your light.

What has come into being in Christ was life,

> *and the life was the light of all people.*

May your people sing a new song for your marvelous work, as we pray in faith for ___.

Hear our gratitude for your glory manifest among us, especially for ___ .

Receive those who have died as heirs of eternal life, especially ___.

What has come into being in Christ was life,

> *and the life was the light of all people.*

Presider: *Loving and gracious Creator, from the beginning you have brightened our darkness with the light of your life: Let your vindication shine out like the dawn, and your salvation like a burning torch, that your Word made flesh may bring grace upon grace to all the earth, in the power of your Holy Spirit, through Jesus Christ our Savior. Amen.*

Images in the Readings

During the fourth century, Christians chose the festival at the winter solstice as an appropriate time to celebrate the birth of Jesus. The prologue of John praises the Word of God as this light come to illumine the world. What has been born into the darkness on the earth is its light—an image especially appropriate for Christians in the northern hemisphere. The light of Christmas awaits the light of the Resurrection.

Too often the church speaks about creation as if it were the task of only God the Father. However, the prologue of John and the introduction to Hebrews see the fullness of God as having created the world. Jesus Christ, the Son of God, "the exact imprint of God's very being," is lauded as creator of all things. For Christians, God is always triune.

The Gospel of John demonstrates its Greek context in its reliance on the imagery of Jesus as the Son of God. Christian theologians stressed that calling Jesus the Son of God does not mean what it commonly signified in Greco-Roman polytheism, where super-humans were born from a human mother who had been impregnated by a god, such as Jupiter. Rather, the image is supreme metaphor for Jesus' origin from God. John also claims that Jesus, as the Father's only Son, makes all believers into children of God.

For John, Christ is the Word. When Jesus speaks, we hear God. When God speaks, we encounter Jesus. Worshipers receive this Word at Sunday worship.

Ideas for the Day

- The Gospel according to John echoes Genesis with its first words: "In the beginning." Readers might understand the word "beginning" as the first of a series of events in time, like the first page of a novel or the opening of a movie. But the Greek word *arché* also means foundation, root, ground of things. So, John's prologue tells us that the Word is at the bottom of things or at the heart of things. The second person of the Trinity—and now the risen Christ—is present to, weaves together, and gives significance to all that is.

- Hear and rejoice! Titus tells us we are saved by God's mercy. Reflect on who was represented at the manger: Jesus' parents, of the lineage of David; angels from heaven; the lowliest in shepherds; the lofty and Gentiles in the magi; and creatures in the barnyard. All of heaven and earth rejoices and is glad about the incarnation of Christ Jesus. Who would be at the manger if it were to happen today? Who are the lowliest? The loftiest?

- Christmas is more than the great celebration and remembrance of the birth of the baby Jesus. It is a joyful proclamation of the Incarnation. God is known in the flesh of human life. People who knew Jesus realized with awe and wonder that to be with Jesus was to be with God. They knew God in their flesh and blood relationships with Jesus. The good news of Christmas is that through the power of the Holy Spirit, we can still know God in the flesh of human life and relationship. God is not a distant creative power. God is a close as the love that binds one to another in a way that points beyond the human encounter to the divine revelation.

Making Connections

This is the day the Lord has made. Let us rejoice and be glad in it. As we celebrate the birth of Christ, the church invites us to allow Jesus Christ to find a home in us.

The Book of Common Prayer offers us several collects for Christmas Day. One way to journey more deeply with gratitude into the mysteries and joys of Christmas is to pray this collect throughout the day:

Almighty God, you have given your only-begotten Son to take our nature upon him, and to be born [this day] of a pure virgin: Grant that we, who have been born again and made your children by adoption and grace, may daily be renewed by your Holy Spirit; through our Lord Jesus Christ, to whom with you and the same Spirit be honor and glory, now and for ever. *Amen.*

Engaging all Ages

Today is Christmas Day. We gather together around tables, Christmas trees, and, fewer of us, around our church's altars. Some of us will gather around hospital beds or pull out old photographs and remember. Today we proclaim with joy the birth of Christ—truly human, born of Mary, yet truly from God. This gift of love incarnate surrounds and fills us. On this Christmas Day, amidst the celebrations, sharing, eating, and, for many, grief, know that life will never be the same and remember your neighbors, strangers, and those who hurt. Let your light shine. Let Jesus' light shine!

Hymns for the Day

The Hymnal 1982
Watchman, tell us of the night 640
Angels, from the realms of glory 93
Dost thou in a manger lie 97
Now yield we thanks and praise 108
Once in royal David's city 102
The first Nowell the angel did say 109
Where is this stupendous stranger? 491
Joy to the world! the Lord is come 100
Let all mortal flesh keep silence 324
Love came down at Christmas 84
O Savior of our fallen race 85, 86
Of the Father's love begotten 82
On this day earth shall ring 92
Sing, O sing, this blessed morn 88
What child is this, who, laid to rest 115

Wonder, Love, and Praise
Where is this stupendous stranger? 726
From the dawning of creation 748

Christmas

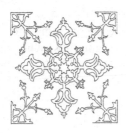

The First Sunday after Christmas

December 31, 2017

God came in Jesus fully to reveal God's love and forgiveness to all.

Color   White

Preface   Of the Incarnation

Collect

Almighty God, you have poured upon us the new light of your incarnate Word: Grant that this light, enkindled in our hearts, may shine forth in our lives; through Jesus Christ our Lord, who lives and reigns with you, in the unity of the Holy Spirit, one God, now and for ever. Amen.

Readings and Psalm

Isaiah 61:10-62:3

In our Hebrew Bible reading, the prophet joyfully responds on behalf of all God's people to the Lord's promises for a redeemed Jerusalem. He is a messenger to those who are poor and have suffered many troubles. Now he feels himself clothed in salvation and integrity, like a bridegroom or bride. In the sight of all people, this nation shall become like a fresh garden. The prophet will not keep silence until the deliverance of Jerusalem is known throughout the world.

Psalm 147 or . . .

A hymn of praise featuring God's power over nature and in history, redeeming those who are faithful.

Psalm 147:13-21

Galatians 3:23-25; 4:4-7

In this epistle lesson, Paul explains what the role of the law has been and how, in our new relationship of faith, we have become sons and heirs of the Father. Before the coming of Christ and justification by faith, we were like small children who had to be closely watched. God's own Son was born a subject of the law. Through him we now are given the status of sons coming into their maturity. We are enabled, through the Spirit of his Son, to call upon God with the same Aramaic word for Father that Jesus is remembered to have used, *Abba*.

John 1:1-18

In the first chapter of John's gospel, Jesus is first introduced from a spiritual point of view, then as the Christ to whom John the Baptist points. Christ is described as the Word who was with God from the beginning and through whom all things come to be. No one has ever seen God. "And the Word became flesh and lived among us, full of grace and truth." John summarizes the Christmas story in this one sentence. Grace and truth, two weighty words in John's gospel, perfectly describe this incarnate Word. The only Son, who is with the Father, has made him known.

Prayers of the People

Presider: *In Christ God's Word has become flesh dwelling among us, full of grace and truth. Let us pray to the true light which enlightens the world, that from the fullness of God all creation may receive grace upon grace, saying: What has come into being in Christ was life, and the life was the light of all people.*

Litanist: Clothe your Church with the garments of salvation and cover her with robes of righteousness, O Gracious One, that we may be your witnesses to testify to the light.

What has come into being in Christ was life,

    and the life was the light of all people.

Inspire the leaders of our nation and all in authority in the ways of grace and truth, that we may no longer be a people enslaved under the law but may know ourselves to be heirs, adopted as God's children.

What has come into being in Christ was life,

    and the life was the light of all people.

Be our light in the darkness for all the world, that the fullness of your heart may be made known for the healing of the earth.

What has come into being in Christ was life,

>*and the life was the light of all people.*

Live among us, O Word made flesh, and reconcile this community to your light.

What has come into being in Christ was life,

>*and the life was the light of all people.*

May your people be a crown of beauty and a royal diadem in your hand, as we pray in faith for ___.

Hear our gratitude for your glory manifest among us, especially for ___.

Receive those who have died as heirs of eternal life, especially ___.

What has come into being in Christ was life,

>*and the life was the light of all people.*

Presider: *Loving and gracious Creator, from the beginning you have brightened our darkness with the light of your life: Let your vindication shine out like the dawn, and your salvation like a burning torch, that your Word made flesh may bring grace upon grace to all the earth, in the power of your Holy Spirit, through Jesus Christ our Savior.* **Amen.**

Images in the Readings

In the Ancient Near East, some religious practice required parents to sacrifice their firstborn son, giving their child to the gods, who would then give to the parents many healthy children. Numbers 18:16 stipulates that instead of death, parents are to present a redemption price. So the infant Jesus is redeemed, and Paul writes of our redemption. When we redeem bottles and cans, we receive value for something that seemed worthless. The New Testament often uses the imagery of redemption as a way to describe salvation.

The white robe of baptism, which is the white robe of the vestment we call an alb, is a sign of our joy in the presence of God. We shine with the light of God.

Julian of Norwich, a fifteenth-century mystic who lived in a hut attached to a church, described believers as being the crown of beauty that God wears.

Most scholars agree that *Abba* was the way in first-century Aramaic that children named their father. Still today, Christians are unlikely to address their prayers to Daddy or Mommy. Yet the access

that Christ gives to believers is surprising, even disorienting.

Ideas for the Day

- John writes that Jesus is the true light that enlightens everyone. He is drawing on a cultural backdrop shaped by Plato and the neo-Platonic thinkers. In *The Republic*, Plato drew an analogy between the sun and the Good (507b–509c). Like the sun, the Good illuminates the truth. Jesus is God's self-revelation. In addition, the sun's light makes all growth possible. Without light, everything would wither and die. By analogy, Jesus is the source of life, eternal life. And finally, the Good shines through the sun and all lesser lights. The Light of the World, Jesus, shines through his disciples.
- The Psalmist (147: 4) says God calls each of the stars by name. What is in a name? What is the story behind your name? In Advent, we hear Isaiah 9:6, the child born would be called Wonderful Counselor, Mighty God, Everlasting Father, Prince of Peace. Jesus calls to us, "Who do you say I am?" Reflect on the attributes each of these names ascribes to God. Which name do you use most often when addressing God? (See: *Praying the Names of God* by Ann Spangler, Zondervan ©2004)
- Though technically Christmas is not a season, since the Sundays are numbered "after Christmas Day," the tradition of the "twelve days of Christmas" is familiar partly from the well-known carol. Twelfth Night, the night before the Feast of the Epiphany, traditionally ends the Christmas "season."

Making Connections

The first Sunday of Christmas is the last day of the year. We remember that Christmas is not a one-day event—there are actually twelve days of Christmas. The fact that the last day of this year is the first Sunday in Christmas comes as a special gift to us.

The gospel reading from this Sunday describes Christ as the Word from the beginning and through whom all things came to be. No one has ever seen God. The only Son, who is with the Father, has made him known.

In Isaiah we hear: "he has clothed me with the garments of salvation." In the early church, those who were baptized were given new white garments to wear as a sign of their redeemed relationship with God and the church. Later, the vesting of the priest became associated with being clothed with "the robe of righteousness."

Engaging all Ages

What we say and how we say it carries a great deal of power. Words matter. Words give life. Words destroy. Today is the first Sunday in the twelve days of Christmas and we celebrate the power of the "Word of God." We read in John "In the beginning was the Word, and the Word was God. He was in the beginning with God." We then read "And the Word became flesh and lived among us." Jesus is the Word. Let us reflect today on Jesus, the Word and how this influences the words we speak.

Hymns for the Day

The Hymnal 1982
Arise, shine, for your light has come S 223ff
How bright appears the Morning Star 496, 497
Father eternal, Ruler of creation 573
Let all mortal flesh keep silence 324
Of the Father's love begotten 82
Word of God, come down on earth 633

Wonder, Love, and Praise
From the dawning of creation 748
Arise, shine, for your light has come 883

Christmas

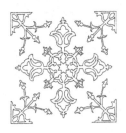

The Holy Name of Our Lord Jesus Christ

January 1, 2018

God's identity is revealed as "merciful and gracious" (Exodus 34:6). Jesus' name has significance: it is the Greek form of the Hebrew name Joshua, meaning "God saves."

Color   White

Preface   Of the Incarnation

Collect

Eternal Father, you gave to us your incarnate Son the holy name of Jesus to be the sign of our salvation: Plant in every heart, we pray, the love of him who is the Savior of the world, our Lord Jesus Christ; who lives and reigns with you and the Holy Spirit, one God, in glory everylasting. Amen.

Readings and Psalm

Numbers 6:22-27

In our opening lesson, Moses, by God's command, instructs those set aside for priestly ministry to bless Israel, putting God's own name upon them. These words have come to be known as the "Aaronic blessing," as they were first entrusted to Aaron and his sons. Because there is a threefold form to the blessing, Christians have often here perceived intimations of faith in the triune God.

Psalm 8

The psalmist glorifies the name of the Lord, sovereign of the earth and the magnificent heavens, who has made human life to have mastery over all other earthly creatures.

Galatians 4:4-7 or . . .

In the fullness of time, God sent God's own Son, born under the law, to redeem those under the law and to give them a new status as adopted children. Christians are not to see themselves as God's slaves, but as children and heirs to whom the Spirit has come, enabling them to speak to God in intimate terms, crying "Abba! Father!"

Philippians 2:5-11

From one of the earliest Christian hymns, we hear how Christ Jesus accepted the condition of a servant, was obedient even to the point of death, and was then given the name above every name. It is possible that this poem was adapted by Paul or another disciple from the hopes for a savior of a people who did not yet know Jesus. Jesus has fulfilled humanity's dream of one who will share fully in the mortal condition before his exaltation. To him every knee shall bow and every tongue confess the great name of the Lord now known in person, Jesus.

Luke 2:15-21

Our gospel tells how the shepherds, after the angelic vision which announced the Savior's birth, come to Bethlehem to see for themselves the child who is to be named Jesus. They share with Mary and Joseph the words of the angels. In this little infant, laid in a manger, the shepherds perceive the fulfillment of the song of the heavenly hosts. After eight days, in accordance with the law, the baby is then circumcised and given the promised name.

Prayers of the People

(using Galatians)

Presider: *O Lord our Sovereign, how exalted is your Name in all the world; hear our prayers of praise and petition, and bless your creation with your glorious Name as we pray: Hear us, Abba, Father; in the Name of Jesus.*

Litanist: Through your Son Jesus you have adopted us as your children, O God, and made us heirs of your eternal promises: Bless your holy family, the church, with the Spirit of Jesus, that we may glorify and praise you for all we have seen and heard.

Hear us, Abba, Father.

in the Name of Jesus.

Visit the leaders of our nation and all in authority with your holy and awesome presence, and quell the enemy and the avenger; that your justice may extend to all the earth.

Hear us, Abba, Father.

in the Name of Jesus.

You have made humanity but little lower than the angels and given us mastery over the works of your hands—beasts and birds and fish: make us wise stewards of our environment and compassionate advocates for all your children.

Hear us, Abba, Father.

in the Name of Jesus.

Bless our community and neighbors as we explore and celebrate your infinite grace, acceptance, and love, that we may treasure all your words in our hearts and honor all creation as the work of your fingers.

Hear us, Abba, Father.

in the Name of Jesus.

You have adorned humanity with glory and honor: Hear our prayers for those for whom we intercede, especially ___.

Join our praise with the angelic messengers as we offer you our thanks, especially for ___.

Hear our prayers for your children who have died, especially ___, that they may be heirs of the kingdom of your Son.

Hear us, Abba, Father.

in the Name of Jesus.

Presider: *Eternal and loving God, bless and keep your children; make your face to shine upon us and be gracious to us; lift up your countenance upon your earth, and give us peace, we pray in the Holy Name of Jesus, our brother and savior.* **Amen.**

(using Philippians)

Presider: *O Lord our Sovereign, how exalted is your Name in all the world; hear our prayers of praise and petition, and bless your creation with your glorious*

Name as we pray: Let every tongue confess, that Jesus Christ is Lord.

Litanist: Through your Son Jesus you have adopted us as your children, O God, and made us heirs of your eternal promises: Bless your holy family, the church, with the Spirit of Jesus, that we may glorify and praise you for all we have seen and heard.

Let every tongue confess,

that Jesus Christ is Lord.

Visit the leaders of our nation and all in authority with your holy and awesome presence, and quell the enemy and the avenger; that your justice may extend to all the earth. Let every tongue confess,

that Jesus Christ is Lord.

You have made humanity but little lower than the angels and given us mastery over the works of your hands—beasts and birds and fish: make us wise stewards of our environment and compassionate advocates for all your children.

Let every tongue confess,

that Jesus Christ is Lord.

Bless our community and neighbors as we explore and celebrate your infinite grace, acceptance, and love, that we may treasure all your words in our hearts and honor all creation as the work of your fingers.

Let every tongue confess,

that Jesus Christ is Lord.

You have adorned humanity with glory and honor: Hear our prayers for those for whom we intercede, especially ___.

Join our praise with the angelic messengers as we offer you our thanks, especially for ___.

Hear our prayers for your children who have died, especially ___, that they may be heirs of the kingdom of your Son.

Let every tongue confess,

that Jesus Christ is Lord.

Presider: *Eternal and loving God, bless and keep your children; make your face to shine upon us and be gracious to us; lift up your countenance upon your earth, and give us peace, we pray in the Holy Name of Jesus, our brother and savior.* **Amen.**

Ideas for the Day

♦ The naming of the person being baptized is an important element in the baptismal rite, as in scripture: "You shall be called by a new name that the mouth of the Lord shall give" (Isaiah 62:2). In some traditions, a child was literally named at baptism and given the name of a Christian saint. Whether or not the name is given at baptism, one's given name takes on new significance as one is adopted into the family of Christ.

♦ Mary Ann Evans wrote under the male pen-name George Eliot. Charlotte, Emily, and Anne Bronte initially published their works with male pseudonyms. Recognized today as outstanding authors, they assumed male names to avoid the negative stereotypes attached to women in the male-dominated publishing industry. More recently, J.K. Rowling assumed the name Robert Galbraith to publish a series of detective novels. She sought to escape the constraining expectations that come with the name of the writer associated with the successful Harry Potter series. Names suggest identity, raise expectations, and sometimes provoke opposition. "Jesus" has all these effects.

♦ Baby Jesus was presented in the Temple for the rite of circumcision. This is a mark of the Jewish faith, a covenant with God. In the Episcopal Church, we are presented for baptism, and are surrounded by the community in reaffirming our covenant with God through the Baptismal Covenant. How are we marked as Christ's own forever?

♦ In the Episcopal tradition, we have blessings. The blessing from Numbers is one of the oldest and most renowned. What is in a blessing? A priest blesses the congregation at the end of worship to "send us forth" before the dismissal. What are other occasions for blessings? Consider offering house blessings to members of your congregation.

Making Connections

This is it. This truly becomes the feast of every believer. The name of Jesus becomes our name and each and every one of us is called into the experience of salvation. Anointed and claimed by Christ in baptism, we become the Holy Name of Jesus.

On this day when we celebrate the Holy Name, a breathing prayer-exercise might be appropriate.

Find a quite spot where you can spend some alone and undisturbed time. It might require putting your phone away.

Close your eyes and for the next few moments breathe in and exhale the names you use for God and Jesus. Imagine that the names you breathe in seek to heal and bless you. Imagine that the names you breathe out seek to heal and bless your family, your church, and the world.

Engaging all Ages

Today we celebrate a major feast day in the church year—The Holy Name of Our Lord Jesus Christ. Holy Name day celebrates the giving of the name of Jesus to the holy child. What is the origin of your name? Were you named after your father or were you named after a much beloved great aunt? Maybe you were named after an actor or maybe you have a name that your parents chose for no other reason than they liked it. What does your name mean? Have you ever looked up the meaning of your name? Today we celebrate the name Jesus—the name given by the angel before he was conceived in the womb.

Hymns for the Day

The Hymnal 1982
Jesus, the very thought of thee 642
How sweet the Name of Jesus sounds 644
Now greet the swiftly changing year 250
O for a thousand tongues to sing 493
To the Name of our salvation 248, 249
Sing praise to our Creator 295
A stable lamp is lighted 104
All hail the power of Jesus' Name! 450, 451
All praise to thee, for thou, O King divine 477
At the name of Jesus 435
From east to west, from shore to shore 77
Jesus! Name of wondrous Love! 252

Wonder, Love, and Praise
God be with you till we meet again 801
You're called by name, forever loved 766

Lift Every Voice and Sing II
Blessed be the Name 78
Glorious is the Name of Jesus 63
There is a name I love to hear 95
There's something about that Name 107
God be with you 234
The Lord bless you and keep you 231

Epiphany

Preparing for Epiphany

Overview

"O God, by the leading of a star you manifested your only Son to the peoples of the earth: Lead us, who know you now by faith, to your presence, where we may see your glory face to face . . ."

(Collect for the Epiphany, BCP 214).

While the Book of Common Prayer gives Epiphany its own season, the day itself—and the season as well—is inextricably tied to Christmas. In the Christmas season, we celebrate "the Word made flesh," "God with us." In Epiphany, this manifestation of God in Christ—God's self-disclosure—begins to be proclaimed to the world. We see this not only in the journey and testimony of the magi, but in the account of Jesus's baptism by John: "And just as he was coming up out of the water, he saw the heavens torn apart and the Spirit descending like a dove on him. And a voice came from heaven, 'You are my Son, the Beloved; with you I am well pleased.'" We see it also in the account of the Transfiguration on the Last Sunday after the Epiphany, when Jesus "was transfigured before them, and his clothes became dazzling white, such as no one on earth could bleach them. And there appeared to them Elijah with Moses, who were talking with Jesus" (Mark 9).

Environment

Look for ways to emphasize light, journey, and manifestation within your space.

Liturgy

Look at the seasonal resources in *Common Worship* (118-207), *Sundays & Seasons* ("Seasonal Rites"), *Book of Common Worship* (191-219), and *New Zealand Prayer Book* (529-531, 560-572).

♦ Eucharistic Prayers. Consider Prayer 1 and Prayer 3 from *Enriching Our Worship I*.

♦ Prayers of the People. Look at the resources in *Common Worship* (124-128, 141-142, 152-153, 164, 198).
♦ Fraction anthems. *Common Worship*, 167.
♦ Blessings. Look at the options in *Book of Occasional Services* (24), *Common Worship* (135-136, 169, 183) and *New Zealand Prayer Book* (530-531).
♦ For the day of Epiphany, unless it falls on a Sunday, it may make sense to celebrate an evening Eucharist. Consider beginning with An Order of Worship for the Evening, "giving candles to the congregation to be lighted after the seasonal prayer for light."[1]

Lectionary

In Year B, we hear about the visit of the wise men (Matthew); the baptism of the Lord (Mark); Jesus calling the disciples (John and Mark); Jesus proclaiming and manifesting the Kingdom of God through teaching, preaching, and healing (Mark); and the Transfiguration (Mark). What does this birth—Emmanuel—God's self-disclosure—mean for the world, and how can we share that?

Music

What hymns or songs focus on the theme of light?

Formation/Activities

Will there be baptisms on the Sunday of the Baptism of our Lord (First Sunday after the Epiphany)? If so, formation for the catechumens/newly baptized continues during these weeks.

---

[1] Leonel L. Mitchell, *Planning the Church Year* (Harrisburg: Morehouse, 1991), 34.

Through the Eyes of a Child

What Jesus did and said helps us to know who God is and what God is doing for us: On the night of Jesus' birth, the giant comet star let the world know that God is with us; magi from far away saw the star and journeyed to visit Jesus. Jesus called his friends to be with him and to help him in his work. Jesus said and did amazing and wonderful things that no one else could do. He healed many people to show how much God loved them. Jesus, the gift of love, came for all the people of the world. Jesus is like a light, helping us to see better. We are a part of Jesus, and in Jesus we are baptized into God's family, the Church. The wonder and mystery of the magi invite us to wonder about the mystery. Jesus, who are you really?

Through the Eyes of Youth

The Church is called to reveal Jesus to the world, and to re-affirm baptismal vows strengthening the ways to seek Christ in all persons, and to continue in the apostles' teachings, breaking of bread, and the prayers. Epiphany is a time to celebrate the mystery of the visit of the magi to the infant Jesus. Epiphany is the sudden realization or comprehension of the essence or meaning of something sacred. Invite the youth to read God's Word every morning; use the lectionary and follow the stories for the season of Epiphany. This is a wonderful season to take each sentence of the Baptismal Covenant and invite the teens to determine how to put it into action, not only for themselves, but for the community.

Through the Eyes of Daily Life

Epiphany is a time to bless the homes of Christians with holy water, incense, and prayers, that those who abide in the home may be empowered to live lives that are an epiphany of God's coming among us in Jesus, into whose body we have been incorporated at our baptism. (See *The Book of Occasional Services*).

Through the Eyes of the Global Community

Many of the collects during this season speak of covenants and commandments. The Baptismal Covenant calls Christians to strive for justice and peace among all people, and to respect the dignity of every human being (BCP 305). Six of the Ten Commandments, which summarize the 613 commandments of the Torah, remind us that to honor God is to love others as we love ourselves. Many of the commandments of the Torah deal with proper treatment of the poor, the stranger, and the disadvantaged in society, as well as ethical business practices. Jesus' "new Law" outlined in the Sermon on the Mount calls the Christian to an even higher standard: reconciliation in all relationships; truthfulness in business, personal, and political matters; justice and respect for human rights; and love for all people, even those perceived to be enemies. In 1997, the General Convention of the Episcopal Church designated the Last Sunday of Epiphany as World Mission Sunday to increase awareness of and participation in the wider global mission of the Church.

Seasonal Checklist

This is a short season. In January, begin to schedule meetings to plan for Lent.

Seasonal Rites for Epiphany

Epiphany Blessing[1]

The following blessing may be used by a bishop or priest whenever a blessing is appropriate. It is a three-fold form with an Amen at the end of each sentence, leading into a Trinitarian blessing. This may be used from the feast of the Epiphany through the following Sunday.

May Almighty God, who led the Wise Men by the shining of a star to find the Christ, the Light from Light, lead you also, in your pilgrimage, to find the Lord. *Amen.*

May God, who sent the Holy Spirit to rest upon the Only-begotten at his baptism in the Jordan River, pour out that Spirit on you who have come to the waters of new birth. *Amen.*

May God, by the power that turned water into wine at the wedding feat at Cana, transform your lives and make glad your hearts. *Amen.*

And the blessing of God Almighty, the Father, the Son, and the Holy Spirit, be upon you and remain with you for ever. *Amen.*

Blessing for a Home

Twelfth Night (January 5), the Feast of the Epiphany (January 6), or another day during the week following, is an occasion for family and friends to gather for a blessing of their home for the coming year.

Following an eastern European tradition, a visual blessing may be inscribed with white chalk above the main door; for example 20 + CMB + 18. The numbers change with each year, with this year being 2018. The three letters stand for either the ancient Latin blessing Christe mansionem benedicat, which means "Christ, bless this house," or the legendary names of the magi (Caspar, Melchior, and Balthasar).

Celebrant Peace be to this house, and to all who dwell in it.

Visit, O blessed Lord, this home with the gladness of your presence, Bless *all* who live here with the gifts of your love; and grant that *they* may manifest your love [to each other and] to all who lives *they* touch. May *they* grow in grace and in the knowledge and love of you; guide, comfort, and strengthen *them*; and preserve *them* in peace, O Jesus Christ, now and for ever. *Amen.*[2]

Candlemas[3]

Candlemas (Candle Mass), on February 2, takes its name from the candles carried at the celebration of the Presentation of Christ in the Temple. It celebrates a ritual of Jewish law related to first-born sons that Joseph and Mary carried out (Luke 2:21-40). Luke's gospel tells how Simeon and Anna, devout Jews, honored the infant Jesus as the promised Messiah.

When circumstances permit, the congregation gathers at a place apart from the church so that all may go into the church in procession, however it can begin just inside the door of the church. All are provided with unlighted candles. These are lit during the opening canticle, which is sung or said.

The Entrance

Celebrant: Light and peace, in Jesus Christ our Lord.
> ***Thanks be to God.***

A Light to enlighten the nations,
and the glory of your people Israel.
> ***A Light to engliten the nations,***
> ***and the glory of your people Israel.***

Lord, you now have set yoru servant free
to go in peace as you have promised.
> ***A Light to enlighten the nations,***
> ***and the glory of your people Israel.***

[1] *The Book of Occasional Services 2003* (New York: Church Publishing, 2004), 24.

[2] Ibid, 49.

[3] Ibid, 53-55.

For thse eyes of mine have seen the Savior,
whom you have prepared for all the world to see.
*A Light to enlighten the nations,
and the glory of your people Israel.*

God our Father, source of all light, today you revealed to the aged Simeon your light which enlightens the nations. Fill our hearts with the light of faith, that we who bear these candles may walk in the path of goodness, and come to the Light that shines for ever, your Son Jesus Christ our Lord. *Amen.*

The Procession

Deacon: Let us go forth in peace.

In the name of Christ. Amen.

All carry lighted candles while an appropriate hymn or canticle is sung, stopping for the following Collect to be read.

O God, you have made this day holy by the presentation of your Son in the Temple, and by the purification of the Blessed Virgin Mary: Mercifully grant that we, who delight in her humble readiness to be the birthgiver of the Only-begotten, may rejoice for ever in our adoption as his sisters and brothers; through Jesus Christ our Lord. *Amen.*

The procession approaches the altar as the following antiphon and Psalm 48:1-2, 10-13 is read.

We have waited in silence on your loving-kindness, O Lord, in the midst of your temple. Your praise, like your Name, O God, reaches to the world's end; your right hand is full of justice.

Great is the Lord, and highly to be praised;
    in the city of our God is his holy hill.
Beautiful and lofty, the joy of all the earth, is the hill
    of Zion the very center o fthe world and the city
    of the great King.
Let Mount Zion be glad and the cities of Judah
    rejoice, because of your judgments.
Make the circuit of Zion; walk round about her; count
    the number of her towers.
Consider well her bulwarks; examine her stronghold;
    that you may tell those who come after.
This God is our God for ever and ever; he shall be our
    guide for evermore.

Other Notable Days in Epiphany

Martin Luther King, Jr. Day, January 15

A federal holiday, this day will fall on Monday, January 15, 2018. Some schools celebrate the day be teaching their pupils or students about the work and ministry of Martin Luther King and the struggle against racial segregation and racism. It has also become a day where Americans give some of their time on this day as volunteers in action in their communities. For congregations, Sunday, January 14, can be a day of focused prayer, preaching, and education on the legacy Dr. King entrusted to us. Resources can be found at http://www.thekingcenter.org/king-holiday and https://www.serve.gov/site-page/mlkday (accessed August 14, 2017).

Lord our God, see how oppression and violence are our sad inheritance, one generation to the next. We look for you where the lowly are raised up, where the mighty are brought down. We find you there in your servants and we give you thanks this day for your preacher and witness, Martin Luther King Jr. Fill us with your spirt: where our human community is divided by racism, torn by repression, saddened by fear and ignorance, may we give ourselves to your work of healing. Grant this through Christ our Lord. *Amen.*[4]

Week of Prayer for Christian Unity, January 18-24

The Week of Prayer for Christian Unity is an international Christian ecumenical observance for eight days, held between the feasts of Peter and Paul. Resources for study, prayer, music, and worship are offered in advance at http://www.oikoumene.org/en/resources/week-of-prayer (accessed August 14, 2017).

Litanist: We have come together in the presence of Almighty God to pray for the recovery of the unity of Christ's Church, and for the renewal of our common life in Jesus Christ, in whom we are all made one.

Silence

Let us give heed to the words of Holy Scripture which set forth God's will and purpose for the unity of his Church.

"Hear, O Israel, the Lord our God is one Lord; and you shall love the Lord your God ith all your heart, and with all your soul, and with all your mind."

Lord, write your word in our hearts.
That we may know and do your will.

"There is one body, and one Spirit, as there is also one hope held out in God's call to you; one Lord, one faith, one baptism; one God and Father of all, who is over all and through all and in all."

---

4 Christopher L. Webber, editor. *An American Prayer Book* (Harrisburg, PA: Morehouse Publishing, 2008), 124.

Lord, write your word in our hearts:
That we may know and do your will.

"For Christ is like a single body with its many limbs and organs which, many as they are, together make up one body. For indeed we were all brought into one body by baptism, in the one Spirit, whether we are Jews or Greeks, whether slaves or free, and that one Holy Spirit was poured out for all of us to drink."

Lord, write your word in our hearts:
That we may know and do your will.

"But it is not for these alone that I pray, but for those also who through their words put their faith in me; may they all be one; as you, Father, are in me, and I in you, so also may they be in us, that the world may believe that you have sent me."

Lord, write your word in our hearts:
That we may know and do your will. Amen.[5]

Theological Education Sunday, February 4

Theological Education Sunday (TES) is officially recognized on the first Sunday in February. It is a day parishioners set aside to pray and give for all laity and clergy whose ministry is Christian education, wherever that ministry happens—in the home, preschool programs, parishes, colleges, universities, and seminaries. Established in 1999 by The Episcopal Church, this Sunday on the church calendar is an occasion for all parishioners to focus on education as a key aspect of mission. Guest preachers and seminarians sponsored by the congregation are often invited to preach.

Litanist: O God of truth, ever beckoning us to loftier understanding and deeper wisdom, we seek your will and implore your grace for all who share the life of divinity schools and seminaries in our day, knowing that, unless you build among us, we who teach and learn will labor but in vain.

Silence

For the men and women who teach, that they may together bring fire and vision to a common task, knowing one field yet eager to relate it to all others; just in their academic demands, yet seeing each student as a child of God; fitted to teach not only by great

learning but by great faith in humankind and in you, their God:

In them and in us, O God, kindle your saving truth.

Silence

For deans and presidents, trustees and development officers, and all others who point the way for theological education in our day, that their chief concern be not budgets and buildings and prestige, but men and women freed to know your whole will and roused to serve you in your Church:

In them and in us, O God, kindle your saving truth.

Silence

For janitors and maids, for cooks and keepers of the grounds, for those who prepare our food and wash our dishes, and for the host of other workers and suppliers whose faithfulness ministers to our common life:

In them and in us, O God, kindle your saving truth.

Silence

For parents and givers of scholarships, who support theological students, that they may not desire for them more income, or social acceptance, or glory of family or of donor, but look rather for new breadth of intelligence, the spirit made whole, and devoted Christian service in life:

In them and in us, O God, kindle your saving truth.

Silence

For the students themselves, that their confusion may be brief, their perspective constantly enlarged, and their minds and spirits alert to all that chapel and classroom, library and fieldwork assignment can mean in their lives.

In them and in us, O God, kindle your saving truth.

Silence

For every member of this community of learning and service, that with them we may be aware of your Holy Spirit leading us all into truth, and may grasp here your special intention for all our learning and striving:

In them and in us, O God, kindle your saving truth.

Silence

[5] "The Week of Prayer for Christian Unity," in *The Wideness of God's Mercy: Litanies to Enlarge Our Prayer* edited by Jeffrey W. Rowthorn (New York: Church Publishing, 2007), 128-129.

Epiphany

We know, O heavenly Father, that a seminary education is but the willing and planning of many men and women, each sought by your great love. Grant that we who would earnestly serve you may witness in the world to the reality of your gospel, as it is shown forth in Christ Jesus our Lord. *Amen.*[6]

Super Bowl Sunday: Souper Bowl of Caring, February 4

Souper Bowl of Caring is a national movement of young people working to fight hunger and poverty in their own communities around the time of the Super Bowl football game. In the weeks leading up to or on Super Bowl Sunday, young people take up a collection (many use a soup pot), asking for one dollar or one item of food for people in need. They give 100% of their donation directly to the local hunger-relief charity of their choice. Learn more at https://souperbowl.org/welcome (accessed August 14, 2017).

We have seen your hand of mercy in the service of those who spread food, shelter, hope, and faith to suffering humankind. Plant more seeds in the bellies of the full, to burst forth in joy, to explode like the ripened grain with life-giving bread. Give us, we beseech you, in the bosoms of our souls, a passion for the powerless and a commitment to place all poverty in the past. *Amen.*[7]

Feast of Lights: An Epiphany Pageant[8]

This service is one of darkness and light, showing how the message of Jesus spread throughout the world and throughout the ages to the present day. It can take the form of a simple liturgy of lighting candles in the sanctuary or can be one in which participants dress in costume to represent each of the persons in history who helped spread the Light of Christ. Traditionally, it is held on the Feast of the Epiphany, or on an evening at the beginning of this season.

Candles can be placed throughout the church, or on the altar. Characters can be seated in the congregation, come forth to stand in front and recite their lines, go light their candle, then return to their seat. Have a candle lighter (taper) at a location so each participant to easily pick it up on their way to light "their" candle. Once the first candle is lit, subsequent candles can be lit from the flame of the previously lit candle.

There are many characters (41+/-), several without speaking roles. Ideally a different person represents each character; however, individuals can represent more than one person, especially if you are not dressing up as the person. This is an excellent pageant to be totally handed over to youth in its production and presentation as an offering to the congregation.

Costumes

Costumes that are used for Christmas pageants can be used—simple robes and headpieces for most of the characters that lived in the first century. Academic robes or period costumes can be used for later period characters.

Props

One candle (in a candlestick, holder, stand, etc.) per character located on the altar, chancel area, or around the sanctuary.

Candle lighter/taper

Candles (with paper followers to catch drips) per every member of the congregation or audience

Script

[NARRATOR]: We come to bear witness to the Light. In the fullness of time, God entered this world in the birth of Jesus, the Word of God, the Light of the world. Jesus grew to adulthood in Nazareth of Galilee. He came to the river Jordan to be baptized by John, and when he came up out of the water, the heavens opened and the Spirit of God descended upon Him, and God said, "You are my beloved Son."

[JESUS]: Let the Paschal candle be lit for Jesus Christ, the light of the world.

[NARRATOR]: Jesus chose twelve ordinary men to receive his light. He spoke to them saying: "While you have the light, believe in the light, that you may become children of light." Then he sent them as apostles to establish the Church, to spread his light to all people, in every race and in every nation on earth. Let a candle be lit for each of the Twelve Apostles . . .

[PETER]: Simon, called Peter. Jesus called me "the rock" on which he would build the Church.

---

[6] John Oliver Nelson, "For Theological Seminaries," in *The Wideness of God's Mercy: Litanies to Enlarge Our Prayer* edited by Jeffrey W. Rowthorn (New York: Church Publishing, 2007), 165-166.

[7] Marcia King, "For an End to Poverty" in *Lifting Women's Voices: Prayers to Change the World* Margaret Rose, Jenny Te Paa, Jeanne Person, and Abagail Nelson, editors (Harrisburg, PA: Morehouse Pubiishing, 2009), 69.

[8] Sharon Ely Pearson, "Feast of Lights: An Epiphany Pageant" part of Church Publishing Incorporated's *Skiturgies: Pageants, Plays, Rites & Rituals* collection. www.skiturgies.com

[ANDREW]: Andrew, his brother. A fisherman.

[JAMES]: James, the son of Zebedee. Also a fisherman.

[JOHN]: John, his brother. A fisherman.

[PHILIP]: Philip.

[BARTHOLOMEW]: Bartholomew.

[MATTHEW]: Matthew, the tax collector.

[JAMES]: James, the son of Alphaeus.

[SIMON]: Simon, the Zealot.

[THOMAS]: Thomas. Following the resurrection, many felt I had doubts of Jesus' rising to new life.

[JUDE]: Jude

[JUDAS ISCARIOT]: Judas Iscariot. I was to betray Jesus with a kiss. Let my candle be extinguished for the light I was unable to carry to the end. *(Light candle, then extinguish by blowing out.)*

[MARY MAGDALENE]: I was the first witness to the resurrection of Jesus, and one who first bore that news to the Twelve. I had accompanied Jesus for much of His ministry, and my special and favored relationship with the Lord is shown in the fact that it was to me that Jesus first spoke after he had risen. From ancient tradition in the Church, I am accorded a status equal to an Apostle.

[MATTHIAS]: I am another who is ranked with the original Twelve. I was elected by the remaining eleven to take the place of Judas in their number.

[NARRATOR]: Let two candles be lit for Matthias and Mary Magdalene, who together show that the Apostolic Succession is proven not only by lineage but also by faithful presence and witness.

[NARRATOR]: Many women have served as disciples, witnesses, and apostles.

[MARY OF BETHANY]: *(Move forward with Martha of Bethany)* Mary of Bethany. I served Jesus many times at my home in Bethany. A week before his crucifixion, I took a jar of expensive perfume, poured it on his feet, wiping it with my hair. I loved to sit at Jesus' feet and listen to him.

[MARTHA OF BETHANY]: *(Move forward with Mary of Bethany)* Martha of Bethany. I was often focused on the details when Jesus came to visit us. But I knew Jesus was the source of eternal life, and believed God would give Jesus whatever he asked. I was right, my brother, Lazarus, was brought back to life.

[SAMARITAN WOMAN]: The Samaritan woman. I met Jesus at Jacob's well and was among the first to confess Jesus as the messiah.

[JOANNA and SUSANNA]: *(Say together.)* We traveled with Jesus through Galilee and financed his journeys.

[MARY]: I was the Mother of our Lord, and was present at the cross and among those gathered at Pentecost.

[PHOEBE and PRISCILLA]: *(Say together.)* We were deacons in the early church.

[JUNIA]: I was an apostle and contemporary of Paul.

[LOIS, EUNICE, and TABITHA: *(Say together.)* We were disciples during the early years of the Church.

[NARRATOR]: Let candles be lit for each of these faithful women of scripture and the early Church, who both led and served their communities of faith.

[NARRATOR]: These apostles went out into the world to spread the light of the gospel of Christ. There were many who opposed their witness and the Word.

[PAUL]: I was one of those who tried to put out the Light. I was known as Saul of Tarsus, a fanatical persecutor of all followers of Jesus until one day I was overcome by a vision of the Light of Christ. Taking the name of Paul, I carried that light throughout the Mediterranean world, establishing the Church far beyond the cities and people of the Jewish culture. From the seeds I planted and those who accompanied me, the light of Christ has spread from a small group in Jerusalem to two billion people in every nation on earth today. Today I am called, "the apostle to the Gentiles."

[NARRATOR]: The story of Jesus spread throughout the world.

[AUGUSTINE]: In the year 596, I, Augustine, was sent from Rome by Pope Gregory the Great to be a missionary to England. I became the first archbishop of Canterbury and reorganized the remnants of the old Celtic churches throughout Britain and Ireland, which had existed since the second century and had been built up by revered predecessors in the faith, such as Patrick of Ireland, Alban in England, David in Wales, and Ninian in Scotland.

Epiphany

[NARRATOR]: Let five candles be lit for these patriarchs of British Christianity.
(Patrick, Alban, David, and Ninian come forward to light candles)

[STEPHEN LANGON]: Reading and studying the Holy Scriptures was greatly facilitated by the system of dividing the Bible's texts into chapters and verses. I, Stephen Langon, introduced this relatively modern idea. I was an Englishman at the University of Paris and later, in 1207, became archbishop of Canterbury.

[THOMAS CRANMER]: I, Thomas Cranmer, became archbishop of Canterbury in 1533. I had been much influenced theologically by the Lutheran reformers in Germany, such as Martin Luther. When the English church rejected the authority of the papacy in 1534, I led the creation and adoption of a new liturgy for the Church, producing the first two versions of the Book of Common Prayer, which has been the lifeblood of Anglican worship throughout the world ever since. I am known as the father of Anglican liturgy.

[QUEEN ELIZABETH I]: It was I, a laywoman, whose genius, leadership, and personal faith truly established Anglicanism as a strong and distinct tradition. As Queen of England, I preserved and brought together into one church the ancient catholic order and the principles of the Reformation. My vision presented the possibilities of unity with diversity.

[SAMUEL SEABURY]: After the American colonies won independence, I was sent from Connecticut to Scotland in 1784 to be consecrated as the first American Anglican bishop. I, Samuel Seabury, thus secured the historic episcopate for the Episcopal Church.

[WILLIAM WHITE]: Three years later, the archbishop of Canterbury presided at the consecration of two others to be bishops for the Episcopal Church. I, William White, was one of these men from of Pennsylvania, and became the first presiding bishop of the Episcopal Church. I was the chief architect and wise overseer for the Church for almost fifty years. Every Episcopal bishop, past and present, can trace their ordinations back to my episcopacy.

[YOUR FIRST BISHOP]: _____ was the first Episcopal bishop of _____, consecrated for this office in _____.
(Note any historical information).

[YOUR FIRST CLERGY PERSON/LAY LEADER]:
(Note the founding of your congregation and any leadership involved, including historical information about your church.)

[NARRATOR]: We, the people of
_____ (name your congregation), are now the recipients of the faith and faithfulness, which has been entrusted to us in _____ (your town or city) as congregations in full communion with each other. With joy and gratitude, we ponder that the faith of Christ, announced by a miraculous star two thousand years ago, has been passed down through the centuries to our places of worship—by magi, apostles, saints, bishops, local clergy and laypeople: men and women, extraordinary and ordinary. The light is passed from the Bethlehem manger to this place and to our homes. Our prayer is that we sustain and grow the Light that is Jesus Christ, and pass it on—to those now beside us, and around us, and to those who come after us. As an outward sign of this, everyone will please light each other's unlit candles.

May Almighty God, who led the wise men by the shining of a star to find the Christ, the Light from Light, lead you also, in your pilgrimage, to find the Lord. Amen.

By the shining of a star to find the Christ, the Light from Light, lead you also, in your pilgrimage, to find the Lord. Amen.

Preparing for Lent

The last Sunday of the season of the Epiphany features the story of the Transfiguration in the gospel reading. This is also the last Sunday the word, "Alleluia" will be used in liturgy, and preparations begin for the coming week's Ash Wednesday liturgy as well as the solemn season that follows.

Here are two traditions for making the transition from Epiphany to Lent.

Burying the Alleluia

As we keep the ancient practice of fasting from singing or speaking "alleluia" through the forty days of Lent, you may consider the practice of "burying" the alleluia at the end of the liturgy on the last Sunday before Ash Wednesday. This might mean simply singing an appropriate song at the end of the service or including the actual lowereing of a visual alleluia banner (perhaps created by children) while singing.

You could bury it in your churchyard or hide it away in a dark place (but remember where you put it!). Bring the alleluia back as part of the first alleluias at the Great Vigil of Easter or your Easter Festive Eucharist.

Leader: O God, make speed to save us, hallelujah, hallelujah.

O Lord, make haste to help us, alleluia, alleluia.

Leader: "Alleluia" is Greek for "Praise the Lord."

Our God is a loving God, worthy of praise.

Leader: The faithful people of God praise him for the great deeds he has done.

God created us out of dust, restored the land, took Israel out of exile, spoke through the prophets, and gives hope and forgiveness through his Son, Jesus Christ.

Leader: The Book of Psalms contains "Hallels" (Psalms 113-118) or special chants. These hymns of praise were sung on each step going up to the Temple during festive celebrations and pilgrimages.

Praise the Lord, all nations! Extol him, all peoples! For great is his steadfast love toward us; and the faithfulness of the Lord endures for ever. Praise the Lord. (Psalm 117)

Leader: Hallelujah! Praise God in his holy temple. (Psalm 150:1)

Let everything that has breath praise the Lord, Hallelujah. (Psalm 150:6)

Leader: We have much for which to be thankful. But there is not always joy in our lives. There is sadness and loneliness in the world. Sometimes we need time to think. Jesus spent forty days in the wilderness praying to God. Lent is our forty days of quiet time to prepare for the mystery of Easter. This is a time when we do not say "alleluia" in church. "Alleluia" is reserved for the great festive celebration of Easter.

How shall we sing the Lord's song in a foreign land? (Psalm 137:4)

(Silently bury the "Alleluia")

Leader: Almighty God, you bid your faithful people to rejoice in praise, but also to repent and reflect in silence. Give us grace and courage to devote our hearts to you and to love others as you would, through Jesus Christ our Lord, who lives and reigns with you and the Holy Spirit, on God, forever and ever. *Amen.*[9]

Fasting

Shrove Tuesday

The day before Ash Wednesday was the day all households were to use up all milk, eggs, and fat to prepare for the strict fasting of Lent. These ingredients were made into pancakes, a meal which came to symbolize preparation for the discipline of Lent, from the English tradition. "Shrove" comes from the verb "to shrive" (to confess and receive absolution) prior to the start of the Lenten season. Other names for this day include Carnival (farewell to meat) and Mardi Gras (Fat Tuesday of the French tradition). Thus, many congregations have Shrove Tuesday pancake suppers.

O Lord, we as we prepare our hearts for our lenten journey, bless these pancakes we are about to share. As they remind us of the rich ingredients from our kitchens that fill our bellies with satisfaction, may we also remember your time in the wilderness when you did not even have bread or water. Be present with us as we get ready to begin the holy season of Lent, strengthening us to be ready to serve you in the days and weeks to come. *Amen.*

Making Pretzels

The pretzel has been used during Lent for over 1500 years. It is thought that originally pretzels were made by monks to resemble arms crossed in prayer. These breads were called "little arms." This can have deep spiritual meaning for us during Lent. Since basically only flour and water are used, pretzels can remind us of fasting.

Heavenly Father, we ask you to bless these little breads. Each time we eat them may we be reminded of the special season we are in and that through prayer we will become better people to each other. Let us not forget those who are in need of our prayers daily. Keep your loving arms around us, O Father, to protect us always. *Amen.*

---

[9] Linda Nichols, "Farewell to Alleluia" as part of Church Publishing Incorporated's *Skiturgies* collection. www.skiturgies.com

The Epiphany

January 6, 2018

The significance of Jesus' birth is revealed to the world beyond Judea.

Color   White

Preface   Of the Epiphany

Collect

O God, by the leading of a star you manifested your only Son to the peoples of the earth: Lead us, who know you now by faith, to your presence, where we may see your glory face to face; through Jesus Christ our Lord, who lives and reigns with you and the Holy Spirit, one God, now and for ever. Amen.

Readings and Psalm

Isaiah 60:1-6

In our Hebrew scripture lesson the prophet envisions the end of exile and the glorious restoration of Jerusalem. Although darkness covers the earth, the Lord will be a light making God's people shine. To this radiance shall come the nations. Rich treasures will be brought from afar to honor God.

Psalm 72:1-7, 10-14

The psalm asks that God endow the king with compassionate justice and righteousness, and that his reign may extend over all nations and throughout all generations.

Ephesians 3:1-12

Here is set forth the great theme of Paul's apostolic commission: the revealed mystery that Christ's salvation extends beyond Judaism to include all peoples. The apostle is near the end of his ministry and in prison at the time of the writing of this letter. Now it is recognized as God's eternal purpose that the Gentiles are to be members of the same body. The wisdom of God is made known through the church even in transcendental realms.

Matthew 2:1-12

Our gospel is the story of the wise men from the east, who, guided by a star, come to worship the child born to be king. Despite the wicked plotting of Herod, the magi are able to bring their gifts to Jesus without betraying his exact location. Early Christians found in the rich symbolism and motifs of the story the fulfillment of both Hebrew scripture prophecy and the dreams of many peoples. The meaning of this birth, amid terrifyingly human circumstances, enlightens and transcends human history.

Or

Isaiah 60:1-6, 9

Psalm 72:1-2, 10-17

Ephesians 3:1-12

Matthew 2:1-12

Prayers of the People

Presider: *Gracious and loving Creator, in the manifestation of Christ you have revealed to all the earth the mystery of your love, spreading your illumination and your abundant promises to all humanity: Hear us now and visit us with that light, as we pray for the needs of all creation, saying: Arise, shine, for the light has come, and the glory of God has risen upon us.*

Litanist: Through the Church, the wisdom of God in its rich variety may now be made known: Help us, O Holy One, to manifest the boundless riches of Christ, becoming servants according to the gift of God's grace that was given us by the working of God's power.

Arise, shine; for the light has come,

     and the glory of God has risen upon us.

Epiphany

Let nations come to your light and rulers to the brightness of your day, O God, that they may rule your people righteously and the poor with justice, to defend the needy among the people, that there may be abundance of peace till the moon shall be no more.

Arise, shine; for the light has come,

and the glory of God has risen upon us.

Thwart the schemes of the powerful against the weak throughout the world, that wisdom may serve justice and the wise may follow the child.

Arise, shine; for the light has come,

and the glory of God has risen upon us.

Manifest your Son to the peoples of our community and lead us to your presence, so all may see your glory face to face.

Arise, shine; for the light has come,

and the glory of God has risen upon us.

Deliver the poor who cries out in distress and the oppressed who has no helper, as we pray especially for ___.

We give grateful praise for Christ, in whom we have access to God in boldness and confidence through faith in him. Hear our prayers of thanksgiving, especially for ___.

We remember those who have entered into the mystery of your eternal life, especially ___.

Arise, shine; for the light has come,

and the glory of God has risen upon us.

Presider: *Gracious and loving God, we come before you with no gifts but ourselves: Accept and receive our lives that we may be manifestations of your presence; let the light of your Spirit shine within and among us, so we may share in the mystery of your purpose of blessing for all creation, through Jesus Christ our Savior.* **Amen.**

Images in the Readings

The main image is light. The star symbolizes a new light in the cosmos. The dawn pierces the thick darkness that has obscured our vision. During January, the northern hemisphere is experiencing a gradual lightening of the darkest time of the year, an appropriate time for the church to praise Christ as the light. This light shines again in the night of the Easter Vigil.

Made popular in hymns, pageants, and crèche sets are the gifts of the magi: gold, frankincense, and myrrh. Gold denotes Jesus as a king. Frankincense and myrrh are sweet-smelling resins that were used in offerings to a god and at status burials. These are symbolic gifts for the divine king who has come to die. The birth narratives contain in them the death of Christ.

The ancient political idea was that monarchs were supposed to insure safety for their subjects. Christ, not Herod, is the true king who gives life, rather than death, to the people.

Ideas for the Day

+ The Creator communicates through the medium of the creation. Drawing on NASA databases, theoretical astrophysicist Grant Mathews suggested that the magi's star was one real natural phenomenon: a supernova, a nova, or a planetary alignment. (Tom Coyne, "Seeking a Star in the East," *Washington Post*, December 22, 2007.) Reflecting upon the universe as a whole, theoretical physicist and Anglican priest John Polkinghorne has argued that the fine tuning of the universe implies a creator without denying evolution. See, for instance, *Belief in God in the Age of Science*. As St. Bonaventure put it in *Journey of the Mind to God*, nature bears the footprints of God.

+ Why magi? And why not a prophet? Prophets do not enter the Christmas narrative (except for John in Elizabeth's womb). Perhaps magi are prophets, like witnesses; people who both connected to the past and witnesses to the future.

+ Dr. Harold Dean Trulear, in an opening address delivered to graduate students at Eastern University's School of Leadership and Development (published November 8, 2013), made an interesting connection with the Hebrew Bible prophet Daniel and the magi from the East: https://youtu.be/F7_oGAgj9VE (accessed August 14, 2017).

+ Two poems make an interesting reflection on light: "The Three Kings" by Henry Wadsworth Longfellow and "The Buddha's Last Instruction" by Mary Oliver.

Making Connections

Do you believe in Jesus Christ, the Son of God?

This is the question we get asked whenever we celebrate baptisms and repeat our baptismal vows.

To believe is to accept the revelation of God to us. To believe is to accept that we are called as a Christian community into a common life of journeying towards God.

Every day God seeks to reveal Jesus Christ to us.

The Feast of Epiphany is a reminder and invitation of how we are called to pay attention to the graces of God around us. The Feast of the Epiphany is an invitation for us to be the presence of God in the world and to manifest God's presence in the world through our commitment to respect the dignity of every human being.

Engaging all Ages

The Twelfth Day of Christmas announces the magi and is celebrated with gift giving in many cultures. Some celebrate with a king's cake. The magi brought gold, frankincense, and myrrh. Gold made it possible for the Holy Family hide safely during the reign of terror of King Herod. Frankincense is believed to carry prayers heavenward to God. Myrrh is oil for anointing the body that enhances the decomposition because family tombs were shared. Are these gifts still significant? These wise gifts took Jesus from womb to tomb. Can you identify gifts today with such profundity? Are they timeless? Would you change any?

What gifts do you bring to the manger? What gifts are you called to share with the world? Are you a singer? An artist? Do you bring the gift of listening? Are you an organizer, a joke-teller, or can you cook? What gifts can you share this day?

Hymns for the Day

The Hymnal 1982
Hail to the Lord's Anointed 616
How bright appears the Morning Star 496, 497
Now the silence 333
Arise, shine, for your light has come S223ff
O very God of very God 672
O Zion, tune thy voice 543
Now my tongue the mystery telling 329, 331
Our God to whom we turn 681
As with gladness men of old 119
Brightest and best of the stars of the morning 117, 118
Duérmete, Niño lindo/Oh, sleep now, holy baby 113
Earth has many a noble city 127
Father eternal, Ruler of creation 573
On this day earth shall ring 92
Songs of thankfulness and praise 135
Unto us a boy is born! 98
The first Nowell the angel did say 109
We three kings of Orient are 128
What star is this, with beams so bright 124
When Christ's appearing was made known 131, 132 (1, 2, 5)
Where is this stupendous stranger? 491

Wonder, Love, and Praise
Arise, shine, for your light has come 883
Where is this stupendous stranger? 726

Lift Every Voice and Sing II
This little light of mine 160

Epiphany

The First Sunday after the Epiphany: The Baptism of Our Lord Jesus Christ

January 7, 2018

The baptism of Jesus.

Color White

Preface Of the Epiphany

Collect

Father in heaven, who at the baptism of Jesus in the River Jordan proclaimed him your beloved Son and anointed him with the Holy Spirit: Grant that all who are baptized into his Name may keep the covenant they have made, and boldly confess him as Lord and Savior; who with you and the Holy Spirit lives and reigns, one God, in glory everlasting. Amen.

Readings and Psalm

Genesis 1:1-5

In our opening lesson we read the beginning of the story of creation. God sweeps like a wind over the chaos and formless void and begins to establish order, bringing forth light and separating that light from darkness. This light precedes the creation of the sun, moon, and stars and may be perceived as an initial revelation of God's character as this first step in creation is declared good.

Psalm 29

The majesty of God is described in the likeness of a thunderstorm: the Lord is mighty over land and sea.

Acts 19:1-7

In our second reading the apostle Paul continues to travel through Asia Minor carrying the good news of Jesus to Jew and Gentile alike. In Ephesus he encounters a group of believers who had received only John's baptism of repentance. Paul baptizes them in the name of Jesus. He then lays his hands upon them and they are filled with the Holy Spirit, speaking in tongues and prophesying as had others among those who first came to faith. The number of believers was twelve, which could reflect a connection with the original twelve disciples, the twelve tribes of Israel, and the ongoing power of the Spirit of God evident in Paul's ministry.

Mark 1:4-11

Our gospel is the story of the ministry of John the Baptist, and of Jesus' baptism. John tells of the mightier one to come whose baptism will be with the Holy Spirit. Jesus is then baptized and the Spirit is manifest. A voice from heaven speaks to Jesus in words that echo ancient oracles concerning the king and the calling of the Lord's chosen servant.

Prayers of the People

Presider: *Let us pray to our God whose Spirit breathes life into being, that through baptism we may be empowered as God's beloved children to share in the healing and reconciling work of Christ, saying: God shall give strength to the people; God shall give us the blessing of peace.*

Litanist: Fill your Church with the power of your Holy Spirit, O God, that we may bring the light of your blessing to the whole world.

God shall give strength to the people;

> **God shall give us the blessing of peace.**

Let your gentle spirit be upon this nation and upon all in authority, that we may share in your work to bring forth justice upon the earth.

God shall give strength to the people;

> **God shall give us the blessing of peace.**

Let your prophets speak powerful words of repentance and transformation to the ends of the earth, that the breath of your creative love and the sound of your blessing may go forth throughout the world.

God shall give strength to the people;

> *God shall give us the blessing of peace.*

Let your grace descend and dwell among the people of this community, that we may be united in love, abounding in compassion, and proactive in peace.

God shall give strength to the people.

> *God shall ive us the blessing of peace.*

May your heavens open and your Spirit descend upon us, bringing your comfort and healing to all for whom we pray, especially ___.

Hear our grateful thanks and praise for your manifestation of presence and grace in our lives and in the lives of others, giving thanks especially for ___.

Welcome with your divine pleasure all who have died, especially ___, that they may have a place in your eternal domains.

God shall give strength to the people;

> *God shall give us the blessing of peace.*

Presider: *Gracious and loving God, you have anointed your people with the waters of baptism and have made us your beloved children: Let your Spirit spread mightily among us, that we may share in the work of your Son, bringing blessing and light to all the world in the power of the Holy Spirit, through Jesus Christ our Savior.* **Amen.**

Images in the Readings

Life on planet earth must have water. Christians see in the waters of baptism the matrix of our new life in Christ. The font is like the River Jordan that leads us to the new land of promise, like the primeval waters over which the Spirit of God hovered in creation. We stand in the river: but we are also with the baptizer in the wilderness.

In several Bible stories, the dove symbolizes the presence of God's Holy Spirit. The white color matches the baptismal garment. Secular culture associates the dove especially with peace, which is the word from God that concludes the tumultuous Psalm 29.

Once again, light is an image for the power of God. God's voice brings light into the earth's darkness. Early Christians referred to baptism by water as enlightenment.

Ideas for the Day

- The words of calling and anointing for ministry heard in connection with Jesus' baptism are the words that frame the church's understanding of the ministry of all the baptized. The radical nature of our calling is to bring justice and to serve the cause of right, to be part of God's mission of liberating the suffering, the oppressed, and the hungry.
- Today we fast forward to Jesus as a young man. First, the Old Testament lesson begins at the very beginning, like the Gospel of John, where the Word was made flesh. Mark's gospel begins with the baptism of Jesus, the start of his public ministry. Baptism announces to the world who Jesus is and to whom he belongs. John baptizes with water, but Jesus with the Holy Spirit. What do we know about the rite of purification? How does our baptism launch us as a child of God? How do we discern our calling and/or purpose?
- Look again closely at the symbols of baptism, especially water, spirit (signified by oil), and light for new revelation about Jesus through the reflection on these texts. More information on baptismal symbols may found in *Baptismal Moments; Baptismal Meanings*, by Daniel B. Stevick, (Church Hymnal Corporation, 1987)
- Several pieces of art and iconography depict Jesus' baptism: Baptism of Jesus (Bogojavlenie, orthodox icon): www.svetigora.com/node/906 (accessed August 14, 2017) and Triptych of Jan Des Trompes (Gerard David, 1505): www.wga.hu/frames-e.html?/html/d/david/2/trompe.html (accessed August 14, 2017).
- In the film *O Brother, Where Art Thou?*, three Depression-era escaped convicts encounter a white-clad congregation making its way to a river for baptism. Delmar—a simple, good-hearted member of the gang—rushes into the water. After being dunked, Delmar announces that he's a new man with a new life. Later, his fellow escapee Everett says, "Even if that did put you square with the Lord, the State of Mississippi's a little more hard-nosed." In baptism, God makes us a new creation. Our struggle is to see each other for who we really are in Christ.

Making Connections

When we celebrate the Baptism of Our Lord, we touch one of the profound experiences we share with Jesus. We have been baptized like Christ and have been claimed as Beloveds of God.

Epiphany

Today we are invited to spend time with the Book of Common Prayer and go through the promises we made or others made for us at our baptism (pages 304–305). Without shaming or blaming yourself, spend some time reflecting on how God is calling you to live out your Baptismal Covenant with more integrity and with deeper faith.

Do you remember the date of your baptism? How does your baptism influence your life today?

Engaging all Ages

The priest holds the infant high in the air—"Let us welcome the newly baptized!" she shouts triumphantly. Today is the day when we celebrate the Baptism of Christ. What a spectacular and curious event. John the Baptizer takes Jesus and pushes him beneath the surface of the River Jordan. Jesus comes out of the water and we hear God speak through a descending dove. Let us remember our baptisms this day and never forget these words from our Baptismal Covenant, "Will you strive for justice and peace among all people, and respect the dignity of every human being?" We will with God's help.

Hymns for the Day

The Hymnal 1982
Songs of thankfulness and praise 135
All creatures of our God and King 400 (1-3, 7)
I sing the almighty power of God 398
Many and great, O God, are thy works 385
Most High, omnipotent, good Lord 406, 407 (1-4, 8)
Thou, whose almighty word 371
Thy strong word did cleave the darkness 381
Baptized in water 294
Christ, when for us you were baptized 121
From God Christ's deity came forth 443
"I come," the great Redeemer cries 116
O love, how deep, how broad, how high 448, 449 (1-3, 6)
The sinless one to Jordan came 120
When Christ's appearing was made known 131, 132 (1, 3, 5)
When Jesus went to Jordan's stream 139

Wonder, Love, and Praise
Baptized in water 767

Lift Every Voice and Sing II
Baptized in water 121
Spirit Song 118

Weekday Commemorations

Tuesday, January 9
Julia Chester Emery
Born in 1852 in Dorchester, Mass., Emery served the Episcopal Church's Board of Missions with loyalty, efficiency, and dedication for 40 years. At 22, she became editor of *The Young Christian Soldier*, a missionary publication of the Woman's Auxiliary of the Board. At first, the Auxiliary assembled and distributed "missionary boxes" to supplement salaries of missionaries; Emery's last report in 1916 recorded branches in two-thirds of the Church's missions and parishes, with receipts of $500,000. Emery traveled extensively for the Church, including, in 1908, attending the Lambeth Conference in London. In retirement, Emery wrote *A Century of Endeavor*, her history of the Domestic and Foreign Missionary Society.

Wednesday, January 10
William Laud, Archbishop of Canterbury, 1645
Laud, born in 1573, was beheaded in 1645 after impeachment for treason. He was seen through his life—and ever since—as either a martyr or a bigot, either compassionate toward commoners against landowners or dispassionate, even murderous, toward "puritans." Made Archbishop of Canterbury in 1635, he emphasized the marriage of church and state, headed by royalty as a Divine Right; raised up the priesthood and sacraments, especially the Eucharist; and demanded reverencing of the altar, which he returned to the eastern wall and fenced in. Laud, who headed the courts of High Commission and the Star Chamber, was fiercely loyal to the Church of England.

Friday, January 12
Abbot of Rievaulx, 1167
Born in 1109, Aelred became a Cistercian monk at the abbey of Rievaulx in Yorkshire in 1133. He soon became very influential in English church life. At a visit to Clairvaux, Aelred impressed Bernard, who encouraged the young monk to write his first book, *Mirror of Charity*, on Christian perfection. But it is on the topic of friendship that Aelred is revered. At the new Cistercian house at Revesby, which he founded in 1143 and where he allowed his monks to show friendly affection, Aelred wrote *Spiritual Friendship*. Friendship, he declared, is a gift of God and a creation of human

endeavor, characterized by loyalty, right intention, discretion, and patience.

Saturday, January 13
Hilary, Bishop of Poitiers, 367

Hilary was born about 315 in Poitiers in Gaul into a wealthy and pagan family. He wrote of his spiritual journey from unbelief to baptism (at about age 30) to bishop in 350, a job he never sought but that he executed with skill and courage. His bravery was tested about 355, when Emperor Constantius ordered all bishops to condemn Athanasius; Hilary refused and was exiled to Phrygia. Uncomplaining, Hilary used those three years to write *On the Trinity*, his principal work. In 360, after great churchly agitation, Hilary returned to his see, where he continued to fight against heresy and to care for his diocese.

Epiphany

The Second Sunday after the Epiphany

January 14, 2018

Responding to God's call to be a "light to the nations."

Color   Green

Preface   Of the Epiphany or of the Lord's Day

Collect

Almighty God, whose Son our Savior Jesus Christ is the light of the world: Grant that your people, illumined by your Word and Sacraments, may shine with the radiance of Christ's glory, that he may be known, worshiped, and obeyed to the ends of the earth; through Jesus Christ our Lord, who with you and the Holy Spirit lives and reigns, one God, now and for ever. Amen.

Readings and Psalm

1 Samuel 3:1-10 (11-20)

In our opening lesson, we hear how Samuel learns that it is the Lord who is calling to him. Three times the boy Samuel misunderstands and thinks that it is his mentor Eli summoning him during the night. Finally Eli realizes it must be the Lord, and tells Samuel to be ready for the prophetic word that will be spoken to him.

If using 1 Samuel 3:1–20:

In our opening reading, we hear how Samuel learns that the Lord is calling him to make him God's prophet. Three times the boy Samuel misunderstands and thinks that it is his mentor Eli summoning him during the night. Finally Eli realizes it must be the Lord, and tells Samuel to be ready. In the morning Samuel informs Eli of the punishment that is about to come upon his house. As Samuel grows, all Israel recognizes that he has been chosen by God to prophesy to the people.

Psalm 139:1-5, 12-17

With marvelous wisdom God alone perceives the heights and depths of life.

1 Corinthians 6:12-20

In this lesson Paul is required to criticize a misguided understanding of Christian freedom that has been adopted by some of the Corinthians. "All things are permitted me," is what some are saying, and evidently then interpreting their freedom in Christ to mean that they are so "spiritual" they can join with a prostitute without doing any harm. But our bodies, Paul contends, like all the rest of us, have now been dedicated to Christ. They are temples of the Holy Spirit through which we may glorify God.

John 1:43-51

Our gospel is the story of Philip and Nathaniel becoming disciples of Jesus. Nathaniel first doubts that the one whom Moses foretold could come from the virtually unknown town of Nazareth. But Jesus astounds Nathaniel by telling him what normal sight could not have disclosed. He then promises Nathaniel that he will have his own still greater vision, a heavenly revelation of the Son of Man as an intermediary between heaven and earth.

Prayers of the People

Presider: *Gracious God, you see into the deepest needs of our hearts and call us to follow you and to listen to your voice: Receive our prayers as we call upon you in your Temple: Speak, Lord, for your servant is listening.*

Litanist: You have called the Church your children and given to us the Holy Spirit, O Gracious One: Grant that we may share with our friends the Good News of Jesus of Nazareth and invite them to "come and see" so that others may share our fellowship in his Name.

We call upon you in your Temple:

Speak, Lord, for your servant is listening.

You search our hearts and know us, Almighty God: Lay your hand upon our nation and upon all in authority throughout the world, that they may be instruments of your compassion and peace, and that we may be known as a people in whom there is no deceit.

We call upon you in your Temple:

Speak, Lord, for your servant is listening.

You have woven our bodies in the depths of the earth, O God our Creator: Look upon the needs of a suffering world and bless all humanity, that your healthful Spirit and presence may do marvelous works for the relief of the world.

We call upon you in your Temple:

Speak, Lord, for your servant is listening.

You visit us in friendship and invite us to be generous and hospitable neighbors to all among whom we live, O Loving One: Fill us with your grace, that we may be a community of kindness and compassion.

We call upon you in your Temple:

Speak, Lord, for your servant is listening.

You fashion our lives day by day in your Spirit. Increase in us your vision that we may see great things for our community.

Hear our prayers for those for whom we intercede, especially ___.

We thank you for your gifts of freedom and blessing, and especially for ___.

By your power, you raise our bodies into union with you, remember those who have died, especially ___.

May all people see heaven opened and the angels of God ascending and descending upon the Son of Man.

We call upon you in your Temple:

Speak, Lord, for your servant is listening.

Presider: *You have freed us from all domination and made us one body in your Spirit, O God: Give us childlike faith to listen to what you are speaking and to follow you in faith, through Jesus Christ our Savior.* **Amen.**

Images in the Readings

God calls. The many call narratives in the Bible testify that this God is the kind of deity who knows us by name and who calls us into new life. Samuel, the Corinthian Christians, Philip, and Nathanael have all been called into a new identity. At baptism we are called both by our secular name and by our adopted name, Christian, that is, "of Christ."

That the heaven opens is a biblical phrase based on the ancient idea that the sky was a fixed dome that separated the earth from the upper sphere of God. The synoptic gospels refer to the heavens opening both at Jesus' baptism and at the end of time, when God will finally "descend" in majesty to bring an end of the cosmos as we know it. For us, this opening of the heaven can mean that in Christ, the separation between divine and human no longer exists.

The story of the boy Samuel has been beloved by Christians as a way to affirm the faith of children.

For Paul, baptism makes us part of the body of Christ, the body that in Jesus died and rose, the body of the church that now contains the Spirit of Christ. This baptismal understanding of the body of the Christian stands in stark contrast to how our culture views the body as the possession of the sovereign individual who inhabits it. John's gospel calls Jesus the temple, and Paul refers to the body of Christian believers as the temple.

Ideas for the Day

- ◆ Nathanael's response to Jesus' call is troubling, biased, and possibly racist. Reflect on Nathanael's response and how your worshipping community responds to people from different communities. For further reflection and a Christian response to racism, read or listen to Dr. Martin Luther King Jr.: http://kingencyclopedia.stanford.edu/encyclopedia/encyclopedia_contents.html (accessed August 14, 2017). A review of the disciples' biographies may be helpful for further reflection. Here is one example: www.bbc.co.uk/religion/0/18395824 (accessed August 14, 2017).

- ◆ In the King James Version, Jesus calls Nathaniel an Israelite "without guile." Nathaniel is the first to recognize Jesus as "the Son of God." Literature and film give us a number of guileless individuals whose wisdom and grace allow them to see the deep truth hidden from others. Most people think them simple or insane. Chanucey Gardiner of Jerzy Kosinski's *Being There*, Elwood P. Dowd of *Harvey*, and Forrest Gump of the eponymous film reveal the grace and goodness and mystery of life hidden from the cunning and cynical and mercenary. Being guileless is our contribution to revelation.

- ◆ This Sunday begins a serialized reading of 1 Corinthians 6–9 and 2 Corinthians 1–3. How might Paul's letters to the Christians in Corinth be explored in preaching or teaching over these next few weeks?

Epiphany

Epiphany

♦ A good poem for reflecting on light is, "Do not go gentle into that good night" by Dylan Thomas, (1914—1953).

Making Connections

God's revelation happens in community and for a world of God. In our gospel reading today, we experience Jesus revealing himself to his first disciples. Jesus called Philip, who then called Nathaniel to meet Jesus. Jesus promises Nathaniel that he will see greater things as he continues his walk and life with Jesus.

John 1: 43-51 reminds us that God is always calling us to call others into the experience of God's love. As we reflect on Jesus' epiphany then and now, we are called to reflect on those who have led us to Jesus and have played a part in our faith journey. We may also want to spend some time reflecting on those we have led to Jesus.

Engaging all Ages

Today we have stories of following with Jesus calling disciples. When asked to follow, Nathaniel asks, how do you *know* me? Is there a person who can finish your sentences? What is that like? How does being thoroughly known affect our actions?

Christians see their baptism as a calling into discipleship. Christ calls all people into servanthood today as the first disciples were called on lakeshore and in the counting house. The baptismal rite includes elements of being called to reflect Jesus' call to the first disciples: "I present N. to receive the sacrament of baptism . . . Do you renounce Satan . . . Do you turn to Jesus?

Hymns for the Day

The Hymnal 1982
Blessed Jesus, at thy word 440
Christ, whose glory fills the skies 6, 7
Christ is the world's true Light 542
How bright appears the Morning Star 496, 497
Lord, thou hast searched me and dost know 702
Thou, whose almighty word 371
God has spoken to his people 536
O Jesus, I have promised 655
Blest are the pure in heart 656
Lift up your heads, ye mighty gates 436
Sing praise to our Creator 295
Strengthen for service, Lord 312

Take my life, and let it be 707
All praise to thee, for thou, O King divine 477
In your mercy, Lord, you called me 706
The great Creator of the worlds 489
The people who in darkness walked 125, 126
What wondrous love is this 439
Ye servants of God, your Master proclaim 535

Wonder, Love, and Praise
I, the Lord of sea and sky 812
Will you come and follow me 757

Lift Every Voice and Sing II
Lord, You have searched my heart 16
I have decided to follow Jesus 136

Weekday Commemorations

Wednesday, January 17
Antony, Abbot in Egypt, 356
Athanasius queried this regarding Antony: "Who met him grieving and did not go away rejoicing?" Antony, born in Egypt to Christians, exemplified the movement of the third century toward monasticism. He followed Christ's invitation to sell all his possessions, and he became an anchorite, or solitary ascetic. Antony dwelt alone for two decades: he prayed, he read, and he worked with his hands. In 305, he walked out of his mountain cave and founded a monastery, its cells filled with monks living in love and peace. He spent his remaining days in the mountains of Egypt, fighting against dissenters through preaching, converting, and performing miracles.

Thursday, January 18
The Confession of Saint Peter the Apostle
Simon Bar-Jona, a boisterous fisher, confessed to Jesus: "You are the Christ." Jesus renamed him Peter, the "rock," on which Jesus built his church. Peter and his brother Andrew were the first disciples; thus, Peter figures keenly in the gospels despite his ill manners. Peter tried to walk on water; Peter wished to build three tabernacles; Peter thrice denied knowing Christ. On the other hand, Peter courageously risked his life to be a disciple, openly declaring his belief in Jesus as the Christ, and he courageously headed the young church's missions. Peter transformed from ordinary Simon, over-bearing and impetuous, to an extraordinary church leader, filled with the Holy Spirit.

Friday, January 19
Wulfstan, Bishop of Worcester, 1095
Wulfstan lived through perilous political times, including the Norman Conquest in 1066. He was born in Warwickshire (about 1008) and schooled by the Benedictines. Wulfstan, who first lived at the cathedral in Worcester as a monk, rose to be bishop, which he did not want but which he executed efficiently and lovingly for 30 years. Perhaps because Wulfstan was admired for his courage and generosity, he numbered among the handful of Anglo-Saxon bishops to retain their sees after submitting to William the Conqueror, and he was one of the compilers of the Domesday Book. By his death, though, he was the only remaining English-born bishop.

Saturday, January 20
Fabian, Bishop and Martyr of Rome, 250
Although he was not among the candidates for Pope in 236, Fabian, a stranger to Rome and layman, was elected without opposition after a dove alighted on his head. He served for 14 years, reforming the office by developing structure among the churches. He set a custom of venerating martyrs at their shrines, and he appointed a committee to record their lives for posterity. He himself became a holy, exemplary martyr when Emperor Decius demanded persecution of the Church across the empire about 240. The Church Fabian had served diligently and with humility stood fast through this time of trouble.

Epiphany

The Third Sunday after the Epiphany

January 21, 2018

The calling of the disciples, yesterday and today.

Color   Green

Preface   Of the Epiphany

Collect

Grant us grace, O Lord, to answer readily the call of our Savior Jesus Christ and proclaim to all people the Good News of his salvation, that we and the whole world may perceive the glory of his marvelous works; who lives and reigns with you and the Holy Spirit, one God, for ever and ever. Amen.

Readings and Psalm

Jonah 3:1-5, 10

In our Hebrew scripture lesson, the prophet Jonah, following his ordeal in the belly of a great fish, receives a second summons to prophesy to the heathen city of Ninevah. Jonah preaches as he passes into the city, proclaiming repentance and predicting forty days before the city's overthrow. The people of Ninevah believe God and respond to the prophet's message, proclaiming a fast and putting on the sackcloth and ashes that signify mourning and repentance. In response to Ninevah's turn of heart, God determines not to destroy the city.

Psalm 62:6-14

God is a rock and shelter. The people are to trust in God alone.

1 Corinthians 7:29-31

In our epistle lesson, Paul encourages the Corinthians to manage their temporal affairs in light of eternal realities. It was thought by Paul and the early Christian communities that the time of the Lord's return was near. The urgency was all the greater, therefore, to keep priorities in order and to be cautious about

attachments to this present world which may distract. The time to labor for God's kingdom is now.

Mark 1:14-20

Our gospel records the beginning of Jesus' ministry: his proclamation of the coming kingdom and the calling of his first disciples. After the arrest of John the Baptist, Jesus returns to Galilee preaching the nearness of God's rule and the need for a change of heart. Two sets of brothers are bidden to leave their nets and become fishers for people.

Prayers of the People

Presider: *In Jesus you have announced the fulfillment of your time, O God: Give us courage to answer readily the call to follow you, letting nothing in us interfere with the good news of your kingdom, as we offer our prayers and intercessions, saying: The time is fulfilled, and the kingdom of God has come near.*

Litanist: God alone is our rock and our salvation: Uphold your church, Almighty One, in your strength, and grant us faithfulness to proclaim the good news of Jesus to all the world.

The time is fulfilled,

> **and the kingdom of God has come near.**

God is our safety and our honor: Put divine trust into the hearts of the leaders of our nation and of all in authority, Almighty One, that they may cooperate with your work to build communities of peace throughout the world.

The time is fulfilled,

> **and the kingdom of God has come near.**

Steadfast love is yours, O Gracious One: Look upon the great cities and lonely villages in your creation, and turn us from our wicked ways, that all who suffer may be relieved, and all who work may find satisfaction.

The time is fulfilled,

> *and the kingdom of God has come near.*

God is our strong rock and our refuge: Be present in our community, O Loving One, that the life of your new world may be manifest in this place.

The time is fulfilled,

> *and the kingdom of God has come near.*

Give your steadfast love to those for whom we pray in intercession, especially ___.

Hear our grateful hearts as we thank you for the blessings of your kingdom, especially for ___.

Bring into your fuller presence those who have died, that they may find life within your reign forevermore, especially ___.

The time is fulfilled,

> *and the kingdom of God has come near.*

Presider: *Put the urgency of your in-breaking kingdom into our hearts, O God, that we may swiftly follow you to do our part in your work of reconciliation, through Jesus Christ our Savior, who with you and the Holy Spirit, lives and reigns, one God, for ever and ever.* **Amen.**

Images in the Readings

The gospel describes the first disciples as fishermen. This may be a memory of the profession of some in the Jesus movement. As well, it establishes the early Christian imagery of baptism as water, believers as water-dwellers, the net as the gospel, and the boat as the church. The Greek of the early Christian creed, "Jesus Christ, God's Son, Savior," presents the acronym *i-ch-th-u-s*, the Greek word for fish, and fish swim through much Christian iconography.

The gospel introduces the image of "the kingdom of God." Arguably the most important image in the New Testament, the kingdom language evoked Israelite memory of a time of political independence. Yet this kingdom is, according to Mark, newly "of God," that is, of a realm in which life belongs to and reflects God. The designation of Jesus as Christ, that is, the one anointed by God for power to reign, relies on the kingdom imagery. It is not an image easily accessible for twenty-first century believers. The Greek word for "kingdom" used in the New Testament, *basileia*, is a complex term, not solely a reference to either the church or an afterlife, but to a life wholly transformed by the death and resurrection of Jesus Christ.

Nineveh was a symbol of the powerful threat of one's earthly enemy.

Forty days ties the repentance of the hearers to many ancient narratives, but here especially to the time that Moses was on Mount Sinai, receiving the word of God.

Ideas for the Day

+ Reflect on these "narratives of receiving a call" in the context of the season of the Epiphany. To that end, could answering the call be a response to seeing the light? *Listening Hearts* by Suzanne G. Farnham (Church Publishing, 2011) and *Called* by Barbara Cawthorne Crafton (Church Publishing, 2017) are resources for anyone discerning a call in their own lives.
+ Thomas Merton wrote: "There exists for me a particular goal, a fulfillment which must be all my own—nobody else's—and it does not really identify that destiny to put it under some category . . ." from *Echoing Silence,* edited by Robert Inchausti.
+ Some people think that one's vocation or calling is a specific job that God has in mind for a person, like being a priest or a doctor or an artist. Former Archbishop of Canterbury Rowan Williams urges us to see things differently. In *Ray of Darkness* he writes, "To talk about God as your creator means to recognize at each moment that it is his desire for you to be, and to be the person you are. It means he is calling you by your name, at each and every moment, wanting you to be you." (p. 149)[1]
+ The psalmist says we are only a breath; the epistle concludes life is short. Jonah does not immediately go to Nineveh, but eventually proclaims the greatness of God who demonstrates compassion when God's mercy and forgiveness is embraced. The Gospel portrays fishermen who follow without hesitancy. There seems to be an urgency, not only to shed lifestyles that are counterproductive, but to fall into the loving arms of God. Why would anyone want to be without the love of God? How can we tell others this good news? What has God done for you lately?

Making Connections

The Kingdom of God has come near. Repent and believe the gospel.

---

[1] Rowan Williams, *Ray of Darkness*, (Boston: Cowley Publications, 1995).

Repent and believe. What do these words signify in our lives? It is said that one of the most important and least practiced activities in the spiritual life is spiritual conversation. Here is a simple spiritual task: Ask seven of your friends or family members what it means to repent and what it means to believe in the gospel.

In the gospel appointed for today, Jesus calls Peter, Andrew, James, and John. He calls them while they are fishing; they leave everything immediately and follow Jesus.

What activity in your life brings you closest to Jesus? Where do you experience God in your day-to-day life? Spend some time with the gospel reading before you go to bed tonight or read it later this week.

Engaging all Ages

Discipleship and repentance are tied together in Jesus' mind and in several of our readings today. Looking at the baptismal liturgy during the season of Epiphany is helpful to understand what it means to be a disciple of Christ. We must make a commitment to change and to grow in Christ's way. This means turning away from evil and separation. We renounce evil and accept Christ. The story of Jonah is a similar call to change. The people had strayed from the God of the covenant. They had followed their own ways and their own gods and consequently had suffered. If they return to God they wil know God's presence and love again. Continue last week's focus on discipleship, but add the dimension of repentence and commitment in the learning community this week.

Hymns for the Day

The Hymnal 1982
Christ for the world we sing! 537
How wondrous and great thy works, God of praise! 532, 533
My God, thy table now is spread 321
Spread, O spread, thou mighty word 530
Give praise and glory unto God 375
God of mercy, God of grace 538
Sing praise to God who reigns above 408
There's a wideness in God's mercy 469, 470
Jesus calls us; o'er the tumult 549, 550
They cast their nets in Galilee 661

Wonder, Love, and Praise
As we gather at your Table 763
Put down your nets and follow me 807

Tú has venido a la orilla/
You have come down to the lakeshore 758
Will you come and follow me 757

Lift Every Voice and Sing II
I'm just a poor wayfaring stranger 19
Soon and very soon 14
I have decided to follow Jesus 136

Weekday Commemorations

Monday, January 22
Vincent, Deacon of Saragossa, and Martyr, 304
Vincent, the so-called protomartyr of Spain, exemplifies the saint raised up because of vehement support of Jesus in a time of persecution, a time of torture and death. Vincent is known for little else than his name, his order (deacon), and the time and place of his martyrdom (early in the fourth century, Saragossa). Vincent and his bishop Valerius were persecuted under the rule of the Roman emperors Diocletian and Maximian, but Vincent preached loudly and fervently in Jesus' name so was punished grotesquely then killed at last by Dacia, governor of Spain. Vincent has been venerated as an outspoken follower of Christ.

Tuesday, January 23
Philips Brooks, Bishop of Massachusetts, 1893
Writer of songs ("O little town of Bethlehem") and sermons ("remember the nearness of God to each one of us"), builder of churches in body and building (Trinity-Boston), innovator, youth-leader, and bishop, Brooks was a tender friend and pastor. He spent ten years serving in Philadelphia before returning to Boston, where he was born in 1835. He was appointed rector of Trinity, where, after three years, the church building burned; Brooks oversaw its rebuilding, with the altar placed daringly in the center of the chancel "as a symbol of unity." He was elected bishop in 1891, and, through the force of his personality and preaching, he provided the spiritual leadership the diocese needed for that time.

Thursday, January 25
The Conversion of Saint Paul the Apostle
Saul, an orthodox Jew, studied under the famous rabbi Gamaliel, but soon after Jesus died, Saul connected to the Christian movement. He determined to crush it as heresy. On his way to Damascus to persecute Christians, Saul converted dramatically, becoming Paul and dedicating himself to Jesus. He planted Christian congregations bordering the eastern Mediterranean. His

letters manifest his alignment with the mind of Christ, thereby founding Christian theology. Although rather frail physically, he was strong spiritually: "I will all the more gladly boast of my weaknesses that the power of Christ may rest upon me." His martyrdom is believed to have occurred in 64 under Nero.

Friday, January 26
Timothy and Titus, Companions of Saul

Timothy, born in Lystra in Asia Minor, and Titus, a Greek, accompanied Paul on his missions. Timothy's missions included encouraging Thessalonians to withstand persecution and Corinthians to strengthen converts' faith; he also represented Paul at Ephesus, becoming, according to Eusebius, the first bishop there. Titus accompanied Paul and Barnabas to Jerusalem for the apostolic council. On Paul's third mission, Titus was commissioned urgently to go to Corinth; later, Titus was entrusted to organize the church in Crete, becoming, according to Eusebius, the first bishop there. Though young, both bore tremendous responsibilities. As they shared a mission with Paul, Titus and Timothy share a commemoration close to the festal day of Paul's conversion.

Saturday, January 27
John Chrysostom, Bishop of Constantinople, 407

John was dubbed "Chrysostom" due to his "golden mouth," an apt description of this legendary preacher, one of the great saints of the Eastern Church. Born about 354 in Antioch, Syria, John followed a call to desert monasticism, but the desert compromised his health. Upon return to Antioch, he was ordained a presbyter; in 397, he became Patriarch of Constantinople, but his ascetic episcopate led to two banishments. He died September 14, 407, during his second exile. John, the patron saint of preachers, believed, "Preaching improves me." His sermons shed light on liturgy and emphasized the voice of the *laos* (the people). A Prayer of St. Chrysostom speaks significantly in the Book of Common Prayer at the end of Morning and Evening Prayer.

Epiphany

The Fourth Sunday after the Epiphany

January 28, 2018

God's word, spoken and embodied in Jesus, is power.

Color   Green

Preface   Of the Epiphany

Collect

Almighty and everlasting God, you govern all things both in heaven and on earth: Mercifully hear the supplications of your people, and in our time grant us your peace; through Jesus Christ our Lord, who lives and reigns with you and the Holy Spirit, one God, for ever and ever. Amen.

Readings and Psalm

Deuteronomy 18:15-20

In our opening reading Moses promises the people that, after his death, God will raise up another prophet for them. The people cannot face God directly but need an intermediary to speak God's words. To him they must listen, for the false prophet who presumes to speak in the Lord's name will die. In later centuries this oracle was interpreted to mean that God would raise up one final prophet to succeed Moses. Some early Christians believed Jesus to be this new Moses.

Psalm 111

A song of praise to the mighty and awesome Lord, who is steadfast and full of compassion.

1 Corinthians 8:1-13

In this lesson Paul gives counsel to the Corinthians who are unsure whether it is permissible to eat the meat of animals that have been sacrificed in pagan temples. Since there is only one true God, such sacrifices are really meaningless, and the meat can be eaten in good conscience. Yet this understanding of the issue must not be treated as superior *knowledge* with respect to those whose consciences are still troubled.

Out of love it is better for those who believe themselves enlightened to avoid eating such meat than to encourage weaker members to do what they regard as sinful and so perhaps to be led back into paganism.

Mark 1:21-28

In our gospel, Jesus both teaches and acts with authority. His teaching was more than interpretation of the law. It was a proclamation of the new possibilities of God's kingdom. He backed his words with his actions. Unclean spirits recognized him and submitted to his power to deliver a man from his disorder.

Prayers of the People

Presider: *Almighty God, in Jesus you have freed us for love and rebuked everything that may threaten us: Let the teaching of your Good News be spread abroad with such authority, that all creation may be reconciled, as we pray: Let us give thanks to God with our whole heart; for you are gracious and full of compassion.*

Litanist: Raise up for your Church prophets like Moses who will speak everything you command, O Holy One, that we may heed your teaching and be an example of goodness for our neighbors.

Let us give thanks to God with our whole heart;

> *for you are gracious and full of compassion.*

Almighty One, rescue the leaders of our nation and all in authority from the knowledge that puffs up and fill them with your love which builds up, that they may accomplish your works with faithfulness and justice.

Let us give thanks to God with our whole heart;

> *for you are gracious and full of compassion.*

Compassionate One, uphold the weak throughout the earth and free the consciences of all people through your love.

Epiphany

Let us give thanks to God with our whole heart;

> *for you are gracious and full of compassion.*

Gracious One, rebuke in us whatever spirit is unclean, that we may so live and teach your gospel of love that your fame may spread throughout our surrounding region.

Let us give thanks to God with our whole heart;

> *for you are gracious and full of compassion.*

Receive our prayers which we offer for all who need you, especially ___.

Hear our gratefulness for all goodness and joy, especially for ___.

Bring into the fullness of your life those who have died, especially ___.

Let us give thanks to God with our whole heart;

> *for you are gracious and full of compassion.*

Presider: *We offer our prayers to God the Father, from whom are all things, and for whom we exist, and our Lord, Jesus Christ, through whom are all things, and through whom we exist, in the power of the Holy Spirit, One God, who lives and reigns forever.* **Amen.**

Images in the Readings

In the New Testament, Jesus heals persons afflicted with an unclean spirit. In some narratives, the person is described as if physically, mentally, or emotionally ill. But the gospels always mean more than a first-century medical diagnosis. The Holy Spirit of our Lord Christ comes then and now to replace the might of evil with the power of God.

In the Bible, holy means not sinless, but set apart, sanctified, whole, filled with the power of God.

Not only in the seventh century BCE, but still today, people hope for a prophet, someone who will speak truth, whose words can conquer evil by the very power of divine authority. We see this archetypal hope, for example, in films when magical words spoken by the good guys are able to obliterate what is wicked and hateful. In the Bible, a prophet is not primarily a seer who foretells the future, but someone who is inspired to know truth from falsehood and who speaks honestly about the outcomes of ignoring such a word of God.

Not only the vegetarians in our assemblies, but many Christians now ask where our food comes from, how ethical was its pathway to our tables, and whether, as Christians, we are to eat in some distinctive way.

Ideas for the Day

- Engaging today's text about "unclean spirits" is a challenging task. One could reflect on this text from a rational perspective or one could take a mystical approach and reflect on good and evil. The moderate approach is to focus on what this text reveals about Jesus. A mystical, yet rational, approach is found in the *People of the Lie: The Hope For Healing Human Evil* (Simon & Schuster, 1983) by M. Scott Peck. *Unclean: Meditations on Purity, Hospitality, and Mortality* (Lutterworth Press, 2012) by Richard Beck deconstructs the category "unclean" as part of a reflection on the challenges toward achieving an inclusive church based on the love of God.
- The psalmist tells of a loving God, gracious and compassionate. Why is that so hard to believe? In Deuteronomy, we are introduced to the role of a prophet: one who speaks on behalf of God. Who are prophets today? What is being said that sounds like something God wants us to hear? The epistle tells us to be careful around others who may stumble. We are to look after those who are weak or less knowledgeable about religious customs. How can we help those who seem to fall by the wayside in our society? Are we patient and kind?
- In Jesus, God liberates us from demonic forces. Carl Jung counseled that being an integrated self involves befriending our shadow lest it become a destructive force within our own soul. More recently, Eleanor Longden gave a TED talk entitled "The Voices in My Head." She tells the story of learning to interpret her own auditory hallucinations as distorted messages from neglected parts of herself. Initially the source of misery and torment, these voices became a source of self-knowledge. Healing began for her when she understood that her fears were an expression of old wounds. www.ted.com/talks/eleanor_longden_the_voices_in_my_head?language=en (accessed August 14, 2017).

Making Connections

Something about the way Jesus talked about God caused the people to follow him and believe in him. They said that he preached with authority. They also noticed that he drove out the demons with authority too.

Following Jesus invites us to live our lives in the authority of our baptismal vows and promises. We seek to know and do the will of God. At times, following Jesus requires that we speak truth to power and cast off and away the things that are not of God.

It is important to remember that Jesus began his public ministry after his baptism. Our baptism calls us to live our faith boldly and to find ways to imitate the words, thoughts, and actions of Jesus in our world today.

Engaging all Ages

From the moment that Jesus entered this world as a baby boy, he was the teacher and we, the students. Through miracles, parables, frustration, tears, silence, and definitely laughter . . . Jesus was forming the people of God. From the manger, at the feet of the elders and priests in the temple, while cooking fish on the beach, walking on water, in the garden, and from the cross, Jesus was teaching us the ultimate lesson—to love one another as he loves us. The poet Mary Oliver reminds us to "Pay attention. Be astonished. Tell about it." May we never stop learning!

Hymns for the Day

The Hymnal 1982
God the Omnipotent! King, who ordainest 569
God has spoken to his people 536
How wondrous and great thy works, God of praise! 532, 533
God is love, and where true love is 576, 577
Lord, make us servants of your peace 593
Where charity and love prevail 581
Deck thyself, my soul, with gladness 339
From God Christ's deity came forth 443
O for a thousand tongues to sing 493
O love, how deep, how broad, how high 448, 449
Spread, O spread, thou mighty word 530
Thine arm, O Lord, in days of old 567
Thou, whose almighty word 371
Ye servants of God, your Master proclaim 535

Lift Every Voice and Sing II
Yield not to temptation 170

Weekday Commemorations

Thursday, February 1
Brigid (Bride)
As Irish as Patrick, and as beloved, Brigid was born to a Druid household in the mid-fifth century. She chose early to dedicate her life to Christ as a nun; in 470, she founded a nunnery in Kildare. To secure the sacraments, Brigid persuaded an anchorite to receive episcopal ordination and escort his community to Kildare, thus establishing the only known Irish double monastery. She effected policy at Church conventions and may have received episcopal orders herself. Stories of her care for the poor include the healing of a leper woman and the taming of a wolf. Her feast day shares sacredness with Imbolg, the Celtic festival of spring.

Friday, February 2
The Presentation of Our Lord Jesus Christ in the Temple
Variously known as the Purification of Saint Mary the Virgin and as Candlemas, in the Eastern Church February 2 also is called the Meeting of Christ with Simeon. These names testify to the wealth of spiritual meanings conjoined to this incident. The "presentation" harkens to the Jewish law that every firstborn son had to be dedicated to God in memory of the Israelites' deliverance from Egypt. When Mary placed her babe in the arms of Simeon, the Old and New Dispensations married: the old oblations were dismissed; the new, perfect offering had entered the temple. The offering was to be made once for all on the cross.

Saturday, February 3
Anskar, Archbishop of Hamburg, Missionary to Denmark and Sweden, 865
Scandinavians regard Anskar (born in France in 801) as their apostle. As archbishop of Hamburg, consecrated in 831, he served as papal legate for missionary work among the Scandinavians. He established a school and a mission in Denmark, where he'd been posted about 826, as he tried, without a lot of success, to convert and evangelize. He persevered, having heard a voice in a vision that exhorted him to "Go and return to me crowned with martyrdom." Around 829, he was called to Sweden and continued his mission in Scandinavia until 848. Three generations later, Anskar's work began to bear fruit from the seeds he had planted.

The Fifth Sunday after the Epiphany

February 4, 2018

God's power to heal is revealed in the life of the prophets and, above all, in the ministry of Jesus.

Color   Green

Preface   Of the Epiphany

Collect

Set us free, O God, from the bondage of our sins, and give us the liberty of that abundant life which you have made known to us in your Son our Savior Jesus Christ; who lives and reigns with you, in the unity of the Holy Spirit, one God, now and for ever. Amen.

Readings and Psalm

Isaiah 40:21-31

In our Hebrew Bible lesson, the prophet Isaiah summons the people to renew their trust and confidence in God. God alone is sovereign, the Lord of all that exists, the creator of the earth and its creatures, and the fount of understanding. Those who turn to the Lord will find their strength replenished; they will not be disappointed.

Psalm 147:1-12, 21c

A hymn of praise to the Lord, who rules over nature in wisdom and has shown faithfulness to Israel.

1 Corinthians 9:16-23

In this reading, we learn how Paul seeks to become all things to all people in order that he may freely and without hindrance share the gospel with them. He takes no special pride in his preaching of the gospel because that is his commission from the Lord. In order not to create unnecessary difficulties, he is willing to live under the law among Jews and outside the law among Gentiles. Some may misunderstand and think him unprincipled, but Paul's only concern is with the essentials of the gospel.

Mark 1:29-39

Our gospel tells of healing events which took place toward the beginning of Jesus' ministry. Peter's mother-in-law is cured of fever. Many flock to Jesus. He heals them and casts out the demons who recognize him for who he is. A brief retreat ends because of the pressing need to continue his mission. The power of the kingdom of God is made manifest through his words and deeds.

Prayers of the People

Presider: *To whom will we compare you, Holy One, the everlasting God, Creator of the ends of the earth, who stretches out the heavens like a curtain: Be near to us in our weakness and uphold us with your might, as we pray: Great is our God and mighty in power; there is no limit to God's wisdom.*

Litanist: Holy One, who never faints or grows weary: Heal and empower your Church, entrusted with a commission to bear the Good News to all the earth, that we may be all things to all people, serving as slaves to all for the sake of the gospel.

Great is our God and mighty in power;

there is no limit to God's wisdom.

Holy One, who brings princes to naught and makes the rulers of the earth as nothing: Guide our nation and all who lead in the whole earth, that they may be servants of healing and may cast out all forms of oppression throughout your creation.

Great is our God and mighty in power;

there is no limit to God's wisdom.

Holy One, who gives power to the faint and strength to the powerless: Reach out your hand and lift up all who suffer from illness or fear, violence or threat, that those who wait upon the Lord shall renew their strength, mount up with wings like eagles, run and not be weary, walk and not faint.

Great is our God and mighty in power;

> *there is no limit to God's wisdom.*

Holy One, who lifts up the lowly and makes grass to grow upon the mountains and green plants to serve humankind: Bless this community with compassion and grace, that we may serve one another with deference and respect.

Great is our God and mighty in power;

> *there is no limit to God's wisdom.*

Holy One, whose understanding is unsearchable:

Touch with your healing compassion those for whom we pray, especially ___.

Hear our gratefulness for all the blessings of our lives, especially for ___.

Enfold into your eternal love those who have died, especially ___.

Great is our God and mighty in power;

> *there is no limit to God's wisdom.*

Presider: *We look toward your eternal glory, O Holy One, and raise our voices to you in prayer: Enter our homes and towns, our solitudes and cities; cast out all that oppresses and threatens your people, heal all who are weak and bring peace in our time, that your whole creation may sing out in praise to proclaim your message of love and hope, through Jesus Christ our Savior.* Amen.

Images in the Readings

What's a fever? We use this medical designation of a heightened body temperature due to some internal malfunction or disease also metaphorically to describe crazed enthusiasm: something is wrong in the body of the person or of the community. The astonishing list of curses in Deuteronomy 28 on those who do not keep the covenant includes fever; whether or not also Mark considered fever as a sign of divine punishment, Jesus brings in the kingdom of God and removes the curse.

The Greek word describing Peter's mother-in-law's activity after being healed is the familiar *diakonia*. We rise to serve others. In 1 Corinthians 9, Paul calls himself a slave of all. Contemporary capitalism suggests that focusing on ourselves will accrue good to the others. The New Testament suggests a more Amish theme: JOY equals Jesus first, others second, yourself last. Even Jesus leaves the "deserted place" to spread the good news and heal others.

The poem in Isaiah 40 is filled with images. Humans are like grasshoppers, withered stubble, who can become soaring eagles. God has stretched out the sky like a tent; God's breath blows away great rulers; yet God numbers and knows everything and everyone by name. In baptism we are called by name, and we are transformed from grasshoppers to eagles. In Christian theology, God's creative might is continuous, just as human weakness is with us forever.

Ideas for the Day

+ Today's gospel is a call to look beyond present circumstance toward hope. Reflect on how the healing of Peter's mother may have inspired others to pursue Jesus for healing. A review of the prayers in "Ministration to the Sick" section of the Book of Common Prayer (p. 453) may offer another lens through which to reflect on today's readings. Look for places in the healing liturgies where people are encouraged to have hope.

+ After Jesus healed Simon Peter's mother-in-law, she began serving others. From one perspective, she is merely resuming the servile role assigned to women in the patriarchal order of her day. And yet, her actions anticipate Jesus's own teachings about servanthood and discipleship (Mark 10:45a). Jesus restores us to wholeness so that we can join him in healing the world. For instance, the twelfth step in AA and other recovery programs says that being sober involves helping others to gain sobriety: "Having had a spiritual awakening . . . we tried to carry this message to [others]."

+ Both the psalmist and Isaiah remind us that God delights in those who put their hope in the Lord. God never grows tired or weary, but renews our strength so we can soar as on eagle's wings. Where do you find strength when you feel down? The gospel conveys the ministry of Jesus was about healing those who are sick. Where do you get hope when you or a loved one is sick? Can you share more? In the psalm, we hear how God cares about the broken hearted. How do we find solace when in sorrow or disappointed?

Making Connections

Today Jesus is revealed to us as a compassionate healer and a man of prayer. He goes to the house of Simon and is moved with compassion to heal Simon's mother in law. He then heals the other sick people brought to him. We then meet Jesus who claims his relationship with God by going off alone to pray.

It is a gift for us to remember that Jesus gets revealed to us in acts of compassionate healing and prayer. As you read Mark's gospel today, place yourself in the story as a companion of Peter and see what you notice about Jesus who heals and prays.

How do you pray? How do you heal others? Where does compassion show up in our life?

Engaging all Ages

We spend a great deal of time running away. We run from fear. We run from commitment. We run from responsibility. We run from Jesus. Today we remember that Jesus is calling us to him. Jesus called the disciples. What a motley crew! Jesus calls us to be his hands, his feet, and his heart. Like the shepherd with his sheep or a mother hen with her chicks, Jesus also calls us to gather closely. "Come to me, all you that are weary and are carrying heavy burdens, and I will give you rest." But we can't rest for long! Today, just before we leave through the church doors, we are reminded to "Go in peace to love and serve the Lord."

Hymns for the Day

The Hymnal 1982
Thy strong word did cleave the darkness 381
Immortal, invisible, God only wise 423
O bless the Lord, my soul! 411
The God of Abraham praise 401
In Christ there is no East or West 529

From thee all skill and science flow 566
Thine arm, O Lord, in days of old 567

Wonder, Love, and Praise
The church of Christ in every age 779
From miles around the sick ones came 774
Heal me, hands of Jesus 773
O Christ, the healer, we have come 772

Lift Every Voice and Sing II
In Christ there is no East or West 62

Weekday Commemorations

Monday, February 5
The Martyrs of Japan, 1597
In the sixteenth century, Christianity was introduced into Japan, first by the Jesuits under Francis Xavier and then by the Franciscans. The missions raised stories of self-sacrifice as well as success: by the end of that century, Japan was home to an estimated 300,000 baptized believers. Soon, however, these pluses were compromised by rivalries between religious orders; in addition, colonial politics—within Japan and between Japan and Spain and Portugal—caused suspicion about Western intents. Christian missions suffered persecution and suppression in a half-century of powerful *shoguns*. The first victims were six Franciscan friars and 20 of their converts in Nagasaki on February 5, 1597.

Epiphany

The Last Sunday after the Epiphany

February 11, 2018

The Transfiguration of Our Lord.

Color   White

Preface   Of the Epiphany

Collect

O God, who before the passion of your only-begotten Son revealed his glory upon the holy mountain: Grant to us that we, beholding by faith the light of his countenance, may be strengthened to bear our cross, and be changed into his likeness from glory to glory; through Jesus Christ our Lord, who lives and reigns with you and the Holy Spirit, one God, for ever and ever. Amen.

Readings and Psalm

2 Kings 2:1-12

From the Hebrew Bible, we hear the story of the taking up of the prophet Elijah into heaven and the passing on of his power to Elisha. The narrative illustrates the great favor Elijah found in the eyes of the Lord as he is carried away in a chariot of fire. Elisha is first in despair and rends his clothing in mourning, yet realizes he himself has been chosen to offer continued prophetic vision to the people.

Psalm 50:1-6

The psalm tells of the majestic and righteous God who requires true sacrifice and thanksgiving of the people.

2 Corinthians 4:3-6

In this lesson, Paul proclaims that Christ is the very image of God, though not all can perceive this truth. This proclamation focuses on Jesus Christ as Lord, and Paul is captive to this message. As light shone forth from darkness in creation, so God has shone forth in the hearts of those to whom the light of the knowledge of God in Christ has been given.

Mark 9:2-9

Our gospel is the story of Jesus' transfiguration. The narrative draws upon themes and symbols from Israel's past and its hopes for the future. Moses and Elijah represent the law and the prophets, whose promises Jesus fulfills. The chosen disciples see divine glory reflected in Jesus' human person. A voice from the cloud declares that he is God's beloved Son.

Prayers of the People

Transfiguration:

Presider: *It is good for us to be here in your glorious presence, O God: Awaken us to the needs of the world, that we may offer all things to your compassionate love and become mediators of your unifying vision, as we pray: Proclaim the greatness of our God; for our God is the Holy One.*

Litanist: Remove the veil when your Church seeks you, O God, and enlighten us with your vision, that we may be eyewitnesses of Christ's majesty and serve the world as people moved by the Holy Spirit.

Proclaim the greatness of our God;

> *for our God is the Holy One.*

Let the glory of your holiness be revealed to the leaders of our nation and be manifest to all in authority, O Mighty One, that they may hear your voice and serve your mission of righteousness and justice, declared by the law and the prophets and fulfilled in Jesus Christ.

Proclaim the greatness of our God;

> *for our God is the Holy One.*

You love justice and establish equity, O Righteous One: Visit with your transfiguring presence every person and home in need of your light and your blessing throughout the world.

Proclaim the greatness of our God;

> *for our God is the Holy One.*

Epiphany

Visit this mountain of holy presence, O Radiant One, and let the cloud of your glory overshadow our community, that with joy we may behold your appearance and be led by your light.

Proclaim the greatness of our God;

for our God is the Holy One.

Listen to our prayers as we speak to you and comfort us with your dawning Spirit.

We remember those who are ill or in any need, especially ___.

Hear our gratefulness and praise for your glorious presence in our lives, especially as we give thanks for ___.

We know our deaths will come soon, even as we recall our transfigured Christ's victory over death. Receive into your eternal light all who have died, especially ___.

Proclaim the greatness of our God;

for our God is the Holy One.

Presider: *Blessed Creator God, let Christ, the morning star, rise in our hearts as we awaken to his glorious presence in our midst: Fill us with gratefulness for your dazzling light which breaks through our cloud of unknowing in every place and time, that we may tell of the things which we have seen and mediate your reconciling presence in all the world, through Jesus Christ our Savior, who with you and the Holy Spirit, lives and reigns, one God, forever and ever.* **Amen.**

Last Epiphany:

Presider: *God of eternal light and everlasting glory, send the Spirit of your Son Jesus Christ upon us that we may be transfigured by the dazzling vision of his goodness, as we bring our prayers to you, saying: Give us the light of the knowledge of the glory of God in the face of Jesus Christ.*

Litanist: You have caused your Church to see the light of the gospel of the glory of Christ: Inspire our witness to him that all the earth may be raised to a new vision of your abiding presence and love.

Give us the light of the knowledge of the glory of God

in the face of Jesus Christ.

Before you, O God, there is a consuming flame and round about you a raging storm: Humble our leaders and all who exercise authority among the nations of the world, that they may keep before them the vision of your peace.

Give us the light of the knowledge of the glory of God

in the face of Jesus Christ.

You see the suffering of people throughout the world who struggle in the midst of poverty, violence, injustice, and illness; you know those desperate ones who have no hope or vision for themselves or their loved ones: Gracious God, let your transfiguring grace bring light and hope to all who yearn for something new.

Give us the light of the knowledge of the glory of God

in the face of Jesus Christ.

Let your light shine in the hearts of this community and overshadow us with the cloud of your presence, that this place may be a place of transfiguring grace.

Give us the light of the knowledge of the glory of God

in the face of Jesus Christ.

You call the earth from the rising of the sun to its setting:

Hear our prayers for all who need your light, especially ___.

We give you thanks for the light of your blessing, especially for ___.

Hear our prayers for those who have ascended with Elijah and Jesus into your eternal light, especially ___.

Give us the light of the knowledge of the glory of God

in the face of Jesus Christ.

Presider: *Holy and everliving God, grant us grace to ascend to your holy mountain and to see the dazzling vision of your transfigured reality in our worship and prayer this day, and then strengthen us to listen to your voice and to follow you in faithful service, even when you are hidden from us, until at last we see you face to face in your eternal and everlasting glory, in the power of the Holy Spirit, through Jesus Christ our Savior.* **Amen.**

Images in the Readings

Once again the readings include the central biblical images of light and mountain. In the Bible, significant religious events occur on a mountain, because according to the ancient cosmology, God was described as dwelling above the earth and, when appearing on earth, coming as far down as the top of the mountain. Still today people speak of "mountain-top experiences."

Epiphany

Yet God is not only brilliant light, but also cloud. Although contemporary people tend to think of clouds as relating to weather conditions, in the Bible the cloud is a mysterious sign of the presence of God. It is as if God covers the earth, brings life, affecting much, yet suddenly vanishes. Christians can add that from God as cloud rain down the waters of baptism.

We are so accustomed to the language of being children of a God who is like a father that we miss that for first-century Jews, this metaphor was a religious surprise. Christ is to God as a son is to a father: we are not pitiful creatures struggling to live in a hostile environment, but rather children cared for by a beneficent God. "Son of man," on the other hand, is the biblical name for the apocalyptic judge, thus only paradoxically also the beloved Son of God. Jesus as "Son" is more and other than a simplistic meaning of "son."

Ideas for the Day

♦ Set the stage for wonder (defined as a feeling of surprise mingled with admiration, caused by something beautiful, unexpected, unfamiliar, or inexplicable). Another approach is to look at the many dimensions within the Transfiguration narrative—the perspective of each of the six characters in this narrative.

♦ Compare the metaphors from the first and last Sundays of Epiphany: the magi and the disciples on the mount of Transfiguration. The light of God's revelation in Jesus has become clearer the past few weeks as disciples are called and the word is proclaimed.

♦ Consider a reflection on the poem, "The Transfiguration" by Edwin Muir (1949) or the painting, "The Transfiguration" by Raphael (1516–20).

♦ In the Transfiguration, Jesus gives a glimpse of his risen self and shows us who we are becoming through him. Cynthia Bourgeault writes, "He's proposing a total meltdown and recasting of human consciousness." (*The Wisdom Jesus: Transforming Heart and Mind*, Cynthia Bourgeault; Shambhala, 2008, p. 27), and Richard Rohr says, "He is the pledge and guarantee of what God will do with all of our crucifixions. At last, we can meaningfully live with hope. It is no longer an absurd or tragic universe. Our hurts now become the home for our greatest hopes." (*Immortal Diamond*, Kindle loc. 1377)[1]

---

[1] *Immortal Diamond: The Search for the True Self*-Richard Rohr, Jossey-Bass, 2013.

♦ Elijah represents the prophets and Moses the law. When Jesus gives us the great commandment, we are told it hinges on the law and the prophets (BCP, p. 324). How important are the law and the prophets today? What spin does Jesus put on these two cornerstones?

Making Connections

What strengthens us? What reminds us that we should not lose hope? Who are the people who come to us with words of wisdom?

The Transfiguration served to encourage the disciples, even if, momentarily. Sometimes a momentary epiphany is all we need and all we can handle.

Moses and Elijah appear with Jesus as a way of reminding us that law and Prophecy are still important dimensions of the Christian life. There are times when we are called to be like Elijah and like Moses. Of course, our faith calls us every single day to be more like Christ and to reveal God's love to the world.

May God continue to bless us as we descend the mountain of transfiguration and may we be God's true presence in the world.

Engaging all Ages

The Transfiguration is a mountaintop experience. Literally. Jesus comes so close to God he glows (like Moses receiving the Ten Commandments). The disciples do not know what to make of it and were changed forever by this experience. How has Jesus changed you?

Can you share a mountaintop experience? Is it hard to find words to describe?

Hymns for the Day

The Hymnal 1982
Songs of thankfulness and praise 135
Alleluia, song of gladness 122, 123
God of the prophets, bless the prophets' heirs 359
Christ is the world's true Light 542
Christ, whose glory fills the skies 6, 7
From God Christ's deity came forth 443
Christ upon the mountain peak 129, 130
O light of Light, Love given birth 133, 134
O wondrous type! O vision fair 136, 137

Lift Every Voice and Sing II
Swing low, sweet chariot 18
Let the heav'n light shine on me 174

Weekday Commemorations

Tuesday, February 13
Absalom Jones, Priest, 1818

Born a slave in 1746 in Delaware, Jones taught himself to read from the Old Testament. He bought his freedom in 1784, having previously purchased his wife's. He served as a lay minister at St. George's Methodist Episcopal Church, evangelizing alongside his friend Richard Allen. The resulting numbers of blacks at St. George's caused the fearful vestry to segregate them into an upper gallery; the blacks indignantly left the building as one body. Jones and Allen were elected overseers of the Free African Society of black Christians in 1787. They worked ceaselessly for blacks to be included within the Episcopal Church, into which Jones was ordained a priest on September 21, 1802.

Wednesday, February 14
Cyril, Monk, and Methodius, Bishop,
Missionaries to the Slavs, 869, 885

These brothers by blood and mission served as apostles to the southern Slavs against mighty barriers from Germany but with equally mighty support from Rome. In 862, the Moravian king asked for missionaries to teach his people in their native tongue; both learned brothers knew Slavonic and accepted the mission, Cyril to the point that he invented an alphabet for transcription. He died in Rome in 869, but Methodius continued despite enmity among Germans and Moravians. While continuing his mission, Methodius translated the Bible into the Slavonic tongue; his funeral, attended by masses, was conducted in Greek, Latin, and Slavonic.

Thursday, February 15
Thomas Bray, Priest and Missionary, 1730

As overseer for the Church in Maryland, Bray, an English country parson, visited the colony in 1702 for the first and only time, but from that visit, Bray gained his *foci*: he felt deep concern over the state of the American churches; over the need for education among clergy and laity, adults and children; for Natives and Blacks. He founded 39 lending libraries, raised funds for missions, and encouraged young English priests to emigrate to America. He founded societies for Promoting Christian Knowledge and for the Propagation of the Gospel. For his own country and for the colony of Georgia, he championed prison reforms.

Epiphany

Lent

Preparing for Lent

Overview

"I invite you . . . therefore, in the name of the Church, to the observance of a holy Lent . . ."

(Ash Wednesday, BCP, 265)

Lent is about, more than anything else, the formation and renewal of a Paschal people.

Lent originally developed as a time of intense catechesis and formation of candidates who would be baptized at Easter. Later, it also became a time during which those who had been separated from the church because of serious sin prepared to be reconciled and restored on Maundy Thursday. Penitence, which many think of as the hallmark of Lent, is perhaps best understood in a baptismal context: it is part of an initial commitment to Christ in baptism and it is an ongoing part of life in Christ. As we live into the Paschal Mystery, we periodically renew our commitment to Christ, particularly as we participate in the baptism of others.

Think about concrete ways to walk with and support those who will be baptized at Easter—shared worship, prayer, meals, study, outreach, fun (every facet of the parish's life and work)—and how to prayerfully and intentionally prepare for the parish-wide renewal of baptismal vows, in which all the baptized participate with various levels of understanding.

Environment

If your seating is flexible, consider orienting it toward the font; alternatively, if the seating is fixed, can the font be moved to a more central place? Can it be decorated or given more prominence and dignity?

Consider arranging a pathway (as was suggested for Advent), leading to the font, that underscores the fact that Lent is a journey, for catechumens and baptized alike.

Liturgy

- The *Gloria* is not used in Lent. Consider instead "A Song of Penitence" (Canticle 14).
- Leonel Mitchell suggests using the Litany of Penitence from the Ash Wednesday liturgy "on one or more Sundays in place of the Confession of Sin."[1]
- Try using Prayers of the People with petitions based on the Baptismal Covenant, with perhaps a sung response. Also see the options in *Common Worship* (215-217), *Book of Common Worship* (236-238), *Sundays & Seasons* ("Seasona Rites").
- Eucharistic Prayer. Prayer A, Prayer C, Prayer 1 (*Enriching Our Worship I*) are especially good choices.
- Fraction anthems. *Common Worship* (232) offers options.
- Blessings. Consider the options in *Book of Occasional Services* (24-26), *Common Worship* (219) and *New Zealand Prayer Book* (533).
- Look for moments when silence would be appropriate.
- Use the Great Litany (BCP, 148). This may be used at the beginning of the liturgy, in place of all that precedes the Collect of the Day.

Lectionary

"For where your treasure is, there your heart will be also" (Matthew); Jesus's temptations in the wilderness (Mark); "take up your cross and follow me" (Mark); the cleansing of the Temple (John); "for God so loved the world" (John); "unless a grain of wheat falls into the earth and dies, it remains just a single grain; but if it dies, it bears much fruit" (John).

---

[1] Leonel L. Mitchell, updated by Ruth A. Meyers, *Praying Shapes Believing* (New York: Church Publishing Incorporated, 2016).

There is an emphasis in Year B on the covenant faithfulness of God and the new life this faithfulness brings (the rainbow, Abram and Sarai, the Decalogue, the bronze serpent as an instrument of healing).

Note the permission in *Book of Occasional Services*: "When there are catechumens who are candidates for baptism at the Great Vigil of Easter, it is appropriate in any year with the consent of the Bishop to use the Sunday lectionary for Year A during Lent and the Great Fifty Days of Easter" (128).

Music

Consider using simple music for Lent, such as songs from Taize and other simple choruses that can be sung a capella or accompanied by instruments like guitar, recorder, or flute.

Formation/Activities

+ The formation of candidates for Easter baptism must be the first priority.
+ An intergenerational event just before the beginning of Lent can be a time for the parish to explore ways to observe a holy and full Lent.
+ Think about holding Lenten programs on the Baptismal Covenant, geared to different ages.
+ Plan a program around footwashing, too, featuring prayer, teaching, and discussion, especially if the practice is new or difficult for your congregation.
+ Stations of the Cross. *Book of Occasional Services* has a form (56-73).

Through the Eyes of a Child

Lent is a time for forgiveness: looking at the things we have done that are wrong, asking God's and other people's forgiveness, and making a promise not to do them again. It is a time for giving up the things that keep us from being loving people; a time for doing extra things that will help us grow closer to God; a time to be more aware of what it means to love as God loves us; a time to ask God to help us to be more loving, remembering that God is always ready to strengthen us; and a time to think about our baptism and what it means to be a child of God. Encourage parents to help their child read the Bible every day.

Invite them to reflect on the stories, particularly inviting reflection on the life of Jesus as he approaches the cross.

Through the Eyes of Youth

Communicating passion during the passion, the church is called to recognize Christ in the poor, the stranger at the gate; follow the Creed as rule of life; faithfully follow daily practices that imitate Christ for the sake of others; and explore the Penitential Order and how we can be reconciled within our families, our schools, our communities, our church. Demonstrating an outward and visible sign of Lenten participation, invite youth to lead a Lenten ingathering that serves the poor either in the church community or local areas. Invite the youth to serve at soup kitchens, at shelters, at the Salvation Army, or any other program or institution that serves the poor and hungry and homeless. Invite the youth to define evil, reflect upon the ways they see evil in the world, and how the mission and ministry of the church responds. Offer overnight or day "retreats" for youth that include contemplation, reflection, and action.

Through the Eyes of Daily Life

The season of Lent is marked by self-examination and repentance, culminating in the Rite of Reconciliation; by prayer and meditating on Holy Scripture; by fasting (not eating between sunrise and sunset on Fridays to remind us what food we need most for life); and by acts of self-denial, best understood as acts or positive practices that enhance an ever-growing and loving relationship with God. However, the main emphasis during Lent is for each person to prepare for the renewal of baptismal vows and covenant at the Easter vigil.

Lent Through the Eyes of Our Global Community

Ethical issues are raised in the Litany of Penitence (BCP 267-269) during the Ash Wednesday liturgy:

+ Exploitation of other people;
+ Dishonesty in daily life and work;
+ Indifference to injustice, human need, suffering, and cruelty;

- Prejudice and contempt toward those who differ from us;
- Waste and pollution of God's creation.

As we explore more fully the Baptismal Covenant and the covenant of the Torah during Lent, we become increasingly aware of how far we have strayed from God's ways.

Seasonal Checklist

- Plan Lenten formation/education programs, especially for those who will be baptized at Easter.

- Plan a Lenten outreach; perhaps weekly meals that welcome the stranger and the needy. Catechumens should play a key role in planning and carrying out this outreach.
- Plan for Holy Week. Make sure rotas are drawn up well in advance and plan rehearsals for each of the key days of Holy Week. In particular, think through how the liturgies will flow, one into the next. Make sure the congregation is well prepared to fully take part.
- As you prepare for Palm Sunday, consider using local foliage instead of palms in geographical areas where palms are not native.

Seasonal Rites for Lent

Lenten Blessings[1]

In Lent, in place of a seasonal blessing, a solemn Prayer over the People is used, as follows:

The Deacon or, in the absence of a deacon, the Celebrant says:

Bow down before the Lord.

The people kneel and the Celebrant says one of the following prayers:

Ash Wednesday

Grant, most merciful Lord, to your faithful people pardon and peace, that they may be cleansed from all their sins, and serve you with a quiet mind; through Christ our Lord. *Amen.*

Lent 1

Grant, Almighty God, that your people may recognize their weakness and put their whole trust in your strength, so that they may rejoice for ever in the protection of your loving providence; through Jesus Christ our Lord. *Amen.*

Lent 2

Keep this your family, Lord, with your never-failing mercy, that relying solely on the help of your heavenly grace, they may be upheld by your divine protection; through Christ our Lord. *Amen.*

Lent 3

Look mercifully on this your family, Almighty God, that by your great goodness they may be governed and preserved evermore; through Christ our Lord. *Amen.*

Lent 4

Look down in mercy, Lord, on your people who kneel before you; and grant that those whom you have nourished by your Word and Sacraments may bring forth fruit worthy of repentance; through Christ our Lord. *Amen.*

Lent 5

Look with compassion, O Lord, upon this your people; that, rightly observing this holy season, they may learn to know you more fully, and to serve you with a more perfect will; through Christ our Lord. *Amen.*

Ash Wednesday Prayer

This collect is appropriate for a service with children, at home, at Morning Prayer, with grace, or at bedtime.

God of all mercy, you love all that you have made. You forgive the sins of all who are truly sorry. Create and make in us clean hearts, that we, humbly confessing our sins and knowing our brokenness, may receive forgiveness and blessing; through Jesus Christ our Lord, who lives with you and the Holy Spirit, one God, for ever and ever. Amen.[2]

Let's Go! An Ash Wednesday Service for Children[3]

This interactive children's service for Ash Wednesday is suitable for children aged four through ten. The service consists of four interactive stations and a fifth station for the Imposition of Ashes and Eucharist. The fourth station includes the shrouding of an Alleluia Banner that can be created on the last Sunday of the Season after the Epiphany or at a Shrove Tuesday Pancake Supper. Ideally it should be cloth and large enough to hang from a banner or chart stand. Choose a location for each station; place the appropriate props at each station. Create a simple tune to go with the words of the chant to use as you process to the stations. Review and memorize a simple version of the two Bible stories. Prepare a take-home Lenten box for each

---

[1] *The Book of Occasional Services 2003* (New York: Church Publishing, 2004), 23-24.

[2] Anne E. Kitch, *The Anglican Family Prayer Book* (Harrisburg, PA: Morehouse Publishing, 2004), 133.

[3] This service was developed by Elizabeth Hammond and is part of the *Skiturgies: Pageants, Plays, Rites, and Rituals* collection from Church Publishing. www.skiturgies.com

child: small wooden boxes, each one with a small container of water, of oil, of ashes, and a votive candle. Tie a purple ribbon around each box.

Scenery/Props: Station One—Water: small table, container of water; Station Two—Oil: small table, container of oil; Station Three—Light: small table, candle, matches or lighter. (A slightly darker location is best, if possible; lighting the candle should make a noticeable difference.); Station Four—Alleluia Banner: Alleluia Banner, banner or chart stand, purple net; Station Five—Ashes/Eucharist: container of ashes, small altar/table (a small child-height table placed in front of the main altar works well), purple cloth, cross, Bible, chalice and paten, Lenten boxes. bread, wine.

Gather/Introduction: Welcome the children and sit together in the area where you will conclude with the Eucharist. Say a short prayer. Using language personalized for your parish and children, explain that we are now in the season of Lent. Share what Lent is, how it is different from other seasons, why we have Lent, and some of your parish customs. Teach the words of the song and practice the first verse a few times.

Process to Station—Water . . . singing . . . Come into God's presence singing: "Alleluia, Alleluia, Alleluia."

Tell the story of Jesus' baptism. (Matthew 3:13-17, Mark 1:4-11, Luke 3:15-17, 21-22.) Invite the children to wonder about all the ways we use water.

Leader: Jesus wanted John to baptize him. Jesus went right under the water so he saw and felt and heard water everywhere! Jesus must have felt clean and refreshed! When we are baptized it is just the same for us. We are clean and refreshed. Jesus shows us how to get ready to follow him.

Invite the children to dip their fingers into the water. They might want to touch their foreheads with their wet fingers. Share a simple prayer of thanks.

Process to Station—Oil . . . singing . . . Come into God's presence singing: "Water that cleans, water that cleans, water that cleans."

Tell the story of the anointing at Bethany (John 12:1-8.)

Leader: Jesus received a very special gift—Mary's gift of extravagant love. Jesus loved Mary. Mary may have felt tears because of so much love. Jesus shows us how to show love to the people around us.

Invite the children to dip a finger into the oil and, if they are comfortable, anoint one another on the backs of their hands. Share a simple prayer of thanks.

Process to Station—Light . . . singing . . . Come into God's presence singing: "Blessed by the oil, blessed by the oil, blessed by the oil."

Leader: Long, long ago, the people felt afraid and uncertain. They were very lonely. Jesus said to them, "I am the Light. I am always with you." When we light a candle, we know Jesus is close and we feel his love in our hearts. Jesus shows us how to shine in the world.

Invite the children to watch as you light the candle. (If you are feeling brave, have a votive for each child to light.) Share a simple prayer of thanks.

Process to Station—Alleluia Banner . . . singing . . . Come into God's presence singing: "Jesus the Light, Jesus the Light, Jesus the Light."

Leader: Alleluia is one of our special church words. It is a word of celebration. We don't say the word Alleluia during Lent, and we won't say it again until Easter.

Invite the children to help you hang/place/attach the banner to a stand or a wall. Shroud it with the purple net. Explain to the children that the net allows us to still see the word but not say it. (If appropriate for your congregation, allow the banner to stay in full view throughout Lent.)

Process to Station—Ashes/Eucharist . . . singing . . . Come into God's presence singing: "We are in Lent, we are in Lent, we are in Lent."

Show the container of ashes and talk about their significance and why we use ashes on this day. Invite the children to be anointed with ashes. The children may want to help say the words each time someone is anointed . . . "Remember that you are dust . . ."

Set the table together with a purple cloth, cross, Bible, chalice and paten. Continue with a Eucharist, a very simple retelling of the Last Supper. Invite the children to serve/share the bread to/with each other. Have an adult administer the chalice. End with a simple prayer of thanks.

Show the Lenten boxes. Remind the children of the stories we shared today. Invite them to find a special place at home for their box. Share a simple final prayer. Offer a blessing.

Enrollment of candidates for baptism[4]

The enrollment of candidates for baptism at the Great Vigil of Easter normally takes place on the First Sunday in Lent. After the Creed, the catechumens to be enrolled are invited to come forward with their sponsors. A book for them (and their sponsors) should be available to sign at the conclusion of this enrollment.

Catechist: I present to you these catechumens, who have been strengthened by God's grace and supported by the example and prayers of this congregation, and I ask that *they* be enrolled as *candidates* for Holy Baptism.

Celebrant: Have they been regular in attending the worship of God and in receiving instruction?

Sponsors: They have. (*He* has.)

Celebrant: Are they seeking by prayer, study, and example to pattern their lives in accordance with the gospel?

Sponsors: They are. (*He* is.)

Celebrant: As God is your witness, do you approve the enrolling of *these catechumens* as *candidates* for Holy Baptism?

Sponsors and congregation: We do.

Celebrant: Do you desire to be baptized?

Catechumens: I do.

Celebrant: In the Name of God, and with the consent of this congregation, I accept you as candidates for Holy Baptism, and direct that your names be written in this book. God grant that they may also be written in the Book of Life.

Welcoming those who are preparing for the reaffirmation of the Baptismal Covenant[5]

This rite is used at the principle Sunday Eucharist for those baptized persons who have returned to the life of the Church after a time away, for those baptized in other traditions, or those seekig to reaffirm their baptism at the Rite of Confirmation. This takes place at the time of the Prayers of the People

---

[4] *The Book of Occasional Services 2003*, 122-123.
[5] Ibid, 140-141.

Member of the community: N., We present to you these persons (*or N., N.,)* who are baptized members of the Body of Christ, and we welcome them to our community as they undertake a process of growth in the meaning of their baptism.

Celebrant: (to each baptized person) What do you seek?

Renewal of my life to Christ.

Celebrant: In baptism, you died with Christ Jesus to the forces of evil and rose to new life as members of his Body. Will you study the promises made at your baptism, and strive to keep them in the fellowship of this community and the rest of the Church?

I will, with God's help

Celebrant: Will you attend the worship of God regularly with us, to hear God's word and to celebrate the mystery of Christ's dying and rising?

I will, with God's help.

Celebrant: Will you participate in a life of service to those who are poor, outcast, or powerless?

I will, with God's help.

Celebrant: Will you strive to recognize the gifts that God has given you and discern how they are to be used in the building up of God's reign of peace and justice?

I will, with God's help.

Celebrant: (to the sponsors/companions/friends) You have been chosen by this community to serve as companions to these persons. Will you support them by prayer and example and help them to grow in the knowledge and love of God?

We will, with God's help.

Celebrant: (to the congregation) Will you who witness this new beginning keep *(N., N.)* in your prayers and help them, share with them your ministry, bear their burdens, and forgive and encourage them?

We will, with God's help.

In full view of all, the baptized write their names in the church's register of baptized persons.

Celebrant: (extending both hands toward the baptized, with sponsors placing a hand on the candidates' shoulders) Blessed are you, our God, our Maker, for you form us in your image and restore us in Jesus

Christ. In baptism, N., N., were buried with Christ and rose to new life in him. Renew them in your Holy Spirit, that they may grow as members of Christ. Strengthen their union with the rest of his Body as they join us in our life of praise and service; through our Savior, Jesus Christ, who lives and reigns with you and the Holy Spirit, now and for ever.

Amen.

Celebrant: Please welcome the new members of the community.

We recognize you as members of the household of God. Confess the faith of Christ crucified, proclaim his resurrection, and share with us in his eternal priesthood.

Lenten Litany[6]

This litany can be used during a weekly Lenten study or at the end of a meal.

Create in us a clean heart, O God.
   And renew a right spirit within us.

Create in me a clean heart, O God.
and renew a right spirit within me.

Have mercy on me, O God, according to your loving-kindness
   In your great compassion blot out my offenses.

Renew a right spirit within me.

Wash me through and through from my wickedness
   And cleanse me from my sin.

Renew a right spirit within me.

For I know my transgressions
   and my sin is ever before me.

Renew a right spirit within me.

Purge me from my sin, and I shall be pure;
   Wash me, and I shall be cleaned indeed.

Renew a right spirit within me.

Give me the joy of your saving help again
   And sustain me with your bountiful Spirit.

Renew a right spirit within me.

Glory to the Father, and to the Son, and to the Holy Spirit.

Create in me a clean heart, O God.
and renew a right spirit within me.

"ONE Sunday"

February 18

The first Sunday in Lent is part of the Episcopal Church's ongoing commitment to fight extreme poverty and achieve the Millennnium Development Goals (MDGs). It is desig-natied as a day of prayer for fulfillment of the eight goals. "As Christians around the world begin their Lenten journeys with commitments to acts of personal devotion, prayer, and almsgiving, congregational celebration of "ONE Sunday' provides an opportunity to deepen our commitment to atively participate in God's mission of healing the world." The Most Reverend Katharine Jefferts Schori[7]

The eight Millennium Development Goals (MDGs) – which range from halving extreme poverty rates to halting the spread of HIV/AIDS and providing universal primary educa-tion, all by the target date of 2015 – form a blueprint agreed to by all the world's countries and all the world's leading development institutions. They have galvanized unprecedented efforts to meet the needs of the world's poorest. The UN is also working with governments, civil society and other partners to build on the momentum generated by the MDGs and carry on with an ambitious post-2015 development agenda.

MDG Prayers of the People[8]

We pray for the one billion people who live on less than one US dollar per day and for each child of God who dies every 3½ seconds from hunger.
Lead us to eradicate extreme poverty and hunger.
Lord in your mercy,

Hear our prayer

---

[6] Adapted from Psalm 51 by Anne E. Kitch. *The Anglican Family Prayer Book* (Harrisburg, PA: Morehouse Publishing, 2004), 134-136.

[7] www.episcopalchurch.org/posts/publicaffairs/jefferts-schori-calls-marking-one-sunday-near-beginning-lent; accessed August 14, 2017.

[8] See more at: http://www.episcopalrelief.org/church-in-action/worship-resources/prayers-and-liturgies#sthash.Tg62fEQB.dpuf; accessed August 14, 2017.

We pray for the more than 100 million children who are not in school this day.
Lead us to achieve universal primary education for all children.
Lord in your mercy,

Hear our prayer

We pray for women who because of their gender never realize their full potential.
Lead us to promote gender equality and empower women.
Lord in your mercy,

Hear our prayer

We pray for those precious children under the age of five who die every 3 seconds due to disease caused by unclean water, sanitation and poor nutrition.
Lead us to reduce child mortality.
Lord in your mercy,

Hear our prayer

We pray for the more than 500,000 women who die each year from complications of pregnancy and childbirth.
Lead us to improve maternal health.
Lord in your mercy,

Hear our prayer

We pray for those who die each day from preventable diseases like HIV/AIDS, malaria, and tuberculosis.
Lead us to combat these diseases.
Lord in your mercy,

Hear our prayer

We pray for our environment. Make us good stewards of your creation so that all of your children may lead productive and fruitful lives.
Lead us to ensure environmental sustainability.
Lord in your mercy,

Hear our prayer

We pray for a fair trading system, increased international aid, and debt relief for developing countries so that all peoples may realize their dreams and their potential.

Lead us to create a global partnership for development.
Lord in your mercy,

Hear our prayer

Presidents' Day

February 19

Almighty God, who has given us this good land for our heritage; We humbly beseech thee that we may always prove ourselves a people mindful of thy favor and glad to do thy will. Bless our land with honorable ministry, sound learning, and pure manners. Save us from violence, discord, and confusion, from pride and arrogance, and from every evil way. Defend our liberties, and fashion into one united people the multitude brought hither out of many kindreds and tongues. Endow with thy spirit of wisdom those whom in thy name we entrust the authority of government, that there may be justice and peace at home, and that through obedience to thy law, we may show forth thy praise among the nations of the earth. In time of prosperity fill our hearts with thankfulness, and in the day of trouble, suffer not our trust in thee to fail; all of which we ask through Jesus Christ our Lord. Amen. (BCP, 820)

World Day of Prayer

March 2

Sponsored by Church Women United, a Christian group of women that strives to work for justice and peace, the origin of World Day of Prayer dates back to 1887, when Mary Ellen Fairchild James, a Methodist from Brooklyn, New York, called for a day of prayer for home missions. Each year, Church Women United selects a women's group from a different part of the world to write a prayer service for the day. Then, everyone, men and women alike, are encouraged to attend a prayer service using what the group wrote. The theme for 2018 is "All God's Creation is Very Good!" and will be written by the women of Suriname. The prayer service will be available here: http://worlddayofprayer.net/national-committees.html and http://www.wdp-usa.org.

International Women's Day

March 8

Grant, O God, that all may recognize women as equal partners in creation and prophesy. By the grace of the Holy Spirit, empower women at home, at work, in government, and in the hierarchies of churches, temples, mosques, synagogues, and all other places of worship. Provide safety and protection, O Gracious Divinity, and inspire just laws against all forms of violence against women. We ask this through Christ our Savior, *Amen.*[9]

The theme for 2018 is "All God's Creation is Very Good!" and will be written by the women of Suriname. The prayer service will be available here: http: //worlddayofprayer.net/national-committees.html and http://www.wdp-usa.org.

World Water Day

March 22

Held annually as a means of focusing attention on the importance of freshwater and advocating for the sustainable management of freshwater resources, the theme for 2018 is "Nature-based Solutions for Water."[10]

We thank you, Almighty God, for the gift of water. Over it your Holy Spirit moved in the beginning of creation. Through it you led the children of Israel out of their bondage . . . In it your Son Jesus received the baptism of John and was anointed by the Holy Spirit as the Messiah, the Christ, to lead us, through his death and resurrection, from the bondage of sin into everlasting life. (BCP, 306)

[9] Christ Knight, "Equal Partners," in *Lifting Women's Voices: Prayers to Change the World,* Margaret Rose, Jenny Te Paa, Jeane Person, Abagail Nelson, editors (New York: Morehouse Publishing, 2009), 101-102.

[10] Learn more: www.unwater.org/new-decade-water/; accessed September 6, 2017.

Ash Wednesday

February 14, 2018

God hates nothing God has made and forgives us when we are truly repentant. We ask God to give us new and contrite hearts, asking for God's perfect forgiveness through Jesus Christ our Lord.

Color   Violet / Lenten Array

Preface   Of Lent

Collect

Almighty and everlasting God, you hate nothing you have made and forgive the sins of all who are penitent: Create and make in us new and contrite hearts, that we, worthily lamenting our sins and acknowledging our wretchedness, may obtain of you, the God of all mercy, perfect remission and forgiveness; through Jesus Christ our Lord, who lives and reigns with you and the Holy Spirit, one God, for ever and ever. Amen.

Readings and Psalm

Joel 2:1-2, 12-17 or

In our Hebrew Bible reading, the prophet pictures the day of the Lord as a time of judgment and darkness, but he holds out the hope of mercy if the people will repent. Some looked to the day of the Lord's coming as an event of great triumph and joy in Israel. But because of sin, the sky will become black with swarms of locusts. The trumpet must be blown, calling for a solemn fast, a time for weeping, rending of hearts, and turning back to a compassionate Lord.

Isaiah 58:1-12

The lesson from the Hebrew Bible is a denunciation of the injustices of those who only act at their religion. There is a promise of the Lord's favor for those who genuinely repent and care for the needy. Fasts and many prayers are of no purpose and may be misused if they do not involve the liberation of the oppressed and help for the weak and afflicted. When there is justice and sharing, then the light of the Lord will rise out of the darkness and all the ruins will be rebuilt.

Psalm 103 or Psalm 103:8-14

A song of praise, this psalm celebrates God's benefits in a comprehensive way, as signaled by the repetition of all throughout. God does whatever is needed to enhance life, as shown through God's steadfast love.

2 Corinthians 5:20b—6:10

In this lesson, Paul urges the new disciples to be reconciled to God in this time of deliverance, and he reminds them of all the hardships he has patiently endured for their sake and for the gospel. The disciples' task is to respond to God's reconciling work in Christ, who has taken upon himself their sinfulness so that they might have a right relationship with God. In order that he might offer his service without presenting any personal obstacles, Paul has accepted many of the paradoxes that were part of Jesus' own ministry. Although himself poor, he brings true riches to many.

Matthew 6:1-6, 16-21

In our gospel, Jesus describes genuine charity, prayer, and fasting. For religious people, the temptation is always strong to want to be recognized as full of piety more than to want honestly to be seeking God and the good of others. Praise and rewards for an outward show of religion all pass away. The real treasure is found in our relationship with God.

Images in the Readings

Although cited only in the reading from Isaiah 58, ashes are the primary image for the day. Since the eleventh century, the ashes, made by burning last year's palms, cycle around from the triumphant celebration of Jesus' entry into Jerusalem to the humiliation of sinners covering their heads with the burnt greens. Ashes also bring to mind the fire of the Easter Vigil. Honesty is always good, if sometimes painful: this day we are honest about sin and death. The ash cross marks one's forehead as if it is the brand of one's owner. We journey forward wearing the sign of the cross.

Lent

The gospel reading is the source for the three disciplines of Lent that have proved useful for many of Christ's disciples: To increase one's giving to the poor, to increase one's attention to prayer, and to decrease one's focus on the self. The idea is that such disciplines open up the self to God and to the neighbor.

The acceptable time, the day of salvation, is how Paul describes the here and now of the life of the baptized. Ash Wednesday calls us each day into life in Christ.

Several beloved hymns call Christ our treasure. The treasure described in both Matthew and Paul— "poor, yet making many rich"—is the countercultural value of the baptized life.

Ideas for the Day

- Ash Wednesday signals our journey to meditate deeply on our mortality, while reminding us of the life everlasting granted to us through Jesus's sacrifice. The themes of repentance and reconciliation are also prevalent in the liturgy. The gospel of the day challenges us to live our faith authentically.
- Many struggle with the challenges of being authentic Christians in our modern world. Marcus J. Borg (*The Heart of Christianity: Rediscovering a Life of Faith*)[1] illuminates the life of faith, deconceptualizing familiar beliefs, focusing on personal transformation and commitment to values of justice and love to God and one another.
- Many of us were not perfect when we were children. In fact, most of us either got in some sort of trouble (or didn't get caught). Time-outs were commonplace in our home. My parents asked us to "go to our room and think about what we had done." In the stillness, in the quiet, it was a fairly effective way to evaluate and learn a good lesson. Lent is the Church's way of telling each of us that it's time to go to our room and think, in the quiet, about those things we have done or left undone.
- Today is one of the designated days for fasting. What if our understanding of this spiritual practice moved beyond a passive posture of self-denial to something bigger and more impactful? What if fasting was a clearing of our own preoccupations so we could take up the necessary work of reconciliation? The invitation today might be for us to unlearn the adoration of busyness so that there is space to do justice in the underserved places of the kingdom and to bind together the broken places of our lives and the world.

[1] HarperOne, reprint edition 2015.

Making Connections

"Come back!" say the readings. "Be reconciled, and rejoice in God's love." And after a Mardi Gras of partying, the Church invites us to remember that we are finite creatures, formed of ashes and stardust. Increasingly, churches are offering "Ashes to Go" on street corners and train platforms and campus malls and office buildings, inviting all to remember, repent, and be reconciled. Engaging the conversation where people "live and move and have their being" begins to build bridges between church and community. To learn more about Ashes to Go, please visit www.ashestogo.org

Engaging all Ages

Ash Wednesday is usually a day focused on adults. How might your church's observances be made accessible to children? The cross of ashes is imposed in the same place as the cross of oil at our baptism, for a similar reason: we are marked as God's own forever; we belong to God, and we will return to God. This can be a simple way of framing the day that will serve as an invitation to families. Young children may prefer to have the cross imposed on the back of their hand, where they can see it.

Hymns for the Day

Note: There is no Entrance Hymn on this day (see BCP, p. 264).

The Hymnal 1982
Eternal Lord of love, behold your Church 149
O bless the Lord, my soul! 411
The glory of these forty days 143
Before thy throne, O God, we kneel 574, 575
Kind Maker of the world, O hear 152
Lord Jesus, Sun of Righteousness 144
Creator of the earth and skies 148
Lord, whose love through humble service 610
Now quit your care 145
O day of God, draw nigh 600, 601
Lead us, heavenly Father, lead us 559
God himself is with us 475
Jesus, all my gladness 701

Wonder, Love, and Praise
Almighty Lord Most High draw near 888
Bless the Lord, my soul 825
Gracious Spirit, give your servants 782

Lift Every Voice and Sing II
Bless the Lord, O my soul 65
Come, ye disconsolate 147
Thou my everlasting portion 122
Give me a clean heart 124

The First Sunday in Lent

February 18, 2018

Turn away from evil and accept the covenant of salvation.

Color   Violet / Lenten Array

Preface   Of Lent

Collect

Almighty God, whose blessed Son was led by the Spirit to be tempted by Satan: Come quickly to help us who are assaulted by many temptations; and, as you know the weaknesses of each of us, let each one find you mighty to save; through Jesus Christ your Son our Lord, who lives and reigns with you and the Holy Spirit, one God, now and for ever. Amen.

Readings and Psalm

Genesis 9:8-17

Our Hebrew scripture lesson tells of God's promise to Noah and to future generations never again to flood all the earth. God establishes this covenant with a sign—the rainbow that is seen in the storm clouds. This covenant is made with the whole creation. It signifies God's purpose to preserve and save the world, not to destroy it.

Psalm 25:1-9

A prayer for forgiveness and guidance and an expression of trust in the Lord.

1 Peter 3:18-22

This reading from the New Testament speaks of the significance of Christ's death and resurrection. In the story of Noah's salvation a prefiguration of our own salvation through the water of baptism is perceived. Portions of this letter are thought to have been originally composed for use in a service of baptism and Eucharist on the eve of Easter. Such a purpose would explain the association of the themes of Christ's death, baptism, and his triumphal resurrection. It is uncertain who is meant by the spirits to whom Christ preached after his death, but this activity may signify God's intention for the salvation of all.

Mark 1:9-15

The gospel is the story of Jesus' baptism followed by his temptation in the wilderness by Satan and his proclamation of the coming kingdom of God. As Jesus comes up from the water, the Holy Spirit descends like a dove and a voice from heaven tells him that he is the beloved Son. The Spirit then guides him out into the wilderness, where ancient Israel also met its temptations. Here Jesus has his first encounter with Satan, and then goes forth proclaiming the nearing reign of God: "Repent, and believe in the good news."

Prayers of the People

Presider: *Come quickly to help us, O Merciful One, for we are assaulted by many temptations and your people suffer from so many ills. Hear our prayer as we cry out: We put our trust in you, O God; let none who look to you be put to shame.*

Litanist: Visit your Church in mercy and compassion, O Gracious One, as we enter these forty days of Lent, and grant us a renewal of your Spirit and a rekindling of your light.

We put our trust in you, O God;

> *let none who look to you be put to shame.*

Almighty One, you guide the humble in doing right and teach your way to the lowly: Let the treacherous be disappointed in their schemes, and show your ways to all in authority, that they may follow your paths of love and faithfulness.

We put our trust in you, O God;

> *let none who look to you be put to shame.*

Let the risen Christ who has suffered for all bring your divine power and hope throughout the world

Lent

to all who live in wildernesses of violence, poverty, oppression and injustice, that your angels may deliver them from their distress and comfort them with your everlasting love.

We put our trust in you, O God;

> *let none who look to you be put to shame.*

You established your covenant with Noah and gave us the rainbow as a sign of your protective care, let your providence extend over us in our day, to protect your creation and inspire us to be responsible stewards of the Earth you have given us.

We put our trust in you, O God;

> *let none who look to you be put to shame.*

Descend upon this community with your gracious Spirit, O God, that we and all our neighbors may embrace the good news of your kingdom and live as beloved children in your new creation.

We put our trust in you, O God;

> *let none who look to you be put to shame.*

Remember, O God, your compassion and love, for they are from everlasting, as we bring to you our intercession on behalf of those for whom we pray, especially ___.

We come to you in grateful thanksgiving for all the blessings of this day, especially for ___.

Let those who have died be made alive in the spirit to dwell with Christ at the right hand of God, with angels, authorities, and powers made subject to him. We remember especially ___.

We put our trust in you, O God;

> *let none who look to you be put to shame.*

Presider: *Send your angels to uphold us, O God, whenever the wild beasts of oppression or the inner beasts of temptation assault your people, that we may be your beloved, living faithfully in the kingdom given to us through your Son, our Savior Jesus Christ, in the power of Holy Spirit, for you are one God, who lives and reigns for ever and ever.* **Amen.**

Images in the Readings

Mark writes that Jesus was tested for forty days and forty nights. In the Bible, forty is always the time between, the necessary span before the gracious conclusion. It is forty, days or years, that numbers the rain of Noah's flood; Moses on Mount Sinai; Israel in the wilderness; the spies scouting out Canaan; Israel in the hands of the Philistines; the taunting by Goliath; the reigns of Saul, David, and Solomon; Elijah's going to Mt. Horeb; Ezekiel's lying on his right side; Nineveh's repentance; and Jesus' appearance after Easter. For us, it is forty days until the resurrection.

The gospel reading describes Satan as the tempter, the power that seeks to lure us away from God by throwing obstacles in our path. The tradition of art has not given us profound enough depictions of this primordial evil, but in Mark's account, Satan is the opposite reality of the angels. The power of Satan is recognized also in the reference to the arrest of John the Baptist.

At least since the writing of 1 Peter, Christians have used the ark as a picture of the Church—the word *nave* likens our buildings to a sailing ship—and the flood as an image for baptism. We know the rainbow to be a spectrum of light that is the consequence of sunlight shining through droplets of moisture in the atmosphere. As readers of the Hebrew scriptures, we can use this natural phenomenon to remind us of divine mercy shining through all that rains upon us. In many places in the Old Testament, the presence of God is described as manifest in a cloud.

Ideas for the Day

- God makes a promise. A rainbow is God's signature in the sky. A covenant between God and all creation that declares God will never again destroy us in order to save us. As we look towards Good Friday, I wonder if there was a rainbow over the cross, for on that day God lived into the covenant, and it was God who died so that we might live in love—not only us as humanity, but all of creation.

- Lent is the time when we are invited to clear the decks and focus on the life and death of Jesus. How might we expand that focus to include the whole narrative of salvation that scripture offers us? How might we actually see that Lent is a gift to remind us of God's many holy promises to us? Maybe what Lent is really about is walking a different way for a bit so that we can see the blessedness around us and renew our desire to respond to that blessedness with generosity and love? How could you respond this week?

- Focus on Jesus's baptism, as one of many ways we experience epiphany in scripture, instead of the temptations. God publicly declares Jesus' nature by claiming him as his own beloved Son. Through Jesus' death and resurrection, we are made heirs to God's kingdom. Through baptism, we are claimed forever as God's children and Christ's property. This reading could inspire people to see their Baptismal Covenant in new and renewed ways. Invite those baptized as adults to share their journeys toward baptism and their experiences of God's love. Invite your congregation to meditate: how do they live their baptismal vows?

♦ Baptism is a foundation of our Christian life. Former Archbishop Rowan Williams in *Being Christian: Baptism, Bible, Eucharist, Prayer* (Eerdmans, 2014) explores baptism, suggesting a set of questions for reflection and discussion to explore more deeply our understanding of baptism and apply it in our own lives.

Making Connections

Peter proclaims the connection between baptism and God's deliverance of Noah's family through water, reminding us that baptism also joins us to Christ's resurrection. The Thanksgiving over the Water of the baptismal rite draws a similar connection, from creation through the miraculously parted Red Sea to the Jordan and on to Golgotha and the empty tomb. Again and again, our God acts to bring deliverance. What liberations, among your faith community, might be part of this great over-arching narrative of God at work, healing, and saving?

Engaging all Ages

What is different in church today? As the season of Lent begins, draw attention to the changes: the color and the texture of the vestments and altar frontal, the absence of flowers, the style of music in worship. In Lent, we often take away things that may distract us in order to come closer to God. What are ways to direct ourselves towards God? If your church does not normally use incense, you could light some half an hour before worship begins, and the scent will linger without being overpowering. Striking a chime or a gong to mark a brief period of silence just before worship begins is another way to involve the senses and sharpen our attention during Lent.

Hymns for the Day

The Hymnal 1982
Eternal Lord of love, behold your Church 149
Lead us, heavenly Father, lead us 559

Eternal Father, strong to save 608
Lord Jesus, think on me 641
O Love of God, how strong and true 455, 456
You, Lord, we praise in songs of celebration 319
Forty days and forty nights 150
From God Christ's deity came forth 443
Lord, who throughout these forty days 142
Now let us all with one accord 146, 147
O love, how deep, how broad, how high 448, 449
The glory of these forty days 143

Wonder, Love, and Praise
Lord Jesus, think on me 798

Lift Every Voice and Sing II
We are often tossed and driv'n on the restless sea of time 207

Weekday Commemorations

Friday, February 23
Polycarp, Bishop and Martyr of Smyrna, 156
Polycarp died at 86, a martyr, burned at the stake. He had filled his life with service to Jesus. He was one of the church leaders who carried on the tradition of the apostles through the Gnostic heresies of the second century. Polycarp, according to Irenaeus, was a pupil of John and had been appointed a bishop by "apostles in Asia." His letter to the Church in Philippi reveals his adhesion to the faith and his concern for fellow Christians. On the day of his martyrdom, probably in 156, Polycarp was ordered to curse Christ. He refused, declaring, " . . . he never did me any wrong." The mob clamored for him to be thrown to the hungry beasts.

Saturday, February 24
Saint Mattias the Apostle
Little is known of Matthias beyond his selection as a disciple. In the nine days between Jesus' ascension and the day of Pentecost, the disciples gathered in prayer. Peter reminded them that the defection and death of Judas had left the fellowship with a vacancy. The Acts of the Apostles records Peter's suggestion that one of the followers from the time of Jesus' baptism until his crucifixion "must become with us a witness to his resurrection." After prayer, the disciples cast lots between nominees Barsabbas Justus and Matthias; the lot fell to Matthias. Tradition holds him as exemplary, a suitable witness to the resurrection, but his service is unheralded by history and unsung by psalms.

The Second Sunday in Lent

February 25, 2018

Saying "yes" to Jesus Christ and offering our lives to God in Christ.

Color Violet / Lenten Array

Preface Of Lent

Collect

O God, whose glory it is always to have mercy: Be gracious to all who have gone astray from your ways, and bing them again with penitent hearts and steadfast faith to embrace and hold fast the unchangeable truth of your Word, Jesus Christ your Son; who with you and the Holy Spirit lives and reigns, one God, for ever and ever. Amen.

Readings and Psalm

Genesis 17:1-7, 15-16

In our opening lesson God appears to Abram and enters into covenant with him, promising to make him an ancestor to multitudes. Abram is now a changed person. He will henceforth be called Abraham, and his wife Sarai will now be called Sarah. The covenant is to be an everlasting covenant made not only with Abraham and Sarah, but with all generations which issue from them. The Hebrew people will come to see this covenant as the originating source of their own identity, and Christians will find an example of saving faith in Abraham's response to God's promise.

Psalm 22:22-30

A song of praise to the Lord, who rules over all and cares for the downtrodden.

Romans 4:13-25

In this reading, Paul explains that the new relationship with God is open to everyone who follows in Abraham's faith. This means that righteousness before God comes through God's free gift and the response of faith—not because of obedience to the law. This was first true in the case of Abraham, who trusted in God's promise before the law even existed. Now it is true for all who have faith and so show themselves to be among Abraham's descendants from many nations.

Mark 8:31-38

In our gospel passage, Jesus teaches his disciples of the true nature of the ministry of the Son of Man and what it means to follow in his way. Peter has just previously stated his belief that Jesus is the Christ. But now he is called Satan because he tempts Jesus with human ideas rather than God's. Peter needs to understand that, as the Son of Man, Jesus' mission leads through suffering and death before resurrection. Disciples must also learn that the true self and true life are found by those who let themselves be lost for the sake of Jesus and the gospel.

Prayers of the People

Presider: Gracious and life-giving God, through the suffering and death of your Son Jesus Christ you have raised us to the new life of grace: Hear our prayers on behalf of all people, that your promise of fruitfulness may extend throughout the world, as we say: We praise you in the great assembly. May your heart live for ever!

Litanist: You have called us to be Christ's followers, O God, to take up our cross and to give our lives willingly for his sake: Set our minds not upon human things but on divine things, that we may proclaim the glory of Christ's resurrection to all the world.

We praise you in the great assembly.

May your heart live for ever!

You rule over the nations, Almighty One, and you hear the voice of the poor when they cry out to you: Bless the multitude of nations with your compassion that they may follow in your ways of justice and mercy.

We praise you in the great assembly.

May your heart live for ever!

Your Beloved suffered rejection from religious and political leaders, O Compassionate One: Uphold with your resurrection power all who suffer, that their faith may be strong until the day of their deliverance.

We praise you in the great assembly.

May your heart live for ever!

You have made an everlasting covenant with your people, O Holy One: Bless the children of Abraham who worship you in the faiths of Judaism, Christianity and Islam, in this community and around the world, that we may be exceedingly fruitful to fulfill the promise that rests on grace, which is guaranteed to all of Abraham's descendants, as we make known to a people yet unborn the saving deeds that you have done.

We praise you in the great assembly.

May your heart live for ever!

You are the God who gives life to the dead and calls into existence the things that do not exist:

Hear our prayers for all for whom we intercede, especially ___.

Bless all who wish to bear children with the promise of Sarah, that their descendants may be known as yours for ever.

We praise you for your promises and the fulfillment of your blessing in our lives, especially for ___.

To you alone all who sleep in the earth bow down in worship; raise to your joyful presence those who have died, especially ___.

We praise you in the great assembly.

May your heart live for ever!

Presider: *Gracious and merciful God, you have taught us through Jesus that there is no profit in gaining the whole world if we lose our own lives, and you have invited us to follow Jesus, for the way of the cross is the way of life: Give us the faith of Abraham that we may trust in your promises and share in the glory of Christ's inheritance, through the power of your Holy Spirit.* **Amen.**

Images in the Readings

The most ancient cross that we have found in Christian art is a small ivory carving on the side of a box from the late fourth century. When execution by crucifixion was commonplace in the Roman Empire,

Christians were understandably horrified by the cross, and only after the emperor Constantine outlawed crucifixions could Christians adopt the cross as a symbol of God's grace.

Ancient Israel had no sense of an afterlife. Rather, a successful patrilineal line constituted the continuation of one's life after death. Thus the biblical desire for a son exemplifies the perennial desire to overcome one's termination at death. (Yet in a biblical corrective to rigid patriarchy, none of the important sons in the Old Testament, from Seth to Solomon, was a firstborn: thus oftentimes the ideal of primogeniture did not actually determine inheritance.) Calling Jesus the Son of God arises from within this patrilineal worldview. As the Son of God, Christ Jesus is our way beyond death.

The usual translation "God Almighty" obscures the archaic image of God as residing above the mountain peaks or as nourishing the people with milk-filled breasts. The circumlocution "Lord" also obscures the non-gendered Hebrew "I AM." The God who promises us life from the cross is bigger than our language suggests.

Paul's language of justification assumes that God is a judge who requires of us a life of righteousness. That justification comes through faith does not eliminate the necessity for such a radical reorientation of the self before God.

Ideas for the Day

- ◆ God makes a promise. For the third time, God tells Abram that he would be the ancestor of a multitude of nations. And why three times? Well, this time Abram finally has figured out what God has been saying about hospitality. Hospitality: offer a safe place; provide some food and drink; give a blessing. One of the benefits of living hospitality was to hear their new names: Abraham and Sarah.

- ◆ Jesus's suffering was inconsistent with the disciples' expectations both of liberation from Roman oppression and resulting human equality. Suffering is part of the human condition; Jesus faced his persecution and suffering, pointing out the differences between the views of humans and those of God. Today's gospel could deepen the understanding of discipleship costs, and of God's mission to restore and reconcile in Jesus.

- ◆ We too often experience an empty cross (exalting the Easter experience) and neglect the Good

Lent

Friday exprience (with the crucifix pointing to Jesus's suffering). Place a crucifix on the altar and encourage congregants to meditate on the cost of leadership and to articulate areas of ministry where they practice their prophetic voice, and perhaps expose their vulnerabilities.

♦ Winnie Varghese (*Church Meets World: Church's Teaching for a Changing World, Volume 4* (Morehouse, 2016) reminds us that the ways of God are found among the some-times unsafe margins, where God's ministry is essential.

♦ At times we want God to be a certain way. We want God to fit into the image of us instead of us being formed in the image of God. It allows us to be comfortable and unchallenged. What if today we intentionally prayed a different way? What if we allowed a space for Jesus' words to Peter to get into our souls? What if our prayers moved from self-interest to those of self-inventory? What if we truly found our bold, unafraid place then shared it with the world?

Making Connections

One scholarly interpretation of the Greek that is rendered "get behind me, Satan" is "walk in my foot-steps." Abram's (Abraham's) willingness to walk God's way—his faith— inspired God to bless him and his wife Sarai (Sarah) in seemingly impossible ways. How do our daily faithful choices—our faith expressed through our everyday actions—bring blessings we have not even imagined, until they show up? Choices like those made by Eric Liddell, Fanny Crosby, George Herbert, and Polycarp, all celebrated this month. (See *Great Cloud of Witnesses* or subsequent Sundays in this book.)

Engaging all Ages

"Take up your cross and follow me," Jesus tells us in today's gospel. Easier said than done. Invite families to try this at idea at home: ask a family member to carry a few things to another room by filling their arms, one at a time, with objects (whatever is handy— books, pillows, laundry). Once their arms are com-pletely full, drop a quarter on the floor and ask them to pick that up, too. It can't be done without dropping everything else. Following Jesus is like that: what do we have to put down first? What are the things that get in our way?

Hymns for the Day

The Hymnal 1982
I to the hills will lift mine eyes 668
Now let us all with one accord 146, 147
Praise our great and gracious Lord 393
The God of Abraham praise 401
How firm a foundation, ye saints of the Lord 636, 637
I call on thee, Lord Jesus Christ 634
My faith looks up to thee 691
Day by day 654
New every morning is the love 10
Praise the Lord through every nation 484, 485
Take up your cross, the Savior said 675

Wonder, Love, and Praise
Will you come and follow me 757
You laid aside your rightful reputation 734

Lift Every Voice and Sing II
My faith looks up to thee 88
We've come this far by faith 208
I can hear my Savior calling 144
I have decided to follow Jesus 136
King of my life I crown thee now 31

Weekday Commemorations

Tuesday, February 27
George Herbert, Priest, 1633
This is what George Herbert preached. "Nothing is little in God's service." Herbert penned prose and poetry, describing the latter as "a picture of the many spiritual conflicts that have passed betwixt God and my soul . . . " Born in 1593, Herbert studied divin-ity as a young man; in 1626, he took Holy Orders. He served as rector of parishes in Fugglestone and Bemerton. According to Izaak Walton, his biographer, Herbert was a model of the saintly parish priest. He wrote *A Priest in the Temple: or The Country Parson* and *The Temple*; two of his poems, "Teach me, my God and King" and "Let all the world in every corner sing," became well-known hymns.

Thursday, March 1
David, Bishop of Menevia, Wales, c. 544
Although David is held in reverence as the patron of Wales, little is known about the boy or the man. He was born in Menevia and founded a monastery near there, becoming abbot and, later, bishop. He wanted most of all to study and meditate in his monastery, but he was nearly dragooned to an assembly of bishops contesting a heresy. There, David was so eloquent that

Archbishop Dubricius chose the young man to be his successor as Primate of Wales. David founded 11 more Welsh monasteries and also made a pilgrimage to Jerusalem. He filled his office as bishop with distinction as a scholar, administrator, and clergyman of moderation and courage.

Friday, March 2
Chad, Bishop of Lichfield, 672
Ordained to the bishopric irregularly, that is, not following Roman Catholic custom, Chad appeared before Theodore, the new Archbishop of Canterbury. Chad tendered his resignation, saying, "Indeed, I never believed myself worthy of it." Such humility prompted Theodore to re-ordain Chad and to appoint him Bishop of Mercia and Northumbria. Chad traveled his diocese by foot until Theodore commanded that he ride when needed. Chad was a devout administrator, who built a monastery at Barrow, near his see in Lichfield. Not three years after his ordination,

Chad fell victim to the plague that killed many in his diocese. Of his death, the Venerable Bede wrote: "He joyfully beheld . . . the day of the Lord . . . "

Saturday, March 3
John and Charles Wesley, Priests, 1791, 1788
Born four years apart (John, 1703; Charles, 1707), the Brothers Wesley entwined their lives until their deaths, three years apart (Charles, 1788; John, 1791). They were the 15th and 18th children of Samuel, a rector of Epworth, Lincolnshire. They preached sermons and wrote theology, but they are best known through their hymns (Charles wrote more than 6,000). They were educated at Christ Church, Oxford, where they convened friends to adhere strictly to the discipline and worship of the Prayer Book (thus, they were called "Methodists"). They adhered confidently to the doctrine of the Church of England, which they loved. The schism of Methodists from the Church occurred after the deaths of the Wesleys.

Lent

The Third Sunday in Lent

March 4, 2018

We are called into covenant in relationship with God at baptism. In Christ there is a new covenant symbolized by Jesus' action of cleansing the temple. In the new covenant, Jesus' body becomes the meeting place between God and creation, rather than the temple in Jerusalem.

Color   Violet / Lenten Array

Preface   Of Lent

Collect

Almighty God, you know that we have no power in ourselves to help ourselves: Keep us both outwardly in our bodies and inwardly in our souls, that we may be defended from all adversities which may happen to the body, and from all evil thoughts which may assault and hurt the soul; through Jesus Christ our Lord, who lives and reigns with you and the Holy Spirit, one God, for ever and ever. Amen.

Readings and Psalm

Exodus 20:1-17

In our first lesson Moses gives the people the ten commandments that God spoke to him on Mount Sinai. These precepts are at the heart of Israel's law or Torah, and form the basis of the covenant with God established through Moses. The first four commandments prescribe Israel's relationship with God. Those which follow require fundamental responsibilities in human relationships.

Psalm 19

A hymn which glorifies the Creator God, with special praise for the law and a prayer for avoidance of sin.

1 Corinthians 1:18-25

In this epistle Paul directs the Corinthians' attention to God's way of using what is weak and lowly—even what the world regards as foolish—to accomplish God's purposes. Paul emphasizes this understanding because a number of these new Christians had come to think of themselves as especially gifted and wise. Yet the cross has shown God active in the world in a manner surprising both to the Jews' expectation of powerful signs and to the Greek's desire for worldly wisdom.

John 2:13-22

Our gospel is the story of Jesus' cleansing of the Jerusalem temple of its commercial activities, and his prediction that his body will be- come the new temple. The fourth evangelist places this incident very early in Jesus' ministry. It signifies the need to cleanse religious practices of corrupting influences and to put in their place a new form of worship. In the future Christians will worship God by sharing together in the risen life of Christ.

Prayers of the People

Presider: *Loving and gracious God, you have given us guidance to create societies of faithfulness and justice: Cleanse your people and drive far away from us all greed and exploitation, that we may be willing servants in your work of healing and reconciliation, as we pray: Let the words of our mouths and the mediation of our hearts be acceptable in your sight, O God, our strength and our redeemer.*

Litanist: O Gracious God, your testimony is sure and gives wisdom to the innocent: Enlighten your Church with such zeal for your house that we may honor your name and liberate your people.

Let the words of our mouths and the meditation of our hearts be acceptable in your sight,

O God, our strength and our redeemer.

Almighty One, your judgments are true and righteous altogether: Let the message of the cross destroy the wisdom of the wise and thwart the discernment of the discerning, that the nations of the world may abandon their idolatries of power and wealth in order to participate in your divine justice and compassion.

Let the words of our mouths and the meditation of our hearts be acceptable in your sight,

> *O God, our strength and our redeemer.*

Loving God, the firmament shows your handiwork: Look upon your world and inspire all nations and societies to follow your commandments, to live justly and honestly with one another, and to offer compassionate relief to all in any need or under any threat.

Let the words of our mouths and the meditation of our hearts be acceptable in your sight,

> *O God, our strength and our redeemer.*

Merciful One, your commandment is clear and gives light to the eyes: Free this community from our addictions and idols and cleanse us from our unwitting sins, our secret faults and our presumptions, that we may be whole and sound and innocent of great offence.

Let the words of our mouths and the meditation of our hearts be acceptable in your sight,

> *O God, our strength and our redeemer.*

Compassionate God, following your will is more to be desired than much fine gold.

Let your healing grace be with those for whom we pray, especially ___

The heavens declare your glory, our Creator, and we bring to you our grateful praise and thanksgiving, especially for ___.

Through the crucified one—Christ the power of God and the wisdom of God—you raise all who have died into your eternal light; we remember especially before you ___.

Let the words of our mouths and the meditation of our hearts be acceptable in your sight,

> *O God, our strength and our redeemer.*

Presider: *Bless and consecrate this day of rest and prayer as we bring our intercessions to you, O God, that we may join in Christ's work, overturning all forms of exploitation and injustice, and leading your people out of the house of slavery into the house of love, where your Spirit reigns in glory everlasting.*
Amen.

Images in the Readings

Historically, a temple is the home of the deity. Like the Lincoln Memorial, it houses a statue of the god or goddess that is honored by devout visitors. Solomon's temple was a near copy of those of his non-Israelite neighbors, but without an effigy of YHWH. Christians use the image of the temple as a metaphor for church buildings, for worship itself, for the baptized community, for the believers' interior faith, and, like John, for Christ himself.

In today's gospel, Jesus is going up to Jerusalem to celebrate Passover. The Christian Passover is Easter. This is less clear in English than in the many languages which call Christ's resurrection day *Pascha*. There is no need for Christians to celebrate some kind of Jewish seder: we already have our Passover meal each Sunday, each Easter.

Christians have dealt in various ways with the Jewish call to keep sabbath. In many societies, Sunday, the day of Christ's resurrection, has not been and is not a day of rest from work. Christians gather to worship on Sunday, which may or may not be also a day of rest from work: it certainly is not for clergy, assistants, and church musicians.

In Greek, wisdom is a grammatically feminine noun, and thus in classical art was depicted as a great woman dispensing truth and knowledge. The New Testament and several hymns praise Christ as our wisdom. More commonly the New Testament refers to Christ as the word, which in Greek is a grammatically masculine noun.

Ideas for the Day

♦ God makes a promise. In the chapter prior to the Ten Commandments is a proclamation of how all the people of this earth are treasured in the eyes of God—God shall carry us as on eagle's wings. The Ten Commandments give us a recipe of how we might discover and experience this love: we are to love God with all that we have (Commandments 1–4) and we are to love our neighbor as our self (Commandments 5–10). The love of Jesus acknowledges our relationship with God—The Commandments might help us see that relationship more fully.

♦ One of the greatest gifts that Jesus gave us was the clear understanding of his purpose and belovedness to God. Many of us have a lot of room for growth in this area. What if we took a cue from

Lent

Jesus and viewed our bodies as temples? How might it change the way we use them? How might it change the way we nourish them? Consider today ways that you might view your body as a precious vessel given to you for goodness and not self-advancement.

♦ The story of the cleansing of the temple foreshadows Jesus's death and resurrection. The temple events show an emotional Jesus, consumed by his disappointment at God's followers forgetting their primary call. Today's gospel could challenge your community to reconnect with their primary purpose—spreading the gospel and living in prayer.

♦ During the Eucharistic Prayer, invite your community to gather around the altar to emphasize the importance of our sacramental life as fundamental to our discipleship and apostleship.

♦ The Episcopal Church website posted a video of Presiding Bishop Michael Bruce Curry (November 2, 2015) in which he explained the nature of the Jesus Movement. Bishop Curry reminded us that the purpose of our church is to bear and share the gospel—the Good News! The video is found here: http://www.episcopalchurch.org/posts/publicaffairs/presiding-bishop-michael-curry-jesus-movement-and-we-are-episcopal-church (accessed August 22, 2017).

Making Connections

The Decalogue—the Ten Commandments—was once (from the time of Thomas Cranmer) the introduction to most celebrations of Holy Communion. With the adoption of the 1979 Book of Common Prayer, with its emphasis on the Baptismal Covenant, the Decalogue came to be used largely as the introduction to the Penitential Rite, used by many congregations only during Lent and other penitential observances. Through our baptism, we become heirs of God's liberation. Just as Jesus liberated the temple from its misuse as a marketplace, God's deliverance of the Israelites from slavery freed them to follow the commands of God, not of their Egyptian masters or of their own sinfulness.

Engaging all Ages

Jesus turns the temple upside-down in order to make a serious point about the purpose it was intended to serve. Invite people to imagine what "a house of prayer for all people" might look like, act like, sound like. In what ways is your church already like that? How might your church change to become more like that?

Hymns for the Day

The Hymnal 1982
Kind Maker of the world, O hear 152
The spacious firmament on high 409
The stars declare his glory 431
Help us, O Lord, to learn 628
Praise the Lord! ye heavens adore him 373
Praise to the living God! 372
The glory of these forty days 143
Hail, thou once despised Jesus! 495
Nature with open volume stands 434
O Love of God, how strong and true 455, 456
Praise to the Holiest in the height 445, 446
There is a balm in Gilead 676 (1-2)
We sing the praise of him who died 471
You, Lord, we praise in songs of celebration 319
Christ is made the sure foundation 518
Lift up your heads, ye mighty gates 436
Only-begotten, Word of God eternal 360, 361
We the Lord's people, heart and voice uniting 51

Wonder, Love, and Praise
God the sculptor of the mountains 746, 747

Lift Every Voice and Sing II
There is a balm in Gilead 203 (1-2)

Weekday Commemorations

Wednesday, March 7
Perpetua and her Companions, Martyrs at Carthage, 202
Vibia Perpetua and her companions—Felicitas, Revocatus, Secundulus, and Saturninus—were martyred for their faith as Christians. Early in the third century, Emperor Septimius Severus decreed that everyone must sacrifice to his divinity. Perpetua could not and would not: she and her companions were arrested. In prison, Perpetua had visions. At her public hearing before the Proconsul, she declared, "I am a Christian," even refusing entreaties of her father. On March 7, the troop was sent to the arena for mangling by a boar, bear, leopard, and a vicious cow. Perpetua exhorted those about to be martyred "to stand fast in the faith." Eventually, she guided the hand of the executioner sent to drive a sword through her throat.

Friday, March 9
Gregory, Bishop of Nyssa, c. 394

Born about 334 in Caesarea, a brother to Basil the Great, Gregory became besotted by Christ and his passion. His faith was heartened when he was 20 by the transfer of relics of the 40 Martyrs of Sebaste, but he dismissed ministry to become a rhetorician like his father. Nevertheless, Basil convinced Gregory to become Bishop of Nyssa; ordination made Gregory miserable because he felt unworthy, knowing little of tact or budgets. Basil and Macrina, their sister, died in 379; his siblings' deaths opened the way for Gregory to develop as a philosopher and theologian (his *Great Catechism* is one of his most respected treatises). In 381, Gregory was honored as a "pillar of the church."

Lent

The Fourth Sunday in Lent

March 11, 2018

God continues to call people back from exile. Salvation comes as a gift of grace. The Eucharist is the proclamation that Christ sustains us on our journey back from exile.

Color Violet / Lenten Array or Rose

Preface Of Lent

Collect

Gracious Father, whose blessed Son Jesus Christ came down from heaven to be the true bread which gives life to the world: Evermore give us this bread, that he may live in us, and we in him; who lives and reigns with you and the Holy Spirit, one God, now and for ever. Amen.

Readings and Psalm

Numbers 21:4-9

In our Hebrew Bible lesson, the impatient Israelites set out from Mount Hor, where Aaron was buried, to detour around the hostile country of Edom. The people complain against God and Moses about challenging conditions, as they have so often since their departure from Egypt. God sends poisonous serpents among the people, and the people respond by repenting of their disobedience. The Lord instructs Moses to make a bronze serpent and set it on a pole so that any who are bitten may look upon this sign of God's faithfulness and live.

Psalm 107:1-3, 17-22

Thanksgiving is offered to the Lord, who saves from storms and other dangers those who will call upon God's name.

Ephesians 2:1-10

This New Testament passage emphasizes the manner in which Christians have been saved by God's free gift. When we were dead in our sins, God raised us up with Christ that we might know the immeasurable riches of God's graciousness. Although we are saved by faith and not by our good deeds, we are now able to do the good works for which God has made us capable.

John 3:14-21

In our gospel, the image of Moses lifting up the bronze serpent in the wilderness is metaphorically related to Jesus' lifting up on the cross. Just as the repentant Israelites could look upon Moses' raised standard and be saved from the poisonous bite of a serpent, so all who look upon the crucified Christ in faith will be saved from their sins. Jesus did not come to condemn, but to be the saving light who draws many to himself.

Prayers of the People

Presider: *Gracious God, you loved the world so much that you sent your only Son not to condemn the world, but in order that the world might be saved through him; let your light renew all things as we pray: We give you thanks, O God, for you are good; your mercy endures for ever.*

Litanist: Loving One, you have shown your church the immeasurable riches of your grace and kindness toward us in Christ Jesus and raised us with him to be seated in the heavenly places: Let your light shine through our deeds, that Christ's love may be known throughout the world.

We give you thanks, O God, for you are good;

your mercy endures for ever.

Almighty One, you resist fools who take to rebellious ways and you deliver those who cry to you in their trouble: Turn the hearts of all who govern or hold authority in the world, that they may love the light rather than darkness and do all such good works as you have prepared for them.

We give you thanks, O God, for you are good;

your mercy endures for ever.

Compassionate and healing One, you are light for those who live in darkness and your saving love extends through all the earth: Be with all who suffer throughout the world, that they may be delivered from their distress.

We give you thanks, O God, for you are good;

your mercy endures for ever.

Saving One, you give us the true bread which gives life to the world, and you raise up signs of hope in our suffering: Send your word into our community that we may be healed and tell of your acts with shouts of joy.

We give you thanks, O God, for you are good;

your mercy endures for ever.

Let your gift of eternal life be manifest in all who turn to you for help, especially those for whom we pray, ___.

Let all give thanks to you for your mercy and the wonders you do for your children. Hear us as we offer our sacrifice of thanksgiving, especially for ___.

You have lifted up the Son so that all may have eternal life. Let your light shine upon those who have died to save them from the grave, especially ___.

We give you thanks, O God, for you are good;

your mercy endures for ever.

Presider: *Almighty God, you are rich in mercy; out of your great love you loved us even when we were dead in our trespasses, and you have made us alive together with Christ: Let your gift of grace shine through our faith, that we may bear your light of eternal life throughout the world, in the power of your Holy Spirit, through Jesus Christ our Savior.* Amen.

Images in the Readings

One important image for the day is light. According to Genesis 1, light is the first creation of God. In John, Christ not only brings light: he is the very light of God. And so the synoptics describe the crucifixion as effecting an eclipse, and when Judas leaves the company for the betrayal, the fourth evangelist writes, "And it was night."

The serpent on the pole is an example of the many layers that a metaphor can acquire. In Canaan, as in some other world religions, the goddess of life was imaged as a serpent. Thus, to oppose devotion to other deities, in the Bible the serpent is used to signify evil. In the narrative, the serpents are giving out death, and the serpent on the pole, Death enthroned, gives life. So for Christians, the man dying of execution on the cross gives life to the world. For the crucifixions in the Roman Empire, a pole was permanently set into the ground, and the victim was attached to the crosspiece and so lifted up onto the pole.

"We were dead" before baptism. This stark biblical language that describes the life that comes only from God helps believers to face their physical death in the peace of Christ: in baptism we have already died, and we already experience life that is eternal.

Ideas for the Day

- God makes a promise. It is easy to believe that people love to complain. It is easy to blame God for pretty much everything bad. It is not so easy to believe that God would send a crate full of serpents to kill a community. The bronze serpent continues a pattern of behavior from God when an instrument of death is ultimately used for healing. God does not curse the people with poisonous snakes, but God does once again live out the statement that we are loved.

- Believing in the Light can be very hard when the dark places of our lives can be so convincing. Trusting in the goodness of God can feel more abstract and distant then the tough (and very real) life situations right in front of us. What would it take for us to lay aside the need to control and simply trust that Jesus' presence in the world two thousand years ago was for all of creation—even us. What misguided fear would we need to let go of this Lenten season to see that we have been given the most remarkable love offering from God?

- John depicts the essence of the history of salvation—it is the gift of Jesus and eternal life through faith in him. There are profound contrasts in this narrative between darkness and light, and Jesus is the light of the world. Explore what it means to be *a person of the light* in a world plagued with darkness and violence.

- At the beginning of your sermon, invite your congregation to join you in singing a hymn related to the theme of light such as *This Little Light of Mine*" (Hymn #221 from *Lift Every Voice and Sing*), and/or *O Christ, You Are Both Light and Day,*" Hymn #41.

Lent

Making Connections

In some congregations, the fourth Sunday in Lent is observed as Laetare Sunday, from the Latin for "rejoice." It is also known as "Mothering Sunday," from the sixteenth century tradition of attending the "Mother Church" on this day, or "Refreshment Sunday," as the mid-point of Lent when some of the disciplines of Lent were traditionally relaxed. Simnel cakes are traditionally baked in the United Kingdom for this day.

Engaging all Ages

The lesson from Ephesians today is that our salvation is through God's grace, a gift freely given of God's great mercy that cannot be earned or deserved. Our response to that gift is how we live, love, and serve God and one another. The gospel, too, emphasizes that God's gift of Jesus is for the whole world. God's love and grace is not a pie—there is enough and more than enough for everyone, everywhere, and what we give away of it does not diminish our share in it.

Hymns for the Day

The Hymnal 1982
Bread of heaven, on thee we feed 323
How wondrous and great thy works,
God of praise! 532, 533
Amazing grace! how sweet the sound 671
Come, thou fount of every blessing 686
In your mercy, Lord, you called me 706
O love, how deep, how broad, how high 448, 449
O Love of God, how strong and true 455, 456
Rock of Ages, cleft for me 685
Sing, my soul, his wondrous love 467
And now, O Father, mindful of the love 337
Lift high the cross 473
My faith looks up to thee 691
Spread, O spread, thou mighty word 530
The great Creator of the worlds 489
When Christ was lifted from the earth 603, 604

Lift Every Voice and Sing II
Amazing grace! how sweet the sound 181
Come, thou fount of every blessing 111
How to reach the masses, those of every birth 159
My faith looks up to thee 88

Weekday Commemorations

Monday, March 12
Gregory the Great, Bishop of Rome, 604
Gregory, born a patrician in 540, is one of only two popes, with Leo the First, to be popularly called "great." Both men reigned during barbaric invasions of Italy, and Gregory served during "plague, pestilence, and famine." He became Prefect of Rome in 573 and Ambassador to Constantinople in 579; in 590, Gregory succeeded Pope Pelagius. Gregory's pontificate was marked by vigorous service: he defended Rome against the Lombards and fed the people from the papal granaries in Sicily. He ordered the Church's liturgy and chant; his legacy remains. He also supported evangelism of the Anglo-Saxons to become "Gregory the Apostle of the English." He is buried in St. Peter's Basilica.

Saturday, March 17
Patrick, Bishop and Missionary of Ireland, 461
Patrick was born in a Christian family on the northwest coast of Britain about 390. As a teen, Patrick was kidnapped to Ireland and forced to served as a shepherd; as a young man, he escaped back to Britain, where he was educated as a Christian and took holy orders. A vision returned him to Ireland about 432. Patrick's missions of conversion throughout Ireland continued until his death. He adapted pagan traditions to Christian: he had Christian churches built on sites considered sacred; he had crosses carved on druidic pillars; and he reassigned sacred wells to Christian status. "St. Patrick's Breastplate," while attributed to him, is probably not his except as it expresses his zeal.

The Fifth Sunday in Lent

March 18, 2018

In Jesus' death and resurrection and through baptism, we have a covenant with God written on our hearts.

Color Violet / Lenten Array

Preface Of Lent

Collect

Almighty God, you alone can bring into order the unruly wills and affections of sinners: Grant your people grace to love what you command and desire what you promise; that, among the swift and varied changes of the world, our hearts may surely there be fixed where true joys are to be found; through Jesus Christ our Lord, who lives and reigns with you and the Holy Spirt, one God, now and for ever. Amen.

Readings and Psalm

Jeremiah 31:31-34

In our opening reading, the prophet Jeremiah foresees a new covenant which God will make with the people, a covenant written not on tablets of stone but on human hearts. Israel and Judah have broken the covenant made when the Lord brought them out of slavery in Egypt. Now they are about to go into exile. Yet the days are coming when their sins will be forgiven, and God will establish a new relationship with them. This covenant will be based not on external law but on an inner knowing of the Lord.

Psalm 51:1-13 or

A confession of sin and guilt and a prayer for a clean heart.

Psalm 119:9-16

Happy are those who walk in the law of the Lord, who guide their ways by God's commandments.

Hebrews 5:5-10

In this New Testament lesson, we hear how through his obedience and suffering Christ reached the perfection of his destiny and was designated by God to be the eternal high priest. The high priesthood of Jesus is the great theme of the Letter to the Hebrews. Like the high priests of the old covenant, Christ is chosen from among human beings and so has sympathy with human weakness. But he is the Son and has now been named high priest forever. He succeeds Melchizedek, a royal and priestly figure from antiquity.

John 12:20-33

In this gospel passage, Jesus presents teaching concerning the meaning of his death. After his prayer to God, a voice from heaven is heard. Greeks wish to see Jesus, but he will not draw all others to himself until after he has died and has risen. Then, like a seed which falls into the earth, he will bear much fruit. Disciples must also learn to serve Jesus by following him in this way. Now is the hour for the Son of Man to be glorified— glorified both by his willingness to be lifted up on the cross to die for others, and afterward to be lifted up to heaven.

Prayers of the People

Presider: *Eternal and loving God, through the glorification of your Son Jesus you have taught us to follow him through death into eternal life: Glorify your name in us, as we bring before you the concerns of the world, saying: Create in us clean hearts, O God, and renew a right spirit within us.*

Litanist: Blessed Father, your Son Jesus has taught your Church that when a grain of wheat falls into the earth and dies, it bears much fruit: Empower your people in our journey of sacrifice and compassion to follow Christ in such faithfulness that we may be glorified with him.

Create in us clean hearts, O God,

and renew a right spirit within us.

Almighty One, you have driven out the ruler of this world through the glorification of Jesus: Put your law of love within the hearts of all who hold authority among the nations, that they may hear of joy and gladness, so that the broken body of the world may rejoice.

Create in us clean hearts, O God,

> *and renew a right spirit within us.*

Bring the joy of your saving help to all who suffer throughout the world, that they may hear of joy and gladness and be healed.

Create in us clean hearts, O God,

> *and renew a right spirit within us.*

Gracious God, you have promised that all who serve your beloved will be honored in your sight: Have mercy upon this community, that all may know you, from the least to the greatest, and follow in the way that Christ has shown us.

Create in us clean hearts, O God,

> *and renew a right spirit within us.*

Let our prayers ascend to Jesus, our eternal high priest, as we offer up our intercessions and supplications, especially for ___.

We thank you for the incarnation of your Son Jesus, who shares our sorrows and our joys. Hear our praise and thankfulness for all the blessings we enjoy, especially for ___.

We entrust into your life all of those who have surrendered their lives into your eternal keeping, especially ___.

Create in us clean hearts, O God,

> *and renew a right spirit within us.*

Presider: *Give us the joy of your saving help again, and sustain us with your bountiful Spirit, O God, as we follow Jesus in service to your world, that the salvation and glorification you have accomplished through his cross and resurrection may extend your eternal life throughout creation, now and forever.* **Amen.**

Images in the Readings

The image of the grain of wheat is especially useful, not only as a historic metaphor for life through death, but also because most Christians have used wheat for Holy Communion. The church uses wheat—the staple of human food in the northern hemisphere—to carry God into the community and so to bear much fruit.

The evangelist makes clear that Christ is "lifted up" by being executed on the cross; his death is what draws the world to God. This death gives us life, and we celebrate that life in the eating of the wheat.

The interpretation of the image of God being the people's husband is complex. Canaanite religion referred to the dominant male deity as the Baal, the lord and master, that is, like a woman's husband, whom in the ancient patriarchal culture she was required to serve and obey. Yet biblical use of the image adds the resonances of love and commitment. Especially medieval celibate Christians found the imagery beloved, since it afforded them religious language of intimacy and affection. Contemporary Christians have struggled with the image, since it accentuates the idea of God as male and seems to sanctify the dominance of the husband over the wife. Recently some Christians have stressed, not husband, but instead marriage as a welcome metaphor for the loving commitment that binds God to believers.

Ideas for the Day

- God makes a promise. Jeremiah proclaims HOPE. It is the essence is what is called the new covenant.
  H = Holy: This is OF God.
  O = Open: There is a wideness in God's mercy.
  P = Practiced: There is a history of God always living in love.
  E = Expectation: We can expect and count on God continuing to be God.
- The whole body of scripture is about God entering into covenant with us and then calling us back when we forget just how beloved we are to God. Each story is a call to come closer. How might we give up a part of what we cling to so that more eternal things can manifest themselves within us? What can we put aside so that God's presence can be more central to us?
- Jesus foretells his ultimate sacrifice for human kind, to the incredulity of his disciples. The analogy of the wheat is instructive—we are encouraged to contemplate seasons and inexorable individual and communal deaths and rebirths, all of which mirror Christ's message—he had to die to live within us.
- Explore, through contemporary examples, what practices or systems take us down paths of death,

perhaps without glimpses of life through God's truth, such as violence and discrimination. To learn more about how our Episcopal Church is working to dismantle deadly practices, visit the Racial Reconciliation Blog at www.episcopal-church.org/blog/RacialReconciliation; accessed 20 August 2017.

♦ The theme of reconciliation is found throughout the Lenten and Easter Seasons. The words in today's gospel are profound and uplifting: "And I, when I am lifted up from the earth, will draw all people to myself." In Jesus, we find common ground and life abundant.

Making Connections

The pulpit in many Episcopal churches is engraved with the line from the Greeks in today's gospel reading: "We would see Jesus." Our preachers are taught to show us Jesus, not simply in the scriptures but in the lives and experiences of everyday people—"holding the Bible in one hand, and the newspaper in the other," as theologian Karl Barth urged. Just as Psalm 51 in our Daily Devotions for Families (BCP p. 137) reminds us, it is God who "create[s] in us a clean heart," opening our eyes to "see [God's] hand at work in the world about us." (BCP, p 372)

Engaging all Ages

The words of the prophet Jeremiah have given comfort and assurance to God's people from generation to generation: "I will put my instructions within them and engrave them on their hearts. I will be their God, and they will be my people." What instructions has God put within you? What are the words God has engraved upon your heart?

Hymns for the Day

The Hymnal 1982
Help us, O Lord, to learn 628
O God of Bethel, by whose hand 709
From God Christ's deity came forth 443
Hail, thou once despised Jesus! 495
O Love of God, how strong and true 455, 456
Lift high the cross 473
My faith looks up to thee 691
O love, how deep, how broad, how high 448, 449
What wondrous love is this 439
When Christ was lifted from the earth 603, 604
When I survey the wondrous cross 474

Wonder, Love, and Praise
O wheat whose crushing was for bread 760

Lift Every Voice and Sing II
How to reach the masses, those of every birth 159
My faith looks up to thee 88

Weekday Commemorations

Monday, March 19
Saint Joseph
The Gospel According to Matthew honors Joseph as open to mysticism while also a man of compassion and devotion. Even so, he may have been perturbed when pressed to be Mary's protector and to be a father to Jesus. He accepted and provided nurturance; he protected Jesus and Mary by escorting them to Egypt to escape Herod's commanded slaughter of boy children. Joseph reared his son as a faithful Jew. Joseph himself, a descendant of David, was a pious Jew, a carpenter by trade. As such, he is enrolled as the patron saint of workers for not only working with his hands but also mentoring his son in this trade. Joseph exemplifies a loving husband and father, a man who trusted God.

Tuesday, March 20
Cuthbert, Bishop of Lindisfarne, 687
Cuthbert, born about 625, entered a monastery after having a vision of angelic light and learning that Aidan of Lindisfarne had died at the time of this vision. Cuthbert was Prior of Melrose Abbey from 651 to 664 and of Lindisfarne for a dozen years. He made it his habit to visit far-flung villages and to preach to the poor people who needed his discipline as a model to withstand the pull of the pagan. He became Bishop of Hexham in 684, but kept his see at Lindisfarne. Cuthbert was the most popular saint of the pre-Conquest Anglo-Saxon Church. Today, his relics and tomb remain at Durham.

Wednesday, March 21
Thomas Ken, Bishop of Bath and Wells, 1711
Born in 1637, Ken became known as a man of integrity during royal upheavals. He publicly rebuked the Prince of Orange's dastardly treatment of his wife and denied hospitality to the mistress of Charles II in 1683. In 1688, under James II, Ken refused to read the king's Declaration of Indulgence; he and his six cohorts were sent to the Tower, acquitted in court, then considered heroes. After the revolution of 1688, Ken refused to swear allegiance to William of Orange, so was deprived of his see. The accession of Queen Anne saw Ken in line again with the Church of England.

He wrote the doxology that begins "Praise God from whom all blessings flow."

Thursday, March 22
James De Koven, Priest, 1879

De Koven advocated for rituals and accoutrements: the "lights and incense and vestments." Born in Middletown, Connecticut, in 1831, he was ordained in 1855 and appointed professor of ecclesiastical history at Nashotah House in Wisconsin. Nashotah House was associated with the Oxford Movement, particularly in emphasizing the sacramental life of the church and practices such as bowing to the altar and at the name of Jesus. At two General Conventions (1871, 1874), where controversy over "ritualism" was rife, De Koven argued that ritualism symbolized "the real, spiritual presence of Christ." Because of this stance, consent for his consecrations as Bishop of Wisconsin in 1874 and of Illinois in 1874 remained ungranted.

Friday, March 23
Gregory the Illuminator, Bishop and Missionary of Armenia, c. 332

Gregory, Apostle of the Armenians, was born about 257. Following his father's assassination of the Persian king, baby Gregory was removed to Caesarea in Cappadocia and raised as a Christian. He married and fathered two sons. About 280, he returned to Armenia and, after much effort, converted the king to Christianity, thereby ending paganism in his native land. About 300, Gregory was ordained a bishop at Caesarea; his cathedral at Valarshapat remains the center of Armenian Christianity. As the first nation-state to become officially Christian, Armenia set a precedent for adoption of Christianity by Emperor Constantine; as a buffer between empires in Rome and Persia, Armenia suffered through the vicissitudes of power and protection.

Holy Week

Preparing for Holy Week

Overview

"On this most holy night, in which our Lord Jesus passed over from death to life, the Church invites her members, dispersed throughout the world, to gather in vigil and prayer. For this is the Passover of the Lord, in which, by hearing his Word and celebrating his Sacraments, we share in his victory over death." (opening address at the Easter Vigil, BCP 285).

Holy Week, and particularly the Triduum (Maundy Thursday evening through Easter Day), is an immersion in the Paschal Mystery. These days are the primary expression and celebration of this Mystery, when the Church knows *anamnesis* as at no other time of the year.

Aim to make these days as rich as possible, both liturgically and spiritually. This doesn't mean, however, that a small parish with limited resources can't celebrate these days well.[1]

Liturgy

- The Proper Liturgies for Special Days should be the priority this week, with other services and events scheduled around them when needed and possible.
- The Triduum is really *one* liturgy in three parts. Emphasize that. Emphasizing that the congregation is to leave in silence after both the Maundy Thursday and Good Friday liturgies fosters the sense that the liturgy then simply picks up where it left off on the previous evening/day. In addition, the rubric at the end of the Good Friday liturgy is clear: after a concluding prayer, "no blessing or dismissal is added" (1979 BCP, 282).
- Think about including simple notes in the bulletin; for example: "We will gather to continue our celebration of the Triduum at such-and-such a time tomorrow."

- *Common Worship* provides forms for the Prayers of the People for Palm Sunday (272-273) and Maundy Thursday (299) and a fraction anthem suitable for any Eucharist this week (275).
- Think about which form of the Eucharistic Prayer to use at each liturgy.
- Make a place for both song *and* silence this week.
- Note the key emphases of each liturgy this week. Carefully look at the rubrics and the available options.
- Make these liturgies accessible for all ages.

Palm Sunday

- Think through the logistics of the day's liturgy:
  - How will the palms or other foliage be distributed?
  - If possible, plan for a true procession, even if just from the parish hall to the church (in other words, avoid the kind of "procession" that simply goes in a circle within a space).
  - How will the procession be arranged and carried out?
  - How will the singing of the processional hymn be supported throughout the length of the procession, so that those at every point can hear and join in the singing?
  - How will the Passion gospel be proclaimed?

Maundy Thursday

- If there will be a footwashing, think through the logistics.
  - Will there be a watch? This needs to be planned (sign-up sheet, arranging for the church to be unlocked and accessible, availability of devotional material and perhaps small flashlights).[2] *Common Worship* provides readings that may be used (304).

---

[1] See Mitchell's suggestions for small parishes and those with limited resources in *Planning the Church Year*, 53-54, 64.

[2] Mitchell notes that if a parish does not wish to have an altar of repose or a watch, the sacrament may simply be reserved "in some convenient place, such as a chapel or the sacristy, from which it can be brought before communion in the Good Friday liturgy" (*Planning the Church Year*, 57).

Good Friday

- ◆ Ideally, there should be only one celebration of the liturgy today.
- ◆ If possible, plan to proclaim the Passion in a markedly different way than was done on Palm Sunday.
- ◆ Explore creative ways to venerate the cross.

Easter Vigil

- ◆ "This is the night."
- ◆ Logistics: where? when? how long? lighting? This liturgy, perhaps more than any other, calls for detailed preparation and rehearsal.
- ◆ Think about movement during this liturgy (perhaps the most important liturgy of the year to plan for this); move from place to place for the different parts of the service, for example:
  - ○ Gather outside for the kindling of new fire and the lighting of the Paschal candle.
  - ○ Process behind the Paschal candle to the parish hall for the singing of the *Exsultet* and the vigil readings (perhaps provide both floor cushions and chairs for an informal seating arrangement)—the vigil portion of the liturgy, when we proclaim key moments in salvation. History, is really the community recounting our family stories by the fire; it is, as well, the final pre-baptismal catechesis for those about to be baptized and ongoing mystagogy for the already-baptized.
  - ○ Think about creative ways of proclaiming these readings; include the children and young people if at all possible.
  - ○ Process behind the Paschal candle to the font for baptism and the renewal of baptismal vows.
  - ○ Gather in the church for the first Eucharist of Easter.

Environment

This is perhaps the most difficult week of the year to plan for and arrange, particularly the transition from the starkness of Lent to the abundance of Easter. If the font is not at the front of the church, it is possible to (quietly) decorate around the altar while the baptisms are taking place. Another option is to make the decorating part of the liturgy, with the entire congregation pitching in during the singing of the *Gloria*.

Lectionary

This is the week when we proclaim our faith in its fulness—the Paschal Mystery in which we live—in the Passion on Palm Sunday (from Mark in Year B); the

account of the Passover, institution of the Eucharist, and footwashing on Maundy Thursday; the Passion according to John on Good Friday; and the sweep of salvation history at the Easter Vigil, culminating in Paul's baptismal theology in the Letter to the Romans ("Do you not know that all of us who have been baptized into Christ Jesus were baptized into his death? Therefore we have been buried with him by baptism into death, so that, just as Christ was raised from the dead by the glory of the Father, so we too might walk in newness of life") and the account of the resurrection from Mark.

Music

There is much to consider and plan for this week, from music for the palm procession to (possible) music during the Maundy Thursday footwashing and Good Friday veneration of the cross to the singing of the *Exsultet* and proclamation of the first Alleluias! during the Easter Vigil.

- ◆ Think about a capella singing this week
- ◆ Think about appropriate times for silence
- ◆ While the Prayer Book includes suggested psalms and canticles to accompany the Easter Vigil readings, "some other suitable psalm, collect, or hymn may be sung" (288). Explore options, and keep in mind the capabilities of your congregation.

Formation/Activities

Is there a time and place for other activities and devotions this week, such as an agapé meal, Stations of the Cross and/or Tenebrae? *The Book of Occasional Services* provides blessings to be used at a Maundy Thursday agapé meal (95-96), a form for Tenebrae on the Wednesday evening of Holy Week (74-92), and a form of the Stations of the Cross (56-73).

Holy Week Through the Eyes of a Child

Talking about death and grief with children is critical to their faith, however, even though it is Holy Week and not yet Easter it is necessary to give the proclamation, "Christ has died and Christ has risen from the dead." Children will be thinking bunny rabbits, Easter eggs and baskets, and time home from school; this is the time to instill in them through prayer and practice the importance of Holy Week in their faith. For example, you might want to do a "foot washing" at home in a special way after sharing the story of Jesus and the last supper. You might encourage the children to participate in a "Good Friday" service. Talk about how sad the disciples and Mary the Mother of Jesus must have been to see Jesus die, but there was a promise Jesus needed to complete. Attend an Easter Vigil service and remind them of the story of our salvation, from Old Testament times to the present. The children will want to act out the Good Friday/Easter story in much the same way they enjoy the Christmas story.

Holy Week Through the Eyes of Youth

The Church is called to proclaim that Christ before his death invited us to remember how much God loves us, so much so that bread and wine mysteriously become what we share at Eucharist when we eat and drink of his flesh and blood, and that through his death new life would be offered for all humanity.

- The idea of an omniscient deity sending his only son to earth to die for the sins of humankind, only to be resurrected from the dead, can be difficult to grasp.
- Fear that we will lose our awareness of a connection with God, or even that we have "lost" God or that our connection with him is invalid. We must be willing to let go of former experiences, no matter how powerful, and continually redefine what it means to be a follower of God at every stage, to be in new life.
- It is not easy to speak about God with friends; many of them see the Church as a reality that judges youth; that opposes their desire for happiness and love. It is a constant Good Friday struggle.

Holy Week is the time to stay current and connected to the youth. Consider with the youth ways in which twenty-first century discipleship calls us to go to the cross. What are the crosses youth will need to bear in the twenty-first century? Practice noticing all kinds of people and responding to them as Christ is in them.

Holy Week Through the Eyes of Daily Life

During Holy Week some communities gather each day to meditate on Jesus' final days before his death on the cross. Begin the journey with Jesus, following his path to Jerusalem through prayer with others or in solitude. At the heart of the Maundy Thursday liturgy is Jesus' commandment to love one another. As Jesus washing the feet of his disciples, we are called to follow his example as we humbly care for one another, especially the poor and unloved. At the Lord's table, we remember Jesus' sacrifice of his life, even as we are called to offer ourselves in love for the life of the world. Plant the cross on your heart, so that in its power and love you can continue to be Christ's representative in the world at work, school, and play.

Holy Week Through the Eyes of the Global Community

Two collects heard during Holy Week set the focus for social justice:

- Palm Sunday: Mercifully grant that we may walk in the way of his suffering. (BCP 272)
- Monday in Holy Week: Almighty God, whose most dear Son went not up to joy but first he suffered pain, and entered not into glory before he was crucified: Mercifully grant that we, walking in the way of the cross, may find it none other than the way of life and peace. (BCP 220)

These collects remind us that we are called:

- To identify with the suffering peoples of the nation and the world and not to remain aloof;
- To have compassion for "all sorts and conditions" of people (BCP 814).

Seasonal Checklist

- These days need and deserve careful planning. Plan and rehearse!
- Be creative and intentional about publicizing Holy Week services and activities: signboards, newspaper, website, Facebook.
- Consider providing detailed teaching regarding this week—in the newsletter, on your website, and/or in the service leaflets, explaining why and how we do what we do.

Holy Week

Holy Week Blessing[1]

The following blessing may be used by a bishop or priest whenever a blessing is appropriate from Palm Sunday through Maundy Thursday.

Almighty God, we pray you graciously to behold this your family, for whom our Lord Jesus Christ was willing to be betrayed, and given into the hands of sinners, and to suffer death upon the cross; who lives and reigns for ever and ever. *Amen.*

Tenebrae[2]

The name Tenebrae (the Latin word for "darkness" or "shadows") has for centuries been applied to the ancient monastic night and early morning services (Matins and Lauds) of the last three days of Holy Week, which in medieval times came to be celebrated on the preceding evening.

Apart from the chant of the Lamentations (in which each verse is introduced by a letter of the Hebrew alphabet), the most conspicuous feature of the service is the gradual extinguishing of candles and other lights in the church until only a single candle, considered a symbol of our Lord, remains. Toward the end of the service this candle is hidden, typifying the apparent victory of the forces of evil. At the very end, a loud noise is made, symbolizing the earthquake at the time of the resurrection (Matthew 28:2), the hidden candle is restored to its place, and by its light all depart in silence.

This service is most appropriate for Wednesday of Holy Week.

Maundy Thursday

Agapé Blessings[3]

Over Wine. *Blessed are you, O Lord our God, King of the universe. You create the fruit of the vine; and on this night you have refreshed us with the cup of salvation in the Blood of your Son Jesus Christ. Glory to you for ever and ever. Amen.*

Over Bread. *Blessed are you, O Lord our God, King of the universe. You bring forth bread from the earth; and on this night you have given us the bread of life in the Body of your Son Jesus Christ. As grain scattered upon the earth is gathered into one loaf, so gather your Church in every place into the kingdom of your Son. To you be glory and power for ever and ever. Amen.*

Over the Other Foods. *Blessed are you, O Lord our God, King of the universe. You have blessed the earth to bring forth food to satisfy our hunger. Let this food strengthen us in the fast that is before us, that following our Savior in the way of the cross, we may come to the joy of his resurrection. For yours is the kingdom and the power and the glory, now and for ever. Amen.*

At the Foot-Washing[4]

Fellow servants of our Lord Jesus Christ: on the night before his death, Jesus set an example for his disciples by washing their feet, an act of humble service. He taught that strength and growth in the life of the Kingdom of God come not by power, authority, or even miracle, but by such lowly service. We all need to remember his example, but none stand more in need of this reminder than those whom the Lord has called to the ordained ministry.

Therefore, I invite you [who have been appointed as representatives of the congregation and] who share in the royal priesthood of Christ, to come forward, that I may recall whose servant I am by following the example of my Master. But come remembering his admonition that what will be done for you is also to be done by you to others, for "a servant is not greater than his master, nor is one who is sent greater than the one who sent him. If you know these things, blessed are you if you do them."

On the Stripping of the Altar[5]

If the custom of stripping the altar is observed as a public ceremonty, it takes place after the Maundy Thursday liturgy. It may be doen in silence; or it may be accompanied by the

---

[1] *The Book of Occasional Services 2003* (New York: Church Publishing, 2004), 26.

[2] Ibid, 75-92.

[3] Ibid, 93-94.

[4] Ibid, 93.

[5] Ibid, 94.

recitation of Psalm 22, which is said with Gloria Patri. The following antiphon may be said before and after the psalm.

They divide my garments among them; they cast lots for my clothing.

The Stations of the Cross for Children[6]

This is a script for a meditation for children, either gathered on the floor, or walking from station to station. Any of the following props may be used and passed around so that children can feel, smell, and taste the story.

Needed are: charoset (chopped apples, honey, and cinnamon) parsley, and salt water (Seder foods); a chalice and wine, flat bread, a bowl with oiled water; rough jute rope, rich purple fabric; a crown of thorns; a large bowl with water for Pilate; nails; Veronika's veil (gauzy fabric with a face vaguely chalked on it); a sponge with vinegar; cotton balls with fragrant oil; linen.

If you wanted to celebrate the beginning of our nation, where would you go to do it? *(Elicit answers: Boston, perhaps, or Philadelphia, or Washington DC.)*

And how would you celebrate? *(Probably with parades, fireworks, food for sure!)*

In Jesus' time, where do you think the Jewish people went to celebrate their liberation? *(To the city of Jerusalem).*

And do you know the name of the holiday that still marks their freedom? *(It is called Passover.)*

When Jesus lived, all the people would go up to Jerusalem for Passover. There they sang and danced and prayed and ate! At the Seder meal, they would tell their children the story of how God had saved them from slavery in Egypt.

"Why is this night different from all other nights?" the children would ask.
"On this night, God opened the Red Sea waters and the Jewish people passed through the sea on dry ground, but the Egyptians who chased them drowned in the sea!"

"Why do we eat charoset?" the children would ask.
"Because of the mortar for the bricks our mothers and fathers had to make in their hard labor in Egypt!"

"Why do we eat parsley dipped in salt?" the children would ask.

"Because of the bitterness and tears of our slavery!"

"Why do we eat unleavened bread?" the children would ask.
"Because there was no time to wait for the bread to rise the night we escaped from Egypt!"

Every spring, the Jewish people have gathered at Passover meals to tell that same story with the children. They say, "Next year, may we celebrate this meal in Israel, our home!"

They sing: "**Da da ye nu, da da ye nu, da da ye nu, dayenu, dayenu!**"
(It would have been enough for us!)
If God had split the sea for us, Dayenu!
If God had sustained us in the wilderness for forty years, Dayenu!
If God had brought us before Mount Sinai, Dayenu!
If God had given us the Torah, Dayenu!
If God had led us to the land of Israel, Dayenu!

Music for Dayenu can be found on line.[7]

In Jesus' time, the people waited for a king to come and free them from the Romans who ruled over them in their own homeland. This king would come at Passover, entering the holy city riding on a colt. He would be like a god, able to heal blindness, and other miracles. So, when Jesus came onto Jerusalem on a colt, many thought he was the Messiah, and they made a huge parade, and shouted "Hosanna! Hosanna!" They made a path with their palms and their clothes. The children sang the loudest, and when people tried to quiet them, Jesus said, "If you silence them, the stones will start to sing!"

The people thought that Jesus would lead them into a great war, a war they could win, and that, after all these years they would be free at last! But there was no war, and the people became sad, scared, and angry. The same people who had welcomed him with such joy and love began to want to kill Jesus.

Jesus knew what was happening. He knew the people wanted him dead. He was sad, scared, and angry, too, because he had thought things would surely turn out differently than this. But he trusted God, and listened to God every minute so that he would know what to do next.

---

[6] Susan K. Bock, *Liturgy for the Whole Church: Multigenerational Resources for Worship* (New York: Church Publishing, 2008), 93-94.

[7] www.chabad.org/multimedia/media_cdo/aid/255530/jewish/Dayenu.htm; accessed 20 August 2017.

Jesus gathered his friends in a small room and they shared their last meal together. As always, he blessed the bread and the wine, but this time he said something different. He said, "From now on, when you eat or drink like this, know I am with you. Remember how I loved you, and how I died on this night."

After supper, Jesus got up from the table and washed his friends' feet, to show them how they ought to serve each other.

Here, the children may share bread and wine and pass the bowl of oiled water around to smell and feel. You may want to do a real foot-washing, while a simple song is sung.

One of Jesus' closest friends, Judas, was so angry that he left and told the police where to find Jesus so they could arrest him. The police paid Judas 30 pieces of silver for this information. Later, when Judas looked at his money and counted it, he realized that no amount of money is worth your love and loyalty.

In the garden of Gethsemane, Jesus was praying, and Roman soldiers came to arrest him. They tied his hands together, like a criminal, though Jesus had never used his hands to hit or hurt anyone, but only to heal and soothe. The soldiers dressed him in a fancy purple robe, and a crown that they made of thorns.

These items may be passed around.

They blindfolded him, and spat at him, and beat him, and shouted, "Some king you are! If you're a prophet, then tell us who just hit you!"

They took him to Pilate, who really wanted to know the truth about things. He said to Jesus, "Who are you?" Jesus was silent. Jesus knew that what was happening to him was not fair, and that, if he spoke, he might be able to save himself. But sometimes we need to be silent, and he knew this was one of those times.

Pilate washed his hands in a bowl of water in front of all the people as a sign that he would not be guilty for whatever might happen to Jesus.

Jesus was led to a hill. He was made to carry his own cross. He was so tired and hungry and sad that he had trouble carrying it. Many people gathered to watch the spectacle. Some made fun of him, some wept, and some helped him, like Veronika.

The legend of Veronika is that the image of Jesus' face remained on her veil when, breaking with tradition and safety, she ran to him, removed her veil, and wiped his face.

Simon helped him carry his cross.

They nailed him to a cross, and his life slipped slowly away from him. He wondered why this was happening to him, and where was his God now that he needed God more than ever. He became very thirsty, and some soldiers held up a vinegar-soaked sponge for him to suck on.

The sponge with vinegar may be passed around.

Just before he died, Jesus gathered up his last little bit of strength and shouted to God in the saddest, loudest cry anyone ever heard. And he died.

He was taken down from the cross and wrapped in white linen. Then he was put in a small cave for a tomb, and a huge stone was rolled in front of it. The next day, some women came with oil and spices to anoint Jesus' body.

The oil-soaked cotton and piece of linen may be passed around.

Only, when they got there, they found that the body was gone! They were angry and confused and ran to tell Peter and the others what they had discovered. This is a Holy Week story, whose end comes at Easter. I wonder how the story will turn out.

Holy Week

The Sunday of the Passion: Palm Sunday

March 25, 2018

We enter into Jesus' death through baptism so that "just as Christ was raised from the dead by the glory of the Father, so we too might walk in newness of life." Romans 6:4b

Color Red/Oxblood

Preface Of Holy Week

Collect

Almighty and everliving God, in your tender love for the human race you sent your Son our Savior Jesus Christ to take upon him our nature, and to suffer death upon the cross, giving us the example of his great humility: Mercifully grant that we may walk in the way of his suffering, and also share in his resurrection; through Jesus Christ our Lord, who lives and reigns with you and the Holy Spirit, one God, for ever and ever. Amen.

The Liturgy of the Palms

Psalm 118:1-2, 19-29

A festival hymn sung in procession in praise of the Lord's salvation.

Mark 11:1-11 *or*

Jesus approaches the holy city of Jerusalem, and his disciples sing praises to God in anticipation of the coming of a new kingdom of David. He has a colt brought to him, and, as did the kings of old in royal celebrations, Jesus rides on it, while his followers spread their garments and leafy branches in the way and shout "Hosanna." Here is great drama as he enters the city and temple he would save, but there is also acute irony for those who know what lies ahead.

John 12:12-16

The crowd gathered in Jerusalem for the celebration of the Passover feast hear that Jesus is coming into the city. They take palm branches and go to meet him, shouting "Hosanna" and proclaiming the arrival of the King of Israel. Jesus was riding on a young donkey, as did the kings of old in royal celebrations. The author of this gospel perceives that all of these actions are in fulfillment of ancient prophecies, as Jesus' disciples would later come to understand.

The Liturgy of the Passion

Isaiah 50:4-9a

Our reading tells of the servant who speaks for the Lord and suffers persecution, but still trusts in God's help and vindication. This is the third of the "servant songs" that come from a period late in Israel's exile. The servant might be thought to be the faithful of Israel, the prophet himself, or another historical or idealized figure. The people are weary and tired of the Lord's calling, but the servant steadfastly continues. Christians have long perceived in these words a foretelling of Jesus' mission.

Psalm 31:9-16

A psalm of trust by one who looks to the Lord for mercy and protection.

Philippians 2:5-11

From one of the earliest Christian hymns, we hear how Christ Jesus accepted the condition of a servant, was obedient even to the point of death, and was then given the name above every name. It is possible that this poem was adapted by Paul or another disciple from the hopes for a savior of a people who did not yet know Jesus. He has fulfilled humanity's dream of one who will share fully in the mortal condition before his exaltation. To him every knee shall bow and every tongue confess the great name of the Lord now known in person, Jesus.

Mark 14:1—15:47 *or*

Our gospel is the story of Jesus' anointing in Bethany, his last supper with his disciples, what took place in the garden of Gethsemane, the trial before Pilate, and his final suffering and death.

Mark 15:1-39 (40-47)

Our gospel is the story of Jesus' trial before Pilate, his final suffering and death.

Prayers of the People

Presider: *Loving God, through the passion of your Son Jesus you have poured out your divine life in love for us despite our evil: Strengthen us to take up our cross and to follow in his way, that we may share in your redeeming work, as we pray: We have trusted in you, O God. We have said, "You are our God."*

Litanist: You have called your Church to be the community of the crucified One, O Gracious One: Help us to walk in Christ's path of obedient humility, that we may be willing to suffer for the sake of your goodness.

We have trusted in you, O God.

We have said, "You are our God."

In Christ's exultation upon the cross you have made a mockery of the pretentions of the rulers and authorities of the world, Almighty One: Grant to all leaders the strength to walk in your way of humble service that we may be saved from all tyranny and oppression.

We have trusted in you, O God.

We have said, "You are our God."

Compassionate One, We bring to your care all whose lives are wasted with grief and their years with sighing, as we pray for all who suffer throughout the world.

We have trusted in you, O God.

We have said, "You are our God."

Our times are in your hand, and you sustain the weary with a word, Our Loving God: Uphold all in our community who endure shame or threat, that they may turn to the cross and be comforted.

We have trusted in you, O God.

We have said, "You are our God."

We pray for those among us who need your saving help, especially ___.

We give you thanks for pouring your divine life into our lives, as we offer our gratefulness in thanksgiving, especially for ___.

We pray for all who have followed Christ along the human journey into death, remembering especially ___. Let them be united in his death and raised into his glory.

Presider: *Gracious God, your Son Jesus endured mockery, pain, and death in order to reveal to us your power that overcomes evil with love and brings life out of death: Guide and guard us in our earthly pilgrimage, that we may gladly share in his passion and be raised with him into your glory, who with the Holy Spirit lives and reigns, One God, forever and ever.* **Amen.**

Images in the Readings

Two opposite images of Christ come in the readings. First, Christ is king. In Mark's passion narrative, he is acclaimed as the descendent of King David; he is the apocalyptic Son of Man, who will judge the world at the end of time; he is accused of falsely presenting himself as Messiah, "king of the Jews," "the king of Israel"; and he is called the "Son of the Blessed," that is, the Son of God, since in the religious worldview of the ancient Near Eastern world, the king was a son of the deity. Much in American culture resists seeing "king" as a positive image. Yet the hope that someone has ultimate power, absolute justice, and endless mercy persists in human imagination.

In an image that derives from the first and second readings, Christ is servant. God will vindicate the servant, even though he is now suffering. We are to adopt the mind of Christ Jesus, who became a servant, indeed a slave, for us. Once again, much in American culture resists "servant" as a positive image. Martin Luther's essay "The Freedom of the Christian" can help us here: through our baptism, we are free, slaves to none, and yet simultaneously servants to all.

Especially in Mark, Jesus is mostly a helpless victim. In his most substantial speech (14:62) he says "I am," and this use of *Ego eimi* may indicate Mark's conviction that Jesus is the incarnate God. Yet later in the trial Jesus speaks only one phrase, and on the cross only a cry of despair that God has abandoned him. The silence of Jesus in Mark contrasts sharply with the speeches that he makes in John's passion narrative proclaimed on Good Friday.

Ideas for the Day

- The temptation is to rush into telling the whole Holy Week story today. Let's push back against that temptation so we can stay in the wild, confusing, noisy, jubilant space of the triumphal entry. What was it like to be that excited about seeing Jesus? What would it be like for us to have that level of anticipation for the coming of the Christ? How would we show our adoration? What would we do to get that close to him? Make a commitment to yourself (and encourage others in your community) to take a Holy Week journey through prayer and worship throughout this week. Relive each part of the Jesus' last days so Easter holds its full significant in your life.

♦ On this day, we are stirred by the glory of Jesus' grand entrance to Jerusalem, horrified by his capture and passion, and redeemed by his sacrifice. These events, prophecy fulfilled in nature, demonstrate both God's endless love for humanity through Jesus, and our inconsistent, ambivalent nature. The gospel reading will challenge your community to consider our Christian life, which compels us to forgiveness, mutual love, and equality among all God's people. Jesus unswervingly committed to reconcile us to God, himself, and each other.

♦ Invite your community to don historic garb and join the procession commemorating the journey to the cross. This procession should include Pilate, Herod, a beaten and exhausted Jesus, Simon of Cyrene carrying Jesus Cross, and some of the women following Jesus to Golgotha. Invite the people to personify these characters as they read the gospel narrative. The narrative may be found here: www.lectionarypage.net/Resources/PassionGospelsInParts.html; accessed 20 August 2017.

♦ As we enter the holiest of weeks
The cosmos beckons to draw near the stone
which bore the cross of death
and ultimately into the depth of the life of God.

Grace filled and beauty overwhelms.
Hosannas cry out as people gather.
Stories circle—family, love, friendship.
Only to find the sound of human sin

"Crucify, Crucify," is the litany sung
And turns the souls of those who surround
Jesus, he only meant to share the divine embrace

What is truth?
Truth is where one is led.
By grace and love
To search for foundations of our souls
We cry as well with arms outstretched.

Making Connections

As the extended reading from Mark tells the story of Christ's Passion, Jesus goes to the cross with the nard of his anointing still perfuming his hair and his body. Jesus himself accepts the anointing as preparation for

his burial. As we move from the triumph of the entry into Jerusalem to the grief of the crucifixion, we can forget that a real human being is at the center of the story—a human being who is also God incarnate. What are the anointings that prepare us for our own death and resurrection?

Engaging all Ages

How does the congregation participate in worship today? Can children be invited to join the procession with choir and clergy, waving palms of their own? Are you able to include the neighborhood by processing around the block, or meet another congregation in procession at a park or near the firehouse? This is a rare opportunity for public witness, and everyone loves a parade. Be sure to have extra palms to pass out to those you meet along the way.

Hymns for the Day

At the Liturgy of the Palms:
The Hymnal 1982
Opening Anthem, Blessing Over the Branches, At the Procession: 153

Processional: *The Hymnal 1982*
All glory, laud, and honor 154, 155
Ride on! ride on in majesty! 156

Wonder, Love, and Praise
Mantos y palmas esparciendo / Filled with excitement 728

Lift Every Voice and Sing II
Ride on, King Jesus 97

At the Liturgy of the Word:
The Hymnal 1982
Alone thou goest forth, O Lord 164
Hail, thou once despised Jesus! 495 (1-2)
To mock your reign, O dearest Lord 170
At the Name of Jesus, every knee shall bow 435
Cross of Jesus, cross of sorrow 160
Morning glory, starlit sky 585 (4-6)
The flaming banners of our King 161
The royal banners forward go 162
What wondrous love is this 439
Ah, holy Jesus, how hast thou offended 158
And now, O Father, mindful of the love 337 (1-2)
Let thy Blood in mercy poured 313
My song is love unknown 458
Nature with open volume stands 434
O sacred head, sore wounded 168, 169
There is a green hill far away 167

When I survey the wondrous cross 474

Wonder, Love, and Praise
O sacred head, sore wounded 735

Lift Every Voice and Sing II
O sacred head, sore wounded 36

Monday in Holy Week

March 26, 2018

We pray that we may find the way of the Cross to be the way of life and peace.

Color Red/Oxblood

Preface Of Holy Week

Collect

Almighty God, whose most dear Son went not up to joy but first he suffered pain, and entered not into glory before he was crucified: Mercifully grant that we, walking in the way of the cross, may find it none other that the way of life and peace; through Jesus Christ your Son our Lord, who lives and reigns with you and the Holy Spirit, one God, for ever and ever. Amen.

Readings and Psalm

Isaiah 42:1-9

In our reading from the Hebrew scriptures, we hear of the mission of the Lord's servant, the one whom God has chosen to bring forth justice and salvation. This is the first of the "servant songs" that form a portion of the Book of Isaiah written at the time when the exile in Babylon was ending and the city of Jerusalem had begun to be restored. The servant is sometimes thought to be an historical individual, or is understood as an idealization of Israel. Christians see in the servant a prefigurement of the ministry of Jesus, who will become a light to the nations of the world.

Psalm 36:5-11

The psalmist celebrates the expansive love of God expressed in faithfulness and justice. God is a river of delight in whose light we see light.

Hebrews 9:11-15

Christ has inaugurated a new covenant, accomplishing all that was anticipated by the rites and rituals of the first covenant, that is, redemption from sin and transgression and the purification of conscience for the right worship of the living God.

John 12:1-11

Six days before the Passover, Jesus gathers with his friends in Bethany at the home of Lazarus, whom he had raised from the dead. Mary, the sister of Martha and Lazarus, anoints Jesus' feet with costly perfume, wiping his feet with her hair. This extravagant devotion is criticized by Judas Isacariot, but Jesus defends the action in ways that seem to prefigure his fast approaching death.

Ideas for the Day

- Mary's actions foreshadow Jesus' death. Jesus may have allowed her this "moment of adoration" in part to prepare the disciples for his imminent death. Jesus's many and varied teachings about the poor, and his insistence that God's Church should care for them, are not undermined by this reading but are *underscored* by it. Through Jesus's death and sacrifice, our commitment to the gospel calls us to serve those less fortunate in compassionate, fervent, and effective ways.
- Invite a member of your community to dramatize an excerpt of Mary's monologue as found in Lindsay Hardin Freeman's book *The Scarlet Cord: Conversations With God's Chosen Women* (Circle Books, 2016). Such a presentation would encourage an exploration of the Jesus experience from the viewpoint of a female disciple.
- Go ahead and try it! Go outside and pick up a little branch or something bruised. Pick it up with the greatest of care and be gentle with it. Or, light a candle with a tiny wick and watch it search for life—gently blow on it enough to keep it going and not to extinguish it. Imagine this branch or this flame is you being embraced by the love of God. This is not a bad way to live a moment of your day.

♦ When was the last time you were shockingly generous? So generous that others found it hard to believe? Mary gives a model of what it is like to lay it all out for Jesus. What could be your way of boldly showing your love and thanksgiving for the saving presence of Christ in your life? How could you give with such a sense of gratitude without counting cost? Today, consider how you might lay your life and gifts at the feet of Jesus without worrying about what others thought of what you had to offer.

Making Connections

Isaiah proclaims that God has called each one of us, "as a covenant to the people, a light to the nations, to open the eyes that are blind, to bring out the prisoners . . . " We are chosen. Jesus eats dinner with Lazarus, the formerly dead man restored to life, and the people crowd the house to see both of them together—each one chosen as a witness to God's good news. How will we proclaim God's resurrection power in our own lives?

Engaging All Ages

In the gospel today, Mary anoints Jesus's feet with expensive perfume and dries them with her hair. "The whole house was filled with the fragrance," we are told. What a strange and intimate act! It was as odd to the people there that evening as it sounds to us today. Scents are known to trigger our strongest memories and equally powerful emotions. What does love smell like to you?

Hymns for the Day

The Hymnal 1982
We sing the praise of him who died 471
Ancient of days, who sittest throned in glory 363
Jesus shall reign where'er the sun 544
Thy strong word did cleave the darkness 381
Weary of all trumpeting 572
Come, thou fount of every blessing 686
Cross of Jesus, cross of sorrow 160
Draw nigh and take the Body of the Lord 327, 328
Glory be to Jesus 479
Holy Father, great Creator 368
Let thy blood in mercy poured 313
God himself is with us 475
Just as I am, without one plea 693
Jesus, all my gladness 701
Jesus, the very thought of thee 642
There's a wideness in God's mercy 469, 470

Lift Every Voice and Sing II
Come, thou fount of every blessing 111
Just as I am, without one plea 137

Tuesday in Holy Week

March 27, 2018

Through God, Jesus's shameful death on the Cross has become the means of life for us.

Color Red/Oxblood

Preface Of Holy Week

Collect

O God, by the passion of your blessed Son you made an instrument of shameful death to be for us the means of life: Grant us so to glory in the cross of Christ, that we may gladly suffer shame and loss for the sake of your Son our Savior Jesus Chrst; who lives and reigns with you and the Holy Spirit, one God, for ever and ever. Amen.

Readings and Psalm

Isaiah 49:1-7

The servant of the Lord reflects movingly on his mission—its sorrows and frustrations—and God's high calling and promise to be with him. The servant is sometimes thought to be an historical individual or is understood as an idealization of Israel. This song was probably composed as the exiles from Jerusalem were preparing to return to their devastated city. Despite appearances, the Lord will make this servant a light to the nations.

Psalm 71:1-14

The psalmist prays that God will continue to be his refuge and stronghold.

1 Corinthians 1:18-31

In this lesson Paul directs the attention of the Corinthians to God's way of using what is weak and lowly—even what the world regards as foolish—to accomplish the divine purposes. Paul emphasizes this understanding because a number of these new Christians had come to think of themselves as especially gifted, powerful, and wise. As the cross has shown, however, God's ideas about what is wise and noble are often quite different from ours. Our only boast can be in the Lord.

John 12:20-36

In this gospel passage, Jesus presents teaching concerning the meaning of his death. After his prayer to God, a voice from heaven is heard. Greeks wish to see Jesus, but he will not draw all others to himself until after he has died and risen. Then, like a seed which falls into the earth, he will bear much fruit. Now is the hour for the Son of Man to be glorified—glorified both by his willingness to be lifted up on the corss to die for others, and afterward to be lifted up to heaven. Disciples must learn to follow Jesus in his way—not walking in darkness but in the light.

Ideas for the Day

♦ There is an endless stream of information that comes into our lives each day. It is hard to see light and goodness in the midst of negative messages and hateful words. If we are to follow Jesus' call to be Children of the Light, what do we need to focus on and what do we need to cut out of our lives? Today, evaluate the social media you view. Do the messages of your "friends" offer you community and insight? Do the posts that you take the time to scroll through offer encouragement and wisdom? Take a few moments to remove what isn't life-giving and inspiring to your faith walk.

♦ At first, we might view Jesus's reaction to the Greeks as dismissive, possibly rude. Jesus seemed to ignore their presence, preferring oratory that might actually have highlighted the moment's urgency. Some think the Greeks represent gentile openness to the gospel, contrasting with Jewish leaders who sought Jesus's demise. How might Greek enthusiasm for Jesus spur us to explore how we might engage the unchurched, seekers, and

Holy Week

those who experience God in different forms and religions?

♦ Your homily might well explore the different and specific ways in which your community experiences God.

♦ Lucinda Allen Mosher's broad perspective of interfaith dialogue in the context of the Episcopal Church is helpful, *Toward Our Mutual Flourishing* (Peter Lang, 2012). In 2004, the Episcopal Church Office of Ecumenical Interfaith Relations and Episcopal Relief and Development published *The Interfaith Education Initiative*, an enlightening resource for addressing interfaith relations.

♦ I am looking outside my window during the final hour of daylight. Photographers say that the temperature is lower and the light enters a moment of perfection. Most of the famous photographs are taken either during the last hour or the first hour of the day. There is a peace about this light. On Christmas Eve, we heard that the people who have walked in darkness have seen a great light. We are well on our way to a perfect light.

Making Connections

God commissions Isaiah to carry God's good news "to the end of the earth," and Charles Henry Brent (remembered this day in *Great Cloud of Witnesses*) responded to that same call. As Missionary Bishop to the Philippines, Brent's determination to assure responsible and ethical treatment of non-Christian Filipinos in the Philippines distinguished him among missionaries. When his health failed, he returned to the U.S. mainland, where he championed the ecumenical movement.

Engaging all Ages

"Unless a grain of wheat falls into the earth and dies, it remains but a single grain; but if it dies, it bears much fruit." This is a mystery well worth exploring at home. Soak wheatgrass seeds overnight in water and drain. Put some pebbles or gravel at the bottom or your container and cover with moist soil, and spread the seeds evenly over it in a thin layer. Cover with a thin layer of soil. Place in a sunny spot; water twice a day. By Easter you'll see sprouts.

Hymns for the Day

The Hymnal 1982
My song is love unknown 458 (1-2, 7)
Christ, whose glory fills the skies 6, 7
God of mercy, God of grace 538
How wondrous and great thy works, God of praise! 532, 533
Beneath the cross of Jesus 498
Cross of Jesus, cross of sorrow 160
In the cross of Christ I glory 441, 442
Nature with open volume stands 434
We sing the praise of him who died 471
When I survey the wondrous cross 474
I heard the voice of Jesus say 692
I want to walk as a child of the Light 490
O Jesus, I have promised 655
The great Creator of the worlds 489
When Christ was lifted from the earth 603, 604

Lift Every Voice and Sing II
Jesus, keep me near the cross 28
On a hill far away stood an old rugged cross 38

Wednesday in Holy Week

March 28, 2018

We ask God for the grace to accept our present sufferings joyfully, secure in the glory that will be revealed.

Color   Red/Oxblood

Preface   Of Holy Week

Collect

Lord God, whose blessed Son our Savior gave his body to be whipped and his face to be spit upon: Give us grace to accept joyfully the sufferings of the present time, confident of the glory that shall be revelaed; through Jesus Christ your Son our Lord, who lives and reigns with you and the Holy Spirit, one God, for ever and ever. Amen.

Readings and Psalm

Isaiah 50:4-9a

Our first reading tells of the servant who speaks for the Lord and suffers persecution, but still trusts in God's help and vindication. This is the third of the "servant songs" that come from a period late in Israel's exile. The servant might be thought to be the faithful of Israel, the prophet himself, or another historical or idealized figure. The people are weary and tired of the Lord's calling, but the servant steadfastly continues. Christians have long perceived in these words a foretelling of Jesus' mission.

Psalm 70

A prayer for help and vindication.

Hebrews 12:1-3

The author of the Book of Hebrews exhorts hearers to persevere in the face of adversity, looking to the example of Jesus and encouraged by all those through the generations who have sought to be faithful to God in difficult circumstances.

John 13:21-32

At his final supper with his disciples Jesus is troubled by the knowledge of Judas's impending betrayal but tells his disciples that God is at work in the glorification of the Son of Man. Judas Iscariot departs into the night to do what he has determined to do.

Ideas for the Day

- Judas gets a bad rap. He had seen the wonderful welcome of Jesus as he entered Jerusalem. It was enough to confirm that if Jesus were to be arrested, the people would rise up and revolt. Freedom! Victory! Today, scripture scapegoats Judas for behavior that most of us have done in some form or another—we do something we believe to be faithful and good, only to discover that God can imagine way so much more than we can.

- People sometimes let us down. At times, it is the very ones we love the most who fall short of our hopes and needs in relationship. Judas' name has come into our popular culture as a term for someone who turns his or her back on us and cannot be trusted. For Jesus, it wasn't the end of the story and it isn't for us either. Today, take the time to touch the broken places of a damaged relationship so that somehow a small place can be healed and forgiven.

- In today's gospel, we glimpse the intimate interactions and social dynamics between the disciples, and the enigmatic role of Judas emerges. Judas represents human weaknesses for greed and power. Some biblical scholars have sought to exonerate Judas, arguing that his treachery was essential to God's plan to reconcile humanity with himself through Jesus's death and resurrection. The reality is that we, as humans, live in inexorable tension between good and evil.

- Invite two congregants to present a skit, using the text of Ruby Jades' poem *A Conversation with Judas* or a similar text to inspire congregants to meditate upon and discuss our inner struggle with good, evil, action, and intention. This poem can be found at https://allpoetry.com/poem/1809722-Conversation-wbr--with-Judas-Iscariot-by-RubyJade; accessed 20 August 2017.

Making Connections

The Book of Occasional Services (BOS) offers a Tenebrae service for use on the Wednesday of Holy Week. The worship, which begins with the lighting of fifteen candles, includes psalms, readings, and responses. One-by-one, fourteen of the candles are extinguished, as the shadows (*tenebrae* in Latin) deepen. The last candle, symbolizing Christ, remains lit. Though hidden for a time during the ceremony, it is later restored, a reminder of Christ's triumph.

Engaging all Ages

"Spy Wednesday" is the day we tell the story of Judas, who betrays Jesus to the authorities. This is when Holy Week takes a darker turn. A tradition in Malta called children to the parish church on this evening, to drum on chairs to make the sound of thunder, an echo of the earthquake at the resurrection, which is also a feature of the Tenebrae service. Even in the gathering gloom of Holy Week, we remember that "the light shines in the darkness and the darkness does not overcome it."

Hymns for the Day

The Hymnal 1982
Alone thou goest forth, O Lord 164
Bread of heaven, on thee we feed 323
Let thy blood in mercy poured 313
To mock your reign, O dearest Lord 170
Hail, thou once despised Jesus! 495
Lo! what a cloud of witnesses 545
The head that once was crowned with thorns 483
Ah, holy Jesus, how hast thou offended 158
Bread of the world, in mercy broken 301
O love, how deep, how broad, how high 448, 449

Maundy Thursday

March 29, 2018

We pray that Jesus will give us grace to receive the Sacrament of his Body and Blood thankfully, remembering that in these holy mysteries we have been given a promise of eternal life.

Color Red, Oxblood, or White

Preface Of Holy Week

Collect

Almighty Father, whose dear Son, on the night before he suffered, instituted the Sacrament of his Body and Blood: Mercifully grant that we may receive it thanfully in remembrance of Jesus Christ our Lord, who in these holy mysteries gives us a pledge of eternal life; and who now lives and reigns with you and the Holy Spirit, one God, for ever and ever. Amen.

Readings and Psalm

Exodus 12:1-4 (5-10) 11-14

In our first reading, instructions are given, and the meaning of the Passover meal is told: it is a remembrance and reenactment of Israel's beginnings as a people when they were saved out of slavery in Egypt. The details indicate that several different traditions stand behind the Passover memorial. Perhaps it was the Israelites' attempts to keep ancient spring rites, derived from their shepherding and agricultural backgrounds, which cause the Egyptians to persecute them. With these traditions the story of God's judgment on Egypt and victory for God's people has become richly entwined.

Psalm 116:1, 10-17

An offering of thanksgiving and praise by one who has been rescued from death.

1 Corinthians 11:23-26

In this lection, Paul recalls the tradition he received concerning the supper of the Lord on the night he was betrayed. The apostle reninds the Corinthians, who

have shown an alarming tendency to divide up into factions, of the message he first delivered to them. This meal is a remembrance and reenactment of the Lord's offering of himself and forming of the new covenant. It proclaims the Lord's saving death and looks forward to his coming.

John 13:1-17, 31b-35

Our gospel tells how Jesus washes his disciples' feet during his last meal with them. This action symbolizes the love and humility of Christ in stooping down to wash those whom he loves from their sins. He has set for them an example, for he must soon depart. His disciples are to be characterized by servant love for one another.

Prayers of the People

Presider: When the hour had come for Christ to be glorified, Jesus washed the disciples' feet, giving us his example of servanthood, and he fed us with bread and wine so that we might participate in his death and resurrection: Loving God, be present with us as we bring into your compassionate heart all of the suffering and need of the world, saying: We love you, O God, because you have heard the voice of our supplication.

Litanist: Gracious One, Christ gave the disciples the new commandment to love one another: Empower us with your Spirit, that we may walk in the way of the cross with such courage and compassion that everyone will know that we are Christ's disciples.

We love you, O God,

> **because you have heard the voice of our supplication.**

Holy, Immortal One, you absorbed the injustice, evil, and violence of every power and principality in Christ's glorification upon the cross: Empower those who work for reconciliation and peace, that everyone exercising a position of authority in the world may share in your work of healing and reunion.

We love you, O God,

> *because you have heard the voice of our supplication.*

Giver of Eternal Life, we ask your compassionate presence to be active in every place where people suffer or mourn or die.

We love you, O God,

> *because you have heard the voice of our supplication.*

Author of Salvation and Lover of Humankind, let the new life of grace enfold those who will be baptized at Easter Vigils around the globe, especially those who will receive the sacrament of new life in our celebration: ___.

We love you, O God,

> *because you have heard the voice of our supplication.*

Healer of bodies and souls, we bring our prayers of intercession and supplication for those we love, especially ___.

We lift our words of thanksgiving and praise to you, especially for ___.

We commend to Christ's cross and resurrection those who have died, especially ___. Precious in your sight, O God, is the death of your servants.

We love you, O God,

> *because you have heard the voice of our supplication.*

Presider: *In Jesus, the divine life has been revealed to us as servant and sacrifice: Hear our prayers on behalf of your whole creation, O God, that you may receive our offering as you received Christ's death for us, consecrating everything into the life of the Spirit, for you live and reign, One God, in glory everlasting.* **Amen.**

Images in the Readings

A primary image for Maundy Thursday is the servant. We recall from Passion Sunday's Servant Song that the image of servant is not a readily accessible symbol in today's society. John's gospel offers us a lowly, even dirty, task as appropriate for a true servant.

The readings are filled with body: the body of the dead lamb, cooked and eaten; the body of Christ, shared in the bread; the body of the neighbor's literal feet. For people who like to keep their individual space, it is countercultural to share in one another's body in this public way.

The first reading says that it is the lamb's blood that reminds God not to punish the Israelites, and Paul says that the wine is a new covenant in Jesus' blood. In the ancient world, life was seen as residing in the blood. Thus, pouring out of blood is giving up of life. Isn't it interesting that small children lick bleeding wounds in hopes of keeping their blood inside their bodies?

In all three readings, the people of God experience themselves as a meal community. Humans must eat to live, and humans eat together to become and maintain community. The Israelites are to keep the Passover meal "as a perpetual ordinance"; Paul assumes and corrects the meal practice of the Corinthians; John describes the last loving meal Jesus had with his disciples before his arrest. So it is that over the centuries most Christian assemblies have shared a meal at their weekly meeting. The liturgy of the Three Days begins with this meal.

Ideas for the Day

♦ "Why is this night unlike any other night?" The words of the Passover feast recall the story of God's love and protection for all generations. How could you make this night different? How could this worship space or home truly be a remembrance of the Hebrew people, of Jesus and his friends, and of the early church finding their way after the death of Jesus? Be intentional about asking the question, "Who is missing from my table?" Consider the justice issues of the food that is placed in your midst. Take time to fully be present to the story and the prayers you offer so that the way you worship will be transformed.

♦ Two pivotal moments in scripture are captured in this today's text: the humble act of the washing of the feet and the gift of a legacy of love. Jesus invited his disciples then, and invites us now, to love one another just as Jesus loves us. The disciples were discussing who among them was the greater. Jesus' perhaps surprising response was not to engage in oratory or discourse, but to wash his disciples' feet and encourage them to wash each other's. In this way, Jesus *showed* his disciples, and *shows us,* that we should be subject to one another, and thus love one another. Jesus chose *action.* Our words are to be accompanied by actions worthy of a follower of Christ.

♦ Invite your congregation to sing or recite the words of the popular Christian song *They'll Know We Are Christian by Our Love* by Peter Scholtes.

♦ God enters. Jesus enters. Spirit enters.
Whole as we might be as we discover purpose and meaning and life.
Oh how good it is when Jesus loves.

Be open, my friends, to Jesus.
Be open, my friends, to love.
Be open, my friends, to the gift of servant with towel tied around himself.

Simplicity in dignity, Jesus gathers all that he was, all that he witnessed, all that he sought.
Simplicity in dignity, a servant's role took he, the towel ready to wash.

Making Connections

Maundy Thursday worship often includes two poignant ceremonies: foot washing, recalling Christ's action at the Last Supper, and stripping of the altar, in preparation for the Good Friday liturgy. In many churches, laity and clergy play a part. The increasingly frequent practice of each person both receiving and giving the foot washing embodies a mutuality of service that speaks volumes. Some congregations engage as many participants as possible in stripping the altar, demonstrating the community work of being church.

Engaging all Ages

We wash each other's feet tonight, we share the bread and wine made holy as we tell the story of the Last Supper, we may even have a simple meal together. One of the most moving moments of Maundy Thursday for many is the stripping and scrubbing of the altar and the removal from the sanctuary of all items used in worship. This is done in solemnity and silence with the help of or in in the presence of the community. Our beautiful worship space is laid bare. We have begun to grieve.

Hymns for the Day

The Hymnal 1982
Go to dark Gethsemane 171
What wondrous love is this 439
Now, my tongue, the mystery telling 329, 330, 331
When Jesus died to save us 322
Zion, praise thy Savior, singing 320
Thou, who at thy first Eucharist didst pray 315

Wonder, Love, and Praise
O wheat whose crushing was for bread 760
As in that upper room you left your seat 729, 730
Three holy days enfold us now 731, 732, 733
You laid aside your rightful reputation 734

Lift Every Voice and Sing II
In remembrance of me, eat this bread 149
This is my body given for you 155
Do this in remembrance of me 272

At the footwashing:
The Hymnal 1982
God is Love, and where true love is 576, 577
Where charity and love prevail 581
Where true charity and love dwell 606
Jesu, Jesu, fill us with your love 602

Wonder, Love, and Praise
Ubi caritas et amor 831

Lift Every Voice and Sing II
Jesu, Jesu, fill us with your love 74

At the stripping of the altar:
Wonder, Love, and Praise
Stay with me 826

Holy Week

Good Friday

March 30, 2018

We ask God to look with kindness at us, the human family, for whom our Lord Jesus Christ died on the cross and lives and reigns forever with God and the Holy Spirit.

Color

Preface

Collect

Almighty God, we pray you graciously to behold this your family, for whom our Lord Jesus Christ was willing to be betrayed, and given into the hands of sinners, and to suffer death upon the cross; who now lives and reigns with you and the Holy Spirit, one God, for ever and ever. Amen.

Readings and Psalm

Isaiah 52:13—53:12

Our opening lesson is the poem of the Lord's servant who suffers and bears the sins of many. The passage is the fourth and last of the "servant songs" that form a portion of the Book of Isaiah written when the exile was coming to an end. The servant is sometimes thought to be an historical individual, or is understood as an idealization of the faithful of Israel. This "man of sorrows," who was "despised and rejected," "wounded for our transgressions," and one who the Lord at last vindicates is perceived by Christians to be a prefigurement of Jesus.

Psalm 22

A psalm of lamentation and a plea for deliverance by one who feels deserted and pressed in on every side, expressing final confidence in God and God's goodness.

Hebrews 10:16-25 or

In this reading, we hear that God has established the promised new covenant through which our sins are forgiven and God's laws are written on our hearts.

Given such confidence, we are to be unswerving in our hope and strong in our encouragement of one another.

Hebrews 4:14-16; 5:7-9

In our New Testament reading, we are encouraged to have full confidence in drawing near to God because Jesus, our great high priest, knows our every weakness and temptation and makes intercession for us. Having learned obedience through suffering, he has become the source of salvation for all who obey him.

John 18:1—19:42

Our gospel is the story of Jesus' trials before the Jewish council and Pilate, followed by his final sufferings and death.

Images in the Readings

The cross was the electric chair of the Roman Empire, the means of execution for low-class criminals. Other cultures have seen in the shape of the cross a sign of the four corners of the earth itself. Christians mark the newly baptized with this sign, God coming through suffering and death, aligned with all who are rejected, and, surprisingly, in this way bringing life to the whole earth. In the suggested sixth-century hymn "Sing, my tongue," the cross is paradoxically likened to the archetypal tree of life.

In John's passion narrative, Jesus of Nazareth is called King of the Jews, the Son of God, and most significantly, I am, the very name of God. Christians see in the man dying on the cross the mystery of God's self-giving love. Along with the witnesses in John's passion, we can sing with the hymn writer Caroline Noel, "At the name of Jesus every knee shall bow, every tongue confess him king of glory now."

In the Israelite sacrificial system, the lamb represented the life of the nomadic herders, and killing the lamb symbolized a plea that God would receive the animal's death as a gift to prompt divine mercy. The New Testament often uses the image of the lamb as one way to understand the meaning of Jesus' death. The book of Revelation recalls Good Friday and Easter in its vision of "a Lamb standing as if it had been slaughtered."

But any single image—such as the lamb—is not sufficient. Thus we are given the opposite image, Christ as the high priest who does the slaughtering. According to Israelite religion, the people needed an intermediary to approach God. Christ, then, is the mediator who prays to God for us. Yet for John, Christ is the God whom our prayers address.

Good Friday lays each image next to another one, for no single metaphor can fully explain the mystery of Christ.

Ideas for the Day

- We shouldn't shy away from the truth—this is the day we remember how Jesus died. However, we miss the point if that is as far as our understanding takes us. As Christians, it is our work to look not only at the significance of his death, but more importantly, to remember (and live out) the many ways Jesus modeled what it meant to *live*. As we quiet our schedules and our lives to remember this holy day, let us also make a renewed commitment of how to live out the ways that Jesus called us into ministry, community, service, and justice in the name of the One who created us and will love us until the end.

- Today's gospel is graphic, and yet gentler than other gospel portrayals of Jesus's suffering and the prophesied fulfillment of the "suffering servant" found in the book of the prophet Isaiah. Jesus experienced abuses of power by the several authorities of his time, culminating in his final suffering and sacrifice. The journey to the cross and the various interactions set forth in the reading may serve as points of meditation or even specific preaching. For instance, the courageous leadership of Joseph of Arimathea, who sought official authorization to bury Jesus' body, is an inspirational story for those who exhibit compassion for others, even when doing so might be a dangerous pursuit.

- A great tool to assist us in connecting Jesus's suffering with our human suffering and experiences of despair may be found in Walter Brueggemann's book *Into Your Hand: Confronting Good Friday* (Cascade Books).

- From the moment Jesus came out of the Jordan River and continuing through the moment of death on the cross, we know that Jesus loved. It was his consistent, non-apologetic, non-negotiable position on how life should be lived. Jesus was killed because he loved. Even in his last breath he loved by forgiving those who were killing him. I want to learn to love like Jesus. That is why I follow him.

Making Connections

The Book of Common Prayer stresses that the Proper Liturgy for Good Friday must not be displaced by the service of The Way of the Cross (or Stations of the Cross). Particularly on Good Friday, some congregations, especially those in urban areas, make a point of taking the Way of the Cross into the streets around the church. Some mark the stations at places where violence has occurred. Making connections with the neighborhoods where churches are located can be a way of acknowledging a community's pain and building relationships for healing.

Engaging all Ages

As dark a day as Good Friday is for us, it is a mistake to keep the children away from it. To know that Jesus suffered and died is painful and sad, but to know that God took his suffering and death and turned it into startling new life is profoundly important. We never leave children at the foot of the cross—after all, we are Easter people—but to go from Palm Sunday to Easter Day is to miss the most important lesson our Christian story teaches us: God's love is stronger than anything, even death on a cross. God's love has the power to transform the most terrible day into Good at the last.

Hymns for the Day

Note: There is no Entrance Hymn on this day (see BCP, p. 276).

The Hymnal 1982
To mock your reign, O dearest Lord
Alone thou goest forth, O Lord 164
Cross of Jesus, cross of sorrow 160
From God Christ's deity came forth
There is a green hill far away 167

Lift Every Voice and Sing II
He never said a mumbalin' word 33

Hymns Appropriate for Singing after the Sermon
The Hymnal 1982
Ah, holy Jesus, how hast thou
  offended 158
O sacred head, sore wounded
  168, 169
At the cross her vigil keeping 159
Go to dark Gethsemane 171
Morning glory, starlit sky 585
Were you there when they crucified my Lord? 172

Wonder, Love, and Praise
O sacred head, sore wounded 735
When Jesus came to Golgotha 736

Lift Every Voice and Sing II
O sacred head, sore wounded 36
Every time I think about Jesus 32
They crucified my Lord 33
Were you there when they crucified
  my Lord? 37 (1-3)

Hymns Appropriate for Singing before the Cross
The Hymnal 1982
In the cross of Christ I glory 441, 442
Sing, my tongue the glorious battle
  165,166
When I survey the wondrous cross 474

Wonder, Love, and Praise
Faithful cross, above all other 737

Lift Every Voice and Sing II
Jesus, keep me near the cross 29
On a hill far away stood an old rugged cross 38

Hymns Appropriate for Singing after the
  Solemn Collects
The Hymnal 1982
Lord Christ, when first thou cam'st to earth 598
O sacred head, sore wounded 168, 169
Sunset to sunrise changes now 163
Were you there when they crucified my Lord? 172

Wonder, Love, and Praise
O sacred head, sore wounded 735

Lift Every Voice and Sing II
King of my life I crown thee now 31
O how he loves you and me 35
There is a fountain filled with blood 39
Were you there when they crucified
  my Lord? 37 (1-3)
When on the cross of Calvary 34

Holy Week

Holy Saturday

March 31, 2018

Through God, Jesus's shameful death on the cross has become the means of life for us.

Color   Red or Oxblood

Preface   Of Holy Week

Collect

O God, by the passion of your blessed Son you made an instrument of shameful death to be for us the means of life: Grant us so to glory in the cross of Christ, that we may gladly suffer shame and loss for the sake of your Son our Savior Jesus Christ; who lives and reigns with you and the Holy Spirit, one God, for ever and ever. Amen.

Readings and Psalm

Job 14:1-14 or

Job reflects on the brevity of human life. Nature may renew itself but not mortals, who have but an impossible hope that they might meet God after the grave.

Lamentations 3:1-9, 19-24

Our first reading is a poem of lamentation and complaint from one who feels besieged by God and circumstance, yet chooses to affirm the steadfast love of the Lord and a belief that confidence in God is ultimately well placed.

Psalm 31:1-4, 15-16

A song of trust by one who looks to the Lord for mercy and protection.

1 Peter 4:1-8

Believers are encouraged to live lives devoted to the will of God, steering clear of all forms of dissipation. Because Christ has suffered in the flesh, his followers must be willing to do likewise, disciplining themselves for the goal of life in the spirit. Of primary importance is the practice of love for one another.

Matthew 27:57-66 or

A man of privilege and a disciple, Joseph of Arimathea, wraps the body of Jesus in clean linen and places the corpse in his own newly hewn tomb. Other disciples of Jesus witness the burial. Jesus' religious opponents appeal to Pilate to place a guard at the tomb lest Jesus' disciples steal his body, and Pilate gives them permission to seal the tomb.

John 19:38-42

Nicodemus and Joseph of Arimathea prepare Jesus' body for burial according to custom, interring Jesus' corpse in a new tomb in a garden where no body had previously been laid.

Hymns for the Day

The Hymnal 1982
My song is love unknown 458 (1-2, 7)
Christ, whose glory fills the skies 6, 7
God of mercy, God of grace 538
How wondrous and great thy works, God of praise! 532, 533
Beneath the cross of Jesus 498
Cross of Jesus, cross of sorrow 160
In the cross of Christ I glory 441, 442
Nature with open volume stands 434
We sing the praise of him who died 471
When I survey the wondrous cross 474
I heard the voice of Jesus say 692
I want to walk as a child of the Light 490
O Jesus, I have promised 655
The great Creator of the worlds 489
When Christ was lifted from the earth 603, 604

Lift Every Voice and Sing II
Jesus, keep me near the cross 28
On a hill far away stood an old rugged cross 38

Easter

Preparing for the Great Fifty Days

Overview

"Almighty and everlasting God, who in the Paschal mystery established the new covenant of reconciliation: Grant that all who have been reborn into the fellowship of Christ's Body may show forth in their lives what they profess by their faith; through Jesus Christ our Lord, who lives and reigns with you and the Holy Spirit, one God, for ever and ever. *Amen*" (Thursday in Easter Week, Second Sunday of Easter, Book of Common Prayer, 223, 224).

"And that we might live no longer for ourselves, but for him who died and rose for us, he sent the Holy Spirit, his own first gift for those who believe, to complete his work in the world, and to bring to fulfillment the sanctification of all" (Eucharistic Prayer D, Book of Common Prayer, 374).

The Book of Common Prayer contains a small, yet momentous, change in wording from previous prayer books, so small that it is easily overlooked or dismissed. In the 1979 book, Easter Sunday is the First Sunday OF Easter, and the subsequent Sundays are OF Easter as well. (At other times, Sundays are named as AFTER feasts (such as the Second Sunday after the Epiphany, for example). This change is wording is meant to underscore the fact that Easter is not just one day. The Great Fifty Days from Easter to Pentecost is, rather, a *season* of rejoicing in the presence of the risen Lord, of continuing to walk with the newly-baptized as they take their first post-baptismal steps of faith and ministry, and of living out the Baptismal Covenant together day by day.

Environment

- To bring out the unity of the season, keep the church decorated with Easter flowers, banners, and hangings throughout the Fifty Days.
- The Paschal candle should be lit at every service from Easter through the Day of Pentecost.

- For the feast of Pentecost, make red and gold windsocks, streamers, etc. These could be used during the procession, as part of the gospel acclamation, and/or at the offertory (possibly by—or including—the children of the parish).

Liturgy

Alleluia!

- If your parish doesn't do this already, consider using fresh-baked bread for the Eucharist. This can provide a fresh experience of the sacrament as well as underscore a truth in one of the gospel readings for Easter Day: when the disciples met Jesus on the road to Emmaus, he was "made known to them in the breaking of the bread" (Luke 24).
- Look at the excellent seasonal resources in *Common Worship*, including Prayers of the People (432-434, 475-476, 485, 497), Fraction Anthems (479, 500), and Blessings (438-439, 481, 488); and the litanies for Pentecost in *Book of Common Worship* (340-343).
- Encourage standing during the Great Thanksgiving and to receive communion.
- Think about celebrating the Eucharist on Pentecost in different languages. At the very least, try to proclaim the epistle reading in more than one language and look at song options (possibly in other languages) in *The Hymnal 1982*; *Lift Every Voice and Sing*; *Wonder, Love, and Praise*; and *Voices Found*.

Lectionary

In Year B on Easter Day, we hear the resurrection account from either John or Mark. Subsequent weeks feature encounters with Jesus and teaching, mostly from John. A reading from Acts is appointed for every Sunday this season—this should never be omitted, even if you have only two readings.

Music

♦ Joyous singing during communion can emphasize that we are feasting with our risen Lord.

Formation/Activities

♦ Will your parish celebrate baptisms at Pentecost? If so, the Great Fifty Days are an excellent time for formation and catechesis (ideally with a role for the new Christians who were baptized at Easter). If not, consider a parish-wide renewal of baptismal vows.

♦ Ongoing mystagogy for new Christians and old-timers alike—consider a season-long program on living out the Baptismal Covenant (that can, perhaps, continue into the Season After Pentecost)— how to be Spirit-filled people in daily life.

♦ Hold an intergenerational event the week before Pentecost to make Pentecost decorations for the church.

♦ Consider holding a parish-wide meal on Pentecost, featuring foods of many nations.

Easter Through the Eyes of a Child

Jesus is risen from the dead! Easter has brought us everlasting life because of Jesus' resurrection. The alleluias are said and sung. God's love is stronger than anything, even death. Because of God's love, we do not have to be afraid of death. Easter is about new life, coming from what we thought was death and bringing unexpected possibilities and surprises. Easter eggs, Easter chicks, Easter flowers all remind us of the new life in Christ. We received new life at our baptism, and during Easter we think about what that baptism means in our lives. Reflect with the children on the ways we keep our baptismal promises:

♦ How do we keep the promises we make?
♦ How do we show our love for God?
♦ How do we show love for each other?

Make an alleluia banner for the table, and talk about why Jesus resurrection would make us so happy. Take a walk and look at all the new life you begin to spot during the walk. Read stories of transformation and new life, such as *The Very Hungry Caterpillar*[1] by Eric Carle. Name the baptismal promises and reflect on them with pictures of how you live each of

them out with your family and friends, at home and at school.

Easter Through the Eyes of Youth

This is the time to encourage youth to Easter reflection and action. Reflect upon the individual baptismal promises found in the Easter Vigil service, and invite the youth to respond to new ways that they can serve within the congregation:

♦ Take Easter flowers to shut-ins
♦ Become part of a lay eucharistic visiting team
♦ Color Easter eggs for the young children and engage them in an Easter egg hunt
♦ Invite someone to church who does not have a "home" church.
♦ Through the Sundays of Easter put closure on their Lenten project

Above all, give youth an opportunity to witness to the fact that they believe Jesus has risen from the dead.

♦ Go: "Where does God need us to go—in school, in our neighborhood, town, and beyond?"
♦ Visit: "Who are the friendless, lonely, outcast people in our lives and how do we connect with them?"
♦ Listen: "Who are the people that no one pays attention to?"
♦ Care: "Why, God, are your people suffering?"
♦ Ask: "What can we do for needy people near and far?"
♦ Pray: "God, open our eyes and ears and hearts. Who will help us to live for others?"
♦ Invite: "Who will go with us? Which adults and teens can we invite to follow, to encounter, and to become Christ today?"

Easter Through the Eyes of Daily Life

On this day the Lord has acted! On the first day of the week God began creation, transforming darkness into light. On this, the "eighth day" of the week, Jesus Christ was raised from the dead. We celebrate this new creation in the waters of baptism and in the feast of victory. Reflect on your baptism and how you live out the promises in every facet of your life. Throughout this season, we hear stories of the men and women who recognized who Jesus really is, after failing to do so during his earthly life. We are enlightened by their visions and their visits with the Risen Christ as they proclaim that our Lord is alive and is life for the

---

[1] Philomel Books; 1 edition (March 23, 1994).

world. As we begin the Great 50 Days of Easter filled with hope and joy, be prepared to go forth to share the news that Christ is risen!

Easter Through the Eyes of the Global Community

The collects for Easter petition the living power of Jesus to open up new life to all. Our prayers and action can reflect God's desire of reconciliation for all. During the Easter season, direct attention is placed in prayer to alleviate the extreme poverty of the world. The Christ-centeredness of the Millennium Development Goals (MDGs) is an example of how making a commitment to others is a commitment to Jesus (John 10:10). For the sake of the poor and suffering of the world, our conversion (turning our lives around) at the individual, congregational, diocesan, national, and global level a difference can be made (Luke 18:1823). Focus on one MDG for the whole liturgical cycle so that during the Easter season, a particular geographic area can be chosen to learn about the people, worship, and need in that area of the world or domestically. The Easter season can be a time to build direct relationships with another location in the Anglican Communion. Enter into mission with another, to help alleviate extreme poverty.

Seasonal Rites for Easter

Easter Season Blessing[2]

The following blessing may be used by a bishop or priest whenever a blessing is appropriate. It is a three-fold form, with an Amen at the end of each sentence, leading into a Trinitarian blessing.

May Almighty God, who has redeemed us and made us his children through the resurrection of his Son our Lord, bestow upon you the riches of his blessing. *Amen.*

May God, who through the water of baptism has raised us from sin into newness of life, make you holy and worthy to be united with Christ for ever. *Amen.*

May God, who has brought us out of bondage to sin into true lasting freedom in the Redeemer, bring you to your eternal inheritance. *Amen.*

And the blessing of God Almighty, the Father, the Son, and the Holy Spirit, be upon you and remain with you for ever. *Amen.*

Blessings Over Food at Easter[3]

These blessings are appropriate for a parish meal following the Easter Vigil or over foods brought to the church for blessing.

Over Wine

Blessed are you, O Lord our God, creator of the fruit of the vine: Grant that we who share this wine, which gladdens our hearts, may share for ever the new life of the true Vine, your Son Jesus Christ our Lord. *Amen.*

Over Bread

Blessed are you, O Lord our God: you bring forth bread from the earth and make the risen Lord to be

for us the Bread of Life: Grant that we who daily seek the bread which sustains our bodies may also hunger for the food of everlasting life, Jesus Christ our Lord. *Amen.*

Over Lamb

Stir up our memory, O Lord, as we eat this Easter lamb that, remembering Israel of old, who in obedience to your command ate the Pascal lamb and was delivered from the bondage of slavery, we, your new Israel, may rejoice in the resurrection of Jesus Christ, the true Lamb who has delivered us from the bondage of sin and death, and who lives and reigns for ever and ever. *Amen.*

Over Eggs

O Lord our God, in celebration of the Pascal feast, we have prepared these eggs from your creation: Grant that they may be to us a sign of the new life and immortality promised to those who follow your Son, Jesus Christ our Lord. *Amen.*

Over Other Foods

Blessed are you, O Lord our God; you have given us the risen Savior to be the Shepherd of your people: Lead us, by him, to springs of living waters, and feed us with the food that endures to eternal life; where with you, O Father, and with the Holy Spirit, he lives and reigns, one God, for ever and ever. *Amen.*

An Easter Pageant

He is Lord: Good Friday becomes Easter[4]

The intention of this play is to help participants get "inside" the Easter story and experience it the way people may have often done with the Christmas story. It may be been done

---

[2] *The Book of Occasional Services 2003* (New York: Church Publishing, 2004), 26.

[3] Ibid, 97-98.

[4] Francis A. Hubbard (New York: Church Publishing, 2011). This Easter pageant is part of the *Skiturgies: Pageants, Plays, Rites and Rituals* collection. www.skiturgies.com

Easter

effectively as the sermon on the Second Sunday of Easter. This timing enhances the celebration of The Great 50 Days of Easter, and if the local schools are on spring break during Holy Week and Easter weekend (and some families are therefore away) may enable people to be involved who may have missed those liturgies in their home church.

Scene 1: *(The scene is just outside Jerusalem, late afternoon on Good Friday. The "house lights" are out except for dim lights at the altar. The congregation softly sings the first verse of "Where you there when they crucified my Lord?" Quietly, a group of men and women carry a man's body towards the altar.)*

NARRATOR: It was the saddest day of their lives. Jesus of Nazareth, their Lord and Master, who had touched their lives more profoundly than anyone else, and who they had *hoped* would lead them to freedom and peace, was dead. He had died the cruel, painful death of crucifixion at the hands of the Roman Empire. *(The group reaches the altar platform and gently slides the body, head first, behind the altar, and kneel there briefly.)* Only the bravest of Jesus' followers have the courage to show up to help bury Jesus. Most of his followers—even Peter and James—are in hiding, afraid that the Romans might grab them next and execute them as well. *(Spotlight shining on the altar goes on. The men and women stand up.)*

JOSEPH OF ARIMATHEA: Well, it's the least I could do, giving him my tomb. I had hoped I would need it long before he would.

MARY, THE MOTHER OF JAMES AND JOSES: You're a good man, Joseph. My sons didn't even have the guts to show up today, when Jesus really needed to see who cared for him.

NICODEMUS: I brought some spices, but there isn't any time to anoint his body properly before burial, the way we Jews usually do. It's almost sundown, and the Sabbath will start soon.

MARY MAGDALENE: Don't worry, Nicodemus. We'll be back after the Sabbath, first thing Sunday morning, and do the right thing. At least I will. *(The women only say "Me too.")*

SALOME: John, you have a really important job. Jesus asked you to take care of his mother. *(John stands silently with his arm protectively around Mary, Jesus' mother; they both nod.)*

ANOTHER WOMAN FROM GALILEE Let's roll this big stone across the opening to his tomb. With all Jesus has had to go through already, the last thing we

would want is to have some of the people who hate him come and steal his body and do *more* things to it.

Amen!

(They all roll the stone across the opening of the tomb, say a silent prayer, and walk sadly offstage. The spotlight shining on the altar goes out. The dim lights at the altar then go out.)

Scene 2: *(While the lights are out, the "body" is removed from behind the altar.)*

NARRATOR: On the Sabbath, they all rested in accordance with the commandment. After the Sabbath was over, at sundown on Saturday, it was too dark to come to the garden where the tomb was. But very early on Sunday morning . . .

(THUNDERCLAP "special effect". Two angels appear from off stage to roll away the stone to reveal—the empty tomb. The lights over the congregation are still out. The dim lights over the altar come on.)

Mary Magdalene, Mary the mother of James and Joses, and Salome walk slowly toward the tomb.

(They all enter from offstage, at the opposite end of the church from the altar. One of them carries a jar of spices for anointing.)

MARY, THE MOTHER OF JAMES AND JOSES: Who will roll away the stone for us? There were lots more of us here on Friday and it was heavy enough then.

SALOME: Oops. Didn't think of that. I feel so stupid.

(Spotlight on the altar goes on.)

MARY MAGDALENE: Look! The stone is rolled away!

(They all run toward the tomb. Ignoring the angels, they stick their heads in and come back out, more upset than ever.)

This gets worse and worse! Somebody stole his body!

ANGEL: Why do you seek the living among the dead? He is not here; he is risen from the dead, and he is Lord! Tell his other followers that he will meet them in Galilee, just as he said he would.

SALOME: I am totally creeped out.

MARY, THE MOTHER OF JAMES AND JOSES: Let's get out of here. I can't handle this.

(Salome and Mary, the mother of James and Joses run away. Angels both exit. Mary Magdalene stays at the tomb, crying buckets of tears. Jesus, who has been out of sight behind the altar, stands and walks toward her.)

JESUS: Ma'am, why are you crying? Who are you looking for?

MARY MAGDALENE: (Still sobbing, her face in her hands.) Mr. Gardener, if you've moved his body someplace, please show me where, and I'll come and take care of him.

JESUS: Mary.

MARY MAGDALENE: (She stops crying and slowly lifts her head and opens her mouth wide while staring at him, then leaps up joyfully.) Rabbi! You ARE alive! (She hugs him.)

JESUS: Now you know it's true, Mary, and you've touched me, so you know I'm not just a vision or a ghost, but real. Now the important thing is for you to go and tell the others!

MARY MAGDALENE: Right! Got it!

(Jesus disappears behind the altar again. The house lights start to come up slowly. Mary Magdalene starts to run down the aisle away from the altar, and encounters three men who are walking very slowly from the back of the church.)

MAN #1: (To Mary Magdalene.) Why are YOU looking so happy today? I thought you loved Jesus! WE all did. This is the worst week of our lives!

MARY MAGDALENE: Guys! Guys! He's alive! Jesus is risen from the dead! He just told me to tell you!

MAN #2: (He looks at Man #3 while pointing at his own head and making circular motions with his finger.)

MAN #3: Yeah, she never was too tightly wrapped.

MAN #1: Cut her some slack, guys! She's stressed out, just like we are. People sometimes think weird things when they're stressed out. (He puts his hand condescendingly on Mary Magdalene's shoulder.) You'll be all right, Mary.

MARY MAGDALENE: (She stamps her foot.) I AM all right! Better than I've ever been, in fact. (Man #2 and Man #3 snicker.) It's true! Go to Galilee and you'll see him too!

MAN #1: Now you not only expect us to believe you, but to travel all the way up there on your say-so?

MAN #2: Women! The stories they tell! (All three men nod, then exit.)

MARY MAGDALENE: ARGH! (Peter and John enter, and start walking slowly from the back of the church.) Oh, wait—there's Peter and John—maybe THEY'LL believe me. I'll start slower. Take a deep breath, Mary, Get a grip. Peter, John! Come quick! The tomb is empty! (Peter and John look up from a distance and start running toward the tomb.) It's empty because . . . (they run past her) because, um, because he is risen from the dead. (Mary sits down, discouraged, while the men ignore her and look in the tomb.)

PETER: Well, it's true, the tomb is empty.

JOHN: I wonder what it means.

PETER: Beats me. And who could possibly tell us? (They shrug and walk right by Mary Magdalene.)

MARY MAGDALENE: I can! I can! Jesus is alive! (Mary Magdalene waves her arms at them, but Peter and John don't notice her and exit, scratching their heads. Mary Magdalene, very frustrated, exits also, to the opposite side of the stage.)

Scene 3: (Cleopas and his companion enter from the back of the church and walk very slowly up the aisle.)

NARRATOR: That same afternoon, two of Jesus' followers, Cleopas and another man, were walking slowly and sadly from Jerusalem to Emmaus.

JESUS (He slips in from off stage alongside them.) What's up, guys? Why the long faces?

COMPANION: Where have YOU been for the last three days?

CLEOPAS: Yeah, are you the ONLY visitor to Jerusalem who doesn't have a clue?

JESUS: A clue about what?

CLEOPAS: About Jesus, the great prophet from Nazareth. Our fellow Jews—the high priest and most of the Council—convinced Pontius Pilate that he was a political revolutionary, so the Romans put him to death. We had thought he would be The One to deliver Israel from them!

COMPANION: That's the sad part; now comes the really strange and confusing part. Some of the women who were really devoted followers of Jesus said they went to his tomb early this morning and couldn't find his body, and they also told people they saw a couple of angels there who told them he was alive.

CLEOPAS: Peter and John went to check it out. They found the tomb empty all right, but that's all they found.

JESUS: What is there about this you don't get? It says in the scriptures that the Messiah would suffer on behalf of the people. "He was wounded for our transgressions." You remember that part? *(They nod.)* And Jesus himself said he would die and rise again. Let me spell it all out for you. *(The three walk together as Jesus pantomimes talking and the others listen.)*

NARRATOR: So, beginning at the beginning, Jesus explained all the things in the Hebrew scriptures which had to do with him.

(The three stop just in front of the altar.)

JESUS: Well, here's the inn you said you were going to stay at tonight. Good to talk with you, I got to keep going.

COMPANION: It's almost dark. Won't you at least have dinner with us?

(Jesus hesitates, and then nods. They all sit down on chairs around the altar, Cleopas and his companion on either side, and Jesus behind the altar, facing the congregation. Jesus stands up, picks up a piece of pita bread from the plate on the altar, raises his eyes to heaven and his hand in blessing, breaks the bread, and gives them each a piece. The men receive the bread and then gasp.)

CLEOPAS AND HIS COMPANION: JESUS!

(Jesus disappears behind the altar. The other two men look at each other with surprise and great joy.)

CLEOPAS: Didn't it feel like our hearts were on fire when he was explaining the Bible to us?

COMPANION: I was getting goose bumps the whole time!

CLEOPAS: We have to run and tell the others!

COMPANION: Amen to that! I don't care if it is dark and it's uphill all the way back to Jerusalem! *(They both exit, running and very excited.)*

Scene 4: *(All of Jesus' male followers except for Cleopas and his companion are gathered together in Jerusalem, seated in front of the altar.)*

PETER: *(He stands.)* I have seen the Lord.

ANOTHER MALE APOSTLE: Well, if YOU say so, I'll believe it.

PETER: Let everyone always remember that the women were the first to see, and the first to believe. I didn't have the guts to show my face at the foot of the cross—I was afraid the Romans would string me up next. Besides, I felt so ashamed after I denied that I even knew him. But Jesus—Jesus forgave me for everything! He says that everyone who believes in him gets a fresh start. *(All nod appreciatively.)*

(Cleopas and his companion run in from off stage.)

CLEOPAS AND HIS COMPANION: It's true! It's true! We've seen him! We've broken bread with him! The women were right. He is risen from the dead, and he is Lord!

(All the women enter from off stage and are greeted joyfully and respectfully by the men. All except Thomas, who stands apart, looking skeptical, sing, "He is Lord.")

THOMAS: Sorry, I won't believe until I see him and get close enough to touch him myself with my own hands.

JESUS: *(He appears suddenly from behind the altar and walks toward them.)* Shalom. Peace to you. *(They ooh and ah and are a little tentative and afraid of him.)* Don't be afraid. I'm not a ghost, or a vision. I'm real. Look at my hands and my feet—you can still see the marks of the nails, but nothing hurts any more. Violence and hatred have no power over me. Even death has no power over me. *(He looks at Thomas.)* Thomas, come on over. Check out my wounds. I'm the same guy who died on Friday.

(Thomas walks to him, reaches out to touch his hand, and then falls on his knees.)

THOMAS. My Lord and my God.

JESUS: *(He looks at Thomas.)* Do you believe because you have seen me? *(He looks out at the whole congregation.)* Even more blessed are those who believe without seeing me. *(He addresses all of the disciples, male and female.)* All of you are to continue to be my followers, even and especially when you can't see me the way you can today. By my power, you can forgive sins and heal people. You do not need to be afraid of anything any more, because through me, you can have abundant life, both now on earth and forever in heaven. I will be with you, coaching you and giving you strength, whatever you have to deal with. So, don't just sit there! Spread this Good News and make disciples of all nations, baptizing them in the Name of the Father, and of the Son, and of the Holy Spirit, and teaching them to believe all that I have taught you. I will be with you always.

(All of the cast and congregation stand and sing the first verse of "Jesus Christ is risen today.")

Earth Day Litany[5]

Sunday, April 22

We have forgotten who we are.
We have become separate from the movements of the earth.
We have turned our backs on the cycles of life.

We have forgotten who we are.
We have sought only our own security.
We have exploited simply for our own ends.
We have distorted our knowledge.
We have abused our power.
We have forgotten who we are.

Now the land is barren
And the waters are poisoned
And the air is polluted.
We have forgotten who we are.

Now the forests are dying
And the creatures are disappearing
And the humans are despairing.
We have forgotten who we are.

We ask forgiveness.
We ask for the gift of remembering.
**We ask for the strength to change,
all for the love of our Creator.** *Amen.*

Rogation Days[6]

The Rogation Days are traditionally observed on the Monday, Tuesday, and Wednesday before Ascension Day. They may, however, be observed on other days, depending on local conditions and the convenience of the congregation.

In ancient times, the observance consisted of an outdoor procession which culminated in a special celebration of the Eucharist. In more recent centuries, the procession has frequently taken place on a Sunday afternoon, apart from the Eucharist.

Hymns, psalms, canticles, and anthems are sung during the procession. The following are appropriate:

Canticle 1 or 12 (Benedicite)
Psalm 102 (Refrain: "Bless the Lord, O my soul")
Psalm 104 (Refrain: "Hallelujah")

At suitable places, the procession may halt for appropriate Bible readings and prayers.

In addition to the readings listed on page 930 of the Book of Common Prayer, any of the following passages are appropriate:

Genesis 8:13-23
Leviticus 26:1-13 (14-20)
Deuteronomy 8:1-19 (11-20)
Hosea 2:18-23
Ezekiel 34:25-31
James 4:7-11
Matthew 6:25-34
John 12:23-26

In addition to the prayers in the Book of Common Prayer, the following can be used:

Almighty and everlasting God, Creator of all things and giver of all life, let your blessing be upon this (see, livestock, plough, forest, _____) and grant that *it* may serve to your glory and the welfare of your people; through Jesus Christ our Lord. *Amen.*

A Prayer on One's Confirmation[7]

God, I am ready.
Jesus, I want to follow you.
Spirit, stay with me.

Be present with me today as I reaffirm my baptismal promises. Thank you for those who have helped me prepare for this day, especially (*names*). Send your Holy Spirit upon me. Give me the strength to be the person you created me to be, to love and serve you to the best of my ability, today and in all the days to come. *Amen.*

[5] United Nations Environment Programme. "Only One Earth," a United Nations Environment Programme publication for Environmental Sabbath/Earth Rest Day, June 1990. UN Environment Programme, DC2-803, United Nations, New York, NY 10017. Used by permission.

[6] *The Book of Occasional Services*, 103-104.

[7] "Confirmation" in *Call on Me: A Prayer Book for Young People*, Jenifer C. Gamber and Sharon Ely Pearson (New York: Morehouse, 2012), 32.

Easter

Easter

An Ascensiontide Litany[8]

Thursday, May 10

Christ was baptized as one of us, but he destroyed sins as God.
He was tempted as a human, but he conquered as God. He wants us to rejoice, for he has overcome the world.

He hungered, but he fed thousands. He is the living bread that comes down from heaven.
He thirsted, but he cried, "If anyone thirsts, let them come to me and drink." He promised that fountains would flow from those who believe.

He was wearied, but he is the rest of those who are weary and heavy-laden.
The demons acknowledge him, but he drives them out. He plunges into the sea the legions of foul spirits and sees the prince of demons falling like lightning.

He prays, but he hears prayers.
He weeps, but he makes tears to cease.

He asks where Lazarus was laid because he was human; but he raises Lazarus because he was God.
He is sold, and very cheap—for only thirty pieces of silver; but he redeems the world at a great price—the cost of his own blood.

As sheep he is led to the slaughter, but he is the Shepherd of Israel—and now of the whole world.
He is bruised and wounded, but he heals every disease and infirmity.

He is lifted up and nailed to the tree, but he restores us by the tree of life.
He lays down his life, but he has the power to take it up again.

He dies, but he gives life; and by his death he destroys death.
He is buried, but he rises again.

He descends into hell, but he raises souls from death.
He ascends to heaven, and he will come again to judge the living and the dead. Amen.

A Mother's Day Prayer[9]

Sunday, May 13

On this Mother's Day, we give thanks to God for the divine gift of motherhood in all its diverse forms. Let us pray for all the mothers among us today; for our own mothers, those living and those who have passed away; for the mothers who loved us and for those who fell short of loving us fully; for all who hope to be mothers someday and for those whose hope to have children has been frustrated; for all the mothers who have lost children; for all women and men who have mothered others in any way—those who have been our substitute mothers and we who have done so for those in need; and for the earth that bore us and provides us with our sustenance. We pray this all in the name of God, our great and loving Mother. *Amen.*

---

[8] "The Mystery of Christ—An Ascenstiontide Litany" in *The Wideness of God's Mercy: Litanies to Enlarge Our Prayer*, ed. Jeffrey W. Rowthorn (New York: Church Publishing, 2007), 89-90.

[9] Leslie Nipps, "For Mother's Day" in *Women's Uncommon Prayers* (Harrisburg, PA: Morehouse Publishing, 2000), 364.

The Great Vigil of Easter

March 31, 2018

Celebrating Christ's glorious resurrection, we pray that we may be renewed in body and mind, being raised from the dead of sin by God's life-giving Spirit.

Color　　White

Preface　　Of Easter

Collect

Almighty God, who for our redemption gave your only-begotten Son to the death of the cross, and by his glorious resurrection delivered us from the power of the enemy: Grant us so to die daily to sin, that we may evermore live with him in the joy of his resurrection; through Jesus Christ your Son our Lord, who lives and reigns with you and the Holy Spirit, one God, now and for ever. Amen.

or

O God, who made this most holy night to shine with the glory of the Lord's resurrection: Stir up in your Church that Spirit of adoption which is given to us in Baptism, that we, being renewed both in body and mind, may worship you in sincerity and truth; through Jesus Christ our Lord, who lives and reigns with you, in the unity of the Holy Spirit, one God, now and for ever. Amen.

Readings and Psalm

Genesis 1:1—2:2

Our lesson is the story of creation. As this ancient narrative opens, the Spirit of the Lord hovers like a great mother bird over the shapeless world. God then forms the heaven and the earth and all its creatures in six days. The seventh day is set aside as a day of rest. God's ultimate creative act is human life, made in God's own image, to whom rulership and responsibility over all other life are given.

Psalm 33:1-11 or

The earth is full of the steadfast love of the Lord.

Psalm 36:5-10

Steadfast love and faithfulness communicate the character of God, while righteousness and acts of justice summarize God's will.

Genesis 7:1-5, 11-18; 9:8-13

Noah and his household are commanded by the Lord to enter the ark, together with pairs of all animals. Forty days and nights of rain and flood cover the earth in water. Finally the waters subside, and the Lord makes a covenant with Noah, promising never again to destroy the earth by flood. As a sign of this covenant, God hangs God's own warrior's bow in the clouds, the rainbow which stretches in the sky's vast expanse.

Psalm 46

The earth may be moved and kingdoms shaken, but God is our refuge.

Genesis 22:1-18

This reading is the story of Abraham's willingness to obey the Lord's command to sacrifice his only son, Isaac, and the Lord's blessing of him. The narrative illustrates Abraham's readiness to abandon all to serve the Lord. Originally it probably also was used as a model story encouraging the substitution of animal for human sacrifices. Ancient Israel was given a better understanding of God's will, and because of his obedience, Abraham received God's promise to him and his descendents.

Psalm 33:12-22 or

Highly placed persons and their resources offer only the illusion of power. Only God, implementing divine love, will deliver.

Psalm 16

Contentment, refuge, and joy are found in the presence of the Lord, who does not abandon God's faithful servant at death.

Easter

Exodus 14:10—15:1

This reading is the story of the deliverance of Israel from bondage in Egpyt. The people are terrified when they see the pursuing army and complain that it would have been better to live in slavery than to die in the wilderness. Moses urges them to courage, for they will see the salvation of the Lord, who has called them to freedom to serve the one true God. the Lord then brings them safely through the sea and destroys the army of the Egyptians.

Canticle 8 (Exodus 15:1-6, 11-13, 17-18)

A song of praise to God for deliverance from captivity in Egypt and from the peril of pursuing armies.

Isaiah 4:2-6

The glory of the New Jerusalem is revealed in God's presence in a renewed Israel.

Psalm 122

A pilgrimage song among the Song of Ascents, in which the psalmist responds to the invitation to visit the Temple.

Isaiah 55:1-11

In this lesson we hear how the return from exile will be a time of prosperity and abundance when God's covenant will be renewed. The prophet pictures the great day: for a people who have been near death there will be food and drink without cost. God's covenant with David is to be extended to all Israel, and other nations will come to see her glory. The life-giving word of the Lord will not fail to produce its fruit and, together with Israel, the natural world will rejoice and reflect God's power.

Canticle 9 (Isaiah 12:2-6) or

A song of praise and thanksgiving to God, the Holy One of Israel.

Psalm 42:1-7

The psalmist laments his inability to come to the house of God and thirsts for the presence of the Lord.

Ezekiel 36:24-28

A time is coming when God will place a new heart and spirit within the people, who will cleave to God and walk in righteousness. Ezekiel prophesies the restoration of the dispersed and humiliated people of Israel.

Psalm 42:1-7 or

See above.

Canticle 9

See above.

Ezekiel 37:1-14

The prophet has a vision of the bones of a dead and hopeless people being restored to new life in their homeland. The Lord calls upon Ezekiel as a son of man to prophesy that the people who have experienced exile and many hardships will live again. The Spirit of the Lord restores their spirit and breath, and they rise from death. Although this passage can be understood to anticipate the hope of individual resurrection, Israel did not yet have this belief.

Psalm 30 or

A song of the dedication of the Temple, giving thanks to God forever.

Psalm 143

The psalmist prays earnestly for the help of God's presence.

Zephaniah 3:12-20

In this lesson, the prophet foretells a time when the judgment of Israel will be ended and the mighty Lord will bring victory and renewal to the people. The city of Jerusalem and its holy Mount Zion may rejoice and sing. All enemies will be defeated and the crippled healed. The fortunes of Israel will be restored, and the nation will be praised by all peoples.

Psalm 98 or

A song of thanksgiving and praise to the victorious Lord, who has made righteousness known and shown faithfulness to God's people.

Psalm 126

The return from exile is expressed in an image from a dream come true, a source of joy and celebration as well as a need to continue to pray for restoration.

Romans 6:3-11

In this reading, we hear that, as Christian disciples have been joined with Christ in his death through baptism, so they are to know a resurrection life like his. In union with Christ, we have died to our sinful selves and have begun to experience a new way of life. In one sense our freedom from death still awaits us in the fuure, but, in another sense, we already know what it means to be alive to God in Christ Jesus and to realize the true meaning of life.

Psalm 114

A song of praise to the Lord, who has brought the people safely out of Egypt and through the wilderness to the promised land.

Matthew 28:1-10

Our gospel tells how three women disciples first learn of Jesus' resurrection. Coming to the tomb early in the morning, they are astounded to find its huge stone covering rolled back. A young man, in appearance like an angel, announces to them that Jesus is risen and will go before his disciples to Galilee. The event is awesome, even terrifying. The women flee from the tomb and, for at least a time, report nothing to anyone because of their fear.

Images in the Readings

At the beginning of the Vigil, Christ is symbolized by the candle which gives light to our darkness and remains bright even when we all share in its flame. The early church called baptism enlightenment. Sharing this light outdoors in darkness makes the image emotionally effective.

Each reading offers an image with which to picture salvation: the earth is God's perfect creation; we are saved in the ark during the flood; we are granted a reprieve from sacrifice; we escape the enemy army; we are enlivened by spring rains; we are instructed by Woman Wisdom; we are given a new heart; our bones are brought back to life; we enjoy a homeland; when we are swallowed by the fish, we do not drown but are coughed up on dry ground; we wear party clothes; thrown into a furnace, we emerge untouched by the fire; we are risen with Christ; and although we do mistake Christ for the gardener, he appears to us and enlivens our faith.

Ideas for the Day

- A beautiful part of the Easter Vigil is the tradition of incorporating baptism into the liturgy. All those gathered make promises on how to support this person in his or her new life in Christ *and* how they intend to renew their *own* lives. Consider: How am I engaging in teaching and fellowship? Where have I resisted evil and practiced repentance? What ways am I proclaiming Good News? How is it going with my attempts to love my neighbor as myself? Am I working for justice and peace? There is always time to live more fully into our Baptismal Covenant. It offers a lifetime of opportunity to unite ourselves with Christ and our community.

- The gospel focuses on the details of Jesus's death and burial. Holy Saturday may be experienced as "The Great Silence," that time of expectation, and the paradoxical feelings of both hope and despair.

- The spiritual *Were You There When They Crucified My Lord?* was likely composed by African-American slaves in the nineteenth century, and first published in William Eleazar Barton's 1899 *Old Plantation Hymns*. It was the first spiritual to be included in the Episcopal Church Hymnal. This inspirational hymn invites us to imagine ourselves in Jesus's time, during the crucifixion and the placement of Jesus's body in the tomb. The lyrics of this spiritual are useful for silence meditation on Holy Saturday.

- Most of us know the first line from the Bible. "In the beginning God created . . ." What we may not notice is that the word translated "created" actually comes from the Hebrew words that mean the "plural of compassion." It is nice to know there was a lot of compassion at creation. "The plural of compassion" is best translated into womb. How would we hear the first words of scripture if it read, "In the beginning God wombed the heavens and the earth?"

Making Connections

The rite and ceremony for the Great Vigil of Easter offers a panoramic view of Christian faith, moving from the kindling of new fire and the lighting of the Paschal candle, through the great stories and prophecy of the Old Testament, to the baptismal rite, and the joyous first celebration of Easter Eucharist. The dramatic re-enactment of the great story of salvation is particularly moving when adults are baptized during the service. What a glorious opportunity for full-immersion liturgy.

Engaging all Ages

Today the earth stands still. Tonight the heavens shine with the light of Christ as we hear the stories of God's saving grace through history, and imagine with great hope what God will do when God's kingdom comes. The Great Vigil of Easter is the jewel of our liturgical year. For the next six weeks, we will celebrate and our church will be filled with beautiful flowers and glorious music. The altar and vestment colors have changed to white and gold. When the gospel of the

Easter

resurrection is read, let everyone present ring bells loudly and long. We cannot—and should not—contain our joy.

Hymns for the Day

The Hymnal 1982
At the Lamb's high feast we sing 174
Christ is arisen (Christ ist erstanden) 713
Christ Jesus lay in death's strong bands 185, 186
Christ the Lord is risen again 184
Christians, to the Paschal victim 183
Come, ye faithful, raise the strain 199, 200
Jesus Christ is risen today 207
The Lamb's high banquet called to share 202
The strife is o'er, the battle done 208
All who believe and are baptized 298
Baptized in water 294
Through the Red Sea brought at last 187
We know that Christ is raised and dies no more 296

O sons and daughters, let us sing 203 (1-3, 5)
On earth has dawned this day of days 201
All who believe and are baptized 298
Over the chaos of the empty waters 176, 177
We know that Christ is raised and dies no more 296

Wonder, Love, and Praise
Camina, pueblo de Dios/
Walk on, O people of God 739
Day of delight and beauty unbounded 738
Baptized in water 767
God's Paschal Lamb is sacrificed for us 880
Wade in the water 740

Lift Every Voice and Sing II
Christ has arisen 41
God sent his Son, they called him Jesus 43
Baptized in water 121
Wade in the water 143
Take me to the water 134

Easter

The Sunday of the Resurrection Easter Day

April 1, 2018

The Resurrection of Jesus the Christ is proclaimed.

Color   White

Preface   Easter

Collect

O God, who for our redemption gave your only-begotten Son to the death of the cross, and by his glorious resurrection delivered us from the power of our enemy: Grant us so to die daily to sin, that we may evermore live with him in the joy of his resurrection; through Jesus Christ your Son our Lord, who lives and reigns with you and the Holy Spirit, one God, now and for ever. Amen.

or this

O God, who made this most holy night to shine with the glory of the Lord's resurrection: Stir up in your Church that Spirit of adoption which is given to us in Baptism, that we, being renewed both in body and mind, may worship you in sincerity and truth; through Jesus Christ our Lord, who lives and reigns with you, in the unity of the Holy Spirit, one God, now and for ever. *Amen.*

or this

Almighty God, who through your only-begotten Son Jesus Christ overcame death and opened to us the gate of everlasting life: Grant that we, who celebrate with joy the day of the Lord's resurrection, may be raised from the death of sin by your life-giving Spirit; through Jesus Christ our Lord, who lives and reigns with you and the Holy Spirit, one God, now and for ever. Amen.

Readings and Psalm

Acts 10:34-43 or

In this lesson Peter realizes that the good news of the gospel is meant for all people, and he proclaims the crucified and risen Jesus. At first Peter was slow to believe that God wanted him to bring the word to a non-Jew. But God has shown this to be the divine will, and Peter gladly responds to Cornelius, a Roman centurion, together with his family and friends. The risen Jesus has appeared to chosen witnesses, and all who trust in him receive forgiveness of sins in his name.

Isaiah 25:6-9

This Hebrew scripture lesson is a prophetic hymn envisioning the day of the Lord's salvation. The prophet uses a rich banquet as an image for the time of festival. It takes place on the mountain of the Lord's temple, Mount Zion, where heaven and earth figuratively meet. This great feast will be for all people, and even the power of death will be overcome.

Psalm 118:1-2, 14-24

A festival hymn sung in procession in praise of the Lord's salvation.

1 Corinthians 15:1-11 or

Paul reminds the Corinthians of his basic proclamation concerning the Lord's resurrection. All these things happened according to the scriptures. Beginning with a manifestation to Cephas, Paul recounts six appearances of the risen Lord to his followers. The last, which must have taken place several years after the others, gave this former persecutor of the church his commission as an apostle.

Acts 10:34-43

See above.

John 20:1-18 or

Our gospel tells of the discovery of the empty tomb and Jesus' appearance to Mary Magdalene. While it is still dark, Mary comes and finds that the stone used to cover the tomb has been moved away. She runs and brings Peter and another disciple whom Jesus loved. Although no human eye catches sight of Jesus' rising from death, these first witnesses see the discarded grave wrappings and the other disciple perceives and believes. Mary remains weeping at the graveside and talks with a man she assumes to be the gardener. He speaks her name, and she knows her Lord.

Mark 16:1-8

Our gospel tells how three women disciples first learn of Jesus' resurrection. Coming to the tomb early in the morning, they are astounded to find its huge stone covering rolled back. A young man, in appearance like an angel, announces to them that Jesus is risen and will go before his disciples to Galilee. The event is awesome, even terrifying. The women flee from the tomb and, for at least a time, report nothing to anyone because of their fear.

Prayers of the People

Presider: *We come with anticipation on this first day of the week to become witnesses, sharing in the resurrection life of Jesus, as we pray: Alleluia! Christ is risen. He is risen indeed. Alleluia!*

Litanist: Almighty One, you have filled your Church with new life and empowered us through the conquering love of Jesus: Raise us with your Spirit that we may live in the power of Christ's resurrection to bring life and light to all the world.

Alleluia! Christ is risen.

He is risen indeed. Alleluia!

The right hand of the Most High has triumphed over evil and death, bringing new hope to all the world: Speak your living truth to everyone who leads and holds authority among the nations, that they may be agents of life and justice.

Alleluia! Christ is risen.

He is risen indeed. Alleluia!

The Apostle Peter has taught us, O God, that you show no partiality, but you accept all who live reverently and do right: Let your peace extend to every person, that the power of evil and injustice may be

banished, and all people may live as beloved children of the divine.

Alleluia! Christ is risen.

He is risen indeed. Alleluia!

Be with us in this community that we may be glad witnesses of your goodness, O Holy One.

Alleluia! Christ is risen.

He is risen indeed. Alleluia!

Christ the wounded healer has overcome all that can threaten us.

Let his resurrection power bring healing and hope to those for whom we pray, especially ___.

Give thanks to God who is good, whose mercy endures for ever. We offer our grateful gladness this Easter Day, especially for ___.

Christ has died and is risen, bringing life and immortality to light. We remember those who have died, especially ___. May they live in him and share in the joy of Easter.

Alleluia! Christ is risen.

He is risen indeed. Alleluia!

Presider: *You have anointed Jesus of Nazareth with the Holy Spirit and with power, O Eternal One, and raised him from death on the cross into resurrection life: Feed us with his life as we eat and drink with him in this Easter Eucharist, that we may be his witnesses, sharing in the Spirit's work of reconciliation and peace, through the Risen One, Jesus Christ our Savior.* **Amen.**

Images in the Readings

The language of being raised from death relies on the commonplace human idea, evident in speech and story, that up is good and down is bad. The ancient three-tier universe placed divine powers on the top level, humans in the middle—between life and death—and the dead below the earth. In today's readings, God raised Jesus (Mark, Paul, Acts), and we feast up on the mountain (Isaiah). Current scientific understandings of the universe teach us that there is no "up." Yet many languages maintain this imagery: the brain is up, dirty feet are down. Thus this language must function for us symbolically: up is life, down is death.

Throughout the Bible, the mountain is an image for the home of God. At Sinai there is "terror and amazement" (see Mark 16:8). But Christians see the empty tomb as changing the mountain from a place of fear to the location of international festivals with fabulous food. For communion today, use bread baked fresh this morning and lots of good-tasting wine.

Isaiah's shroud—that white sheet enwrapping a dead body—is now the fair linen, the tablecloth we spread on the altar. Perhaps at communion today, several people can spread and lay the altar cloth in everyone's sight as part of the offertory procession.

Ideas for the Day

+ As modern Christians, we have the luxury of knowing the whole story. Imagine being the friends and followers of Jesus standing at the empty tomb. For them the initial feelings were fear, anger, and dread. What we must remember is the message given to them was "Do not be afraid. Jesus has gone ahead of you." Even though we know how this part of our biblical story ends, the call for us is the same. Do not be afraid. Jesus is already where we are heading. We are not alone.
+ The message of Easter Sunday is always a kind of "new old news." The meaning of the empty tomb is unmistakable—it unequivocally signifies the resurrection, conveys God's might and love, and marks the beginning of a new era for all believers. Being called by name (Mary Magdalene at the tomb) is a highlight in today's gospel, and a reminder to us of our personal and unique relationships with Jesus, who knew us before we were in our mother's wombs.
+ A good resource to sustain the joy of Easter Day throughout the season is Kate Morehead's devotional book *Resurrecting Easter* (Morehouse, 2013).
+ I know there is a lot of theology that can be offered about Easter. I am sure that it is all very important. But as I begin to look forward to Easter, the one thing that is noticeable is just how happy a group of people can be! They seem to come out even more than Christmas time. There are folks of all ages with smiles on their faces. There are lots of people holding hands. I am glad that Jesus is alive to see all of this!

Making Connections

The Great 50 Days of Easter—ten days longer than Lent—are meant to be a glorious extended celebration of our deliverance. The "alleluia" returns in hymns and worship. The Book of Common Prayer allows for omitting the General Confession during Eastertide. The Paschal candle—lit at the Easter Vigil—remains burning through Pentecost, as well as during baptisms and funerals. Many congregations stand for all prayers during the season. How might your congregation's liturgy express Easter joy for all seven Sundays of the season?

Engaging all Ages

The account of the resurrection in the Gospel of Mark is the oldest one we have, and ends unsettlingly with the women running from the empty tomb, terrified. For some, this is its strength: if ever a story was confusing and strange, it's this one. We, like the women, wonder, too. What happened here? What does it mean for us? How do we go on from this place? What happens now? What if living into the mystery of Easter is means challenging our assumptions and changing the way we approach everything?

Hymns for the Day

The Hymnal 1982
At the Lamb's high feast we sing 174
Christ is arisen/Christ ist erstanden 713
Christ Jesus lay in death's strong bands 185, 186
Come, ye faithful, raise the strain 199, 200
Good Christians all, rejoice and sing 205
Jesus Christ is risen today 207
Look there! the Christ our brother comes 196, 197
The day of resurrection 210
The Lamb's high banquet called to share 202
The strife is o'er, the battle done 208
Hail thee, festival day 175
In Christ there is no East or West 529
Sing, ye faithful, sing with gladness 492
"Welcome, happy morning!" age to age shall say 179
This is the feast of victory for our God 417, 418
This is the hour of banquet and of song 316, 317
Alleluia, alleluia! Hearts and voices heavenward raise 191
Love's redeeming work is done 188, 189
Now the green blade riseth 204
We know that Christ is raised and dies no more 296
Christ the Lord is risen again 184
Christians, to the Paschal Victim 183
Lift your voice rejoicing, Mary 190
O sons and daughters, let us sing (1-3, 5) 203
On earth has dawned this day of days 201

Easter

Wonder, Love, and Praise
Christ is risen from the dead 816, 817
Day of delight and beauty unbounded 738
God's Paschal Lamb is sacrificed for us 880

Lift Every Voice and Sing II
Christ has arisen 41
Amen 233
In Christ there is no East or West 62
I come to the garden alone 69
They crucified my Savior 40

The Second Sunday of Easter

April 8, 2018

We know the risen Christ through faith. We may not see the risen Christ but we will know the risen Christ as we gather in faith-filled community on the "eighth day."

Color White

Preface Easter

Collect

Almighty and everlasting God, who in the Paschal mystery established the new covenant of reconciliation: Grant that all who have been reborn into the fellowship of Christ's Body may show forth in their lives what they profess by their faith; through Jesus Christ our Lord, who lives and reigns with you and the Holy Spirit, one God, for ever and ever. Amen.

Readings and Psalm

Acts 4:32-35

In this reading we hear of the enthusiasm and spirit of sharing and caring for one another in the early Christian community. The apostles continue their powerful witness to the resurrection. Greed and anxiety with regard to material possessions are overcome by grace. The author of Acts may present a somewhat idyllic picture, but there is no denying the power of the gospel to bring disciples to a profoundly new way of life.

Psalm 133

The psalm celebrates the blessing of a harmonious people.

1 John 1:1—2:2

The theme of this passage is the word of life by which Christians are called to walk in the light of God. Confessing their sins, they and all others can find forgiveness through Jesus. The beginning of this letter leaves open the possibility that the *word* may be understood as Jesus himself, or Jesus as he is revealed in scripture, or in the bread of the Eucharist. When his followers share a common life in the light that is God, they can be free to be honest about their sins and then be cleansed from them.

John 20:19-31

Our gospel presents two appearances of the risen Lord to his disciples. The first takes place on the very evening of the day of his resurrection. The disciples are gathered in fear, but Jesus brings them peace, gives them their mission, and bestows on them the Holy Spirit. A week later, Thomas, who had been absent when Jesus first appeared and who doubted his resurrection, now knows Jesus by his wounds and worships him as his Lord and God. Future disciples will not have Jesus' physical presence, but they will be blessed in their belief.

Prayers of the People

Presider: Through the incarnation, death, and resurrection of Jesus, God brings a new gift of peace into the world. Let us offer our prayers with thankful hope, saying: God has ordained the blessing; life forevermore.

Litanist: Breathe your Holy Spirit upon your Church, O Gracious One, that we may be of one heart and soul, live together in unity, and bring the light of your reconciling gospel of forgiveness and peace to the whole world.

God has ordained the blessing;

life forevermore.

Inspire the leaders of our nation and all in authority throughout the world with the breath of your peace, that they may share their possessions with the poor and bring justice and comfort to all who live in fear or need.

God has ordained the blessing;

life forevermore.

Be present to any who huddle fearfully behind closed and locked doors and let the healing touch of the wounded Jesus come to comfort all who suffer anywhere on the earth.

God has ordained the blessing;

life forevermore.

Let this community walk in your light and do our work of reconciliation, revealing the eternal life that was with the Father and has been revealed to us.

God has ordained the blessing;

life forevermore.

Hear the cries of all who grieve like Thomas and of all who suffer from any form of anguish, illness, or hurt, especially ___; that they may touch the healing presence of the risen Christ.

Complete our joy as we offer our words of thanksgiving to you, especially for ___.

Receive into your eternal life all who have died, especially ___, that they may have life in Christ's name.

God has ordained the blessing;

life forevermore.

Presider: *Oh, how good and pleasant it is, when kindred live together in unity: Fill your people with the breath of your Holy Spirit, O God, and bring us the assurance of forgiveness, that we may be enlivened to participate in Christ's work of reconciliation on behalf of all the world, and share in his eternal life, here and now, and forevermore.* Amen.

Images in the Readings

Usually depictions of the crucified Christ include the marks on his hands and side. Our archaeological knowledge that for crucifixions nails were driven through the wrist ought not negate the symbolism of the palm, which is central to a person's hand. Neither need we get fascinated by the accounts of the stigmata, for we all carry the mark of the crucified and risen Christ on our palm each time we receive the body of Christ at communion. Easy talk about healing from one's wounds can be replaced with the Johannine image of the wounds: like Christ, we may scar, rather than heal. In John 19:34, blood and water flow from the wound on Jesus' side, and church tradition has seen in this detail not an erroneous description of human anatomy, but rather the proclamation that baptism and eucharist flow from the death of Christ.

Each year on the second Sunday of Easter we meet Doubting Thomas. He is all of us, and we doubters are glad to share with all other doubters the peace of the risen Christ. It is not easy to believe that we too have felt the wounds of Christ. Faith is trust in what is unseen.

From the earliest decades, Christians were renowned for their generosity in contributing money for those in need. Some Christians advocate that every single gathering of Christians, certainly every celebration of holy communion, include a collection for the poor. Current congregational systems of automatic withdrawals from bank accounts require us nonetheless to find a way to connect our own reception of grace and our consequent sharing with the needy.

Ideas for the Day

- As in Year A, in Year B we read selections from the Acts of the Apostles for the six weeks of Easter following Easter Sunday because we need to hear the story of the first-century church in order to understand our mission in the world today.
- What would the world be as if we lived together in community as the fourth chapter of Acts suggests? How would we spend our time? Our money? Our energy? Who would be better served? Who would be finally accepted? Where would we finally find peace? Who would finally have justice? We need to be asking ourselves these questions during Eastertide (and always).
- Thomas is the archetype of the inquirer-believer who somewhat paradoxically seeks concrete evidence on matters of faith. Jesus's response to Thomas' doubt about the resurrection shows how our Lord *meets us exactly where we are*. The themes of faith and the gift of the Holy Spirit as a post-resurrection experience permeate this passage.
- *When Thomas Heard from Jesus*, a hymn written by Presbyterian Pastor Carolyn Winfrey Gillette, depicts Thomas's growing faith as a model for us Christians. Sung to the tune of *The Church's One Foundation*, it can be found at http://www.carolynshymns.com/ (accessed 26 August 2017) Permission for usage is required.
- The power of a greeting: Jesus says three times "Peace be with you." Good that we can rehearse this greeting each Sunday during the exchange of the Peace. We have other powerful greetings: In Spanish people say "Adios" which is to say "To God." In English we say "Good-bye" which is to

say "God be with you." Imagine a world where when these words are said, they are also offered as a blessing!

Making Connections

"Peace be with you," says Jesus, as he appears to the terrified disciples, as Luke tells the story. In every resurrection appearance, Jesus proclaims *shalom*. Then they all break bread together. "Then he opened their minds to understand the scriptures," writes Luke. In each celebration of Holy eucharist, we exchange the Peace. And when the eucharistic bread is broken, we proclaim, "Christ our Passover is sacrificed for us." In the breaking of the bread and the exchange of the peace, Christ is revealed to us, and reminds us that we are all connected.

Engaging all Ages

The gospel today is the story of "Doubting Thomas," who needed to touch Jesus before he could believe in his resurrection, and the gospeller has Jesus speak to us, who have not seen and yet believe. We, however, are unlike Thomas in one important way: our doubts do not vanish. We have them still. Children, youth, and adults need to hear that "doubt is not the opposite of faith; it is an element of faith" (Paul Tillich). Being free from fear of doubt is more important than being free of doubt, and surely more attainable.

Hymns for the Day

The Hymnal 1982
Christ the Lord is risen again 184
Good Christians all, rejoice and sing 205
Jesus is Lord of all the earth 178
Jesus lives! thy terrors now 194, 195
Sing, ye faithful, sing with gladness 492
This joyful Eastertide 192
I want to walk as a child of the light 490
Just as I am, without one plea 693
Awake, arise, lift up your voice 212
By all your saints still striving 231, 232 (2: St. Thomas)
How oft, O Lord, thy face hath shone 242

O sons and daughters, let us sing 206
We walk by faith and not by sight 209

Wonder, Love, and Praise
From the dawning of creation 748
We are marching in the light of God 787

Lift Every Voice and Sing II
Just as I am, without one plea 137
We walk by faith and not by sight 206

Weekday Commemorations

Monday, April 9
William Law, Priest, 1761
Law typified the devout parson to many a parishioner, although he chose to live outside the law when he refused to swear allegiance to the House of Hanover. This so-called Non-Juror was born in Northhampton-shire (1686) and ordained in 1711. Because he refused allegiance to George I, he was relieved of his teaching duties at Cambridge. A quiet, free-lance tutor (the father of historian Edward Gibbon was a pupil, 1727-37) and inspired preacher, Law led a revolution by modeling a devout life, influencing churchmen such as Henry Venn, George Whitefield, and John Wesley. Law rigorously defended the sacraments and scriptures against attacks, and he inveighed against war.

Wednesday, April 11
George Augustus Selwyn, Bishop of New Zealand, and of Lichfield, 1878
Selwyn was selected as the first Bishop of New Zealand in 1841. He vigorously began his office by learning the Maori language on the voyage to the mission field. He was born April 5, 1809, at Hampstead, England; he prepared at Eton and graduated from St. John's College before being ordained in 1833. New Zealand and England fought for ten years, during which time Selwyn ministered to both sides, gaining their affection and admiration. The constitution he laid down at his first general synod in 1859 was influenced by the Episcopal Church and significant to all English colonial churches. He visited America twice, preaching at General Convention in 1874.

The Third Sunday of Easter

April 15, 2018

We know Christ in sacramental life. Jesus appears to the disciples and in eating with them, he is able to show that he appears not as a ghost but as the risen Christ. Then he opens "their minds to understand the scriptures" (Luke 36:45), relating what they have experienced with him to what they know of the Hebrew scriptures.

Color   White

Preface   Easter

Collect

O God, who blessed Son made himself known to his disciples in the breaking of the bread: Open the eyes of our faith, that we may behold him in all his redeeming work: who lives and reigns with you, in the unity of the Holy Spirit, one God, now and for ever. Amen.

Readings and Psalm

Acts 3:12-19

Peter has just healed a crippled man, and in this passage, he proclaims the fundamentals of the gospel to those who come running to hear him. From the beginning, the new faith showed its power through such healings, and these occasions were used for preaching the good news. Many of these speeches are presented as summaries of basic themes. The role of the apostles as witnesses to Jesus' resurrection is stressed, as is the theme of scriptural fulfillment.

Psalm 4

The prayer of one falsely accused, and an expression of confidence in God, who instills confidence and peace in all circumstances.

1 John 3:1-7

In this lesson, we learn that through the Father's love, disciples are now children of God, and they no longer live in sin. Their destiny is to be like Christ. Those who live without God do not understand what it means to be a child of God any more than they recognized Jesus. But Christians know that a dramatic change has taken place in their lives, and that the mystery of what they are fully to become still awaits them.

Luke 24:36b-48

In our gospel, the risen Jesus shows himself again to his disciples, and he interprets to them the scriptures which reveal that his death and resurrection were part of God's plan. This Jesus is no ghost or phantom (as some later interpretations of the resurrection might have suggested). His appearance is real; his friends touch him and he eats with them. Now they are to be his witnesses and to carry the message of repentance and forgiveness to all peoples.

Prayers of the People

Presider: Gracious and Loving God, Christ's peace penetrates our startled and terrified hearts: Open our minds to understand the scriptures and to know ourselves to be your beloved children, as we pray, saying: Know that God does wonders for the faithful; when we call, God will hear us.

Litanist: You have called your Church to be witnesses of the resurrection and to proclaim in your name repentance and forgiveness of sins: Lift up you countenance upon us, O God, that we may see and touch the presence of the Risen One.

Know that God does wonders for the faithful;

when we call, God will hear us.

Though the nations of the earth act in ignorance and reject the call of the Holy and Righteous One, fulfill what you have foretold through all the prophets, that we might see better times.

Know that God does wonders for the faithful;

when we call, God will hear us.

We praise our Wounded Healer, Christ, who suffered, and rose from the dead on the third day, that your divine re-creative power may be at work throughout the world to confront injustice, disease, poverty, and sadness.

Know that God does wonders for the faithful;

when we call, God will hear us.

Answer the people of this community, Almighty One, defender of our cause, and set us free when we are hard-pressed, that we may dwell in safety until the day when we will see you as you are.

Know that God does wonders for the faithful;

when we call, God will hear us.

Hear our prayers for all for whom we intercede, especially ___.

We celebrate the goodness of your blessings among us, especially for ___.

We remember all who have died, that they may be revealed to be like you, O God, in the resurrection life of Christ, especially _____.

Know that God does wonders for the faithful;

when we call, God will hear us.

Presider: *O God of our ancestors, you have glorified your servant Jesus: Fill our wondering hearts with your joy and love, that we may live faithfully and may be righteous as he is righteous, living in your life-giving Spirit, through Christ our Savior.* **Amen.**

Images in the Readings

Fish became a significant Christian symbol in the church's early centuries, perhaps in memory of disciples having been fishermen, but perhaps because of a Jewish poetic tradition that described fish as the main course served at the messianic banquet. Eating fish may have symbolized faith in the demise of the ancient evil sea monster. The acronym for "Jesus Christ, God's Son, Savior," spelled the Greek noun for fish. Some early Christian art depicting the last supper shows a great fish on the plate in front of Jesus, as does the frontispiece for Holy Communion by He Qi in *Evangelical Lutheran Worship*, page 89.

In the biblical worldview, one's name embodied one's self and carried one's being. In our baptism, we are given the name of the triune God and thus live within and because of God's power. Our culture is getting further away from this ancient sense of the name, although perhaps when we dread "identity theft," we are close to a sense of the authority of one's name. This biblical imagery needs explication, when, for example, we baptize "in the name of" the triune God.

Later Trinitarian doctrine made the language of Jesus as Son of God privileged divine speech. But earlier Christian writing, as in 1 John, understood that Jesus' sonship was the inauguration of all believers: using categories important in a patriarchal society, we all were to become sons of God who inherit what the Father could bestow.

Ideas for the Day

- A life in Christ is about moving out into the world. Just as the disciples were commissioned to go out so that all nations would hear and know the greatness of God through Christ, it is also our commission to share this Good News. When could we take the time to sit with scripture this week? Who do we know who needs a message of hope? Where can we place ourselves so that the healing power of Jesus can be shown and spread to others? Where will you start?

- Jesus greets his disciples, recognizing their emotional state—"Peace be with you." Jesus declares a new status for the disciples. They are "Witnesses." As the disciples experience the risen Christ, their understanding is opened and their lives transformed. It is the experience of the risen Christ that led them later to spread the Good News of the gospel through the known world. Preach about the intersection of transformation by faith and evangelism.

- Invite those members of your congregation who serve in outreach ministries to share specific ways in which those in your community engage in neighborhood evangelism. They may do so through art, music, or photo collage.

- In a world that is hectic and we grab a bite to eat on the fly, Jesus offers us the option to sit down, enjoy some food and conversation. There is a wonderful little boy who pops up in another gospel and in the midst of 5,000 people offers his lunch. When we are willing to bridge eating, time, and conversation, we are offered the opportunity to enter the Reign of God.

Making Connections

The collects for Easter petition the living power of Jesus to open up new life to all. Our prayers and action can reflect God's desire of reconciliation for all. The

Easter

collect for this Third Sunday of Easter asks God to "open the eyes of our faith, that we may behold him in all his redeeming work." It reminds us that the actions of the church and of individual Christians must be judged as to whether they are redeeming or demeaning works. Also, the healing ministry of the church involves the healing of society as well as individuals.

Engaging all Ages

Jesus appears to the disciples, who take him for a ghost until he eats with them. We, too, know Jesus through the food we eat together each week as we gather at God's table. It's just as well we don't serve fish at communion, but whenever our senses are fully engaged we have a richer experience in liturgy. We get to know each other at another level when we share a meal together. How can the parish family, all ages together, gather for meals?

Hymns for the Day

The Hymnal 1982
Christ is alive! Let Christians sing 182
Come, let us with our Lord arise 49
Good Christians all, rejoice and sing 205 (1, 3-5)
Sing, ye faithful, sing with gladness 492
Baptized in water 294
Sing praise to our Creator 295
Awake, arise, lift up your voice 212
Blessed Jesus, at thy word 440
Come, risen Lord, and deign to be our guest 305, 306
Come, ye faithful, raise the strain 199, 200
Look, there! the Christ our brother comes 196, 197
O sons and daughters, let us sing 203
That Easter day with joy was bright 193

Wonder, Love, and Praise
Day of delight and beauty unbounded 738
Baptized in water 767
You're called by name, forever loved 766

Lift Every Voice and Sing II
Christ has arisen 41
Baptized in water 121
Children of the heavenly Father 213

Weekday Commemorations

Thursday, April 19
Alphege, Archbishop of Canterbury, and Martyr, 1012
"And his holy blood fell on the earth, whist his sacred soul was sent to the realm of God." Thus, the Anglo-Saxon Chronicle recorded the death of Alphege (or Aelfheah) at the hands of the Danes, who "smote him with an axe-iron . . . " Alphege, born in 954, served the Church during the second series of Scandinavian invasions and settlement in England. Following a time as a monk at Deerhurst and an abbot at Bath, Alphege became Bishop of Winchester. He helped bring Norse King Olaf Tryggvason to King Aethelred in 994 to make peace and be confirmed. Captured by the Danes in 1011, Alphege refused to satisfy the ransom and was killed seven months later.

Saturday, April 22
Anselm, Archbishop of Canterbury, 1109
Anselm, born in Italy about 1033, took monastic vows in 1060 in Normandy and became Archbishop of Canterbury in 1093. Although his greatest gifts lay in theology and spiritual direction, he served in a time of conflict between Church and State. Anselm exploited the so-called "ontological argument" for God's existence: God is "that than which nothing greater can be thought." Anselm is also the most famous exponent of the "satisfaction theory" of the atonement, explaining Christ's work in terms of the contemporary feudal society. Supporting his thinking and arguing was profound piety, captured in the words, "unless I first believe, I shall not understand."

The Fourth Sunday of Easter

April 22, 2018

The risen Christ is known through the ministry of the church modeled by Jesus, the Good Shepherd.

Color   White

Preface   Easter

Collect

O God, whose Son Jesus is the good shepherd of your people: Grant that when we hear his voice we may know him who calls us each by name, and follow where he leads; who, with you and the Holy Spirit, lives and reigns, one God, for ever and ever. Amen.

Readings and Psalm

Acts 4:5-12

In this story from the Acts of the Apostles, Peter and John, having cured a crippled man, are called to account before the high Jewish council. Peter testifies that the source of their healing power is the same Jesus whom the leaders rejected. Referring to scripture, Peter speaks of the stone rejected by the builders, which is nevertheless meant to be the cornerstone of the new faith. Evidently there were a number of encounters like this in the life of the early church, but the disciples continued to heal and to preach in Jesus' name.

Psalm 23

The Lord is shepherd and guide. God is present in the time of danger and is generous and merciful.

1 John 3:16-24

In our epistle lesson, we learn that the followers of Jesus are to emulate his love by laying down their lives for one another. Such love is demanding and practical, requiring believers to share what they have with those who lack. By acting in ways consistent with the kindness of God, disciples will know that they do indeed believe in Jesus the Son of God. They will know that he abides within them and they in him, and that the Spirit has been given them.

John 10:11-18

In our gospel reading, we are taught that Jesus is the good shepherd who is willing to die for his sheep. He is not like one who has been hired to tend the sheep, and who runs away in time of danger. Rather, he knows the sheep with the same intimacy that he has with the Father. Jesus has shared fully in their circumstances. Together with those who are yet to be called, there will be one flock under the one true shepherd.

Prayers of the People

Presider: O God our Shepherd, you spread a table before us and reassure our hearts with your guiding care: Hear our prayers for all your people, as we say, the Lord is our shepherd; we shall not be in want.

Litanist: You know your own and your own know you, good Shepherd of the sheep: Guide the Church in gentleness and peace, that we may obey your commandment to love one another and live out that love in truth and action.

The Lord is our shepherd;

we shall not be in want.

The rejected stone has become the cornerstone for the whole world's salvation, the power and name for all healing: Be present, O God, among our leaders and with those who exercise authority for the nations of the world, that they may guide us along right pathways for your Name's sake.

The Lord is our shepherd;

> *we shall not be in want.*

You have given your life for the protection of your people: Open our eyes to see our brothers' and sisters' need throughout the world, and then empower us to respond with generous help.

The Lord is our shepherd;

> *we shall not be in want.*

The Spirit that you have given us is alive in this community: Revive our souls that we may abide in Christ, lay down our lives for one another, and lie down in green pastures beside the still waters of fellowship and reconciliation.

The Lord is our shepherd;

> *we shall not be in want.*

Hear us as we bring the prayers of our hearts to you, O Gracious One, remembering especially ___.

We thank you that we abide in Christ and that Christ abides in us. Receive our prayers of gratefulness and thanksgiving, especially for ___.

Hear our prayers for those who have walked through the valley of the shadow of death; grant that they may dwell in the house of the Lord forever. We remember especially ___.

The Lord is our shepherd;

> *we shall not be in want.*

Presider: *Reassure our hearts, O God, with the comfort of your guiding presence, that we may know that you are with us, and we will fear no evil. Strengthen us to join in the Spirit's work of leading all people into your divine abundant love, that goodness and mercy may follow us all the days of our life, through Jesus Christ our Savior.* **Amen.**

Images in the Readings

To deepen our contemplation of the metaphor of Christ as shepherd, it is good to review the positive use that the Bible makes of the image of sheep. The Hebrew scriptures tell of the nomadic life of sheep and goat herders. Sheep signified the communal life of the people, constituted a source of food and clothing, and functioned as the primary sacrificial gifts to God. The single wandering lamb from Luke's parable of the lost sheep is not the image in John 10; nor does the Bible describe sheep as being dirty; nor is a barefooted white-robed man a realistic depiction of the shepherd, who by the first century was thought of as lower class and religiously unclean. Yet on the wall of the third-century baptismal room in Dura, Christ the shepherd is leading the sheep to the font. In Genesis 29, Rachel is a shepherd.

In Psalm 118, we can trace the career of a metaphor. At its origins, to celebrate an ancient military victory, this communal song likened Israel to a stone, once rejected, but now the cornerstone. The later psalmist uses this image in an individual song of thanksgiving, to give more weight to personal praise. Even later, Peter's speech cites the metaphor as a description of Jesus' death and resurrection. Christians sing Psalm 118 on Easter Day, since already in the New Testament, Christians used this metaphor to describe Christ as the cornerstone of the church. Now often merely decorative and ceremonial, in antiquity the cornerstone was the foundation that carried the weight of the building.

Ideas for the Day

- ◆ Psalm 98 calls for us to "sing to the Lord a new song." What does your song sound like now? Is it one of praise? Lament? Whining? Demands? Gratitude? Doubt? Worry? Love? Shame? What would it take to write a new song to God in your heart and mind? What chorus of voices would you like to join together? What could be your unique way to praise God? Take a moment this week to pen a few lines of praise then post it in a location you will see each day.
- ◆ The image of the Good Shepherd pervades Christianity, symbolizing the very nature of God's loving care both for us and for the ministry of those who serve in ordained life. Preaching themes for this Sunday may include intimacy with God, as a portrait of the relationship of shepherd and flock.
- ◆ In lieu of a homily or during coffee hour (depending on the style of the congregation), lead the congregation in a guided meditation on Psalm 23, which emphasizes God's role as our shepherd and ours as God's flock. As you lead them in meditation, you may invite them to paint using Ember Canada's coloring book *Beside Still Waters: Coloring the Psalms* (Broadstreet Publishing, 2015).
- ◆ Guideline #1: Jesus said to love our neighbor as ourselves. Jesus did not say love your neighbor more than yourself—that would be co-dependent. Jesus did not say love yourself more than your

neighbor—that would be selfish. Jesus offers the great *equal* sign (=). Guideline #2: We *always* have the option to love.

Making Connections

The Fourth Sunday of Easter is known as "Good Shepherd Sunday." The lectionary this year assures us that the Good Shepherd knows us by name, protects us from evil, and lays down his life for us sheep. The images of the Good Shepherd remind us that he seeks out the lost and restores them to their community. How can these words and images inspire us to imitate the Good Shepherd, offering our lives—our skills, our resources, our time, and our love—for others?

Engaging all Ages

Today is Good Shepherd Sunday. We do not, by and large, have much experience of sheep these days, and still the good shepherd, the one who calls us each by name, is beloved by young and old. The 23rd Psalm is perhaps the best known of all paslms, often the first one learned and the last one spoken. The good shepherd was "the gate" and laid "down his life for the sheep" quite literally in ancient Israel, by being the human barrier between the sheep inside the stone sheepfold and the dangers (wolves, thieves) outside. Children love to take turns enacting this.

Hymns for the Day

The Hymnal 1982
Christ the Lord is risen again 184
Good Christians all, rejoice and sing! 205 (vs 1, 3-5)
My Shepherd will supply my need 664
Sing, ye faithful, sing with gladness 492
The King of love my shepherd is 645, 646
The Lord my God my Shepherd is 663

The strife is o'er, the battle done 208
At the name of Jesus 435
Christ is made the sure foundation 518
How sweet the Name of Jesus sounds 644
The Church's one foundation 525
To the Name of our salvation 248, 249
God is Love, and where true love is 576, 577
I come with joy to meet my Lord 304
Lord, whose love through humble service 610
Where charity and love prevail 581
Where true charity and love dwell 606
You, Lord, we praise in songs of celebration 319
Jesus, our mighty Lord 478
Praise the Lord, rise up rejoicing 334
Savior, like a shepherd lead us 708
Shepherd of souls, refresh and bless 343

Wonder, Love, and Praise
Ubi caritas et amor 831

Lift Every Voice and Sing II
The Lord is my Shepherd 104

Weekday Commemorations

Wednesday, April 25
Saint Mark the Evangelist
All New Testament references to a man named Mark may not be to the same man, but if they are, he was the son of a woman householder in Jerusalem—perhaps the house in which Jesus ate his Last Supper. Mark may have been the naked young man who fled when Jesus was arrested in the Garden of Gethsemane. Paul referred to Mark in a letter to the Colossians as the cousin of Barnabas, with whom he was imprisoned; Paul was not satisfied by the reasons Mark gave for not accompanying Paul and Barnabas, so Paul refused Mark's company on a second journey. Early tradition names Mark as the author the Gospel of Mark.

Easter

The Fifth Sunday of Easter

April 29, 2018

A new community is formed out of the resurrection; the indwelling of the Holy Spirit is the life of that community. Those who follow the commandments of love will find new life in intimate association with Jesus and the Father.

Color   White

Preface   Easter

Collect

Almighty God, whom truly to know is everlasting life: Grant us so perfectly to know your Son Jesus Christ to be the way, the truth, and the life, that we may steadfastly follow his steps in the way that leads to eternal life; through Jesus Christ your Son our Lord, who lives and reigns with you, in the unity of the Holy Spirit, one God, for ever and ever. Amen.

Readings and Psalm

Acts 8:26-40

This is the story of how Philip brought the Ethiopian eunuch to faith in Jesus. Early Christians doubtless loved to tell and retell this narrative. It shows how a significant foreign personage, who was apparently an inquirer into Judaism, learned about Jesus and was baptized. It also illustrates the way an important passage from the Old Testament, which tells of the Lord's servant who suffered for others, was interpreted as prophecy about Jesus.

Psalm 22:24-30

A song of praise to the Lord, who rules over all and cares for the downtrodden.

1 John 4:7-21

This reading teaches that God's love is made known to us through Jesus. In response, we are to love one another. No one has ever seen God, but to experience God's love and to recognize Jesus as God's Son is to know God. Only by not loving other humans made in God's image would we show that we do not know and love God. When we do love one another, then we live in union with God and fear is driven away.

John 15:1-8

In our gospel reading, we hear that Jesus is the true vine to which each branch must be united if it is to bear fruit. The vine and the vineyard were well-known symbols for God's people. A living relationship with Jesus in the following of his teaching is the source of fruitful discipleship. God will cut away the dead branches and prune the healthy ones so that they will bear more abundantly.

Prayers of the People

Presider: As branches of Jesus, the living Vine, seeking to abide in the Spirit of love, we bring our prayers to God: Eternal Loving One, accept the wishes of our hearts as we pray faithfully, saying: For God is love; and perfect love casts out all fear.

Litanist: Gracious One, you have called us to abide in your life and to bear witness to Christ the lamb: Grant that the Church may reveal your love through Jesus, that we might live in him and so bear much fruit.

For God is love;

> *and perfect love casts out all fear.*

Light of the Word, dominion belongs to you, for you rule over the nations: Raise up bold witnesses like Philip who will testify to the rich and powerful about God's good news which is perfected in love, so that peace may abound in our time.

For God is love;

> *and perfect love casts out all fear.*

Attentive Vinegrower, you tend the braches and fruit of your vine extending to the ends of the earth: Let your loving attention reach out to all people who live in suffering and threatening conditions, that they may be restored to life and fruitfulness.

For God is love;

and perfect love casts out all fear.

Everyone who loves is born of God and knows God: Inspire all in our community to seek to expand the fruits of compassion and care so that the poor shall eat and be satisfied and that all the ends of the earth shall remember and turn to the Lord.

For God is love;

and perfect love casts out all fear.

You have first loved us and called us to love our neighbors as ourselves: Hear our prayers for all for whom we intercede, especially ___.

Accept our grateful thanks for your abundance in our lives, especially for ___.

Gather into your banquet all who have died, especially___; may their hearts live forever!

For God is love;

and perfect love casts out all fear.

Presider: *You have planted us in the nurturing ground of your steadfast love, O God, and grafted us into the life of your resurrected Son, Jesus our Savior: Keep us evermore abiding within your Spirit of love, that we may bear the fruit of your reconciliation for all that is and is to come, through Jesus Christ our Savior.* **Amen.**

Images in the Readings

Perhaps because Palestine has abundant vineyards, the vineyard is an image for the promised land and for the people Israel that recurs repeatedly throughout the Old Testament. In contrast to a religion that focuses on the processes of nature, Judaism praises God as the source of the vineyard. Promises of restoration from the prophets include the picture of flourishing vineyards, since where water might be polluted, wine remains the preferred drink. In the synoptic gospels, the vineyard is an image of the kingdom of God, and in John, the vine is Christ. When we drink the wine at Holy Communion, we can feel our very bodies respond to the transformative power of the vine. That the joy which is wine can turn into the horrors of alcoholism is a poignant example of how good can mutate into evil. Grape juice, invented in 1869 by Thomas Welch, is a fruit of the vine that does not warm the body and

unites the community in the same way as does wine. When it is advisable to replace wine with grape juice remains a pastoral issue.

According to the ancient Israelite worldview, the eunuch is seriously maimed, a man who, because unable to procreate, was not a whole person who could approach God in worship. Cultures differ in how they understand sexuality, yet it is usual for a society to view as less than fully human those who are outside the acceptable sexual parameters. The reading in Acts 8 is pertinent for our time, in which, for example, the Christian status of homosexuals is widely debated. Acts 8 could be used to suggest that in Christ, societal distinctions about sexuality no longer apply, even if they had been religiously significant in the past.

Ideas for the Day

- Pruning is a painful process. We often let our physical and emotional places become overgrown because cutting back can be hard. Somehow, an image of abundance is more desirable than a carefully cut back existence. The truth is that overgrown and untended things rarely yield good fruit. So it is with our lives. What places in you need to be pruned so that you can be more fruitful? How might you ask God to come into your life to cut back the dead or dying places? What might be revealed when the underbrush of your life is cleared?
- On the very first day of Sunday school, my daughter (now age 27) ran up to me and cried "I love you, Daddy, because God loved me first—first Jesus 3:19." Now the citation may have been off a bit, but I am thankful to her Sunday school teachers, for on the very first day Elizabeth learned one of the most important lessons of life: we love because God loved us first.
- The imagery of the vine reminds us of our connections to God and one another. This gospel provides a great opportunity for your community to explore and reflect on the ways they are being fruitful, living their discipleship in daily life as individuals and as a community.
- In the book *Radical Sending: Go to Love and Serve* (Morehouse Publishing, 2015), Demi Prentiss and J. Fletcher Lowe masterfully describe our ministry in daily life and our discipleship, using the analogy of mountain climbing, while raising awareness in all areas of our Christian life. This book is a good tool for adult Bible study and Christian formation forums as well as personal devotion.

Easter

Making Connections

The new life Christ promises is lived in relationship with God, as intimate as the connection between vine and branches. The Holy Spirit flows through us because of our connection to Christ, and, apart from him, we can do nothing. In the Baptismal Covenant, we promise to nurture those connections—through the apostles' teaching and fellowship, the breaking of bread, and prayer.

Engaging all Ages

"I am the vine, you are the branches," Jesus tells us. We are connected to God and to one another in very real ways, and those connections need attention and care in order to grow and stay healthy. What are your favorite ways of staying connected to God? How do you maintain healthy relationships with family and friends? What do our connections to others in our community allow us to do that we couldn't do alone? What are the new connections we need to make?

Hymns for the Day

The Hymnal 1982
Christ is alive! Let Christians sing 182
Come away to the skies 213
Come, my Way, my Truth, my Life 487
Good Christians all, rejoice and sing! 205 (vs 1, 3-5)
He is the Way 463, 464
Sing, ye faithful, sing with gladness 492
Thou art the Way, to thee alone 457
Descend, O Spirit, purging flame 297
In Christ there is no East or West 529
We know that Christ is raised and dies no more 296
God is love, and where true love is 576, 577
God is Love, let heaven adore him 379
I come with joy to meet my Lord 304
Lord, whose love through humble service 610
Love divine, all loves excelling 657
The great Creator of the worlds 489
Where charity and love prevail 581
Where true charity and love dwell 606
You, Lord, we praise in songs of celebration 319
Bread of heaven, on thee we feed 323
Like the murmur of the dove's song 513
Thou hallowed chosen morn of praise 198

Wonder, Love, and Praise
Here, O Lord, your servants gather 793
Ubi caritas et amor 831
Muchos resplandores/Many are the light beams 794
O blessed spring, where Word and sign 765

Lift Every Voice and Sing II
In Christ there is no East or West 62
The angel said to Philip 50

Weekday Commemorations

Tuesday, May 1
Saint Philip and Saint James, Apostles
Philip and James are known but a little—and that through the gospels. James has been called "the Less" to distinguish him from James the son of Zebedee and from Jesus' brother James—or maybe he was young, or short. He was listed among the Twelve as James the son of Alpheus, and he may also be the person labeled in Mark's gospel as "James the younger," who witnessed the crucifixion. In John's gospel, Philip has a greater presence: Jesus called Philip as a disciple right after naming Andrew and Peter; in turn, Philip convinced his friend Nathaniel to see the Messiah. Philip, at the Last Supper, declared, "Lord, show us the Father, and we shall be satisfied."

Wednesday, May 2
Athanasius, Bishop of Alexandria, 173
Athanasius significantly determined the direction of the Church in the fourth century. Born about 295 in Alexandria, he was ordained a deacon in 319. He attended the first council at Nicaea in 325 as secretary and adviser to Alexander, the Bishop of Alexandria. Athanasius won approval for the phrase in the Nicene Creed that expresses the godhead of Christ, "one Being with the Father." Athanasius succeeded Alexander in 328. He defended the Nicene Christology against powers political and clerical, and he was exiled five times. He wrote volumes, from treatises to theology, sermons, and letters. His *On the Incarnation of the Word of God* is classic.

Friday, May 4
Monnica, Mother of Augustine of Hippo, 387
Tucked into *The Confessions of Saint Augustine* is the story of his mother Monnica, who was born in North Africa around 331. Within her deepening life of prayer, she converted her husband Patricius to Christianity, and she longed to bring her son to Christ as well. He was baptized in Milan in 387. Monnica became sick as she and her two sons awaited a ship in the port of Rome to return them home to Africa. As she lay dying, she asked that her sons remember her "at the altar of the Lord." Her mortal remains were buried in 1430 at the Church of St. Augustine in Rome.

The Sixth Sunday of Easter

May 6, 2018

The theme of the new community formed out of the resurrection and the indwelling of the Holy Spirit in the life of that community is grounded in love.

Color   White

Preface   Easter

Collect

O God, you have prepared for those who love you such good things as surpass our understanding: Pour into our hearts such love towards you, that we, loving you in all things and above all things, may obtain your promises, which exceed all that we can desire; through Jesus Christ our Lord, who lives and reigns with you and the Holy Spirit, one God, for ever and ever. Amen.

Readings and Psalm

Acts 10:44-48

In our New Testament lesson, Peter has gone to visit Cornelius, a Gentile and Roman centurion, and has proclaimed to him the good news of Jesus, that all who believe in Jesus will receive forgiveness of sins. Even as Peter is speaking, the Holy Spirit falls upon the gathered and they extol God and speak in tongues, as had happened to Jewish disciples with the arrival of the Spirit. The Jewish believers who had come with Peter are astounded that the Spirit has fallen impartially also upon Gentiles, and Peter is persuaded that baptism must be extended to these new believers.

Psalm 98

A song of thanksgiving and praise to the victorious Lord, who has made divine righteousness known and shown faithfulness to the people of God.

1 John 5:1-6

In this lesson we hear that belief in Jesus as the Christ, together with love of all God's children, form the heart of the Christian faith. This faith is victorious over the world; that is, over godless society. To love God means to obey God's commandments, and the essence of the commandments is the love of all who are of God. The one who overcomes the world believes that Jesus is the Son of God, who was present in the world not only through the water of his baptism but in the blood of his crucifixion.

John 15:9-17

In our gospel, Jesus speaks of his great love for his disciples and calls upon them to show this same love toward each other that has come to him from the Father. Jesus is talking with his disciples shortly before his death, when he will be taken away from them. But this love has now formed his followers into a new community in relationship with Jesus and the Father. They are no longer servants but friends.

Prayers of the People

Presider: Gracious and loving God, your Son Jesus has laid down his life and called us his friends, and you have promised to give whatever we ask you in Christ's name: Hear our prayers for the whole human family and for the world, as we say: Sing to the Lord a new song, for he has done marvelous things.

Litanist: Your Church is the community of those who believe that Jesus is the Christ, and you have taught us that we have been born of God: Help us to show our love for you, O God, by loving your children and thus fulfilling Christ's command to us.

Sing to the Lord a new song;

for he has done marvelous things.

You have shown your righteousness openly in the sight of the nations, O Mighty One, and with your right hand and your holy arm have you won for yourself the victory: Extend your dominion over all the earth and imbue all in authority with your Spirit of love and

Easter

compassion, that they may serve the world in peace and justice.

Sing to the Lord a new song;

for he has done marvelous things.

All creation witnesses to God's goodness; the sea and the lands, the rivers and hills ring out with joy before the Lord: Bless and protect this world and its fragile environment, and grant to all your children their necessities for daily life and peaceful freedom from all that may threaten.

Sing to the Lord a new song;

for he has done marvelous things.

You have taught us to keep your commandments by abiding in your love, O God: Bless this community with such faithfulness that your joy may be in us and that our joy may be complete.

Sing to the Lord a new song;

for he has done marvelous things.

Hear our prayers for our friends and for all who suffer, especially ___.

Accept our grateful thanksgivings as we lift up our voice, rejoice and sing, especially for ___.

We entrust to your never failing victory those who have died, especially ___. Let our faith in you witness to the victory that conquers the world.

Sing to the Lord a new song;

for he has done marvelous things.

Presider: *Blessed One, you have loved us, chosen us, and appointed us to go and bear fruit, fruit that will last: Honor the faithful prayers of your people, that all the earth may abide in your love and know the joy of your friendship, through Jesus Christ our Savior, who with you and Holy Spirit, lives and reigns one God, for ever and ever.* **Amen.**

Images in the Readings

The word "commandments" has more negative than positive connotations. Yet in today's readings, the commandments display God's love, serve to hold the community together in God's love, and provide the way that believers can live as did Christ.

One friend is, in some ways, equal to another, neither above nor below. "Friend" can be a powerful metaphor for God, but not if it stands alone: it needs to be the surprising balance to ourselves as servants of God, as mere humans before the Almighty.

The fruit that comes from a life that abides in God is fruit that lasts. Thus, even the image of fruit is insufficient to speak of life that manifests God's love, since normally fruit is short-lived and does not last.

Speaking in tongues is a phenomenon found in various religious traditions and is valued by some Christians. As if the worshiper has been taken over by the power of divine, normal human speech is replaced by ecstatic sounds. In extreme emotion, for example, in sorrow, terror, joy, or orgasm, humans make noises that are other than language.

Victory evokes massive military engagements and countless dead bodies. Yet, in 1 John, we hear about a victory that is our faith in Jesus as the Son of God.

Ideas for the Day

- ♦ We do a disservice to Jesus when we paint him to be a peaceful, permissive, and always loving Savior. When Jesus instructs us to love one another as He has loved us, it means so much more than just being nice and tolerant of one another. How might we love others with the clarity, passion, forcefulness, and unconditional love that Jesus has shown in scripture? How might we put aside our meek, passive love so that a wild and authentic realm of real relationship can emerge?

- ♦ To offer a blessing is to look into the eyes of another and state how you see God working in that person that very minute. To offer a blessing is to tell them how much you love them and that God has loved them without condition or without exception. To offer a blessing is to say this moment between you and me is sacred.

- ♦ During the tumultuous years of the Civil Rights struggle, Dr. Martin Luther King, Jr wrote a sermon book *Strength to Love*. In a sermon written in jail, entitled *Loving Your Enemy*, Dr. King stresses the irresistible power of love to overcome hate. In our increasingly fractious nation and world, today's gospel animates us to foster love, promote nonviolence, and strive to end gender bias, racism, and the many other "isms" that often divide us.

- ♦ Following the gospel reading, invite a soloist to sing Hymn 353 from "The Hymnal 1982", *Your love, O God, has called us here.*

Making Connections

"This is my commandment, that you love one another as I have loved you." Christ's commandment opens us to lives transformed by his love. Each time we renew our baptismal promises, we remind ourselves and one another that we will "seek and serve Christ in all persons, loving [our] neighbor as [ourselves] . . . strive for justice and peace among all people, and respect the dignity of every human being."

Engaging all Ages

The lections today continue to speak to the role of the community in fulfilling God's purpose, by loving God and each other. We tend to think of this love in the abstract, but love is concrete and practical, too. Families and congregations can brainstorm acts of love to take out into the neighborhood and world, such as homemade cookies or yard work for a neighbor, making get well and birthday cards for shut-ins, or assembling baby boxes of diapers, blankets, and formula for a local shelter.

Hymns for the Day

The Hymnal 1982
Alleluia, alleluia! Hearts and voices heavenward raise 191
As those of old their first fruits brought 705
Now the green blade riseth 204
O Jesus, crowned with all renown 292
Descend, O Spirit, purging flame 297
In Christ there is no East or West 529
O Love of God, how strong and true 455, 456
Sing, ye faithful, sing with gladness 492
Come, we that love the Lord 392
In your mercy, Lord, you called me 706
Lord, dismiss us with thy blessing 344
Lord, we have come at your own invitation 348
Lord, whose love through humble service 610

Wonder, Love, and Praise
Ubi caritas et amor 831

Lift Every Voice and Sing II
In Christ there is no East or West 62
One bread, one body 151

Weekday Commemorations

Tuesday, May 8
Dame Julian of Norwich, c. 1417
Little is known of Julian's life. Born about 1342, the only writing of hers we have is *Revelations of Divine Love*, the description of her "showings," or visions, which she experienced after an illness when she was 30. Prior to her illness, Julian had desired three gifts from God: "the mind of his passion, bodily sickness in youth, and three wounds—of contrition, of compassion, of will-full longing toward God." Although she forgot about the first two until after her illness, the third was always with her. After recovering, she became an anchorite at Norwich, living alone in a hut attached to the Church of St. Julian (hence, her name) and gaining fame as a mystic.

Wednesday, May 9
Gregory of Nazianzus, Bishop of Constantinople, 389
This Cappadocian Father loved God, *belle lettres*, and humankind. Born about 330, he studied rhetoric in Athens; with his friend Basil of Caesarea, he compiled the works of Origen. He was ordained a presbyter against his will in 361 and attempted a life of austerity; however, the times were against living peacefully. He became Bishop of Sasima ("a detestable little place," he wrote) before moving to Constantinople in 379 with hope renewed. There, he preached five sermons on the doctrine of the Trinity: therein rests his reputation. Among the Fathers of the Church, he is known as "The Theologian."

Easter

Ascension Day

May 10, 2018

We recall the Lord's exaltation, when he was taken gloriously up into heaven, to be "seated at the right hand of God the Father."

Color   White

Preface   Ascension

Collect

Almighty God, whose blessed Son our Savior Jesus Christ ascended far above all heavens that he might fill all things: Mercifully give us faith to perceive that, according to his promise, he abides with his Church on earth, even to the end of the ages; through Jesus Christ our Lord, who lives and reigns with you and the Holy Spirit, one God, in glory everlasting. Amen.

or this

Grant, we pray, Almighty God, that as we believe your only-begotten Son our Lord Jesus Christ to have ascended into heaven, so we may also in heart and mind there ascend, and with him continually dwell; who lives and reigns with you and the Holy Spirit, one God, for ever and ever. Amen.

Readings and Psalm

Acts 1:1-11

In our gospel, Jesus prays for his disciples shortly before his death, asking for their unity and sanctification in truth. He prays that they may be protected in the Father's name, that is, by God's true character as it has been made known by Jesus. Because of Jesus' revelation to them, the disciples are set apart from a disbelieving worldly society. Yet, in another important sense, they remain a part of this world and are consecrated to witness to the truth in it.

Psalm 47 or

A hymn of praise to the mighty king who is raised up and enthroned on high.

Psalm 93

God reigns, the Lord of all creation, and has established the earth and subdued the great waters.

Ephesians 1:15-23

In this lesson, Paul gives thanks for the faith and love of the Ephesians and prays that they may see with their inward eyes the power of God, who has raised and enthroned Jesus far above all earthly and heavenly dominions. How vast is the treasure that God offers to those who trust in God! The Lord Christ now reigns as head of the Church, which is his body and which experiences the fullness of his love.

Luke 24:44-53

In our gospel, Jesus leaves his followers with the promise of the Holy Spirit and is carried up into heaven. The disciples are to await their empowerment from on high before beginning their mission to the world. Joyfully they return from Bethany, the town where Jesus had stayed before his Passion. They enter the temple and praise God.

Prayers of the People

Presider: Christ has ascended high that he might fill all things: Listen to our prayers, O God, as we proclaim the riches of your glorious inheritance and the immeasurable greatness of your power for us who believe, saying, Clap your hands, all you peoples; shout to God with a cry of joy.

Litanist: O Gracious God of our Lord Jesus Christ, the Father of glory, give to your Church a spirit of wisdom and revelation as we come to know you, that we may be your witnesses to the ends of the earth.

Clap your hands, all you peoples;

shout to God with a cry of joy.

You reign over the nations, and the rulers of the earth belong to you: Put your power to work among those who hold authority throughout the world, that they may establish your peace and reconciliation among all people.

Clap your hands, all you peoples;

shout to God with a cry of joy.

Cover the earth with your grace, O Compassionate One, that all who suffer from any threat or oppression may know the power of your goodness.

Clap your hands, all you peoples;

shout to God with a cry of joy.

Fill our community with your blessing, O Loving One, that with the eyes of our hearts enlightened, we may know the hope to which you have called us.

Clap your hands, all you peoples;

shout to God with a cry of joy.

Receive our prayers, dear God, for all for whom we are called to pray, especially ___.

Hear our song of praise and thanksgiving as we lift our gratefulness to you, especially for ___.

You raised Christ from the dead and seated him at your right hand: Receive into your divine dwelling those who have died, especially ___.

Clap your hands, all you peoples;

shout to God with a cry of joy.

Presider: *Wonderful and Everliving God, your Christ reigns far above all rule and authority and power and dominion, and above every name that is named: Put all things under Christ's feet and fill the earth with the fullness of him who fills all in all, through the power of your Holy Spirit, One God, for ever and ever.* Amen.

Images in the Readings

Ascension Day plays with the ancient cosmological picture of the three-tier universe, the highest level of which is heaven, or "the heavens." Over the centuries, Christians have speculated in quite different ways about what this heaven is. By the nineteenth century, heaven came to be described as a kind of family summer camp, perfection in populist human terms. However, in the Bible, "heaven" is often a synonym for God, a way to speak about divine majesty and mercy. In Acts, the ascending Jesus is covered with a cloud, which in the Hebrew scriptures usually refers to the elusive presence yet cosmic power of God. It is important that today's references to heaven not suggest that it is a place that is far away. The risen Christ is here in the assembly of believers.

Luke has two men in white robes speaking with the disciples. The Christian church has regularized the wearing of white robes as the sign of baptism. We all can speak of the power of the ascended Christ.

In Ephesians, the body of Christ is the church imagined like Atlas, a giant standing on earth holding up the skies, the head being Christ, and the body being the church that fills the world. Today we blend this understanding of "body of Christ" with the bread we eat and the assembly gathered to worship.

Ideas for the Day

- The Feast of the Ascension reminds us that, although Jesus is *spiritually* among us, it is *we* who are his hands and voice in the world, and thus we are called to witness.

- The theme of evangelism and witnessing is a consistent narrative exhibited in scriptures following the resurrection. As we continue exploring what it means to be part of The Jesus Movement, as Presiding Bishop Michael Curry describes it, we are inspired to embrace a concrete form of witnessing God's love and grace in our lives as individuals and parts of a community. Today's readings provide an opportunity to further explore The Jesus Movement and our participation in it.

- When Jesus returned to heaven, the disciples were left there looking up to the sky. Jesus told them to prepare for a gift that would fortify them for their ministry. So much of our lives are spent looking down. We look down at our phones. We bury our lives in work, hobbies, social engagement, and many other forms of distraction. How could you look up today? How might you listen for the voice of God in the midst of your life? How might you be more willing to look up and around so that a ministry might be born in you?

Easter

♦ Most people don't really worry about what happened to Jesus when he ascended into heaven. However, many people worry about the judgment that will come to them when it comes time for each of us to make that journey. Easter says that the judgment of God comes in the words Jesus asked Peter, "Do you love me?" This might be a good time to think about how we might answer.

Making Connections

Catechesis of the Good Shepherd (a Montessori-based approach for children) teaches about the Ascension using the Paschal candle and imagery from the Eastern Church. With the children sitting in a circle around the lit candle, the catechist snuffs it out, and then silently watches the wisps of smoke dispersing into the air. "I wonder where the smoke goes," she muses. "I wonder where Jesus goes." How might we increase awareness—among all believers—of Jesus' unseen presence all about us?

Engaging all Ages

Ascension, like resurrection, is a fancy word for a simple concept. Let children know ascension means "going up." Go outside, look at the clouds, imagine what it must have been like for Jesus's friends when he went into heaven. How did they feel? What did they think? What might it be like when Jesus comes again?

Do not release helium balloons outside in deference to the damage they can do to wildlife, but by all means let some loose inside. Whipped cream clouds with berries might be a lovely conclusion to this day.

Hymns for the Day

The Hymnal 1982
And have the bright immensities 459
Hail thee, festival day! 216
A hymn of glory let us sing 217, 218
Alleluia! sing to Jesus! 460, 461
Hail the day that sees him rise 214
See, the Conqueror mounts in triumph 215
The Lord ascendeth up on high 219
Crown him with many crowns 494
Hail, thou once despised Jesus! 495
It was poor little Jesus, yes, yes 468
Lord, enthroned in heavenly splendor 307
O Lord most high, eternal King 220, 221
Rejoice, the Lord is King 481
Rejoice, the Lord of life ascends 222
A hymn of glory let us sing 217, 218
Alleluia! sing to Jesus! 460, 461
Hail the day that sees him rise 214
See, the Conqueror mounts in triumph 215
The Lord ascendeth up on high 219

Lift Every Voice and Sing II
"Go preach my gospel," saith the Lord 161
He is king of kings, he is Lord of lords 96

The Seventh Sunday of Easter
The Sunday after Ascension Day

May 13, 2018

The Church is consecrated as the Body of Christ, becoming a living sacrament to the world, and "outward and visible sign" of Christ's redeeming presence in history, through the power of the Holy Spirit.

Color   White

Preface   Ascension

Collect

O God, the King of glory, you have exalted your only Son Jesus Christ with great triumph to your kingdom in heaven: Do not leave us comfortless, but send us your Holy Spirit to strengthen us, and exalt us to that place where our Savior Christ has gone before; who lives and reigns with you and the Holy Spirit, one God, in glory everlasting. Amen.

Readings and Psalm

Acts 1:15-17

In this lesson, we hear of the selection of Matthias to take Judas's place as one of the twelve apostles. Peter perceives that it is prophesied that another should replace Judas, and lots are cast to select between two men who had been among the larger band of Jesus' followers. Matthias is chosen as one of the companions of Jesus who is able to witness to the resurrection.

Psalm 1

The Lord makes fruitful those who choose the way of righteousness.

1 John 5:9-13

In this lection, disciples are bid to believe in the testimony that God has borne to Jesus, the Son of God. They are to have confidence that their prayers are heard and that in the Son they have eternal life. Elsewhere in this letter it is indicated that God's witness to Jesus is especially made known through the experience of love, a love made manifest in Jesus. Those who trust in Jesus as the Son of God realize this testimony

within their own hearts. Refusal to accept this witness means to lose the possibility of true life.

John 17:6-19

In our gospel, Jesus prays for his disciples shortly before his death, asking for their unity and sanctification in truth. He prays that they may be protected in the Father's name, that is, by God's true character as it has been made known by Jesus. Because of Jesus' revelation to them, the disciples are set apart from disbelieving worldly society. Yet, in another important sense, they remain a part of this world and are consecrated to witness to the truth in it.

Prayers of the People

Presider: Benevolent God, hear our prayers through Jesus who intercedes on behalf of the Church, and fulfill the joy of your Son by sending your blessing upon your creation, as we pray: As you have sent Christ into the world; so Christ has sent us into the world.

Litanist: Gracious One, through Christ you have made your name known and your Church has been given everything from the Father: May we be one as Christ and the Father are one.

As you have sent Christ into the world;

> *so Christ has sent us into the world.*

Loving One, you have given all nations the testimony of God in their hearts: Extend your providence to protect them from the evil one and to bestow the liberating blessings of justice and peace to humanity.

As you have sent Christ into the world;

> *so Christ has sent us into the world.*

Compassionate One, you have promised to lose nothing that you have made: Look upon all who suffer from illness, violence, poverty, or threat: Protect them in your name and sanctify them in your truth.

Easter

As you have sent Christ into the world;

> *so Christ has sent us into the world.*

Ever-present One, you have planted this community like trees by streams of water: Empower us to bear fruit in due season and to make Christ's joy complete in this place.

As you have sent Christ into the world;

> *so Christ has sent us into the world.*

Honor our prayers on behalf of those for whom we pray, especially ___.

Accept our thanksgiving for the many blessings of this life, especially ___.

Let your eternal life raise all who have died, especially ___.

As you have sent Christ into the world;

> *so Christ has sent us into the world.*

Presider: *Loving God, you have kept your word through Jesus your Son and sanctified your Church in truth: Fulfill the testimony of scripture and inspire our witness to the resurrection of Jesus, that we may share in the eternal life which reconciles all creation in the unity of the Spirit, through Jesus Christ our Lord.* **Amen.**

Images in the Readings

John writes about the name of God. When we say, "Stop in the name of the law," we mean that our very invoking of "the law" brings with it the authority behind the law, the power of the law. So the name of God conveys divine mercy and might. Jews still today, careful not to misuse God's name, invoke "Hashem," "the Name," as a circumlocution for God. Christians can call upon the name of the Lord by invoking Jesus Christ. Baptism lays upon us the name of the triune God.

Both the fourth evangelist and the author of 1 John see their writings as essential testimony to the truth of belief in Christ. A testimony is a sworn statement about the facts and meaning of a situation.

Many ancient societies, including biblical Israel, made "allotments" and chose leaders by casting lots, in the belief that the result was divinely ordered. Amish communities still today choose their annual leader by a method of casting lots: whichever man picks up the hymnal that includes the piece of paper marked with a black spot is the preacher for the next year. Some

Protestants find the language of "God's plan" helpful, while others find Job's baffled silence a more truthful way to think about our inability to know the will of God.

Ideas for the Day

- Today's gospel illustrates the profound intimacy between God, the Son, and God, the Creator. We are given a glimpse of both Jesus' love and care for his disciples and his profound knowledge that their faith would expose them to dangers and perhaps terrible costs in a world after the Resurrection.
- Jesus' prayer asks for unity among believers. Explore the concept of unity versus uniformity and the ways in which God's diverse people are united in our earthly pilgrimage and in our role in the world—to bear witness of our faith.
- Dramatize the reading of the gospel by using a monologue style to help your congregation experience this reading in a new light.
- The film "Of Gods and Men," about a community of Benedictine monks who will ultimately be assassinated, includes a scene near the end where all have gathered for a meal. It is clear that they know that death is at hand and yet, in the midst of the silence, they begin to laugh and then cry out of pure joy. They are connected to each other and to Jesus. It appears that they are able to touch perfection.
- Imagine being seated at the table in the Upper Room. Many have wondered what the intimate conversations would have sounded like amongst Jesus and his disciples. The gospel reading for today shows an achingly tender side of Jesus and his prayer for his closest friends and companions. The hope is for unity, joy, the ability to stay away from evil, and that Jesus' purpose would be spread throughout the world. How are you working for unity? Where are you cultivating joy? How are you fending off evil? How are you making the saving help of Jesus known?

Making Connections

In Christ's high-priestly prayer in today's gospel, he asks God to protect us, guard our unity, and help us witness to the truth. Our baptismal promises to "persevere in resisting evil, . . . repent and return to the Lord, . . . and proclaim by word and example the Good News of God in Christ" are the way we live into Christ's prayer for us.

Engaging all Ages

In the final gospel of Eastertide, Jesus prays for his disciples and, by extension, us, that we will be one, united, not only with God but with each other. That takes intentionality, humility, and effort. Being reconciled to God and to one another is the work of Christian community and one of the ways God's love for the whole world is modeled. Praying is certainly a key element to creating this unity. How else do we work to create unity among other Christians? What is our role or responsibility in being united with those of other faiths?

Hymns for the Day

Hymnal 82
All hail the power of Jesus' name (450, 451)
Alleluia! sing to Jesus! (460, 461)
Hail, thou once despised Jesus! (495)
Lord, enthroned in heavenly splendor (307)
Rejoice the Lord is King (481)
The head that once was crowned with thorns (483)
By all your saints still striving (231, 232)
All who believe and are baptized (298)
Crown him with many crowns (494)
Draw nigh and take the Body of the Lord (327, 328)
Eternal light, shine in my heart (465, 466)
Many and great, O God, are thy works (385)
For the bread which you have broken (340, 341)
Humbly I adore thee, Verity unseen (314)

Praise the Lord through every nation (484, 485)
Thou, who at thy first Eucharist didst pray (315)
Word of God, come down on earth (633)

Wonder, Love, and Praise
Come now, O Prince of peace (795)
Unidos, unidos / Together, together (796)
We are all one in mission (778)

Lift Every Voice and Sing II
"Go preach my gospel," saith the Lord (161)

Weekday Commemorations

Saturday, May 19
Dunstan, Archbishop of Canterbury, 988
Although the phrase, "contemplatives in action," sounds like a contradiction in terms, the work of Bishops Dunstan, Aethelwold of Winchester, and Oswald of Worcester (his former pupils), manifested just that. After King Edgar named Dunstan Archbishop of Canterbury in 960 (about age 50), Dunstan exploited the vigorous currents of the Benedictine monastic revival by raising the monastic prayer life to the attention of the English Church. The three men sought better education and discipline among clergy, the end of landed family influence in the Church, restoration and establishment of monasteries, revival of the monastic life for women, and closer ordering of the liturgy. Effects of the "Monastic Agreement" lasted long.

Easter

Pentecost

Preparing for the Season after Pentecost

Overview

"Almighty God, by the Passover of your Son you have brought us out of sin into righteousness and out of death into life: Grant to those who are sealed by your Holy Spirit the will and the power to proclaim you to all the world; through Jesus Christ our Lord. *Amen*" (collect from The Great Vigil of Easter, Book of Common Prayer).

This period of time is not a true season in the sense that Advent or Lent or the Great Fifty Days are, and no organic theme binds these Sundays together. Nevertheless, the lessons appointed lend themselves to a serious exploration of the demands of the Baptismal Covenant and of our mission in and to the world. It is a time of working to advance the reign of God by being the Body of Christ; a time, as Taylor Burton-Edwards reminds us, to "challenge and support one another in living out" the ministries to which we are called.[1] It is punctuated—book ended, really—by feasts—Trinity Sunday, All Saints' Day, Christ the King (while The Episcopal Church doesn't call the last Sunday of this time Christ the King, the propers do reflect the theme)—that remind us about who God is, about the great cloud of witnesses that stands with us, that we already see the first glimmers of Christ's reign.

Environment

- This is a good time to think about the space you have and to figure out how to use it as creatively and effectively as possible. The old adage that the architecture always wins doesn't always have to be (completely) true.
- If possible, use local flowers, plants, and fruits, perhaps out of parishioners' gardens.
- If your situation allows for it, consider worshiping out of doors.

---

[1] http://www.umcdiscipleship.org/resources/worship-planning-for-the-season-after-pentecost-ordinary-time-year-c; accessed 5 December 2016.

Liturgy

- Think about using new prayers (e.g., perhaps the resources in *Enriching Our Worship I*, if your parish is not familiar with them).
- Because there is nothing that inherently ties this season together, well-thought-out liturgical choices can provide coherence. For example, choose one way to sing or say the psalm, one form of the Prayers of the People, and one form of the Eucharistic Prayer, and use these throughout the season.
- *Common Worship* provides important resources on mission and unity that could be useful during this season (138-158).

Lectionary

Year B is the year of Mark; since it is a short gospel, it is supplemented by several weeks of John during the summer. The readings from Mark feature teaching (parables re: the Kingdom of God, take up your cross, let the children come) and healing. The selections from John feature the feeding of the 5000 and the bread of life teaching.

Music

- This is a good time to teach new music.
- Look at songs about the Baptismal Covenant, mission, the stewardship of creation.
- If your parish does decide to hold services outdoors, explore options for leading/accompanying the singing: guitar, recorder, other instruments, a person (or persons) with a strong singing voice. Some in the parish very likely have talents that would be especially useful for this.

Formation/Activities

- Start the season off with an intergenerational event, perhaps one focused on being the Body of Christ in the world.

Pentecost

- Offer a variety of formation activities/events over the summer, even if the regular programs are on a break.
- Will there be baptisms on All Saints' Day or Sunday? If so, formation should begin by September at the latest.

Pentecost Through the Eyes of a Child

Indwelling inspiration: breathing in and out reminds us that our very life is dependent upon the gift of the Holy Spirit. Words and thoughts for young children include: mighty wind, teacher that leads into all truth, New Covenant proclaiming renewal, tongues of fire, witnesses all gathered with new awareness of God and each other. God promises to be with us always, and we are strengthened from within by the Holy Spirit, whose power, like a strong wind, we can feel even though we cannot see it. Now the church will continue to grow and learn more about Jesus, even after his death and resurrection.

Mission, building and re-building the church (what some call "congregational development") with and for children is critical during the season of Pentecost. This is the time the children will wonder what are the adventures of building the early church? How was the early church built? The travels of St. Paul with maps and cities where Paul founded churches, as well as the travels of St. Peter, St. James, and St John can be inspiring for children as they enjoy the concept of building something new.

Pentecost Through the Eyes of Youth

Developing an authentic faith in the understanding of "God as Three" (Creator, Redeemer, Sustainer) is a vital part of youth spirituality. Youth are developing their identity and part of that identity is formed through the gifts God has given them, including gifts of the spirit. Questions to consider with youth:

- What will be and what will we leave to the next generation?
- Are we building our lives on firm foundations, building something that will endure?
- Are we living our lives in a way that opens up space for the Spirit in the midst of a world that wants to forget God, or even rejects him in the name of a falsely conceived freedom?

Pentecost is a perfect time to invite the youth to reflect upon the gifts that God has given them. Not only the gifts they see in themselves, but the gifts they see in each other. Retreats can be most helpful to give the young people some time to remember the gifts the Spirit gave to the disciples, and the gifts that the Spirit gives to them.

Pentecost Through the Eyes of Daily Life

On the fiftieth day of Easter, we celebrate the Holy Spirit as the power of God among us that heals, forgives, inspires, and unites. Images of wind and fire describe the Spirit poured out on disciples of all nations. In John's gospel, the risen Christ breathes the Spirit on his followers on Easter evening. In the one Spirit we were baptized into one body, and at the Lord's table, the Spirit unites us for witness in the world. The Spirit calls us to follow in the way and in the pattern and in the shape of the life of Jesus.

Pentecost Through the Eyes of Our Global Community

The Day of Pentecost opened the way of eternal life to every race and nation. On this day it is appropriate to study racism, sexism, and all other attitudes and actions that deny God's love for all people. It is common to see in the gift of the Spirit at Pentecost a sign that reveals God's purposes to heal and restore creation, including overcoming the disorder and confusion of languages that was told to have happen at Babel.

The Spirit of God crosses over the boundaries of language and culture to create a new people of God, a human family renewed and made whole. Consider the global perspective of how the Church has made its journey from the time of Paul to today and how the message of Christ has spread throughout the world in its many forms and traditions.

Seasonal Checklist

- Schedule meetings for July and/or August to plan the program year. Note when and where more intensive planning and preparation will be needed. Review previous years, noting what worked, what did not, what might need to be tweaked.
- If your leadership team is contemplating changes in the schedule of services/church school/weekly activities, the beginning of the program year (usually at some point in September after Labor Day) is a logical time to put these changes into effect.

Seasonal Blessings[1]

The following blessings may be used by a bishop or priest whenever a blessing is appropriate for the following season and noted Sundays.

The Day of Pentecost

May the Spirit of truth lead you into all truth, giving you grace to cnfess that Jesus Christ is Lord, and to proclaim the wonderful works of God; and the blessing of God Almighty, the Father, the Son, and the Holy Spirit, be among you, and remain with you always. *Amen.*

Trinity Sunday

May God the Holy Trinity make you strong in faith and love, defend you on every side, and guide you in truth and peace; and the blessing of God Almighty, the Father, the Son, and the Holy Spirit, be among you, and remain with you always. *Amen.*

All Saints

May God give you grace to follow his saints in faith and hope and love; and the blessing of God Almighty, the Father, the Son, and the Holy Spirit, be among you, and reemain with you always. *Amen.*

A Prayer for Memorial Day[2]

Monday, May 28

Lord God, in whom there is life and light: Accept our thanks for those who died for us, our prayers for those who mourn, our praise for the hope you have given us. Refresh our hearts with dedication to heroic ideas, with appreciation for the honesty of the just, with obedience to upright laws. Forgive us when our patriotism is hollow, when our nationalism is arrogant, when our allegiance is halfhearted. Stir within us thanksgiving for all we have inherited, vigilance for the freedoms of all people, willingness to sacrifice for fellow citizens. Comfort us with the joy that Christ died for all those who died for us, bringing life and immortality to light for all who believe in Him. *Amen.*

Graduation Prayers

A Graduation Collect[3]

Precious Father, *I* especially pray for out teenagers and young adults at this time of school graduations; where they are lost, find them; when they are afraid, bring them comfort and love; and where they are confused, show them your will. Protect them, Father, and be with parents as they ride the roller coaster of these years with their children. May they have the courage, the strength, the wisdom through your Holy Spirit to help guide them and in many cases just to hold on, and to be there as their children take on adult responsibilities in a chaotic, sinful world. *I* now place them under your loving wings. *Amen.*

A High School Graduation Litany[4]

Each section of this litany may be used separately, or the whole may be used as one continuous litany for those who are graduating from high school.

Leader 1: Lord, it is your will for us to welcome new freedom.

Leader 2: We welcome new freedom to embark on a career; freedom to earn our money, or train to earn it; freedom to spend our money, or save it; freedom to

[1] *The Book of Occasional Services 2003* (New York: Church Publishing, 2004), 27-28.

[2] "The Last Monday in May," in *An American Prayer Book,* edited by Christopher L. Webber (Harrisburg, PA: Morehouse Publishing, 2008), 141-142.

[3] Stephanie Douglas, "Protect Them and Lead Them," in *Women's Uncommon Prayers,* edited by Elizabeth Rankin Geitz, Ann Smith, Marjorie A. Burke (Harrisburg, PA: Morehouse Publishing, 2000), 155.

[4] "At a High School Baccalaureate," in *The Wideness of God's Mercy: Litanies to Enlarge Our Prayer,* edited by Jeffery W. Rowthorn (New York: Church Publishing, 2007), 232-233.

fashion new routines; freedom to plan leisure; freedom to bear new responsibilities; freedom to make fresh meaning out of life.

Leader 1: We welcome new freedom to grow in the world you have given us, to travel to the destination you have prepared for us, to meet and serve the people you have waiting for us.

Leader 2: In the challenge of freedom

> *Equip us.*

Leader 1: In the decisions of freedom

> *Direct us.*

Leader 2: In the art of freedom

> *Discipline us.*

Leader 1: In the dangers of freedom

> *Protect us.*

Leader 2: In the raptures of freedom

> *Steady us.*

Leader 1: In the life of freedom

> *Give us joy.*

Leader 2: In the use of freedom

> *Grant us wisdom.*

Leader 1: Against all the victimization of the world,

> *God has set us free, we are free indeed.*

Leader 2: So in the freedom given us by God,

> *We shall make money honestly, we shall love honorably, we shall make time for those who need us, we shall make friends of our enemies, we shall make amends right away, we shall make God supreme, for God's service in the world is perfect freedom. Amen.*

An Independence Day Litany[5]

Wedesday, July 4

> *This litany is designed for use on days of national celebration (like Independence Day), or in times of national crisis.*

---

[5] "Litany for the Nation," in *An American Prayer Book,* edited by Christopher L. Webber (Harrisburg, PA: Morehouse Publishing, 2008), 39–41.

Mighty God: the earth is yours and nations are your people. Take away our pride and bring to mind your goodness, so that, living together in this land, we may enjoy your gifts and be thankful.

> *Amen.*

For clouded mountains, fields, and woodland; for shoreline and running streams; for all that makes our nation good and lovely;

> *We thank you, God.*

For farms and villages where food is gathered to feed our people;

> *We thank you, God.*

For cities where people talk and work together in factories, shops, or schools to shape those things we need for living;

> *We thank you, God.*

For explorers, planners, diplomats; for prophets who speak out, and for silent faithful people; for all who love our land and guard our freedom;

> *We thank you, God.*

For vision to see your purpose hidden in our nation's history, and courage to seek it in human love exchanged;

> *We thank you, God.*

O God, your justice is like a rock, and your mercy like pure flowing water. Judge and forgive us. If we have turned from you, return us to your way; for without you, we are lost people. From brassy patriotism and a blind trust in power;

> *Deliver us, O God.*

From public deceptions that weaken trust; from self-seeking in high political places;

> *Deliver us, O God.*

From divisions among us of class or race; from wealth that will not share, and poverty that feeds on food of bitterness;

> *Deliver us, O God.*

From neglecting rights; from overlooking the hurt, the imprisoned, and the needy among us;

> *Deliver us, O God.*

From a lack of concern for other lands and peoples; from narrowness of national purpose; from failure to welcome the peace you promise on earth;

Deliver us, O God.

Eternal God: before you nations rise and fall; they grow strong or wither by your design. Help us to repent our country's wrong, and to choose your right in reunion and renewal.

Amen.

Give us a glimpse of the Holy City you are bringing to earth, where death and pain and crying will be gone away; and nations gather in the light of your presence.

Great God, renew this nation.

Teach us peace, so that we may plow up battlefields and pound weapons into building tools, and learn to talk across old boundaries as brothers and sisters in your love.

Great God, renew this nation.

Talk sense to us, so that we may wisely end all prejudice, and may put a stop to cruelty, which divides or wounds the human family.

Great God, renew this nation.

Draw us together as one people who do your will, so that our land may be a light to the nations, leading the way to your promised kingdom, which is coming among us.

Great God, renew this nation.

Great God, eternal Lord: long years ago you gave our fathers this land as a home for the free. Show us there is no law or liberty apart from you; and let us serve you modestly, as devoted people; through Jesus Christ our Lord.

Amen.

Labor Day[6]

September 3

Lord God, our Creator. We deserve to labor among thorns and thistles, to eat by the sweat of our brow, to work without reward. For we confess we have spoiled your creation by our sin, we have marred your work by our neglect, we have hurt your work by our rebellion. We pray you, bless our labor by him who was once a carpenter, by him who came to be our servant, by him who saved us to serve. For his sake, keep us and all who labor from false dealing and unfair practice, from excessive profit and unjust gain, from slovenly service and irrational demands. Help us to labor with love, to labor with joy, to labor with faithfulness. Teach us that the best labor we give you is loving service to others. In Christ's name we ask it. *Amen.*

Back to School

Marking the Beginning of a School Year[7]

God of all wisdom, we praise you for wisely gifting us with sons and daughters. Give to each one a clear sense of your love, that they may feel your presence supporting them throughout this school year. Guide their choices, direct their quest for knowledge, bless their relationships, and use their successes and failures as opportunities to grow in understanding of who you would have them be. Continue, we pray, to shape them as branches of the one true vine, that they may ever walk in the way of Christ, grow strong in your Spirit's love for all people, and know the complete joy of life in you. In the name of Christ, we pray. *Amen.*

The Blessing of Backpacks[8]

(Children are invited to gather in the chancel with their backpacks. Following the blessing, small wooden crosses may be given out for the children to place inside the backpacks.)

God of Wisdom, we give you thanks for schools and classrooms and for the teachers and students who fill them each day. We thank you for this new beginning, for new books and new ideas. We thank you for sharpened pencils, pointy crayons, and crisp blank pages waiting to be filled. We thank you for the gift of making mistakes and trying again. Help us to remember that asking the right questions is often as important as giving the right answers. Today we give you thanks for these your

[6] "The First Monday in September," in *An American Prayer Book*, edited by Christopher L. Webber (Harrisburg, PA: Morehouse Publishing, 2008), 148-149.

[7] Linda Witte Henke, "From the Vine," in *Marking Time: Christian Rituals for All Our Days* (Harrisburg, PA: Morehouse Publishing, 2001), 63.

[8] Wendy Claire Barrie, in *Skiturgies: Pageants, Plays, Rites, and Rituals* (New York: Church Publishing, 2011). www.skiturgies.com, accessed 27 August 2017.

children, and we ask you to bless them with curiosity, understanding, and respect. May their backpacks be a sign to them that they have everything they need to learn and grow this year in school and in Sunday School. May they be guided by your love. All this we ask this in the name of Jesus, who as a child in the temple showed his longing to learn about you, and as an adult taught by story and example your great love for us. *Amen.*

Remembering September 11, 2001[9]

A prayer to be used in observances of the anniversary of September 11, 2001.

God the compassionate one, whose loving care extends to al the world, we remember this day your children of many nations and many faiths whose lives were cut short the fierce flames of anger and hatred. Console those who continue to suffer and grieve, and give them comfort and hope as they look to the future. Out of what we have endured, give us the grace to examine our relationships with those who perceive us as the enemy, and show our leaders the way to use our power to serve the good of all for the healing of the nations. This we ask through Jesus Christ our Lord, who, in reconciling love, was lifted up from the earth that he might draw all things to himself. *Amen.*

A Litany for the International Day of Peace[10]

September 21

Remember, O Lord, the peoples of the world, divided into many nations and tongues. Deliver us from every evil that gets in the way of your saving purpose; and fulfill the promise of peace to your people on earth, through Jesus Christ our Lord. *Amen.*

From the curse of war and the human sin that causes war;

> *O Lord, deliver us.*

From pride that turns its back on you, and from unbelief that will not call you Lord;

> *O Lord, deliver us.*

From national vanity that poses as patriotism; from loud-mouthed boasting and blind self-worship that admit no guilt;

> *O Lord, deliver us.*

For the self-righteous who will not compromise, and from selfishness that gains by the oppression of others;

> *O Lord, deliver us.*

From trusting in the weapons of war, and mistrusting the councils of peace;

> *O Lord, deliver us.*

From hearing, believing, and speaking lies about other nations;

> *O Lord, deliver us.*

From groundless suspicions and fears that stand in the way of reconciliation;

> *O Lord, deliver us.*

From words and deeds that encourage discord, prejudice, and hatred; from everything that prevents the human family from fulfilling your promise of peace;

> *O Lord, deliver us.*

O God our Father: we pray for all your children on earth, of every nation and of every race, that they may be strong to do your will.

Silence

We pray for the Church in the world;

> *O Lord, give peace in our time.*

For the United Nations;

> *O Lord, give peace in our time.*

For international federations of labor, industry, and commerce;

> *O Lord, give peace in our time.*

For departments of state, ambassadors, diplomats, and states persons;

> *O Lord, give peace in our time.*

For worldwide agencies of compassion, which bind wounds and feed the hungry;

> *O Lord, give peace in our time.*

For common folk in every land who live in peace;

> *O Lord, give peace in our time.*

[9] Frank W. Griswold, "Remembering September 11, 2001," from *An American Prayer Book,* edited by Christopher L. Webber (Harrisburg, PA: Morehouse Publishing, 2008), 113.

[10] "World Peace," from *There's a Wideness in God's Mercy: Litanies to Enlarge Our Prayer,* edited by Jeffrey W. Rowthorn (New York: Church Publishing, 2007), 334-335.

Eternal God: use us, even our ignorance and weakness, to bring about your holy will. Hurry the day when all people shall live together in your love; for yours is the kingdom, the power, and the glory forever. *Amen.*

The Feast of St. Francis

October 4

A Litany for St. Francis Day[11]

With all our heart and with all our mind, we pray to you, O God:

> *Lord, make us instruments of your peace.*

For our President and for all who are in authority, and for the people and leaders of every nation, that we may truly respect each other and learn to live together peacefully, we pray to you, O God;

> *Where there is hatred, let us sow love.*

For this community gathered, for our families and friends, our neighbors and co-workers, especially for those whom we have hurt, we pray to you, O God;

> *Where there is injury, let us sow pardon.*

For all those who seek you, God, and for those who shut you out, that they may be touched by your presence, power and grace, we pray to you, O God;

> *Where there is doubt, let us sow faith.*

For the poor, for prisoners, for refugees, for those who are oppressed and persecuted, that they may be delivered from danger and fear, we pray to you, O God;

> *Where there is despair, let us sow hope.*

For the people of God throughout the world, that the good news of God's redeeming love may be known in all places, we pray to you, O God;

> *Where there is darkness, let us sow light.*

For those who are sick, unhappy, lonely or bereft, that they may be healed and comforted, we pray to you, O God;

> *Where there is sadness, let us sow joy.*

For those who have died, especially those we now name, we pray to you, O God. *(People may add their own petitions)*

For what is in our hearts today, we ask you to hear us, O God. *(People may add their own petitions)*

For all the gifts of your creation, and for the trust and joy you have given us in these our pets, we thank you and praise you, O God. *(People may add their own thanksgivings.)*

> *Grant that we may not so much seek to be consoled as to console, to be understood as to understand, to be loved as to love, for it is in giving that we receive, it is in pardoning that we are pardoned, and it is dying that we are born to eternal life. Amen.*

A Blessing of Pets[12]

The Lord be with you.

> *And also with you.*

O Lord, how manifold are your works!

> *You stretch out the heavens like a tent. You set the earth on its foundations. You make springs gush forth in the valleys and give drink to every animal.*

You plant trees where birds may build their nests.

> *You cause the grass to grow for the cattle and plants for people to use. You open your hand and give all creatures their food in good season. (Psalm 104)*

We have come together to acknowledge with gratitude the goodness of God in all creatures, great and small, and to seek God's blessing on the pets that are our companions in life. Let us pray:

On this day, O God, we offer thanks for these, our pets, who are your daily instruments of joy and comfort in our lives. Even as you demonstrate care for us, so also move us to demonstrate care for these and all your creatures, knowing that, in do doing, we are privileged to share in your love of creation. We pray in the name of Jesus, in whose power we are made a new creation.

> *Amen! May it be so!*

> *[As the leader approaches each pet, the pet's owner speaks the pet's name aloud so that all those gathered may hear. The leader then raises his/her hand above the pet and speaks a word of blessing.]*

[11] Intecessions by Wendy Claire Barrie from "Liturgy for the Feast of St. Francis," in *Skiturgies: Pageants, Plays, Rites, and Rituals* (New York: Church Publishing, 2011). www. skiturgies.com, accessed 27 August 2017.

[12] Linda Witte Henke, "All Creatures Great and Small," in *Marking Time: Christian Rituals For All Our Days* (Harrisburg, PA: Morehouse Publishing, 2001), 80-82.

May God Creator bless you and keep you through all the days of your life.

Thanks be to God!

[If some participants have brought mementos of former pets, the leader may touch each memento, while speaking these or similar words.]

May God bless the memory of this pet's presence in your life!

Thanks be to God!

[If children have brought stuffed animals to receive a blessing, the leader may touch each toy, while speaking these or similar words.]

May this animal's presence be a source of joy and comfort in this child's life.

Thanks be to God!

May God Almighty, Father, Son, and Holy Spirit, use us as intsruments of blessing for all creatures, great and small.

Amen! Thanks be to God!

A Native American Thanksgiving for the Americas and Their People[13]

Columbus Day: October 6

For our ancestors, who built nations and cultures; who thrived and prospered long before the coming of strangers; for the forfeit of their lives, their homes, their lands, and their freedoms, sacrificed to the rise of new nations and new worlds.

We offer a song of honor and thanks.

For the wealth of our lands; for minerals in the earth; for the plants and waters and animals on the earth; for the birds, the clouds and rain, for the sun and moon in the sky and the gifts they gave to our people that enabled the rise of new world economics.

We offer a song of honor and thanks.

[13] "1492-1992: A Celebration of Native American Survival. Earth and All the Stars" in *There's a Wideness in God's Mercy: Litanies to Enlarge Our Prayer,* edited by Jeffrey W. Rowthorn (New York: Church Publishing, 2007), 298-299. This litany was prepared for use at a service commemorating the quincentenary of the landing of Christopher Columbus in 1492 with its fateful impact on the Native American peoples, who despite all have survived to the day. The service was held on October 12, 1992 in the National Cathedral in Washington, D.C.

For the many foods coaxed from the heart of Mother Earth; for the skills we were given to develop foods that now belong to the world: potatoes, corn, beans, squash, peanuts, tomatoes, peppers, coffee, cocoa, sugar, and many, many more.

We offer a song of honor and thanks.

For the medicinces first disocvered by our ancestors and now known to the world: quinine, ipecac, iodine, curare, petroleum jelly, witch hazel, and others; for the healing skills of our people and those how now care for us. For tobacco, sage, sweet grass, and cedar that give spiritual healing by the power of their meaning.

We offer a song of honor and thanks.

For oceans, streams, rivers, lakes, and other waters of our lands that provide bountifully for us; for clams, lobsters, salmon, trout, shrimp, and abalone; for the pathways the waters provide.

We offer a song of honor and thanks.

For the friendship that first welcomed all to our shores; for the courage of those who watched their worlds change and disappear and for those who led in the search for new lives; for our leaders today who fight with courage and great heart for us.

We offer a song of honor and praise.

For the friends who suffered with us and stand with us today to help bring the promise and the hope that the New World meant to their ancestors.

We offer a song of honor and thanks.

For the strength and beauty of our diverse Native cultures; for the traditions that give structure to our lives, that define who we are; for the skills of our artists and craftspeople and the gifts of their hands.

We offer a song of honor and thanks.

For the spiritualty and vision that gave our people the courage and faith to endure and that brought many to an understanding and acceptance of the love of Christ, our Brother and Savior.

We offer a song of honor and thanks.

Accept, O God, Creator, our honor song, and make our hearts thankful for what we have been given. Make us humble for what we have taken. Make us glad as we return some measure of what we have been given. Strengthen our faith and make us strong in the service of our people, in the name of our Brother and Savior, Jesus Christ, your Son, in the power of the Holy Spirit. *Amen.*

A Litany for Children's Sabbath[14]

October 21

Tortured by hunger and thirst, ravaged by disease and pollution;

> *Save all your children, Lord.*

Savaged by the brutalities of war, victimized by violence and abuse

> *Save all your children, Lord.*

Broken by exploitative child labor, stunted by suffering;

> *Save your children, Lord.*

Thwarted by prejudice, deprived of beauty, joy, and laughter;

> *Save your children, Lord.*

Uprooted by famine, war, and disaster, burdened by the debts of preceding generations;

> *Protect all our children, Lord.*

Aged before they could be young, denied freedom, justice, and peace;

> *Protect all our children, Lord.*

Nurtured and guided with love and undertanding, provided with food and clothing and shelter;

> *Care for all your children, Lord.*

Enriched by a safe and clean environment, empowered by education and opportunity;

> *Care for all your children, Lord.*

Welcome and honored in our midst, brought to know and to love you as their Savior;

> *Care for all your children, Lord. Amen.*

An All Hallows' Eve Liturgy[15]

October 31

All Hallows' Eve, which later became known as Halloween, is celebrated the night before All Saints' Day, November 1. You may use this simple prayer service

in conjunction with Halloween festivities to mark the Christian roots of this festival. Begin in partial darkness.

Light and peace, in Jesus Christ our Lord.

> *Thanks be to God.*

If I say, "Surely the darkness will cover me, and the light around me turn to night," darkness is not dark to you, O Lord; the night is as bright as the day; darkness and light to you are both alike. (Psalm 139:10-11)

Let us pray. Lord Christ, your saints have been the lights of the world in every generation: Grant that we, who follow in their footsteps, may be made worthy to enter with them into that heavenly country wehre you live and reign for ever and ever. Amen.

Candles are now lighted as all say recite the Phos hilaron:

> *O gracious Light,*
> *Pure brightness of the everliving Father in heaven,*
> *O Jesus Christ, holy and blessed!*
>
> *Now as we come to the setting of the sun,*
> *And our eyes behold the vesper light,*
> *We sing your praises, O God:*
> *Father, Son, and Holy Spirit.*
>
> *You are worthy at all times*
> *to be praised by happy voices,*
> *O Son of God, O Giver of life,*
> *And to be glorified through all the worlds.*
>
> *Glory to the Father, and to the Son, and to the Holy Spirit; as it was in the beginning, is now, and will be for ever. Amen.*

Election Day[16]

November 6

Holy God, throughout the ages you have called men and women to serve you in various ways, giving them gifts for the task to which they were called and strengthening and guiding them in the fulfillment of their calling; in this free land, you share with us that great responsibility and enable us to choose those who will serve you in positions of leadership in various offices of government.

---

[14] Mary Ford-Grabowsky, "For Children at Risk," in *The Wideness of God's Mercy: Litanies to Enlarge Our Prayers,* edited by Jeffrey W. Rowthorn (New York: Church Publishing, 2007), 356.

[15] Anne E. Kitch, *The Anglican Family Prayer Book* (Harrisburg, PA: Morehouse Publishing, 2004), 148-149.

[16] Christopher L. Webber, "Before an Election," by Christopher L. Webber in *An American Prayer Book,* edited by Christopher L. Webber (Harrisburg, PA: Morehouse Publishing, 2008), 150.

Help us in so choosing to seek those who have an understanding of your will for us, a commitment to justice, a concern for those in greatest need, a love of truth and a deep humility before you; Send your Spirit among us that we may be guided in the choices we make that your will may be done on earth as it is in heaven. *Amen.*

A Stewardship Litany[17]

God of life and love: We are quick to accept bounteous gifts from you, but slow to give thanks and to express our gratitude.
We hold too tightly the things of this life, giving them the allegiance we owe only to you.

> *Take my life and let it be*
> *consecrated, Lord, to thee.*
> *Take my moments and my days;*
> *let them flow in ceaseless praise,*
> *let them flow in ceaseless praise.*

Gracious God, we admit that our lives are too often out of balance; we are more willing to receive than to share, more ready to take than to give.
Create in us grateful and generous hearts, we pray, and restore to us the joy of our salvation.

> *Take my hands and let them move*
> *at the impulse of thy love.*
> *Take my feet, and let them be*
> *swift and beautiful for thee,*
> *swift and beautiful for thee.*

Merciful God, from whom comes every good and perfect gift, we praise you for your mercies:
your goodness that has created us, your grace that has sustained us,
Your discipline that has corrected us, your patience that has borne with us,
> *and your love that has redeemed us.*

> *Take my will, and make it thine;*
> *it shall be no longer mine.*
> *Take my heart, it is thine own;*
> *it shall be thy royal throne,*
> *it shall be thy royal throne.*

Help us to love you, and to be thankful for all your gifts by serving you and delighting to do you will.
Accept now, Gracious God, our offerings, these our pledges of resources and talents for your service, and the commitment of our lives, through Jesus Christ, who gave his all for us.

> *Take my silver and my gold,*
> *not a mite would I withhold;*
> *take my intellect, and use*
> *every power a sthou shalt choose,*
> *every power as thou shalt choose.*

> *Take my love; my Lord, I pour*
> *at thy feet its treasure store,*
> *Take myself, and I will be*
> *ever, only, all for thee,*
> *ever, only, all for thee. Amen.*

The Nicene Creed: A Chancel Drama[18]

This chancel drama may be appropriate for Trinity Sunday, involving three readers and a narrator.

[NARRATOR]: We believe in one God, the Father, the Almighty, maker of heaven and earth, of all that is, seen and unseen.

[READER 1]: When I stop to think about God the creator, I stand in awe!

You must admit, whether you believe in creationism or evolution, it's all pretty astounding. God created out of nothing, out of chaos. When we make something new, it's with the gifts of creation at our disposal. We can only create from what is already here; all the raw materials God made. Reminds me of the joke when Man told God he was going to do a better job with Woman and God told him to get his own dirt . . .

God created everything that is, from the vast expanse of interstellar space, to galaxies and suns, to the planets in their courses (ref. BCP, 370) and Mother earth, to humans and the smallest of atoms. Is there any detail God didn't consider when making all this? Think about how big God's love must be! It's enough to make you stop and pause.

[READER 2]: What does "We believe" mean? Are we affirming that we have love of neighbor and self? Really? Are we unified in Christ? And to take it

---

[17] W. Alfred Tisdale Jr, "A Stewardship Litany," in *The Wideness of God's Mercy: Litanies to Enlarge Our Prayer,* edited by Jeffery W. Rowthorn (New York: Church Publishing, 2007), 124-125. Hymn stanzas by Frances Ridley Havergal; a shorter version is found as #707 Take my life, and let it be, *The Hymnal 1982.*

[18] Linda W. Nichols, *The Nicene Creed: A Chancel Drama* (New York: Church Publishing, 2011). Part of the Skiturgies collection. www.skiturgies.com

further, are "we" those who are already with Christ, those living now and those believers yet to come? Hopefully, we really are the Body of Christ; one big happy family, past, present, and future.

[NARRATOR]: We believe in one Lord, Jesus Christ, the only Son of God, eternally begotten of the Father, God from God, Light from Light, true God from true God, begotten, not made, of one being with the Father. Through him all things were made.

[READER 3]: It reminds me of that passage: In the beginning was the Word, and the Word was with God. He was in the beginning with God; all things were made through him, and without him not anything was made . . . John 1:1-3

Let's face it; there's been debate around the identity of Jesus since the beginning of the Church. I believe Jesus is the Son of God. Why can't Jesus be human *and* divine? It's a paradox and a mystery of faith. Why can't Jesus be both?

If you think about it, it is hard to believe. But, if God created all that is, *and* God is God, why can't God create someone both human and divine? And as human beings, baptized into the Body of Christ with God's spirit dwelling within us, we can now believe we are truly sons and daughters of God. We somehow know we belong to God's family.

Doesn't this mean that God loves us a lot? God loved us enough to come face to face with us.

[NARRATOR]: For us and for our salvation he came down from heaven: by the power of the Holy Spirit he became incarnate from the Virgin Mary, and was made man.

[READER 2]: The age-old question is: what does it mean to be made man and be the Incarnate Son of God? Middle Eastern culture dictates that Mary was a virgin *or* she would have been stoned. Her age meant she was a mere child. So what does this mean for us today?

Does my belief in Jesus as Savior depend on a virgin birth? Well maybe this means more, and is expressing something deeper. Can't God use any individual to express the plan for our salvation? God does not need to show his face through miracles. But for me, God knew in our weakness that we need signs to give us hope. Believing in the Incarnation, come to think of it, makes it easier to believe in the Resurrection. Talk about God's amazing plan for us! God sent the Son, because the Virgin Mary said "yes"!

This is the deeper meaning, even though it's hard for us to believe. After all, it's a matter of childlike faith, isn't it?

[NARRATOR]: For our sake he was crucified under Pontius Pilate; he suffered death and was buried. On the third day he rose again, in accordance with the Scriptures; he ascended into heaven and is seated at the right hand of the Father.

[READER 2]: See what I mean, this is the hard part for me. Think about the Resurrection. In one moment, sin and death no longer has power over us. Christians have spent centuries talking about forgiveness and love of our neighbors as well as ourselves. We are to forgive as we have been forgiven. How many times? Seven times seventy, and God wants us to forgive those who persecute us. That's hard.

God made life never ending with the Resurrection of Jesus. We will be resurrected too! God wants to be with us forever. God loves each of us that much. Eternity is a long time to love me! Now that's something worth believing.

[NARRATOR]: He will come again in glory to judge the living and the dead, and his kingdom will have no end.

[READER 3]: Where is God's Kingdom? Are we talking heaven here on earth or a heaven yet to come? Are we talking present or future? Sometimes kingdom language is confusing. The Parables say the Kingdom of God is like: a Mustard Seed, the Good Shepherd, the Found Sheep, the Lost Coin, Use of Talents, a Heavenly Banquet . . . I guess Jesus wasn't understood any better in back then. I suppose the best we can do is try to use our talents for the advancement of the Kingdom.

It seems like I've attended many funerals, and I find great comfort with fellow believers that there's a place with no more sorrow and pain. I'm still not sure about that whole Day of Judgment thing. Do we ever really talk about that subject? May your Kingdom come, your will be done.

[NARRATOR]: We believe in the Holy Spirit, the Lord, the giver of life, who proceeds from the Father and the Son. With the Father and the Son he is worshiped and glorified. He has spoken through the Prophets.

[READER 1]: Finally, we complete the Trinity. I know folks who think it's just about the Father and the Son. I must admit, the Holy Spirit is ghostly, no

Pentecost

pun intended. It's a mystery that God breathed over creation to start everything and keeps it going. In the medical profession, isn't it breath that pronounces us dead or alive? Sometimes it's easier to comprehend the living God with the Spirit as one rather than God and Jesus as one . . .

Then there's the whole Pentecost—the Spirit or breath of God moved to give us prophesies, dreams, and visions. It's about hope. The Spirit is our Counselor, companion, and guide to help us see ourselves in God's plan. It seems like it's only by the Spirit of God that we can begin to understand all the prophets spoke about, the life of Christ, and all that proceeds from the Giver of Life.

[NARRATOR]: We believe in one holy catholic and apostolic Church. We acknowledge one baptism for the forgiveness of sins.

[READER 2]: Here's where my friends get tripped up: the whole "one holy catholic Church" thing. Some say denominations don't matter and others are so sure they have all the answers that they think everyone else is wrong. This doesn't make any sense! Either we're all baptized as Christians or we're not . . . Why can't we focus on what Jesus taught in the Upper Room the night before he died, "That we all be one"? If we really thought we were One Body, we would get along better with others and be good neighbors to those who do not know Jesus yet. Actions do speak louder than words.

[NARRATOR]: We look for the resurrection of the dead, and the life of the world to come.

[READER 1]: "Parousia" is a word we're hearing more and more in children's formation. It refers to when God's creation comes together; the Alpha and the Omega; the Beginning and the End; when all of creation is complete; when the lion lies down with the lamb. I resonate with the thought of paradise restored! *(Pair-a-see-a* OR *Pa-roo-ze-a—one pronunciation is Greek & one is Latin)*

There's an acclamation in the Eucharistic Prayer when we say after the Consecration: Christ has died, Christ is risen, Christ will come again (BCP, 363). What do we mean by this faith response? Well, it sums up what God did for us and what that means for us as we are now living in the Kingdom, which will last to the world to come, to the Age of Ages!

[NARRATOR]: Amen.

So it is. May the love of God be so forever and ever.
Amen.

A Chancel Drama for the Pentecost Season

St. Barnabas: Son of Encouragement[19]

Scene 1: In Jerusalem on the Day of Pentecost and soon afterwards *(As the scene opens, several disciples are sitting on the altar platform (or stage, if either is available); the crowd is sitting on the floor in front of the altar platform or stage.)*

NARRATOR: Jesus rose from the dead on Easter, showing that he had defeated Death itself, and the Holy Spirit came to Jesus' followers seven weeks later, on Pentecost. Suddenly, the disciples were courageous and eager to speak in public about Jesus.

PETER: This Jesus God raised up, and of that we are all witnesses. *[The other disciples nod.]* God has made him both Lord and Messiah.

MEMBER OF THE CROWD: *[Stands.]* Brothers, what should we do?

PETER: Repent, and be baptized every one of you in the Name of Jesus Christ so that your sins may be forgiven; and you will receive the gift of the Holy Spirit. *[Everyone in the crowd nods. Peter and the other disciples start to pantomime baptizing the new converts.]*

NARRATOR: Three thousand people were baptized that day. They devoted themselves to the apostles' teaching, to the breaking of bread, and to the prayers. They also made sure that no Christian, no matter how poor, went hungry. They became really good at sharing. All these, like the original followers of Jesus, were Jews, mainly from the Holy Land. But the faith and good deeds of the community of believers started drawing in people from out of town as well—Jews who were visiting Jerusalem. One of them was a man named Joseph, from the island of Cyprus. *[Enter Barnabas, stage left.]*

BARNABAS: Jesus is the Messiah we've been waiting for! I want to help to spread the Good News of Jesus and to feed the poor, which is what he also wants us to do. Peter, here's the money I got from selling a piece of land that belonged to me. *[He gives a stack of play money to Peter.]*

PETER: Thank you! That really helps. I've heard a lot about you already—not only do you believe in Jesus

[19] Francis A. Hubbard, (New York: Church Publishing, 2011). This is part of the *Skiturgies: Rites, Rituals, Pageants, and Plays* collection. www.skiturgies.com

and follow his teaching, you're a good coach—always encouraging other believers. You should be called Barnabas, the name which means "son of encouragement." *[They shake hands and Barnabas leaves, stage left.]*

NARRATOR: However, not everyone loved Jesus or liked his followers. Some people hurt those who believed in Jesus, or tried to get them locked up. One of the people who tried to get believers in Jesus locked up was called Paul. *[Paul enters, stage left, looking sinister and pantomiming going after members of the crowd.]* One day, Jesus himself appeared to Paul and convinced him to take a U-turn with his life. *[Paul takes a U-turn and exits, stage left.]* Suddenly, Paul started talking about Jesus as the Savior, and he himself got in trouble with the enemies of Jesus' followers.

PETER: *[To the other leaders.]* I've heard stories about Paul changing, but I'm not sure I really trust him.

BARNABAS: *[Walks in from stage left with his arm around Paul.]* Trust me, Peter, Paul is the real deal! I've heard him preach about Jesus, and he's great! He shows a lot of guts, too.

THE APOSTLES: *[In unison.]* Barnabas, if he's O.K. with you, he's O.K. with us. *[Everyone shakes hands with Paul and pats Barnabas on the back. Barnabas and Paul then exit, stage left.]*

NARRATOR: The community of believers inn Jesus spread beyond the Holy Land, and the leaders had to figure out how to lead a movement which included followers who were far away.

MESSENGER FROM ANTIOCH: *[Enters from stage left and addresses the apostles.]* I come from Antioch. We have many people who believe in Jesus as the Savior, and we want to learn more about him and about how to be a community of faithful believers who help others. Can you send someone to guide us?

APOSTLE #1: *[To Peter.]* Wow, Antioch's almost 400 miles from here. The Word is really getting around.

APOSTLE #2: It's all part of God's plan. Jesus told us we were supposed to make disciples of ALL nations.

APOSTLE #3: Hey, how about we send Barnabas to them? He's a terrific teacher and coach, and he leads by example, showing them how to be good followers of Jesus by how he treats people, and by

his generosity. Plus, he gets along with all kinds of people.

APOSTLE #4: But he's from out of town. Can somebody who's not from where WE grew up become an important leader of the Church?

APOSTLE #5: I think it's an advantage that Barnabas is from someplace else. He's traveled a lot, knows more languages than I do, and is comfortable with people from all over the place.

PETER: I think that the Holy Spirit is calling us, as leaders, to open the leadership to anyone from anywhere who the Holy Spirit has picked to be a leader among believers in Jesus.

APOSTLE #4: I think you're right, Peter. I need to be more open-minded. God does have the whole world in his hand, after all, not just my home town.

PETER: Let's pray and ask the Holy Spirit to guide us. *[The apostles, including Peter, all join hands and bow their heads. After a brief time, they all raise their heads and nod to each other.]* It's settled, then. We'll send Barnabas.

[Apostle #4 exits stage left and returns with Barnabas. They all lay hands on Barnabas' head and shoulders, and he goes off, stage left, with the Messenger from Antioch. The apostles exit stage right while a few bars of "He's got the whole world in his hand" are played.]

Scene 2: Barnabas in Antioch *[A crowd is seated in front of the altar or stage.]*

NARRATOR: Barnabas came to Antioch. *[He enters, stage left, led by the Messenger from Antioch, and addresses the group.]*

BARNABAS: Wow! You have a great community of believers in Jesus here! Keep up the good work! *[He stands on the altar platform or stage and assumes a teaching pose.]*

NARRATOR: He was a good man, full of the Holy Spirit and of faith. Barnabas didn't talk about himself, he talked about Jesus, and he encouraged people all the time to do their best.

[More people join the crowd from stage right.]

BARNABAS: We're getting so many new followers of Jesus, I need an assistant. I know! I'll send for Paul.

(He sends the Messenger from Antioch, who exits stage left, and returns with Paul. Barnabas and Paul then take turns pantomiming teaching the crowd.]

NARRATOR: For whole year they met with the church and taught a great many people.

FOLLOWER FROM ANTIOCH: Barnabas, the people in town who don't like Jesus are calling us "Christians." They think it's a "dis", but I think it's a badge of honor to be called a Christian!

BARNABAS: You're right! We should all call our-selves Christians! *[Everyone nods.]*

NARRATOR: This was the first time and place that followers of Jesus were called Christians. The name stuck.

BARNABAS: O.K., let's have a roll call of the lead-ers of the Christian Church of Antioch, besides me. Simeon, the black man? *[He stands.]* Lucius, from Libya in North Africa? *[He stands.]* Manaen, who works for Herod the ruler? *[He stands.]* Paul, from Tarsus? *[He stands.]* Let us pray. *[They join hands and bow their heads.]*

THE HOLY SPIRIT: *[A woman's voice, from over the p.a. system if one is available. If not, loudly and from off-stage.]* Set apart for me Barnabas and Paul for the work to which I have called them. *[The circle of men look up as the Holy Spirit speaks.]*

SIMEON: O.K., you heard the Holy Spirit's voice. Barnabas and Paul have to leave on a mission trip to tell people about Jesus who have never heard of him.

[Barnabas and Paul kneel, and Simeon, Lucius and Manaen lay hands on their heads and pray silently. All then leave, stage left. The crowd leaves, stage right.

Scene 3: Barnabas and Paul on a mission trip. *[Barnabas and Paul enter from stage left. They walk up and down the aisle while the Narrator is speaking.]*

NARRATOR: Barnabas and Paul traveled widely through Cyprus, Barnabas' homeland, and through what is now the nation of Turkey. They told many people about the love and power of God, about the second chance everyone could have because they have forgiveness of sins thanks to Jesus, and about the new kind of community they could have in which no one was mean to anyone because of what they looked like, how much money they had, or where they came

from. Some people didn't like their ideas at all, and in some places they even got beaten up, but they were strong and courageous. They returned to Antioch and reported to the church there.

[Barnabas and Paul walk around the back of the sanctuary and up the side aisle to off stage, where they get their bandages and are ready to enter from stage left.]

Scene 4: Back in Antioch *[Simeon, Lucius, Manaen and other Christians of Antioch enter stage right; Barnabas and Paul enter stage left. Barnabas has bandages placed conspicuously on his face and arms and Paul has an arm in a sling and a big band-aid on his face. The Christians of Antioch gasp when they see Barnabas and Paul so injured.]*

BARNABAS: *[Addresses the Christians of Antioch.]* Many people are becoming Christians—even people who had never heard of the one true God before, never mind Jesus.

PAUL: Not everyone "got it"—in one town we after we healed someone by the power of God, the pagan people thought Barnabas was the pagan god Zeus and that I was the pagan god Hermes. *[The Christians of Antioch looked shocked.]*

BARNABAS: Paul straightened them out, saying "We're not Zeus and Hermes, and actually Zeus and Hermes are bogus. We come to tell you about the real God. Those people were so mad they attacked Paul. *[Paul motions with his arm in a sling.]* But we kept going.

PAUL: You gotta be tough sometimes to be a Chris-tian. But my point is, there are Gentiles, not just our fellow Jews, who are becoming Christians. Lots of them.

SIMEON: God, I believe, has opened up a door of faith for anyone from anywhere. But this is so impor-tant that you need to go to Jerusalem to talk to the original leaders of the Church about this.

[All nod and exit stage left, as a few bars of "He's got the world world in his hand" are played.]

Scene 5: Back in Jerusalem and finale *[Peter and the other original apostles enter stage right. Paul, now leading, and Barnabas enter stage right.]*

PETER: *[To Paul and Barnabas.]* You both are true apostles. I have heard of your travels, your suffering, and the people you have won for faith in Jesus Christ. We here in Jerusalem have talked a lot about how you are converting even people who had never heard of God into believers! You have risked your lives for Jesus' sake. Keep up the good work!

NARRATOR: Paul and Barnabas returned to Antioch. Later, Paul decided to go back to Asia Minor on another mission trip, while Barnabas returned to Cyprus. Barnabas had the wisdom—and self-confidence—to take on as his assistant Paul, who would become a bigger star than Barnabas. Both were very important in spreading the Good News of Jesus hundreds of miles away from the places Jesus himself had been during his time on earth. Other people later said, "Let's be missionaries and encouragers like Paul and Barnabas," and that's how WE became Christians. And we, too, can be like them, for Jesus' sake.

[The entire cast returns to the stage to bow and lead the congregation in the first verse of "He's got the whole world in his hand."]

A Play for the Feast of St. Francis or the Blessing of Animals

St. Francis and the Wolf[20]

(As the play begins, all the actors, except the WOLF, gather in the chancel or in front of the congregation, if performing outside)

NARRATOR ONE: St. Francis loved God, and he loved everything God had created: the sun, moon and stars, trees, flowers, people . . . and animals. Francis *loved* animals.

NARRATOR TWO: Once, he preached to a flock of birds—and they listened!

NARRATOR ONE: Everywhere Francis went, he spoke about God's love and helped others to see and feel that love in the world around them.

NARRATOR TWO: And then one day, Francis came to the town of Gubbio, where the people hid in their houses and lived in fear.

---

[20] Wendy Claire Barrie, "St. Francis and the Wolf," (New York: Church Publishing, 2011) is part of *Skiturgies: Pageants, Plays, Rites, and Rituals*. www.skiturgies.com

FRANCIS: (approaching a VILLAGER) What is making you so afraid?

VILLAGER: There's a ravenous wolf on the prowl.

VILLAGER: He makes his meals on our sheep.

VILLAGER: Even our cows aren't safe from his attacks.

VILLAGER: Even our children aren't safe from his attacks!

FRANCIS: I will go and find this wolf, for it is God's will that people and animals should live together peacefully.

(He strides off, the villagers chasing after him.)

VILLAGER: Don't be so foolish!

VILLAGER: You don't know what he will do to you!

NARRATOR ONE: The villagers protested. But Francis didn't listen. He walked to the edge of the woods and followed the wolf's tracks.

NARRATOR TWO: The tracks ended, and out jumped the snarling, beady-eyed wolf! (The WOLF jumps out!)

FRANCIS: (making the sign of the cross before the WOLF) Brother Wolf! Do you know what you have done? You have terrorized a village! Have you no shame?

NARRATOR ONE: After these words, the wolf stopped.

(The WOLF bows his head in sadness. FRANCIS pats his head, and rubs his ears.)

FRANCIS: I know you have acted out of hunger, my brother. Please promise never to harm any of God's creatures. I will tell the villagers to feed you as long as you never hurt them or their animals again.

NARRATOR TWO: The wolf followed Francis back to the town square.

(The VILLAGERS gather around FRANCIS and the WOLF. The WOLF places his paw in FRANCIS' hand)

VILLAGERS: (cheering) Hooray! Francis has tamed the hungry wolf!

(The VILLAGERS now surround the WOLF, patting him and playing with him)

Pentecost

NARRATOR ONE: After that, the wolf went from door to door in Gubbio, and the townspeople fed him well, breakfast and dinner every day.

NARRATOR TWO: When, after two years, the old wolf died, the villagers wept with sorrow.

NARRATOR ONE: Gubbio was, for that brief time, like God's Peaceable Kingdom.

FRANCIS: As the prophet Isaiah foretold, the wolf shall live with the lamb,

NARRATOR TWO: the leopard shall lie down with the kid,

FRANCIS: the calf and the lion and the fatling together,

YOUNGEST VILLAGER: and a little child shall lead them.

VILLAGERS: The cow and the bear shall graze, their young shall lie down together; and the lion shall eat straw like the ox.

They will not hurt or destroy on all God's holy mountain; for the earth will be full of the knowledge of the Lord as the waters cover the sea.

FRANCIS: Amen, and amen!

The Day of Pentecost

May 20, 2018

The Spirit of God crosses over the boundaries of language and culture to create a new people of God, a human family renewed and made whole. In the one Spirit we were baptized into one body, and at the Lord's table the Spirit unites us for witness in the world.

Color   Red

Preface   Pentecost

Collect

Almighty God, on this day you opened the way of eternal life to every race and nation by the promised gift of your Holy Spirit: Shed abroad this gift throughout the world by the preaching of the Gospel, that it may reach to the ends of the earth; through Jesus Christ our Lord, who lives and reigns with you, in the unity of the Holy Spirit, one God, for ever and ever. Amen.

or this

O God, who on this day taught the hearts of your faithful people by sending to them the light of your Holy Spirit: Grant us by the same Spirit to have a right judgment in all things, and evermore to rejoice in his holy comfort; through Jesus Christ your Son our Lord, who lives and reigns with you, in the unity of the Holy Spirit, one God, for ever and ever. Amen.

Readings and Psalm

Acts 2:1-21 or

This lesson tells the story of the Holy Spirit filling the apostles and empowering them to share the message of the gospel with people of different languages. Clearly this was a most dramatic moment in the life of the early church, an experience described in terms of wind and fire. From this time forward, the mighty works of God done in Jesus will be told to all the peoples of the earth, crossing barriers of language and culture.

Ezekiel 37:1-14

In our opening reading, the prophet has a vision of the bones of a dead and hopeless people being restored to new life in their homeland. The Lord calls upon Ezekiel as son of man to prophesy that the people who have experienced exile and many hardships will live again. The Spirit of the Lord restores their spirit and breath, and they rise from death. Although this passage can be understood to anticipate the hope of individual resurrection, Israel did not yet have this belief.

Psalm 104:25-35, 37

The psalm describes the wonders of the world created and renewed by the Lord's Spirit.

Romans 8:22-27

In this New Testament reading, the apostle Paul understands the whole of creation to be linked with human destiny as we await our redemption. We await our adoption in hope, dependent on the indwelling Spirit of God, who intercedes for us in all things in ways we cannot achieve for ourselves.

Acts 2:1-21

See above

John 15:26-27; 16:4b-15

In our gospel, Jesus tells his disciples that his going away will mean the coming of the Advocate, the Holy Spirit, who will guide them into all truth. The Counselor-Spirit will bring true judgment into the world. Everything the Spirit declares will have been received from Jesus, even as all which the Father has belongs to Jesus. The Spirit, then, reveals Jesus, who himself has made the Father known.

Prayers of the People

Presider: *Pour out your Spirit upon all flesh and inspire us, O Holy One, that we may proclaim your prophesy of justice and speak your message of compassion and love, saying: I will sing to God as long as I live; I will praise my God while I have my being.*

Litanist: Let your Spirit rest upon your Church like tongues of fire, O God, to inspire us to do your will.

I will sing to God as long as I live;

> *I will praise my God while I have my being.*

God looks at the earth and it trembles; God touches the mountains and they smoke: Let your glory go forth into all the world to guide the leaders of the nations and all in authority, that they may obey your Spirit and bless your people.

I will sing to God as long as I live;

> *I will praise my God while I have my being.*

O Holy One, how manifold are your works; in wisdom you have made them all. Let your glory go forth to comfort all who live under poverty, violence, or threat, that everyone who calls upon the name of the Lord shall be saved.

I will sing to God as long as I live;

> *I will praise my God while I have my being.*

You open your hand and fill all with good things, O gracious One: Bless this community, that our children may see visions and our elders dream dreams.

I will sing to God as long as I live;

> *I will praise my God while I have my being.*

Comfort with your life-giving Spirit those for whom we pray, especially ___.

We will rejoice in the Holy One, and praise God with words of thanksgiving, especially for ___.

The breath of the Spirit breathes new life into all creation: Raise into your resurrection life those who have died, especially ___.

I will sing to God as long as I live;

> *I will praise my God while I have my being.*

Presider: *Let the fire of your divine love descend upon us, O God, to inspire and heal, to renew and empower, that the earth may be filled with your glory, and all creation sing to you in praise, through Jesus Christ the Risen One, in the power of the Holy Spirit, one God, for ever and ever.* **Amen.**

Images in the Readings

Anthropologists describe fire as one of the markers of the human species. For tens of thousands of years, humans gathered around fire for light, warmth, protection, community, and better food. Many passages in the Bible liken God to fire. The Holy Spirit of God appeared on Sinai in flames of fire, which on Pentecost appeared on the forehead of each believer. Moses experienced God in fire; through fire the Israelites presented offerings to God; God led the people through the wilderness with a pillar of fire. Seraphim are fire-spirits, extensions of the divine. Yet fire is also a sign of divine judgment: the angel in Eden hides the tree of life from humanity with a sword of fire, and John the Baptist predicts that fire will consume the chaff. Fire both occasions human life and has the power to destroy. Think fire, think God.

The Hebrew noun *ruah* can be translated into English as "spirit," "breath," or "wind." Spirit is the most amorphous of these words. In Christian theology, the Spirit we experience is the Spirit of the risen Christ, a spirit of service, a spirit of love, a spirit of resurrection beyond death.

According to the New Testament, the resurrection of Christ has inaugurated the very end of this world. In Acts 2, Luke uses characteristic eschatological imagery to describe the last days and the Day of the Lord. Throughout much of Christian history, those believers who are suffering the most from the current situation and who see no way out are those for whom the anticipation of the Day of the Lord is most comforting. The immensely popular *Left Behind* novels are based on a fundamentalist view of the Rapture and the last days, but there is no way to know how fully this theology is accepted by the series' millions of readers.

Ideas for the Day

- Pentecost pushes the church forward. While the ability given to the apostles to preach in many languages serves, like Jesus' miracles, to confirm God's powerful presence, the gift of the Holy Spirit is more than confirmation. The Spirit propels Jesus' followers forward. The Book of Acts tells us that after Pentecost the disciples are sent out beyond Jerusalem to all of those hard to pronounce places like Cappadoica and Pamphylia. The word *apostle* comes from the Greek root "sent out." What if following the apostles means being similarly sent? Where is the Holy Spirit leading the church today?

- Love sings us new life and warmth when hatred drains us cold. Standing in the midst of the winter brought about by people's hatred, we must speak truth with fire. We must learn to be peace educators and warriors. As Ezekiel, empowered by the spirit, caused flesh to appear on the dry bones in the valley, we too must raise to life those who are deadened by hatred. Just as the Apostles, with tongues of fire, broke the barriers of language to deliver a message of an awesome God, we too must speak in new ways, so that those who hear us will understand. The fire of love, faith, and peace within us cannot be extinguished by anyone and will easily thaw the ice of those who live by the laws of hatred.

♦ The author of Luke and Acts saw history as divided into three periods: the time of Israel and the prophets (with John the Baptist as the last prophet); the time of Jesus' earthly ministry; and the time of the church, which began at Pentecost and in which we are living now. Pentecost is the first event of the church's history.

Making Connections

Pentecost is the celebration of when the Holy Spirit came upon the disciples in Jerusalem. While the Episcopal tradition is not generally thought of as charismatic—speaking in tongues or practicing spontaneous healings—we do rely heavily on the Holy Spirit. One might characterize us as "stealth charismatic." Observe the ordination services: in each rite, the bishop leads the congregation in a specific prayer, bidding the Holy Spirit to alight upon the new ordinand. Following the sung prayer, the community observes a moment of silent prayer, as we await the answering of the prayer we've just said.

We invoke the Holy Spirit in each Eucharist as well—asking the Holy Spirit to come upon the gifts of bread and wine and transform them and us for Christ's purpose in the world.

We tacitly rely on the Holy Spirit at nearly every point in our liturgical lives, yet most of us never really notice!

Engaging all Ages

This is a day of celebration for all ages. Draw the generations in as you mark the birth of the Church—use different languages as you read from the Acts of the Apostles, distribute flame colored streamers to the children to wave during the scripture reading, and design worship to be as interactive as possible. It is a day for us to remember that we are continually granted new life in the Spirit, and so it is also a day

for gratitude. Encourage everyone to speak a word of thanks in other languages they know. Make a joyful noise together!

Hymns for the Day

The Hymnal 1982
This day at thy creating word 52
We the Lord's people, heart and voice uniting 51
A mighty sound from heaven 230
Hail thee, festival day! 225
Hail this joyful day's return 223, 224
Spirit divine, attend our prayers 509
Breathe on me, Breath of God 508
Go forth for God; go to the world in peace 347
Put forth, O God, thy Spirit's might 521
Eternal Spirit of the living Christ 698
Like the murmur of the dove's song 513
Come, gracious Spirit, heavenly Dove 512
Holy Spirit, ever living 511
Spirit of mercy, truth, and love 229
To thee, O Comforter divine 514
All who believe and are baptized 298
Baptized in water 294
Descend, O Spirit, purging flame 297
Over the chaos of the empty waters 176, 177
Spirit of God, unleashed on earth 299

Wonder, Love, and Praise
Veni Sancte Spiritus 832
Filled with the Spirit's power, with one accord 741
Baptized in water 767

Lift Every Voice and Sing II
There's a sweet, sweet Spirit in this place 120
Let it breathe on me 116
Spirit of the living God 115
Baptized in water 121

Weekday Commemorations

Thursday, May 24
Jackson Kemper, First Missionary Bishop in the United States, 1870
Kemper, born in New York State on Christmas Eve 1789, served as the first missionary bishop. He was assigned to the wilderness in Missouri and Indiana, but he planted other churches throughout the Midwest, the South, and Southwest; he is known as "The Bishop of the Whole Northwest." He was ordained a priest in 1814 and a missionary bishop in 1835, after which he immediately ventured to the frontier. He founded a clergy-training school in St. Louis, but

Pentecost

it failed from lack of funds in 1845. Kemper founded Nashotah House in 1842 with the help of James Breck. He encouraged translation of services into languages of Native Americans.

Friday, May 25
Bede, the Venerable, Priest, and Monk of Jarrow, 735

Of his life's work, Bede wrote: "... I always took delight in learning, teaching, and writing." He was ordained a deacon at 19, a presbyter at 30. Bede, the greatest scholar of his time in the Western Church, also boasted of exemplary character as a model monk, a devout Christian, and a man of manners. The title "*Venerable*," added a century after his death, was unusual but deserved. Bede commented on the scriptures based on patristic interpretations, and his treatise on chronology was a standard. His most famous work, *The Ecclesiastical History of England*, remains the primary source for Anglo-Saxon culture of the period 597-731.

Saturday, May 26
Augustine, First Archbishop of Canterbury, 605

Pope Gregory the Great sent to the pagan Anglo-Saxons in 596 a mission, led by Augustine, the prior of Gregory's own monastery in Rome. They carried a silver cross and an iconic image of the Christ. About 601, King Ethelbert was converted and became the first Christian king in England; around the same time, Augustine was ordained bishop somewhere in France and named "Archbishop of the English Nation" (the chair of St. Augustine in Canterbury Cathedral dates from the thirteenth century). A remnant of Gregory and Augustine's correspondence from this time deals with "unity in diversity" in the young English Church, foundational to the modern ecumenical movement.

The First Sunday after Pentecost: Trinity Sunday

May 27, 2018

God is revealed to us in three persons existing in a mutual relationship of love. It is the total revelation of God: God the Father as Creator; God the Son as Redeemer; and God the Holy Spirit as Sanctifier and Comforter.

Color   White

Preface   Trinity Sunday

Collect

Almighty and everlasting God, you have given to us your servants grace, by the confession of a true faith, to acknowledge the glory of the eternal Trinity, and in the power of your divine Majesty to worship the Unity: Keep us steadfast in this faith and worship, and bring us at last to see you in your one and eternal glory, O Father; who with the Son and the Holy Spirit live and reign, one God, for ever and ever. Amen.

Readings and Psalm

Isaiah 6:1-8

Our first reading is Isaiah's vision of the Lord and his prophetic commission. The earthly temple becomes an icon for the temple in heaven. Isaiah is purged of his guilt and sin and responds to the Lord's call. The Church hears in the thrice-holy song of the seraphim an anticipation of its praise of God as Father, Son, and Holy Spirit.

Psalm 29 or

The majesty of God is described in the likeness of a mighty thunderstorm.

Canticle 12 or

A song of creation

Canticle 13

A song of praise

Romans 8:12-17

In this lesson, we hear that if we follow our lower nature, we are enslaved and destined to death, but when we are moved by God's Spirit, we become God's children and heirs with Christ. The Spirit makes this experience possible by prompting our lips to call upon God as Father with the same Aramaic word (*Abba*) that Jesus used. This new relationship means that we are no longer required to be led by baser instincts. Our heritage is life, while we must also learn to share in Christ's sufferings.

John 3:1-17

In our gospel story, Nicodemus, one of the Pharisees, comes during the night to talk with Jesus. Nicodemus is a figure used by the evangelist to represent a type of person who wants to believe but has difficulty understanding spiritual realities. Jesus tells him that no one can enter the kingdom of God unless he is born anew through water and the Spirit. The inner meaning of the passage partly turns on the fact that "born anew" can also be understood as "born from on high," and that the same Greek word means both wind and spirit. Jesus then tells Nicodemus of the Son of Man come down from heaven who will be lifted up, both on the cross to die for the world and to return to heaven in glory.

Prayers of the People

Presider: Holy Trinity, One God, the whole world is filled with your glory: Hear the prayers of your children as we say: Ascribe due honor to God's holy Name; worship the Most High in the beauty of holiness.

Litanist: Abba! Father! You have filled your Church with your Spirit and adopted us as your own children: Inspire us to speak of what we know and testify to what we have seen.

Ascribe due honor to God's holy Name;

worship the Most High in the beauty of holiness.

Your Son Jesus, the Son of Man, was lifted up to give the whole world eternal life: Send Christ's compassion and understanding to all who exercise roles of power and authority, that they may be led by the Spirit of God in the ways of justice and peace.

Ascribe due honor to God's holy Name;

> *worship the Most High in the beauty of holiness.*

Through the ever-present and energizing Spirit, your presence sustains the world and brings all life into being: Protect, comfort, and heal all who live with illness, threat, poverty, or oppression throughout the world, that they may enjoy the goodness of your blessing.

Ascribe due honor to God's holy Name;

> *worship the Most High in the beauty of holiness.*

Glorious Trinity, One God, enable our community to be born from above, born of water and Spirit, that we may manifest your loving compassion and peace toward all.

Ascribe due honor to God's holy Name;

> *worship the Most High in the beauty of holiness.*

Your children, O God, have not received a spirit of slavery to fall back into fear, but we have received a spirit of adoption, through which we ask for your aid:

Hear our prayers for ___.

Accept our praise and thanksgiving for ___.

Embrace with your eternal life those who have died, especially ___.

For you did not send the Son into the world to condemn the world, but in order that the world might be saved through him.

Ascribe due honor to God's holy Name;

> *worship the Most High in the beauty of holiness.*

Presider: *Let our prayers and praises fill your temple, O Father, as you send forth your Spirit into the world to empower your children to do the deeds of your Son and to be signs of your divine presence; we pray in the name of our Savior Jesus Christ who lives and reigns with you, O Father, in the unity of the Holy Spirit, one God, now and for ever.* **Amen.**

Images in the Readings

One of the primary Christian emphases during the twentieth century was a rediscovery of the wealth of imagery for God in the Bible and throughout Christian history, and today's readings exemplify this effort by surrounding the classic terminology for the Trinity with other language and imagery. Isaiah describes God as residing above the earth, as king with ultimate power, as wearing an endless robe, as leader of the armies. Paul gives us God as Abba, one to whom we, as children, can pray. It is interesting that the Church has not been able to use this shocking term, but instead has replaced it with the more commonplace religious title "Father." John's description of God as the one from whom we are born has been applied to baptism more than to God's very being.

There is coal on the altar because of the burnt offerings that signified confession of sin. In Isaiah's vision, the coal becomes a blessing, transforming the prophet's lips so he can speak the word of God. The Israelite temple was a near copy of the temples of neighboring Canaanite religions, but without a statue of the deity. The Jewish adaptation of a temple is like our language for God: we use what is religiously available, but then make alterations, as if to say, "Well, that is not what we mean: we mean instead endless divine mercy."

Being "born from above" is a contemporary translation of what earlier English bibles rendered as being "born again." Christian tradition interpreted this birth imagery as applying to baptism. Only recent centuries introduced another interpretation: a personal experience of conversion into active participation in the faith community. The fourth evangelist uses the metaphor of birth to lead into perhaps the world's most famous sentence about God's actions through Christ to love and save the world, John 3:16.

Ideas for the Day

♦ Andrei Rublev, a famous Russian iconographer, created an image of the Trinity depicting the three divine persons seated for a meal. As the viewer looks closer at the icon, she realizes that there is room for her at the table, an implicit invitation. Similarly, in Orthodox theology, the Trinity is described with the term *perichoresis*, dance. God's life is a dance, and we are invited to kick off our shoes and join in. Will we take our seat at the table? Will we dance?

♦ Take a look at the symbols for the Trinity that may exist in your sanctuary, such as *fleur de lis*, three interconnected circles, triangles, or clover. Consider the prayers found in the Book of Common Prayer that refer to the Trinity. The *Perichoresis*—the Greek term for the mysterious exchange of God (as the Divine) and the love between the Father, the Son, and the Holy Spirit are in all of these forms. What is the relationship in each, one to the other?

♦ We are children of God, born of the Holy Spirit. We are in a constant state of spiritual growth. As we grow in the Spirit, we become better able to handle the challenges of being a Christian. We need strength to follow the path of the Lord. That strength does not come from man. "The voice of the Lord is powerful and full of majesty." We must have faith in its power to speak across time. We are instructed not to live according to the flesh but to live by the Spirit. Living by the flesh stunts our spiritual growth. We must not put obstacles in the way of our spiritual growth, we must let the fire within us flourish so that the Spirit will bear witness with our spirit.

Making Connections

Ah, the dreaded stumbling block of preaching—the Trinity: hard to explain, and even harder to really care about. Outside of the twisty-turny phrases of the Athanasian Creed, there's a reason preachers avoid it. Yet, like the Holy Spirit last week, it undergirds our entire liturgical life. Our Collects all end by invoking the Father, Son, and Holy Spirit. The Eucharistic Prayers all address the three-in-one. The creeds we recite also reiterate the foundational quality of this unique aspect of our faith. There's no magic answer to explain the Trinity, but the time and energy expended by the writers of the creeds (even more can be found in the Historical Documents section of the prayer book) suggest that the Trinity was an important part of what was different about Christianity. God as manifest in relationship, and in a variety of ways to us, is a powerful idea, and one we shouldn't shy away from. It makes us who we are—singular and diverse.

Engaging all Ages

In today's gospel, Nicodemus shows us that at times we may have to take a risk to approach Jesus. Children and youth in particular know that their questions may not always be welcome. When we ponder the question, "Why did God send Jesus?" can we allow ourselves to also ask, "Why did God send me?" Posing questions opens the door to imagination and creativity and one that all ages can be asked to consider in the days ahead is, "What is my question for Jesus?" Consider making available a bulletin board or display area for worshippers to post their questions.

Hymns for the Day

The Hymnal 1982
Holy Father, great Creator 368
Holy God we praise thy Name 366
How wondrous great, how glorious bright 369
I bind unto myself today 370
O Trinity of blessed light 29, 30
Sing praise to our Creator 295
Holy, holy, holy! Lord God Almighty! 362
Let all mortal flesh keep silence 324
My God, how wonderful thou art 643
O day of radiant gladness 48
O God, we praise thee, and confess 364
Round the Lord in glory seated 367
The God of Abraham praise 401
Baptized in water 294
And now, O Father, mindful of the love 337
Lift high the cross 473
O love, how deep, how broad, how high 448, 449
The great Creator of the worlds 489
When Christ was lifted from the earth 603, 604

Wonder, Love, and Praise
God, beyond all human praises 745
God the sculptor of the mountains 746, 747
O threefold God of tender unity 743
O Trinity of blessed light 744
I, the Lord of sea and sky 812
Santo, santo, santo 785
Thuma mina/Send me, Lord 808
Every time I feel the spirit 751
Baptized in water 767

Lift Every Voice and Sing II
Oh Lord, how perfect is your name 57
Baptized in water 121
Children of the heavenly Father 213
Every time I feel the spirit 751, 114

Weekday Commemorations

Thursday, May 31
The Visitation of the Blessed Virgin Mary
This Feast commemorates the visit of the Mary to her cousin Elizabeth (Luke 1:39-56). The pregnant Elizabeth greeted Mary: "Blessed are you among women, and blessed is the fruit of your womb." Mary responded with a song of praise, a thanksgiving known as the *Magnificat:* "My soul proclaims the greatness of the Lord." The dramatic scene places the unborn John the Baptist, who was to prepare the way of the Lord to all Israel, in proximity with that Lord Himself. The gospel weaves in the story that when Elizabeth heard her cousin's greeting, John leapt for joy in his mother's womb.

Pentecost

May/June
The First Book of Common Prayer

1549, the second year of the reign of King Edward VI, the first Book of Common Prayer began its service to Anglicans. Through subsequent editions and revisions, the BCP continues to serve the Anglican Communion. The book was prepared by a commission, comprising learned priests and bishops, but Thomas Cranmer, Archbishop of Canterbury (1533-1556), stamped the book in style, substance, and format. Bishops and priests compiled the book from, among other sources, medieval Latin service books, Greek liturgies, ancient Gallican rites, and vernacular German forms. The English "Great Bible" (authorized by King Henry VII in 1539) supplied the Psalter, and the Litany came from the English form going back to 1544.

Friday, June 1
Justin, Martyr at Rome, c. 167

While strolling on the beach at Ephesus, Justin (born about 110 in Samaria) met a stranger. He told Justin about Jesus. Justin wrote that "a flame was kindled in my soul." He became a Christian. About 150, he moved to Rome, started a school of Christian philosophy, and became a debater and a writer. He wrote a dialogue with a Jew in the Platonic style, and he wrote two defenses ("apologies"): against the Greek charge of irrationality and against the Roman charge of disloyalty to the empire. His works offer insight into developing theologies and liturgies. His debates with a philosopher resulted in martyrdom when Justin would not renounce his faith.

Saturday, June 2
The Martyrs of Lyons, 177

Sanctus. Attalus. Maturus. Blandina. Pothinus. A deacon, a recent convert, a slave, a bishop—these are the some of the martyrs of Lyons, who refused to deny their faith. "I am a Christian," Blandina declared before the mob. Before persecution began in 177, Christians had lived under the guidance of Pothinus, Bishop of Lyons, in parts of Gaul, which had drawn them from Asia and Greece. After public torments, the Christians were subjected to public spectacle. Blandina, the last one living, was finally beaten, torn, burned with irons; having been wrapped in a net, she was thrown to and by a wild bull. Her endurance impressed the mob.

The Second Sunday after Pentecost: Proper 4

June 3, 2018

Jesus has ultimate authority, even over the commandments of the Torah.

Color   Green

Preface   Of the Lord's Day

Collect

O God, your never-failing providence sets in order all things both in heaven and earth: Put away from us, we entreat you, all hurtful things, and give us those things which are profitable for us; through Jesus Christ our Lord, who lives and reigns with you and the Holy Spirit, one God, for ever and ever. Amen.

Readings and Psalm

1 Samuel 3:1-10 (11-20) (SEMI-CONTINUOUS) or

In our Hebrew scripture reading, we hear how Samuel learns that the Lord is calling him to make him God's prophet. Three times the boy Samuel misunderstands and thinks that it is his mentor Eli summoning him during the night. Finally Eli realizes it must be the Lord, and tells Samuel to be ready. In the morning, Samuel informs Eli of the punishment that is about to come upon his house. As Samuel grows, all Israel recognizes that he has been chosen by God to prophesy to the people.

Deuteronomy 5:12-15 (GOSPEL-RELATED)

In our Hebrew scripture lesson, we hear the commandment to keep the Sabbath day holy. Six days are sufficient for labor, but the Sabbath is to be kept free from work and set aside for the Lord, a remembrance of the former captivity in Egypt and of God's deliverance.

Psalm 139:1-5, 12-17 or

With marvelous wisdom, God alone perceives the heights and depths of life.

Psalm 81:1-10

A psalm of festival praise and an exhortation to worship the Lord alone.

2 Corinthians 4:5-12

In this lesson, Paul teaches that although human weakness is all too apparent in those who preach the gospel, what is proclaimed is the glorious light of the revelation of God in Jesus Christ. The same divine light which first shone at the creation has now been manifested in Jesus. Human frailty becomes the means for God to prove that God is the source of the power of the gospel. Paul's sufferings and mortality are a way of sharing in the weakness and death in which Jesus himself participated. Yet through perseverance, they point beyond themselves to the source of life greater than death.

Mark 2:23—3:6

In the gospel, Jesus proclaims in word and sign that the Son of Man is sovereign over the Sabbath law. The interpretation of the Torah prevailing during this period regarded both the plucking of grain and healing to be forms of work, and therefore activities forbidden on the Sabbath day. Jesus, however, teaches that human need and the doing of good must always take precedence over rigid interpretation, for "the Sabbath was made for humankind, and not humankind for the Sabbath." Many Jewish teachers of the time agreed that the Sabbath must always be seen as a blessing for human life and not as an arbitrary requirement. Jesus goes beyond this in announcing that he possesses an even greater authority for human behavior than the law.

Pentecost

Prayers of the People

Presider: In freedom you have created us and called us to work and rest in your generous love, hear our prayers on behalf of all your creation, and empower us to share in your healing and reconciling work, as we pray: You call to us and we answer. Speak, Lord, for your servant is listening.

Litanist: Search out and purify your Church, O Holy One, that we may proclaim Jesus Christ as Lord not only in our words but in our deeds, living with freedom and courage to do good and to save lives at all times and in all places.

You call to us and we answer.

Speak, Lord, for your servant is listening.

Let your dominion guide all rulers and authorities that they may know that extraordinary power belongs to God and does not come from us, and that they may exercise their own power in wisdom, compassion, and love.

You call to us and we answer.

Speak, Lord, for your servant is listening.

May your compassionate power be present to heal all who suffer throughout the world, that though afflicted, they may not be crushed; if perplexed, not driven to despair; when persecuted, not forsaken; and when struck down, not destroyed, that the risen life of Jesus may be made visible in their lives.

You call to us and we answer.

Speak, Lord, for your servant is listening.

Let your light shine in our community and in our hearts: the light of the knowledge of the glory of God in the face of Jesus Christ, and the light present in every person we encounter.

You call to us and we answer.

Speak, Lord, for your servant is listening.

We bring to your healing compassion all for whom we pray on this our Christian Sabbath day, especially ___.

We raise voices of thanksgiving for all of your grace toward us and for our abundant blessings, especially for ___.

We return to your enfolding heart those who have died, especially ___.

You call to us and we answer.

Speak, Lord, for your servant is listening.

Presider: Holy and Wondrous God, by your never-failing providence you set in order all creation: Put away from us all hurtful things and give us those things which are profitable for us, through Jesus Christ our Savior, who lives and reigns with you and the Holy Spirit, one God, for ever and ever. **Amen.**

Images in the Readings

By the year 100, more Christians were Gentiles than Jews. Thus it was not long in Christian practice that the Jewish Sabbath no longer functioned religiously. To meet one another in the risen Christ, Christians met on the first day of the week, not the seventh, and both then and now for many people, the first day was not a vacation day. The Emperor Constantine decreed that some occupations, mostly those dealing with trade, keep Sunday as a day of rest. John Calvin sought to reestablish regulations about Sabbath as applicable to Sunday, and the strong Calvinist influence in the eastern colonies of what became the United States led to an American sense of Sunday as Sabbath. Still today, there are places where one cannot purchase alcohol on Sunday. Many contemporary Christians agree that the pace of our society is unhealthy and that a Sabbath is a good idea. Yet Christians must always remain aware of those whose occupation does not allow for a day off each week, as well as the unemployed for whom "a day of rest" is not what they desire. For clergy and church musicians, of course, Sunday is never a day of rest.

In the miracle story, the human hand can function as a symbol of the self. The Old Testament speaks of God having a mighty hand, and in some art, a hand is used to depict God the Father.

At Holy Communion, we receive the bread in our hand. Early theologians taught communion recipients to make a "throne" of their hands for the bread, the left hand below the right hand, as if the weaker hand supports the stronger. It was not until the Middle Ages that the bread was put into the communicants' mouths, in order to insure that they did not take the bread home with them to plant it in the garden for good luck or set it up in their home to revere. This problem is not ours. Thus we welcome the reception of bread into the hand, a sign of the self receiving Christ.

Ideas for the Day

◆ Some smart phones and watches now remind us to breathe, to take a break from life's constant din. Jesus' take on Sabbath got him into trouble, but

Jesus' didn't disregard Jewish teaching. Jesus valued the Sabbath so much that he invited others to consider: "why do you practice Sabbath?" Do we meditate just because our smart watches told us to? Can practicing Sabbath help us unplug from the busy-ness not simply to rest? Can Sabbath help us ask deeper "why" questions? Take a break and consider, "Why do I do the work I do? Why do I practice faith?"

- Let us remember where we have come from and how far the Lord has brought us. Time to reflect on this reality is sacred. When our mind is quiet we can hear the Lord calling us to ministry. As Samuel heard the Lord's call, we too must be ready to hear what the Lord is saying. The Lord commands us to recall the time of our physical bondage in order that we not take our current freedom for granted. Too often, we don't create the sacred space and time to reflect on our journey. Lord, teach us to stop, slow down the pace of our lives, so that we might hear your call to us.

- The twenty-nine Collects for the Sundays that follow Pentecost fall broadly under four themes. Each theme is a statement of a basic Christian truth, which applies to us at any age: We are God's children. We have a personal relationship with Jesus Christ and a ministry of love to other people. God calls us to be open to the reality of the presence and action of the Holy Spirit. We believe in the Church as the Body of Christ in the world and in the Church's mission

Making Connections

A smart professor I had in seminary was known for being the spikiest of all High Church clergy—the highest of the very high. But when it came time for him to instruct us on how to celebrate the Eucharist, he refused to let us become entrapped in layers of tradition. "You shouldn't do anything unless you find it meaningful, unless it deepens your own connection to Christ," he told us. No solemn bow, no swoop of the hands, no chanted note was useful unless it pointed us to the greater reality of the Divine. As Episcopalians, we love our liturgy—and with good reason. But occasionally, we can become entranced by the liturgy itself, and all the trappings thereof. The liturgy's true gift is not its beauty, its age, or its commonality. Its true gift is the liturgy's ability to connect us to God in Christ, and remind us of the pattern our lives should take.

Engaging all Ages

God calls a child—imagine! In the story of Samuel woken by God's call and then seeking guidance from a wise adult in his life, we receive a model for welcoming the young and inexperienced in our community. And yet it is a meaningful and necessary exercise for all ages. How do we experience God's call? Who helps me discern what God is asking of me? These are intimate questions. As we consider how personally God approaches each of us, we do well to identify the mentors, the wise elders who will guide us as we ask and then listen.

Hymns for the Day

The Hymnal 1982
Blessed Jesus, at thy word 440
Christ, whose glory fills the skies 6, 7
Eternal light, shine in my heart 465, 466
Lord of all being, throned afar 419
Spread, O spread, thou mighty word 530
Thy strong word did cleave the darkness 381
God of mercy, God of grace 538
I call on thee, Lord Jesus Christ 634
There is a balm in Gilead 676
Thine arm, O Lord, in days of old 567
God has spoken to his people 536 (SEMI-CONTINUOUS)
Lord, thou hast searched me and dost know 702 (SC)
O Jesus, I have promised 655 (SC)
O day of radiant gladness 48 (GOSPEL-RELATED)

Wonder, Love, and Praise
No saint on earth lives life to self alone 776
Heal me, hands of Jesus 773
O Christ, the healer, we have come 772
I, the Lord of sea and sky 812 (SC)

Lift Every Voice and Sing II
Nobody knows the trouble I've seen 175
There is a balm in Gilead 203
Lord, You have searched my heart 16 (SC)
Jesus, we want to meet 81 (GR)
This is the day that the Lord hath made 219 (GR)

Weekday Commemorations

Tuesday, June 5
Boniface, Archbishop of Mainz, Missionary to Germany, and Martyr, 754
Boniface was born Winfred in Devonshire, England, about 675, and decided to be a missionary after being professed a monk then ordained to the presbyterate.

Pentecost

He traveled to Frisia (Netherlands) but met little success; before traveling next in 719, he first went to Rome for approval from Pope Gregory, who named him Boniface. Thereafter, Boniface dedicated his life to reforming, planting, and organizing churches, monasteries, and dioceses in Hesse, Thuringia, and Bavaria. In 722, Gregory ordained Boniface a bishop and, in 732, an archbishop; he was given a fixed see at Mainz in 743. After resigning his see, Boniface and his fellow missionaries were murdered by pagans.

Saturday, June 9
Columba, Abbot of Iona, 597

Almost immediately upon being ordained a monk, Columba, born in Ireland in 521, set forth on his mission; before being ordained a presbyter in 551, he had founded monasteries at Derry and Durrow. Twelve years later, Columba and a dozen companions journeyed to northern Britain to evangelize among the Picts. Columba was encouraged to preach, convert, and baptize; he was also given the island of Iona, where, according to legend, his small boat had washed ashore. There, he founded the famous monastery. From Iona, for 30 years, Columba founded other monasteries and traveled through the Highlands, thereby establishing Iona as a link between Irish and Pictish Christians. He died while copying the Psalter.

The Third Sunday after Pentecost: Proper 5

June 10, 2018

Doing the will of God.

Color   Green

Preface   Of the Lord's Day

Collect

O God, from whom all good proceeds: Grant that by your inspiration we may think those things that are right, and by your merciful guiding may do them; through Jesus Christ our Lord, who lives and reigns with you and the Holy Spirit, one God, for ever and ever. Amen.

Readings and Psalm

1 Samuel 8:4-11 (12-15) 16-20; (11:14-15) (SEMI-CONTINUOUS) or

In our Hebrew Bible lesson, the elders of Israel insist that the aging prophet Samuel anoint for them a king such as governed the surrounding nations. The biblical account refers to the military threat of the Philistines as the primary motivation for this request, but other pressures were likely at work as the tribal structure of Israelite society underwent change. God tells Samuel to consent to the request of the elders, but to make clear the cost involved in submission to the arbitrary power of a human monarch.

Genesis 3:8-15 (GOSPEL-RELATED)

In our Hebrew scripture lesson, we hear of the results of Adam and Eve's act of disobedience in the Garden of Eden. Adam and Eve now experience alienation from God and hide from the divine presence. The text also offers explanation for the estrangement between humankind and other creatures of the earth, symbolized by the serpent. Because of their disobedience and coming to the knowledge of good and evil, the man and woman now live in disharmony with the world and one another.

Psalm 138 or

A hymn of praise and thanksgiving to the Lord on high, who has saved God's servant and cares for the lowly.

Psalm 130

A plea for mercy offered in patient hope to the faithful Lord.

2 Corinthians 4:13—5:1

In this passage, Paul speaks of the eternal and glorious hope that belongs to Jesus' disciples even in the midst of trouble and mortality. The apostle has just told of the difficulties that beset his ministry. These, however, have not prevented his preaching of the gospel. Now he quotes scripture to express his conviction that the belief of Christians can and must be proclaimed in all circumstances. Although our physical being is gradually decaying, we are inwardly being renewed in accordance with what is unseen and eternal.

Mark 3:20-35

In our gospel lesson, Jesus is accused of being possessed by the prince of demons. He responds by describing his battle against Satan and indicating that true relationship with him is based in the doing of God's will. The passage suggests a certain separation between Jesus and his own relatives due to the intensity of his ministry. To those who charge him with doing good by the power of evil, Jesus answers with figures of speech—one implies that Jesus himself is the man who must first bind Satan before destroying his power. A warning is given not to blaspheme against the Holy Spirit—by which perhaps is meant calling good evil.

Prayers of the People

Presider: *Holy God, ruler of heaven and earth, you have raised us into your eternal life, and you have brought into Christ's family all who do your will: When we call you, answer us and increase our strength within us; hear us as we pray for the needs of your creation, saying: Make good your purpose for us; O God, your love endures for ever.*

Litanist: You have filled the Church with your Spirit, O Holy One, and you renew us day by day: Empower our mission of witness and service, so that your grace, as it extends to more and more people, may increase thanksgiving, to the glory of God.

Make good your purpose for us;

O God, your love endures for ever.

You are on high, yet care for the lowly, and perceive the haughty from afar: Reveal your glory to all who exercise power and authority and halt their deeds of pride, greed, and violence, so that all the rulers of the earth will praise you.

Make good your purpose for us;

O God, your love endures for ever.

Do not abandon the works of your hands: Look upon those who walk in the midst of trouble to keep them safe.

Make good your purpose for us;

O God, your love endures for ever.

Visit this community with your compassion and your grace, that we may glorify your Name and your word above all things.

Make good your purpose for us;

O God, your love endures for ever.

We do not lose heart as we pray for those who need our intercession, especially ___.

We will give thanks to you, O God, with our whole heart, especially for ___.

We know that the one who raised the Lord Jesus will raise us also with Jesus, and will bring us into his presence. Hear our prayers for those who have died, especially ___.

Make good your purpose for us;

O God, your love endures for ever.

Presider: We believe and so we pray, O God, that your glory may enter our lives and infuse the world with resurrection power, through Jesus Christ our Savior, who with you, and the Holy Spirit, lives and reigns, One God, for ever and ever. **Amen.**

Images in the Readings

Painted depictions of Satan, like those of angels, are not profound enough to convey what these biblical figures embody. Often depictions of Satan are racist, by having darker skin than the people looking at the image. In much medieval art, the snake has the same face as the woman. Contemporary pictures of the devil often merely evoke Halloween. Ancient Israel knew of no devil. By the time of Jesus, Jews had adopted into popular piety the figure of Satan from the dualism of Zoroastrianism. For some Christians, the devil is nearly an alternate deity. Yet Christian doctrine proclaims that there is only one ultimate power, not two, and that the power of evil, although still fighting against good, has already been conquered in the death and resurrection of Christ.

About the woman and the man of Genesis 3 there has been much nonsense written, from which especially countless women have suffered. However, we are all the man and the woman, eating food that brings us not life but death. This story is a profound legend filled with truths about the human condition, but Christians need not teach it as though it is factual, thus disregarding what centuries of science have taught us about how God actually formed and shaped the earth and its many creatures.

Our life here is only a tent. An evil wind can blow it down, a snake slither in during the night. Together we take shelter in the building that is Christ.

Ideas for the Day

♦ "You have to tie up the strong man," Jesus tells the disciples. His image asks us to identify his social location, and our own. The term "looting" has become problematic when the news media covers a natural disaster or a protest. The word is controversial because it carries a bias. "Looting" usually describes the activity of the poor and people of color. In today's gospel, Jesus gives advice on looting. What does this say about the community he ministered among? What does our reaction say about our own economic status?

♦ In Old Testament times, anointing involved smearing a person's head with scented oil as a way of designating the person for a particular office. We are "anointed" or "sealed" with oil (Chrism) at baptism and marked as Christ's own forever (BCP, 308).

♦ We live in a day and age where it is easy to become estranged from our family. Society is often pushing us to pursue our personal interests and goals above those that support family relationships. We use technology to disconnect from those around us. Jesus shows us that we must make brothers, sisters and mothers of everyone we come in contact through work in ministry. Love knows no limit. We don't have to choose loving others over loving our family. We can love others and our family. We do this by staying true to the teachings of Christ at home and outside the home, building positive relationships with everyone we come in contact with.

Making Connections

There's a recurring theme in these readings about conformity. In 1 Samuel, the Israelites want to be just like the other nations, and have their own king. In Mark, Jesus' mother and siblings wish he would come home and start acting like other sons. In neither case does this turn out to be where God is leading. Conformity can be tempting because it takes away the stress of having to discern God's will. You can rely on what someone else has already discerned, and your work is done! However, conforming too quickly also denies God's unique work in your own life. Had God wanted you to be a clone of the person down the street, surely that is something God could have arranged. But God created us all in diversity, whether we be people, cultures, or churches.

Engaging all Ages

In today's gospel, Jesus calls his followers brother and sister. In a large and diverse congregation or one where everyone knows everyone it is important for us to continually look around and say, "You are my sister. You are my brother." Are the children and youth accepted as full members? Are the elders invited to share the benefit of their experience? Consider offering today's Prayers of the People using generations of voices. The best kind of family is where the generations form a close, loving bond, where individual families, in their own unique configuration, feel part of the larger family.

Hymns for the Day

The Hymnal 1982
Before the Lord's eternal throne 391 (SC)
God the Omnipotent! King, who ordainest 569 (SC)
How wondrous and great thy works, God of praise! 532, 533 (SC)

From deepest woe I cry to thee 151 (GR)
Out of the depths I call 666 (GR)
We walk by faith, and not by sight 209
Creating God, your fingers trace 394, 395
God of grace and God of glory 594, 595
Jerusalem, my happy home 620
Jesus lives! thy terrors now 194, 195
Light's abode, celestial Salem 621, 622
O what their joy and their glory must be 623

Wonder, Love, and Praise
Hallelujah! We sing your praises!/
Haleluya! Pelo tso rona 784

Lift Every Voice and Sing II
Sing the wondrous love of Jesus 20
We walk by faith, and not by sight 206
When peace like a river attendeth my soul 188

Weekday Commemorations

Monday, June 11
Saint Barnabas the Apostle
Barnabas, born Joseph, was called an apostle, along with the Twelve, for his missions. Like Paul, Barnabas was a Jew of the Dispersion; Barnabas presented Paul to the apostles with the story of Saul's conversion to Paul. Later, Barnabas, having settled in Antioch, sent for Paul to help lead the Christian Church there. The two men, sent by the disciples, carried food and relief to the Church during a famine in Jerusalem. Afterwards, the Church sent out the pair, starting from Cyprus. Their friendship split over Mark, who had left the mission to return to Jerusalem. Barnabas and Mark traveled to Cyprus, where tradition honors Barnabas as the founder of the Church and places his martyrdom.

Thursday, June 14
Basil the Great, Bishop of Caesarea, 379
Born a Christian about 329 in Caesarea, Basil knew wealth and education. He was baptized in 357, then ordained a deacon. His sister Macrina's faith fired his own to study the anchorites in Egypt and beyond. Following his sister, who had founded the first monastic order for women at Annesi, he founded the first monastery for men at Ibora. The *Rules* he wrote with Gregory Nazianzus lay the foundation for all Eastern monastics. Basil was ordained presbyter in 364. The road to Bishop of Caesarea was not so smooth, but he persevered in his effort to restore discipline to the clergy, defend the Nicene faith, adore God, and care for the poor.

Pentecost

Friday, June 15
Evelyn Underhill
Born December 6, 1875, Underhill was a fine writer whose essays and books appealed to many also drawn by her definitive mysticism. She grew up in London and was confirmed in the Church of England. In the 1890s, she began journeying to Europe, especially Italy, enticed by art and religion. Despite 15 years' wrestling with profound interest in the Roman Catholic Church, she stayed true to her Anglican roots. Although she had little formal religious education, she was curious about religion and spirituality from childhood, when she met Hubert Moore. They married in 1907 and are buried together in London. She believed mysticism belongs not just to a few saints but to any nurturing soul.

Saturday, June 16
Joseph Butler, Bishop of Durham, 1752
Butler, born in 1692, became an Anglican despite having been raised a Presbyterian and educated at Dissenting schools. He was ordained in 1718. He rose to be called "the greatest of all the thinkers of the English Church." His sermons on human nature, preached during his eight years at Rolls Chapel, first brought him to prominence. After a series of rectorships, he was appointed Bishop of Bristol. He declined the primacy of Canterbury and accepted the bishopric of Durham (1750). His fame resides in his profound support for orthodox Christianity against the Deist thinking in England; in 1736, he published *The Analogy of Religion, Natural and Revealed, to the Constitution and Course of Nature.*

The Fourth Sunday after Pentecost: Proper 6

June 17, 2018

The kingdom of God arrives through God's grace, not by human striving for power.

Color   Green

Preface   Of the Lord's Day

Collect

Keep, O Lord, your household the Church in your steadfast faith and love, that through your grace we may proclaim your truth with boldness, and minister your justice with compassion; for the sake of our Savior Jesus Christ, who lives and reigns with you and the Holy Spirit, one God, now and for ever. Amen.

Readings and Psalm

1 Samuel 15:34—16:13 (SEMI-CONTINUOUS) or

In our Hebrew Bible story, the Lord sends Samuel to anoint David to be the new king over Israel. God has rejected Saul as king, but he remains in power and Samuel must go secretly on his mission. As so often happens in the Bible, one who seems least likely in the eyes of others is chosen by God to carry out the divine will.

Ezekiel 17:22-24 (GOSPEL-RELATED)

In our Hebrew Bible lesson, we hear how from a mere sprig God will bring forth on the mountain height of Israel a noble cedar that will provide protection for all kinds of birds. The analogy describes how God uses the low and insignificant to high and great ends.

Psalm 20 or

A prayer and petition for victory in time of conflict.

Psalm 92:1-4, 11-14

A psalm of thanksgiving and praise. Those who choose righteousness are like a great tree planted in the house of the Lord.

2 Corinthians 5:6-10 (11-13) 14-17

In this lesson Paul speaks of his confident hope and his longing to experience the transformed body of heavenly existence. It will be like having a new house or set of clothes replaced or—better—be put on over this tent of a body. In any case, we will not be left just as souls without form, but will have some manner of personal existence. God's Spirit is already our guarantee, born from the conviction that Christ has died and risen. We must live, therefore, no longer for ourselves alone, but for Christ, for we will be judged for our use of this earthly life.

Mark 4:26-34

In our gospel, Jesus tells the parables of the seed growing secretly and of the mustard seed in order to suggest what the kingdom of God is like. God's activity is often unseen and mysterious, but it will produce its fruit and bring about the time for harvest. To human eyes, the beginning of the kingdom seems insignificant, but suddenly it will break forth. The great bush which the mustard seed becomes is a symbol for the kingdom of God's protection. The evangelist closes the passage with his understanding that only faithful disciples can perceive the significance of Jesus' parables.

Prayers of the People

Presider: Our Holy God, you have planted the Kingdom of God among us like seeds scattered on the ground: Let your creation flourish and grow into the fullness of your abundant life, as we pray: If anyone is in Christ, there is a new creation.

Litanist: Gracious One, the love of Christ urges us on: Lead your Church to walk by faith and live for him who died and was raised for us.

If anyone is in Christ,

there is a new creation.

Eternal One, we will shout for joy at your victory and triumph in your Name: Guide the nations of the earth to put not their trust in chariots and horses, in tanks and in planes, but rather to call upon the Name of God and to listen to your direction.

If anyone is in Christ,

there is a new creation.

Mysterious One, let your quiet strength work in our sleep and in our rising, night and day, to nurture your purpose for all people, that new life may sprout and grow, we do not know how, and produce a harvest of abundant life for all your creatures.

If anyone is in Christ,

there is a new creation.

Loving One, you have planted your Spirit into all humanity: Let us regard no one from a human point of view any longer, but open our eyes to see Christ's presence in all persons.

If anyone is in Christ,

there is a new creation.

Compassionate One, you plant hope in our hearts and you bring newness to life.

Hear our prayers for those for whom we intercede, especially ___.

Hear our grateful thanks for the abundance of your grace, especially for ___.

With Paul, we, also, are convinced that one has died for all, therefore all have died and will be raised to newness of life. Raise into your eternal life those who have died, especially ___. If anyone is in Christ,

there is a new creation.

Presider: *We are always confident, O Gracious One, whether we are at home or away, for our life is hidden in you: Nourish our growth in you that we may become mature and fruitful disciples producing an abundant harvest for the sake of your Name, through Jesus Christ our Savior, who with you and the Holy Spirit, live and reign, one God, forever and ever.* **Amen.**

Images in the Readings

Oftentimes people have used the metaphor of the mustard seed growing into a massive tree to illustrate the truism that small things can grow into big things. However, mustard seeds do not develop into massive trees, but rather into scraggly annual plants. Mark is

using the image ironically: the cross is, ironically, a tree of life. It is as if Mark is saying, "You want a cosmic tree that holds up the sky and shelters all the birds of the air? It is hidden in the cross."

The tree of life, an archetypal image common in past and present, was employed by ancient Near Eastern monarchies as a depiction of the power of the monarch, and thus of the nation-state. The detail that it houses "all the birds of the air" is commonplace in religious art through the centuries. In the fourth century of the Roman Empire, Queen Helena led an archeological dig of Jerusalem and claimed to have excavated Christ's cross from the hill of Calvary. The story goes that she placed the cross onto the corpse of a dead man, who then came back to life, and thus Helena knew that this wood was Christ's cross, and so was the tree of life. Later storytellers wove an elaborate tale that traced the wood of the cross back to a sprig taken by Seth from the tree of life in Eden and planted in Adam's mouth in the grave. Many medieval churches display an image of the cross as a tree of life, and often birds are in its branches, or are resting on the side arms of the cross of Christ.

Ideas for the Day

+ Both Jesus' parable about the mustard seed and the story of Samuel anointing David invite us to pause and reflect on our initial impressions. We live in a busy world. The tiny mustard seed could be easily overlooked. Don't miss unexpected potential. Our gender biases can also prove problematic for clear sight. God instructs Samuel to pass over David's tall masculine brother in favor of David who is described using more culturally feminine adjectives (in Hebrew). Left to our own prejudices, we might reject the very building blocks of God's reign.

+ The traditions associated with Rogation Days emphasize God's presence in the mystery of creation and growth in the natural world. The proper for Rogation Days includes the text from today's gospel (BCP, 930).

+ God plants the Kingdom in us and in creation. Sometimes growth comes so slowly that it is imperceptible. We may become discouraged, but God's kingdom is happening nevertheless.

+ We must be comfortable understanding that there are certain things in life we simply can't know. Science is a wonderful tool in helping us understand the world around us, however, it is only half of the story. Understanding the science of how a plant grows does not tell us about the Spirit within it. The seed does not belittle itself for being small, it simply grows without thought. The natural impetus to grow is the Spirit of the Lord, living inside every creature. Science can often get in the way of our spiritual growth because it asks to explain in logic things that we simply know through experience. Let us not seek to explain the fire within us, let us simply live fully within it.

Making Connections

I feel fairly confident in asserting that Jesus' disciples must have gotten irritated at his parables. "Another one? Again?! Why can't he just *tell* us something like a normal person?!" I picture them grumbling to themselves like teenagers. Stories, however, are how humans construct meaning out of our experience. I understand what happens to me because I can relate it in a story. As someone else hears my story, they not only learn of my experience, they can also discover meaning I did not consciously impart. Stories are how humanity makes and discovers meaning—and so they are far richer and denser than any one telling. Our liturgical year, too, constructs a certain type of story. We wait for Christ's arrival, celebrate his birth, observe his ministry, mourn his death, then celebrate his resurrection. And around again. As we view our place in history from our place in the cycle, the story of God informs how we understand the story of our lives, too.

Engaging all Ages

Mustard seeds are some of the tiniest things imaginable. Invite worshippers to hold a seed during the reading of the gospel and marvel at how it holds the potential to grow into a magnificent tree sheltering birds. And marvel also that the Kingdom of God holds just such potential, growing and growing while offering shelter for those who live God's way. A worthy challenge is for us to consider what we are offering to the growth of the tree, the Kingdom. What can we each do, in the days ahead, to share the love and good news of God's Kingdom?

Hymns for the Day

The Hymnal 1982
Lord, whose love through humble service 610
God moves in a mysterious way 677 (SC)
Seek the Lord while he wills to be found S217ff (SC)
How wondrous and great thy works, God of praise! 532, 533 (GR)
All glory be to God on high 421
All who believe and are baptized 298
Come away to the skies 213

Lord Christ, when first thou cam'st to earth 598
Love divine, all loves excelling 657
Rejoice, the Lord is King! 481
The Church's one foundation 525
We know that Christ is raised and dies no more 296
We walk by faith, and not by sight 209
Almighty God, your word is cast 588, 589
Come, ye thankful people, come 290 (2-4)
Father, we thank thee who hast planted 302, 303
For the fruit of all creation 424

Wonder, Love, and Praise
Camina, pueblo del Dios/
Walk on, O people of God 739
When from bondage we are summoned 753, 754
God the sculptor of the mountains 746, 747

Lift Every Voice and Sing II
We walk by faith, and not by sight 206
Sing the wondrous love of Jesus 20

Weekday Commemorations

Monday, June 18
Bernard Mizeki, Catechist and Martyr in Rhodesia, 1896
Born about 1861 in Portuguese East Africa (Mozambique), Mizeki escaped to Capetown, South Africa. There, he was harbored by Anglican missionaries and baptized (1886). Five years later, Mizeki voluntarily joined a pioneer mission in Mashonaland as catechist. In 1896, native peoples arose against Europeans and their African allies. Mizeki was targeted, and despite being warned to flee, he would not desert his converts. He was stabbed to death. His body has never been found, nor his burial site. A shrine at the site of his martyrdom draws pilgrims. The Anglican Churches of Central and South Africa honor Mizeki as their main martyr and witness.

Friday, June 22
Alban, First Martyr of Britain, c. 304
According to tradition, Alban is the first British martyr. He was a Roman soldier, stationed in a city now called St. Alban's, 20 miles northeast of London. He sheltered a Christian priest fleeing from persecution and then dressed as the priest to be tortured and martyred in his place. The site became a shrine soon after the incident: a monastery was established there in 793 and was ranked in the Middle Ages as the premier abbey in England. The Cathedral of St. Alban's, begun in 1077, stands on the site of Alban's martyrdom; it is the second longest church in England. Alban's remains lie in a chapel east of the choir.

Pentecost

The Fifth Sunday after Pentecost: Proper 7

June 24, 2018

God's power to still the storms of nature and evil are revealed in Jesus.

Color   Green

Preface   Of the Lord's Day

Collect

O Lord, make us have perpetual love and reverence for your holy Name, for you never fail to help and govern those whom you have set upon the sure foundation of your loving-kindness; through Jesus Christ our Lord, who lives and reigns with you and the Holy Spirit, one God, for ever and ever. Amen.

Readings and Psalm

1 Samuel 17:(1a, 4-11, 19-23) 32-49
(SEMI-CONTINUOUS) or

In our Hebrew scripture lesson, the young man David, already secretly anointed by Samuel as king over Israel, arrives in Saul's encampment. Here the Israelites have engaged the Philistines. Goliath, a large and impressively arrayed Philistine warrior, has challenged the Israelites to produce anyone equal to him in battle, and David, hearing the challenge, volunteers. He goes to battle without the customary armor and fells Goliath with a single stone from his slingshot.

1 Samuel 17:57—18:5, 10-16 or

In this Hebrew scripture story, we find David in Saul's court following his defeat of the Philistine warrior Goliath. We are told of Saul's son Jonathan's love for David, and of the covenant by which they bound themselves to one another. Saul quickly becomes jealous of the allegiance David commands among his family, court, and the nation at large. The Spirit of God has departed from Saul and is bringing success to David.

Job 38:1-11 *(GOSPEL-RELATED)*

In our first reading, God appears to Job out of the whirlwind and demands to know whether he is wise enough to question the Creator of the heavens and earth. The challenge seems almost brutal. Job, out of all his distress, had complained about the unfairness of life. He is now forced to recognize how little he understands the ways of the world and of God.

Psalm 9:9-20 or

A petition for personal deliverance to God who will not forget the poor, the needy, or the oppressed.

Psalm 133 or

The psalm celebrates the blessing of a harmonious people.

Psalm 107:1-3, 23-32

Thanksgiving is offered to the Lord, who saves from storms and other dangers those who call upon God.

2 Corinthians 6:1-13

In our epistle reading, Paul continues to commend himself, together with the ministry of his coworkers, to the troubled Corinthian church. Paul and his colleagues have proven the value of their ministry through multiple and profound sufferings, and also in the tenor and quality of their labors. They do all of this in service to Christ and for the benefit of those for whom they strive, and at great personal cost. They have opened their hearts in every way to the Corinthians, and now Paul asks that their love and care find reciprocation.

Mark 4:35-51

The gospel is the story of Jesus' stilling of the storm. The narrative was used in the life of the early church to stress the importance of faith in difficult times. Still more significantly, it served to emphasize the majesty of the Lord Jesus, whose power could control destructive natural forces and, symbolically, the cosmic forces of evil. Audiences of that time would recognize the parallel between Jesus' sovereignty over the storm and the power of God shown when he, according to myth, conquered the watery chaos and formed the world.

Prayers of the People

Presider: *Your powerful presence comforts us, O God, for when we are threatened by chaos and storm, Christ is our peace: Hear us as we call to you, and answer our prayers as we say: You are a refuge in time of trouble; you never forsake those who seek you, O God.*

Litanist: Loving God, your Church works together with Christ to accept your grace for all people: Fill us with purity, knowledge, patience, kindness, holiness of spirit, genuine love, truthful speech, and your Godly power, that there may be no fault found with our ministry.

You are a refuge in time of trouble;

> *you never forsake those who seek you, O God.*

Almighty One, you are known by your acts of justice: Let your goodness be sustained by all who hold authority in the nations, and let not the ungodly have the upper hand; for the needy shall not always be forgotten, and the hope of the poor shall not perish forever.

You are a refuge in time of trouble;

> *you never forsake those who seek you, O God.*

Your peace dwells continually at the center of our being, O Gracious One: Give peace to all whose lives are swamped by waves and winds, and defend those who face giant threats, that they may know the comfort of your presence and face their troubles with David's courage.

You are a refuge in time of trouble;

> *you never forsake those who seek you, O God.*

Help us to commend ourselves in this community with hearts wide open to our neighbors for your Name's sake.

You are a refuge in time of trouble;

> *you never forsake those who seek you, O God.*

Compassionate God, at an acceptable time you have listened to us—now is the acceptable time; now is the day of salvation:

Hear our prayers for those for whom we intercede, especially ___.

We tell of all your praises and rejoice in your salvation as we bring our prayers of gratitude and thanksgiving, especially for ___.

Bring into your eternal peace those who have died, especially ___.

You are a refuge in time of trouble;

> *you never forsake those who seek you, O God.*

Presider: *Gracious and Loving Father, be known to your people in the storms and anxieties of our lives so that we may hear the call of our ever present Savior saying "Peace! Be still!", through the power of the Holy Spirit, One God, for ever and ever.* **Amen.**

Images in the Readings

Throughout the centuries, Christians have used the boat as a picture of the church, which like Noah's ark carries us in safety across the seas of life.

That God speaks to Job out of the whirlwind is a reminder that as we become more attuned to the well-being of nature—see the petition suggested for the weekly intercessions, *Evangelical Lutheran Worship*, page 105—we think of the great array of natural forces as somehow manifestations of God. Not only lovely sunsets but also terrifying whirlwinds are part of the creation for which we intercede. Yet the whirlwind is only one image for God; when Elijah is hiding from Jezebel, he hears the word of God, not in the whirlwind, but in the sound of sheer silence. Each image of God comes closer to truth when it meets a contrary image.

In the creation poem in Job, God describes the primeval ordering of the universe very differently from what we find in Genesis 1 or Genesis 2. Had Job 38 been at the opening of the biblical corpus, would Christians be still quarreling over evolution?

Ideas for the Day

♦ Holding the story of David and Goliath and the disciples' storm together brings out interesting relief. In each story we can ask: what was expected? Goliath makes fun of David. He does not imagine this pipsqueak could beat him. The disciples expect Jesus to do something, to save them, but it becomes clear that they didn't expect enough. Maybe they thought Jesus would just help row the boat to safety. Instead, he calms the storm. Sometimes our expectations get us into trouble, and sometimes God does more for us than we could ask or imagine.

♦ Our faith has been scattered by the wind. Our hopes caught in windswept rains. The boat we journey on surely feels as if the sea of life will smash it to pieces. We frantically look around for a solution. Our friends are unable to help, for they live in fear as well. We are tossed around feeling disoriented, unsure of where we are going and how we can make the storm stop. Just as Jesus rebuked the wind and the sea with the words, "Peace, be still," we must have faith that he will do the same for us. We have the power to hold on to our faith in such a way that neither wind nor rain will pull it away from us.

♦ The passing of the peace in the liturgy dramatizes the role of the Christian in the world. Reconciliation is expressed as an essential component in congregational life, which is precisely why the peace is shared every time Christians gather for Eucharist. Evil is taken seriously in the liturgy, in counseling, and in social witness.

Making Connections

In the worldview of most ancient people, the natural world was notable for being chaotic. Oceans roared, volcanoes exploded, animals came and snatched up the weak—all without seeming rhyme or reason. Chaos (and therefore, mindless evil) was recognized in natural forces that no one could understand or control. Nowadays, through the growth of rational science, we have a clearer view of the reason that lies behind much of this. But back then, disorder seemed to reign. The God who created the universe was powerful chiefly because God brought order out of this confusion. God was knowable, in a world that often wasn't. God could be spoken to, pleaded with; the plague that swept thru your village couldn't. In this story about the storm, Jesus impresses the disciples by being able to bring order out of the frightening storm. He can command the unruly powers of nature the way they understand God can, and best of all—he intercedes for them. As impressive as it is that Jesus can calm storms, it is more wonderful that he calms storms for his friends, out of a sense of love and compassion.

Engaging all Ages

". . . they were filled with great awe . . ." Today's gospel invites us to search for signs and wonders that fill each day. And we may well ask, "What kind of person is this Jesus?" This is a good day to let the poetry of our liturgy inspire us to have faith in Jesus' calming

presence and to commit to taking that inspiration with us into our everyday lives. In a few moments of silence after the reading of the gospel, invite worshippers to imagine a great storm, caused by weather or some life event, then place Jesus in the midst, restoring peace.

Hymns for the Day

The Hymnal 1982
Praise to the living God! 372
He who would valiant be 564, 565 (SC)
God is Love, let heaven adore him 379 (GR)
Many and great, O God, are thy works 385 (GR)
Songs of praise the angels sang 426 (GR)
Lead us, heavenly Father, lead us 559
Ye servants of God, your Master proclaim 535
Almighty Father, strong to save 579
Eternal Father, strong to save 608
Jesus, Lover of my soul 699

Wonder, Love, and Praise
As newborn stars were stirred to song 788 (GR)

Lift Every Voice and Sing II
Little David, play on your harp 211 (SC)
If when you give the best of your service 190
I've been 'buked and I've been scorned 195
Jesus, Lover of my soul 79
Jesus, Savior, pilot me 80
When the storms of life are raging 200
When the waves of affliction sweep over the soul 204

Weekday Commemorations

Thursday, June 28
Irenaeus, Bishop of Lyons, c. 202
Recognized by Protestants and Catholics as the first great systematic theologian, Irenaeus learned Christianity in Ephesus from Polycarp, who had known John the Evangelist. In 177, when Irenaeus was probably still a teenager, a flood of heresy threatened to wash away the Church. Irenaeus, whose name means "the peaceable one," was sent to Rome as mediator. Upon his return to Lyons, he was elected Bishop of Lyons to succeed Pothinus. Irenaeus' chief work, *Against Heresies*, which brought him fame, addressed the major Gnostic systems (often with sharp wit) and stressed the resurrection of the body and the goodness of creation. He may have been martyred about 202.

Friday, June 29
Saint Peter and Saint Paul, Apostles

Peter and Paul, each with his own commemoration as a renowned Church leader, are also remembered together because, by tradition, they were martyred together in Rome under Nero in 64. Paul was a well educated, urbane Jew of the Dispersion; Peter was an untutored fisher from Galilee. The two disagreed on the issue of mission to the Gentiles in the early years of the Church, but they were committed to Christ and to proclaiming the gospel, which they bore to Rome. According to tradition, Paul was decapitated by sword swipe, as befitted a Roman citizen; Peter suffered death on the cross, it is said, with his head pointed downward.

Pentecost

The Sixth Sunday after Pentecost: Proper 8

July 1, 2018

God's power to heal and bring life even out of death is revealed in Jesus.

Color   Green

Preface   Of the Lord's Day

Collect

Almighty God, you have built your Church upon the foundation of the apostles and prophets, Jesus Christ himself being the chief cornerstone: Grant us so to be joined together in unity of spirit by their teaching, that we may be made a holy temple acceptable to you; through Jesus Christ our Lord, who lives and reigns with you and the Holy Spirit, one God, for ever and ever. Amen.

Readings and Psalm

2 Samuel 1:1, 17-27 (SEMI-CONTINUOUS) or

In our Hebrew scripture reading, the report of Israel's devastating defeat by the Philistines at Mount Gilboa is brought to David at Ziklag. Saul and his three sons have been slain, including Jonathan. David might have been expected to show relief at the death of Saul, who had so relentlessly hunted him, but instead David grieves both publicly and privately. Israel has lost her king and finest prince to war, and David, who served Saul so long and loved Jonathan, is bereft. David's elegy was likely set to music, extolling Saul's heroism, Jonathan's might in battle, and the profound national and personal loss embodied in their deaths.

Wisdom of Solomon 1:13-15; 2:23-24 (GOSPEL-RELATED)

In our first lesson, the author of the Wisdom of Solomon meditates on the fact of death in a world created by a loving God. God has brought us into life for incorruption, and the generative forces of the world are manifestly good. Death does not come from God, but is a consequence of trespass and evil, here personified in the figure of the devil.

Psalm 130 or

A plea for mercy offered in patient hope to the faithful Lord.

Canticle: A Song of God's Mercy (Lam. 3:22-33) or

Our Hebrew scripture reading is a canticle of profound and abiding trust in God in every circumstance. The one who waits patiently for the Lord and seeks after God with humility will know the compassion and abundance of the Lord's love. God is just and merciful.

Psalm 30

A hymn of praise and thanksgiving by one whom the Lord has saved from death.

2 Corinthians 8:7-15

In this New Testament lesson, the apostle Paul encourages the Corinthians to be generous in their contributions to a collection he has been gathering for the relief of the church in Jerusalem. It seems the Corinthians had begun to raise money for this cause in the previous year but have not completed the project despite the means available to them. In sharing from their abundance with those in need, these new disciples will be following in the way of the Lord Jesus who, though rich, became poor that the Corinthians might become rich.

Mark 5:21-43

The gospel tells of the healings of a woman with hemorrhages and of the daughter of Jairus, an official of the local synagogue. Here are two remarkable stories of healing, one told within the other. As Jesus is responding to Jairus's plea for his sick daughter, a woman who has suffered with hemorrhage for twelve years reaches out in faith, and is healed and given new life. By the time Jesus reaches Jairus's house, the twelve-yearold daughter is seemingly dead, but Jesus raises her to new life.

Prayers of the People

Presider: Through Christ, your healing touch reaches into our suffering and our fear, O God, raising us to new life and wholeness: Empower our hearts with your generosity, that we may reach out also in concern for others, as we pray: We wait for you, O God; for with you there is mercy.

Litanist: Bless your Church with your gracious Spirit, O Holy One, that your people may excel in everything—in faith, in speech, in knowledge, in utmost eagerness, and in love, but especially that we may excel in generosity.

We wait for you, O God;

for with you there is mercy.

Fill our nation and its leaders with the spirit of freedom, that we may live into the ideals of liberty and justice for all and may extend the benefits of self-determination and peace throughout the world.

We wait for you, O God;

for with you there is mercy.

Let your healing and protection be powerfully present with all who are vulnerable throughout the world, especially women and children, that they may have the love and security that all people deserve.

We wait for you, O God;

for with you there is mercy.

Extend prosperity and equity to all people, and open our hearts with your generosity: Let those who experience abundance share with those who experience need, so that the one who has much does not have too much, and the one who has little does not have too little.

We wait for you, O God;

for with you there is mercy.

Be near to those who suffer with chronic pain or illness and with women who wish to bear children: Let your healing presence raise up those for whom we pray, especially ___.

Our hearts wait for you with thankful hope as we offer our words of gratitude and praise, especially for ___.

Out of the depths we call to you to comfort those who grieve and to give your resurrection life to all who have died, especially ___. We wait for you, O God;

for with you there is mercy.

Presider: Out of your eternal abundance, O God, you gave to us your Son Jesus Christ, who though he was rich, yet for our sakes became poor, that by his poverty we might become rich: Let all who draw near to you be healed and empowered to serve your generous intentions for all your creation, in the power of your Spirit that dwells among us, through Jesus Christ our Savior. **Amen.**

Images in the Readings

Some historians speculate that the openness of the primitive Christian community to women was part of its rapid growth. In today's gospel reading, Jesus welcomes the plea of a bleeding woman, even though her bleeding has rendered her both religiously unclean and personally frustrated by medical failures. Jesus also touches the hand of a corpse, and that of a young girl, whose life would have been undervalued by a patriarchal society. The picture of Jesus meeting needs without any worry about religious restrictions continues to challenge the church.

Traditional religion has honored even the clothing of saintly persons, as if the holiness transferred from one's inner being to one's garment. Medieval Christianity regarded such clothing as relics worthy of reverence because they symbolized the baptismal life of the deceased. For example, in Assisi is displayed the robe of St. Francis, a believer who literally followed Jesus by embracing the sick and dying.

In the lament, the Lord is called portion. For the Levites, who were given no land allotment in Israel, God was their portion of the people's inheritance.

The lament urges the suffering warrior to sit in silence. This is a complex image: yes, the suffering one is urged to patience and silence, but this advice is given to a warrior, not, for example, to an abused woman. We must be careful not to misuse poetic imagery.

Ideas for the Day

- ♦ Today's reading from Mark asks us to question cultural silence around women's bodies. Sensing that power went out from him, Jesus refuses to keep quiet. A woman, socially shamed about her body, snuck a blessing and is caught out. She is frightened, but Jesus calls her "daughter." He makes clear that she is beloved. In counter point, after raising Jairus' daughter he instructs his inner circle of disciples to be quiet. Jesus questions social mores requiring women to suffer in silence, and he also sometimes asks the men who follow him to quiet down.

♦ We often falter in the faith of touch. We find ourselves in moments when we simply don't want to be touched. We also find ourselves in times when we fear touching others. Yet, touch can heal. The woman simply touched the garment of Jesus and was healed. It was her belief that the touch would heal her, and she was healed. Jesus felt he was touched and once he understood the context, he allowed the woman to go in peace. Touch is one of the most elemental human senses, and we must not deprive ourselves of it. Whether it be a hug given or a hug received, let us not shun those who surround us in our everyday lives. Touch can heal.

♦ Acts 2:43–47 describes a church in which everything was held in common and distributed to each person as needed. This vision of congregational life, as idealistic as it may seem, shaped the church's understanding of community, stewardship, and the Baptismal Covenant, which calls for the Christian to "seek and serve Christ in all persons" (BCP, 305).

Making Connections

This is the only place in the gospels where we get a second healing story inserted into the middle of the first healing story. But the two have similarities. In both instances, the person asking for healing receives an initial rebuke for their daring. The woman who bleeds expects to get in trouble; the crowd tells the little girl's parents to give up.

Before we say the Lord's Prayer, we acknowledge that "we are bold to say" it. Our boldness to approach Jesus with familiarity comes not from disrespect or overconfidence, but the sureness of his love and care for us. We know how we are broken, but more than that—we know that Jesus loves us and wants us to be healed.

Engaging all Ages

Jesus amazes again! In these remarkable stories of healing, Jesus demonstrates the power of faith. This is a good day to share stories of healing, both experienced and observed. The children may have stories of pets being helped—honor these as well. And let today's prayers reflect our reliance on the one who heals and the importance of making our requests

known. When we speak aloud our pleas for healing and wholeness, we also reveal our faith and belief in the one who hears and heals us. Celebrate the stories of healing and restoration in your community. Yes, Jesus amazes!

Hymns for the Day

The Hymnal 1982
Christ is made the sure foundation 518
The Church's one foundation 525
From deepest woe I cry to thee 151 (SC)
Out of the depths I call 666 (SC)
Immortal, invisible, God only wise 423
Praise to the living God! 372
As those of old their first fruits brought 705
Father all loving, who rulest in majesty 568
God of grace and God of glory 594, 595
Lord, whose love through humble service 610
Not here for high and holy things 9
O Jesus, crowned with all renown 292
Take my life, and let it be 707
O bless the Lord, my soul! 411
O for a thousand tongues to sing 493
Thine arm, O Lord, in days of old 567

Wonder, Love, and Praise
Give thanks for life, the measure of our days 775 (GR)
The steadfast love of the Lord never ceases 755 (GR)
Heal me, hands of Jesus 773
O Christ, the healer, we have come 772

Lift Every Voice and Sing II
Great is thy faithfulness 189 (GR)

Weekday Commemorations

Wednesday, July 4
Independence Day
Ten years after July 4, 1776, General Convention called for observance of Independence Day throughout "this Church, on the fourth of July, for ever." Proper Psalms, Lessons, and Prayers were appointed for the national recognition of this day; however, they were rescinded in 1789 by General Convention with the intervention of Bishop William White. Although he supported the American Revolution, White revolted against observing the day, given that the majority of the Church's clericals remained loyal to the British government. Not until 1928 was provision made again for the liturgical notice of the day.

The Seventh Sunday after Pentecost: Proper 9

July 8, 2018

Jesus' rejection of his own people, but God's grace overcomes all.

Color   Green

Preface   Of the Lord's Day

Collect

O God, you have taught us to keep all your commandments by loving you and our neighbor: Grant us the grace of your Holy Spirit, that we may be devoted to you with our whole heart, and united to one another with pure affection; through Jesus Christ our Lord, who lives and reigns with you and the Holy Spirit, one God, for ever and ever. Amen.

Readings and Psalm

2 Samuel 5:1-5, 9-10 (SEMI-CONTINUOUS) or

In our first lesson, we hear the culmination of the narrative charting the rise of David. David has already been anointed king of the southern tribes, but these actions in Judah carry no weight among the northern tribes of Israel. Now the tribes of Israel come to David at Hebron to form an alliance, entering into a covenant and anointing David their "shepherd-king." David will go on to capture Jerusalem and will rule the united kingdom of Judah and Israel from that city, now called the city of David. God's providential care for Israel is manifested through David, God's chosen instrument.

Ezekiel 2:1-5 (GOSPEL-RELATED)

In our Hebrew scripture lesson, Ezekiel receives his prophetic commission: he is to speak the words of the Lord fearlessly to the rebellious people of Israel. Throughout this book, God addresses Ezekiel as *son of man*, meaning human being. But while only a mortal, the Lord's Spirit is with him so that the people will know that a prophet is in their midst. He will pronounce stern judgment on a nation that has sinned and is being sent into exile.

Psalm 48 or

A celebration of God's providential care and defense of Mount Zion and the holy temple.

Psalm 123

Those who are lowly and scorned place their trust in the merciful Lord.

2 Corinthians 12:2-10

In this epistle lesson, Paul tells of both exaltation and infirmity, and the discovery of a strength that comes through weakness. The Corinthians wanted to boast of their revelations and visions. Well, Paul knows a man (he means himself) who once had an ecstatic experience. God has, however, revealed something still more important to him: that the divine power comes to its full strength when acting through human frailty.

Mark 6:1-13

In our gospel story, Jesus returns to his hometown and finds suspicion and lack of faith. He can do no mighty works in such a climate. The passage reminds us that God's action is often clothed in the commonplace. Though rejected, Jesus perseveres and expands his ministry, commissioning his disciples by twos and sending them out to the surrounding villages to preach and to heal. They are to travel in radical dependence upon God, making little provision for their own maintenance or well-being.

Prayers of the People

Presider: *Ever present God, you come to us through the teaching of your Son Jesus Christ, risen and manifest in every place and time: Grant that our eyes and ears may be open to his wisdom and his healing, that we may be sent forth in his name to do the work that he calls us to, as we pray: To you we lift up our eyes, for your power is made perfect in our weakness.*

Litanist: Gracious God, you have given authority to your Church over many things that threaten your

Pentecost

creation: Grant us the grace of your Spirit, that we may teach with Christ's wisdom and perform his deeds of power for the healing of the world.

To you we lift up our eyes,

> *for your power is made perfect in our weakness.*

Let our nation hear the words of your prophets to reveal our impudence and stubbornness and to change our hearts: Give us just and compassionate leaders and protect our bulwarks and strongholds, that we may be a people of hospitality, welcoming your work of reconciliation and obeying your right hand of justice.

To you we lift up our eyes,

> *for your power is made perfect in our weakness.*

Let your compassionate spirit go forth throughout the world to comfort and uphold all who suffer any form of weaknesses, insults, hardships, persecutions, and calamities, that they may be upheld by your strength and justice.

To you we lift up our eyes,

> *for your power is made perfect in our weakness.*

Enable this community to see and to hear heavenly things and to treasure the mystery of your revelation so dearly that we may recognize and accept the unexpected gifts offered to us by our neighbors, family, and friends.

To you we lift up our eyes,

> *for your power is made perfect in our weakness.*

Strengthen us humbly to persevere through our tribulations, O God, and heal all who need your gift of mercy, especially ___.

We thank you for your goodness revealed in all the blessings of life, especially for ___.

Receive into Paradise all who have died, especially ___.

To you we lift up our eyes,

> *for your power is made perfect in our weakness.*

Presider: *Let your infinite grace, O Father, free us from all attachment, cynicism, and fear, that we may participate in your universal mission of teaching and healing through the reconciling Spirit of your Son, Jesus Christ our Savior.* **Amen.**

Images in the Readings

Going out two by two is an image of the companionship that is more characteristic of the church than are personal mystical visions, such as what Paul is devaluing.

That believers are sent out on a journey has been a beloved image throughout church life. Taking this passage literally, many missionaries have journeyed throughout the world. Christianity is a missionary religion, infused with the commission to spread the work of repentance and healing everywhere. In medieval times, a journey to a sacred shrine was sometimes ordered as penance for sin. Especially in Europe, pilgrimages are again popular. But even in one's regular secular life, the image of one's years as a journey remains important for many people. For Christians, the journey through life to death is always a journey with and toward God.

Our translations of the New Testament include three occurrences of the term paradise: this account of Paul's mystical vision, Jesus' words to the thief on the cross, and the location of the tree of life at the end of time. The Greek word, a loan word from Old Persian, means an enclosed garden and came into Jewish vocabulary during the exile. The Old Testament and intertestamental literature include many poetic references to such a royal garden as a symbol for the people's perfect life with God.

Ideas for the Day

- Paul's words "whenever I am weak, I am strong" are hard won. It takes time and work to find strength through suffering. In the second season of The West Wing, the character Josh suffers from Post Traumatic Stress Disorder after a shooting. He lashes out at co-workers, even yells at the president. Thankfully Josh's boss Leo knows trauma personally. Leo is a recovering alcoholic. He doesn't fire Josh. He gets him a therapist. When we can say, "I've been there," another sufferer may not feel as alone, might even find a way to heal.

- The role of the prophets is central to the biblical story. We read the words of Jesus in the gospels to see what he might be saying to us "in the flesh" of our human experience. The gospel readings are offered as a way of moving us to discover how Christ is encountering us personally in our daily lives.

- Bring nothing for your journey. Take no material possessions with you. How hard that would be to do in today's society. We leave our houses strapped with material things, whether it be a cell phone, a laptop, nice clothes, comfortable shoes, etc. Could we simply give them up? Occasionally, I accidently leave my cell phone home. It is such a liberating feeling. It can be so much easier to feed one's spirit when one is not connected to an electronic device. There is nothing wrong with having material possessions; however, we must not let them cloud our spirit. Jesus instructs us that we need no material possessions for our journey as ministers. We only need our mind, body, and spirit.

Making Connections

Behold, the most practical passage in the gospels! If you ever attempt to minister in the church in which you grew up, then you have lived this story. For whatever reason, the people who knew you when . . . have a hard time shifting their view of you as you grow, change, and mature. Jesus' advice, however, gives us permission not to expend our energy on those who cannot hear the gospel from us. We must trust that God will send others to them. As amazing as we are, we may not be the best instrument to reach them. We aren't called to do everything, all the time. We are only called to the things to which God has called us.

Engaging all Ages

Often, "where we are from" holds great significance. We may still be there or have traveled a great distance from the place of our birth. There is the potential to be forever known as the "girl or boy who . . . " But our greatest identity lies in the invitation to be named as a follower of Jesus. Today we can speak the words of the liturgy knowing we are chosen by Jesus and appointed to continue his ministry. The challenge that lies ahead is to offer what we know to those who are interested and accept rejection from those who are not.

Hymns for the Day

The Hymnal 1982
Love divine, all loves excelling 657
Hail to the Lord's Anointed 616 (SC)
O God of Bethel, by whose hand 709 (SC)

Open your ears, O faithful people 536 (GR)
Amazing grace! how sweet the sound 671
Go forth for God; go to the world in peace 347
How firm a foundation 636, 637
If thou but trust in God to guide thee 635
Christ the worker 611
Lord, you give the great commission 528
Spread, O spread, thou mighty word 530
Ye servants of God, your Master proclaim 535

Wonder, Love, and Praise
Lead me, guide me, along the way 756
Lord, you give the great commission 780
We are all one in mission 778

Lift Every Voice and Sing II
Be not dismayed, whate'er betide 183
Amazing grace! how sweet the sound 181
Lead me, guide me, along the way 194
"Go preach my gospel," saith the Lord 161 (vs 1-4)

Weekday Commemorations

Wednesday, July 11
Benedict of Nursia, Abbot of Monte Cassino, c. 540
Benedict, "the father of Western monasticism," was born about 480 in Nursia in central Italy during a time rife with barbarism. Benedict secluded himself from the noise by removing to a cave above Lake Subiaco. He does not seem to have been ordained or to have considered founding an "order;" however, a community grew up around him. Between 525 and 530, he moved south with a few disciples to Mount Cassino to establish another monastery. There, about 540, he laid out his monastic *Rules*. In the Anglican Communion today, many religious orders' rules have been influenced by Benedict's. He is buried in the same grave with his sister, Scholastica.

Pentecost

The Eighth Sunday after Pentecost: Proper 10

July 15, 2018

New life following a time of death and mourning.

Color   Green

Preface   Of the Lord's Day

Collect

O Lord, mercifully receive the prayers of your people who call upon you, and grant that they may know and understand what things they ought to do, and also may have grace and power faithfully to accomplish them; through Jesus Christ our Lord, who lives and reigns with you and the Holy Spirit, one God, now and for ever. Amen.

Readings and Psalm

2 Samuel 6:1-5, 12b-19 (SEMI-CONTINUOUS) or

In our Hebrew scripture reading, King David sets out to bring the ark of the covenant into the new royal city of Jerusalem. With extravagant liturgy, the ark proceeds into the city that David has captured. David leads the procession in exuberant dance. One of his wives, Saul's daughter Michal, perhaps representing the old order which David is replacing, despises him. With the arrival of the ark, Jerusalem becomes both the cultic and religious center of David's kingdom.

Amos 7:7-15 (GOSPEL-RELATED)

In the first lesson, Amos is given a vision of a plumb line, and he prophesies God's judgment regardless of the personal consequences. A plumb line hangs down and shows whether a wall is vertical. Israel's heart is out of line, and God is out of patience. The priest of the royal shrine at Bethel reports Amos's words to the king and tells him to prophesy elsewhere. Amos replies that he is not one of the official, professional prophets that do others' bidding. God has called him.

Psalm 24 or

As pilgrims go up to God's holy place for worship, they cleanse themselves and praise the just Lord, who has created all things.

Psalm 85:8-13

The psalm both celebrates and prays for the Lord's gracious favor, God's forgiveness, deliverance, and justice.

Ephesians 1:3-14

In this reading, Paul praises God for the glorious inheritance that has been ordained for those who are now the children of God. Redeemed by the sacrifice of Christ, our freedom from sin is made possible. Now we share in the mystery of God's plan to form a universal community in association with Christ. In all this, we have the Holy Spirit as a kind of pledge or down payment for the fullness of the heritage to come.

Mark 6:14-29

Our gospel story is of the death of John the Baptist by order of King Herod. John the Baptist's preaching sharply criticized Herod for his marriage to Herodias, who had been the wife of Herod's brother Philip. Herod was intrigued and also fearful of John, but at a banquet at which Herodias' daughter performed, the king rashly promised the girl whatever request she might make. At her mother's prompting, the girl asks for the head of John the Baptist. John's fearlessness, Herodias' brutality, and Herod's expediency thus intersect and lead to John's martyrdom.

Prayers of the People

Presider: *Blessed be the God and Father of our Lord Jesus Christ; your wisdom and insight has made known to us the mystery of your will to gather up all things in Christ: Move with power and justice throughout the earth, to unite all people into your divine life, we pray: The earth is God's and all that is in it, the world and all that dwell therein.*

Litanist: You chose your Church in Christ before the foundation of the world, O gracious One: Fill us with such gladness and love of you that we may sing and rejoice in your presence, and bless all people in your name.

The earth is God's and all that is in it,

the world and all that dwell therein.

Raise up and protect prophets as of old who will challenge the rulers of this age and inspire us to be holy and blameless before you in love: Protect us from political intrigue and from the abuse of power, so that our nation may be a people of clean hands and pure hearts.

The earth is God's and all that is in it,

the world and all that dwell therein.

In Christ, you have blessed us with every spiritual blessing in the heavenly places; let your holy presence, strong and mighty: Be with all who live in places of injustice or violence; strengthen all who suffer for the sake of conscience; protect whistleblowers and those who confront injustice with truth; visit the prisoners with your mercy and wisdom.

The earth is God's and all that is in it,

the world and all that dwell therein.

Give this community wisdom and insight to hear the word of truth and to live in the glorious grace that you freely bestow on us in the Beloved, that your glory may dwell in our land.

The earth is God's and all that is in it,

the world and all that dwell therein.

We have set our hope on Christ as we offer our prayers of intercession:

We pray for those who are ill, or who live with any threat or trauma, especially ___.

Hear our glad words of thanksgiving, especially for ___.

Raise to your eternal presence all innocents who die because of the decisions of the powerful. Remember all who have died, that they may be marked with the seal of the promised Holy Spirit, the pledge of our inheritance, especially ___.

The earth is God's and all that is in it,

the world and all that dwell therein.

Presider: Hear us as we call upon you, O God, and establish among us your rule of justice and truth, that we may be protected from all evil and live according to the riches of the grace that you have bestowed upon us through Jesus Christ, who lives and reigns with you and the Holy Spirit, One God, forever and ever. **Amen.**

Images in the Readings

The head of John the Baptist on a platter is a memorable image of this cruel and unjust world. However, as with most martyrs, John's voice has survived his decapitation, and centuries later we continue to hear his preaching. At this Sunday assembly, we approach a transformed platter, on which is not a dead man's head, but instead the bread of heaven for us. John's blood was poured out to make Herod look good, but Christ's blood gives us redemption.

A plumb line was used by builders to ensure the precise verticality of a building. We still speak of a wall being on or off plumb. Our covenant with God is one such plumb line that calls us to straighten up. Yet, thanks be to God, there is another plumb line that saves: the cross of Christ.

Ideas for the Day

+ Today's readings feature two very different dances. David dances madly before the ark of the Lord. Herod's daughter, sometimes called Salome, also dances. Her mother Herodias has a grudge against John the Baptist. She uses her daughter's dance to seduce the court. At Salome's urging Herod orders John's death. Contrasting these two dances, and their results, allows us to examine our attitudes towards our bodies. Consider contrasting how we value men's bodies and women's bodies. Consider asking tough questions about body image. Invite the congregation to dance, not to please society, but to glorify God.

+ Music, song, and dance are central ways we praise God in our worship today. Adoration is a form of prayer in which we lift up our hearts and minds to God, asking nothing but to enjoy God's presence.

+ Gifts rooted in the spirit, service grounded in the Lord, and activities empowered by God become means by which we can live a fruitful life. We must give of ourselves using the talents God has bestowed on us. We must be prepared to serve the Lord at all times, in a variety of different ways that facilitate our growth as Christians. We must choose activities that fill our time with things that glorify God. This life we lead benefits ourselves and the people we come in contact with everyday. Each aspect collaborates with the other to give us the strength to persevere.

Making Connections

What's fascinating about the stories of the "villains" in the gospel is that they are depicted as so feckless. Herod (then Pilate, then Caiaphas) doesn't hate John, isn't possessed by Satan, and he isn't depicted as crazy (which contemporary historians of the time might have actually disputed.) He is just spineless enough to allow a grave injustice occur in his name. Herod just doesn't care enough to stand up for a man's life. For those of us with institutional power, or the power of privilege, our greatest sins occur not when we actively choose, but when we fail to act. To be neutral in the face of injustice causes just as much damage as to act with malice.

Engaging all Ages

Today the Hebrew scripture offers great stories of celebration. King David dances and the psalmist sings of God's glory and invites us to lift up our hands. Use a variety of musical instruments to enhance the readings and invite all ages to join in the celebration. Consider what, in our worship today, inspires us to sing and to dance and to display the joy of these two readings. Invite people to name where they find joy. In the music? The prayers? The Eucharist? The presence of children, youth, and families? Name the sources of joy and give thanks to God.

Hymns for the Day

The Hymnal 1982
Lift up your heads, ye mighty gates 436 (SC)
O day of God, draw nigh 600, 601 (GR)
Praise to the living God 372 (GR)

Amazing grace! how sweet the sound 671, 181
Baptized in water 294
Come, thou fount of every blessing 686
Hail, thou once despised Jesus! 495
In your mercy, Lord, you called me 706
Sing praise to our Creator 295
Sing, ye faithful, sing with gladness 492
Awake, thou Spirit of the watchmen 540
By all your saints still striving [2: June 24] 231, 232
King of the martyrs' noble band 236
"Thy kingdom come!" on bended knee 615

Wonder, Love, and Praise
Baptized in water 767
Loving Spirit, loving Spirit 742
You're called by name, forever loved 766

Lift Every Voice and Sing II
Amazing grace! how sweet the sound 181
Baptized in water 121
Come, thou fount of every blessing 111

Weekday Commemorations

Tuesday, July 17
William White, Bishop of Pennsylvania, 1836
The founding of the American Episcopal Church and the United States of America followed many parallel lines, not least of which were drawn by the venerable White. The chief designer of the Church's constitution was born (1747) and educated in Philadelphia. He was ordained a deacon in England in 1770, priest in 1772; returning home, he ministered at Christ and St. Peter's for seven years, whereupon he began a rectorship that continued until his death. He served as chaplain to the Continental Congress (1777–1789) and of the Senate until 1800. He was Presiding Bishop at the Church's organizing General Convention in 1789, then from 1795 until he died.

The Ninth Sunday after Pentecost
Proper 11

July 22, 2018

God dwells with us through Jesus.

Color Green

Preface Of the Lord's Day

Collect

Almighty God, the fountain of all wisdom, you know our necessities before we ask and our ignorance in asking: Have compassion on our weakness, and mercifully give us those things which for our unworthiness we dare not, and for our blindness we cannot ask; through the worthiness of your Son Jesus Christ our Lord, who lives and reigns with you and the Holy Spirit, one God, now and for ever. Amen.

Readings and Psalm

2 Samuel 7:1-14a (SEMI-CONTINUOUS) or
In our Hebrew Bible lesson, the enemies of David have been subdued, and David turns his thoughts to building a temple to the Lord. Through the prophet Nathan, God declares to David that the construction of an earthly temple is not among the purposes for which God has anointed David. God has chosen David from among the lowly, a mere shepherd boy, and given him victory over his enemies. Now God will make of David a great house, securing the hopes of the people of Israel. David's throne shall be established forever, the prophet declares.

Jeremiah 23:1-6 (GOSPEL-RELATED)
In our opening lesson, the Lord denounces the rulers who have so poorly shepherded the people Israel. God will gather the flock together and give them new shepherds, especially a just ruler in the line of David. Jeremiah prophesied during the year that Babylon was conquering his country, and while Judah's last king, Zedekiah (part of whose name means *righteousness*) was ruling in Jerusalem. God would now have to act as shepherd to this people, and will finally fulfill Israel's dream by raising up a wise and truly righteous ruler.

Psalm 89:20-37 or
The Lord is praised for faithful love and mighty justice. As a Father, God promises to the anointed servant David and everlasting kingdom.

Psalm 23
The Lord is shepherd and guide. God is present in the time of danger and is generous and merciful.

Ephesians 2:11-22
This passage is a celebration of the new community of a unified humanity which God has formed and built up through Christ Jesus. Before this time, Gentiles lived a life distant from God and the hope of God's promises. Now, through the sacrifice of Christ, the power of the law to separate and the wall of hostility are broken down. Former strangers have found peace and become fellow citizens who share in the Lord's spiritual temple.

Mark 6:30-34, 53-56
In our gospel lesson, the apostles return from their first mission and are summoned away by Jesus to a place of solitude and restoration. There is such urgent need among the people, however, that Jesus and his disciples are met by large crowds everywhere they go. Jesus is a compassionate shepherd and responds to the need of the multitude in teaching and healing, and all who come to him find solace.

Prayers of the People

Presider: *Comfort us, gracious God, in our anxiety and worry, and grant us such rest and renewal that we may be strengthened to share in your reconciling and healing work of bringing peace to the world, as we pray: You are our God, our savior and the rock of our salvation.*

Litanist: Your Church has been built upon the foundation of the apostles and prophets, Christ Jesus as the cornerstone: Break down the dividing walls within

Pentecost

your Body and be our peace, that we may act no longer as strangers and aliens but as citizens with the saints and all the members of the household of God.

You are our God;

our savior and the rock of our salvation.

Give us rest from all our enemies and guide our leaders to be instruments of peace to those who are far off and to those who are near.

You are our God;

our savior and the rock of our salvation.

Bring your reconciling love and infinite peace to all who suffer from any trouble or injustice throughout the world, that they may be touched by your healing presence.

You are our God;

our savior and the rock of our salvation.

Let your faithfulness and love be with us and among all with whom we live, that no one shall be a stranger or alien, but everyone may live together in your new humanity.

You are our God;

our savior and the rock of our salvation.

Touch with your healing grace all who are sick, anxious, or fearful, as we pray especially for ___.

You keep your love for us forever, and so we offer our prayers of thanksgiving, especially for ___.

You have promised that you will not take your love from your people, let those who have died rest in your love and be given an eternal name, especially ___.

You are our God;

our savior and the rock of our salvation.

Presider: *You are our peace, O God: Give us renewing rest that we may rise daily to share in your healing and reconciling work, through Jesus Christ our Ruler and Shepherd, who lives and reigns with you and the Holy Spirit, one God, for ever and ever.* **Amen.**

Images in the Readings

Many sets of lectionary readings include the image of Christ as our shepherd. The task is twofold: to avoid a sentimental interpretation of an image that is distant from the experience of most worshipers, and to respect the metaphor of sheep, which the Bible uses to suggest the goodness of the caring Creator.

Jesus wore fringes on his cloak. Numbers 15:37-41 interprets the fringes worn by observant Jewish males as reminders that God's commandments are more important than one's own desires. A parallel for Christians might be the wearing of a cross or crucifix. Mark's gospel suggests that the holiness symbolized by Jesus' fringes was so powerful that it could be transferred to the sick to make them whole.

The imagery of the Branch of David has been popularized throughout Christian history in artistic depictions of the tree of Jesse.

In the famous poem "Mending Wall" by Robert Frost is the line, "Good fences make good neighbors." Ephesians says just the opposite: in Christ the walls have been broken down. We live together as one building.

Ideas for the Day

♦ This story of Jesus' search for rest appears in the middle of summer, a time when many churches are sparsely attended due to the congregation's summer vacations. The Book of Common Prayer includes a Collect for the "Good Use of Leisure" (BCP 825). The prayer asks for times of "refreshment and peace" and that we might use our leisure to "rebuild our bodies" and "renew our minds." Do our vacations leave us refreshed, rebuilt, and renewed? How can our leisure be used well?

♦ Christ has compassion for the people of the church and the world who hunger for God's word and healing. Our churches are sanctuaries for prayer and healing. The Ministration of the Sick is a service that includes the Laying on of Hands and Anointing. Many call these "healing services" (BCP 453–461).

♦ How difficult it is to preach peace in a hostile world. So many people are far from the Lord. They are disconnected with their spirits. They find it easier to tear down than to build up. Yet, we must continue to preach peace. Jesus helps us to reconcile the warring factions within ourselves, creating a new person in peace. We become close to him, living as fellow citizens with the saints and members of the household of God. We are no longer far from him, and our peace of spirit gives us strength. We put our resources into building a dwelling place for the Lord. This will be a place that will bring those from afar to take the opportunity to become close with the Lord.

Making Connections

For fellow progressive Christians, many times our faith is about doing things. Clearly, the things we do are good and needed things: serving the impoverished, feeding the hungry, empowering the oppressed, but occasionally the drive to fix the world becomes exhausting. While Christ calls us to serve the least of these, Christ also sees us and has compassion for our weariness. We cannot show the love of God to others until we ourselves are rested within it.

Engaging all Ages

Perhaps the most important focus for us today, in the midst of our busy lives, is to heed Mark's poignant words . . . "For many were coming and going and they had no leisure even to eat." Are we listening to Jesus' directive, "Come away to a deserted place . . . and rest awhile"? Provide a time of reflection in today's worship for each person to ponder the busyness of everyday life and then commit to some quiet time—to eat, pray, share stories, and simply to "be" as a follower of Christ. There is healing for us, too, as we draw near to the Savior.

Hymns for the Day

The Hymnal 1982
Hosanna to the living Lord! 486 (SC)
Only-begotten, Word of God eternal 360, 361 (SC)
Savior, again to thy dear Name we raise 345 (SC)
We the Lord's people, heart and voice uniting 51 (SC)
Give praise and glory unto God 375 (GR)
Hail to the Lord's Anointed 616 (GR)
My shepherd will supply my need 664 (GR)
Savior, like a shepherd lead us 708 (GR)
The King of love my shepherd is 645, 646 (GR)
The Lord my God my Shepherd is 663 (GR)
Christ is made the sure foundation 518
Hail, thou once despised Jesus! 495
In Christ there is no East or West 529
Just as I am, without one plea 693
The Church's one foundation 525
Dear Lord and Father of mankind 652, 653
O for a thousand tongues to sing 493
Thine arm, O Lord, in days of old 567

Wonder, Love, and Praise
Come now, O Prince of Peace 795
Now let us rise and hymn the grace 781
From miles around the sick ones came 774

Heal me, hands of Jesus 773
O Christ, the healer, we have come 772

Lift Every Voice and Sing II
The Lord is my shepherd 104 (GR)
In Christ there is no East or West 62
Gentile or Jew, servant or free 151
Just as I am, without one plea 693

Weekday Commemorations

Tuesday, July 24
Thomas à Kempis, Priest, 1471
He was born Thomas Hammerken in the Duchy of Cleves (about 1380) and educated by the Brethren of the Common Life. He joined its order (1399) in Zwolle, where he took his vows (1407), was ordained (1415) and made sub-prior (1425). The order, founded by Gerard Groote, comprised laity and clergy. The Brethren cultivated biblical piety, more practical than speculative, and stressed living the inner life and practicing virtue. The members supported themselves by teaching (Erasmus was a pupil) and copying manuscripts. Thomas is renowned for *The Imitation of Christ*, which Thomas composed, or compiled; the work has been widely translated, nearly as often as the Holy Scriptures.

Wednesday, July 25
Saint James the Apostle
James' familiar name, James the Greater, distinguishes the brother of John from the other apostle named James (commemorated with Philip) but also from the other James, "the brother of our Lord." This James was the son of Zebedee, a prosperous Galilean fisher; with his brother John, James left his home and business to follow Christ's call. He seems to have belonged among those chosen for the privilege of witnessing the Transfiguration, the raising of Jairus' daughter, and the agony in the garden. Jesus called the brothers "Sons of Thunder" because of their boiling tempers. James was the first apostle to die for Jesus.

Thursday, July 26
The Parents of the Blessed Virgin Mary
Their names, Joachim and Anne, are apocryphal, and little is known about either of the parents of the mother of Jesus. Anne, thought to have descended from David, was presumably brought up in a good Jewish family that longed for the kingdom of God. In the second century, an apocryphal gospel, *Protoevangelium of James,* appeared to tell legendary stories of Anne and Joachim. In 550, the Emperor Justinian

Pentecost

I built the first church to St. Anne, but not until the twelfth century was her feast day known in the West. The Roman Catholic Church joined Joachim's several dates with Anne's in 1969.

Friday, July 27
William Reed Huntington, Priest, 1909

Born in 1838 in Massachusetts, Huntington served his Church not only as ecumenist and statesman but also as a liturgical scholar. When the Church faced schism in the late nineteenth century, Huntington encouraged reconciliation from his position as a member of the House of Deputies (1871 to 1907). His passion for unity resulted in *The Church Idea* (1870); the grounds he laid were accepted by the House of Bishops in Chicago in 1886. The sixth rector of Grace Church in New York City, he guided the parish with breadth and generosity. He exemplified boldness in 1871 when he moved to support women's roles in the church by reviving the ancient order of deaconesses, which was met with resistance until 1889.

The Tenth Sunday after Pentecost: Proper 12

July 29, 2018

Jesus' compassion for the people leads him to respond with food for mind and body. God's power is revealed in Jesus.

Color Green

Preface Of the Lord's Day

Collect

O God, the protector of all who trust in you, without whom nothing is strong, nothing is holy: Increase and multiply upon us your mercy; that, with you as our ruler and guide, we may so pass through things temporal, that we lose not the things eternal; through Jesus Christ our Lord, who lives and reigns with you and the Holy Spirit, one God, for ever and ever. Amen.

Readings and Psalm

2 Samuel 11:1-15 (SEMI-CONTINUOUS) or

In the Hebrew scripture reading, King David, secure in Jerusalem while his troops carry on a battle against the Ammonites, conceives a child with Bathsheba, a married woman. David is concerned to cover up his impropriety and summons her husband, Uriah the Hittite, from battle. The king's first intent is for Uriah to have relations with Bathsheba, but the Hittite will take no comfort for himself while his comrades are militarily engaged. When this plan fails, David sends Uriah back to the fight carrying orders for Joab, the commander, as to how Uriah's necessary death is to be achieved. David, so favored by God, transgresses woefully.

2 Kings 4:42-44 (GOSPEL-RELATED)

In our Hebrew Bible lesson, God's abundant provision for the people is shown in the multiplication of the first fruits from the village of Baal-shalishah. The prophet Elisha insists that the people be fed with limited supplies, and when they are set before the people, God gives increase. In accordance with the prophet's word, there is food left over when all have eaten. This miracle recalls the manna sent from God in the Sinai wilderness, and, for Christians, anticipates Jesus' feeding of the multitude.

Psalm 14 or

Those who reject God are foolish and perverse, but God will be vindicated.

Psalm 145:10-19

A hymn of praise to the Lord, who is mighty in deeds yet tender and compassionate.

Ephesians 3:14-21

In our epistle lesson, the author, in the language of praise, expresses fervent hope that the community of the church might know the rich abundance of God's indwelling Spirit. There is a power and wisdom which comes only from Christ, surpassing all knowledge. The blessing of knowing Christ exceeds all that can be imagined, and will be at work for every generation of those who are, through faith, members of Christ Jesus and his church.

John 6:1-21

Our gospel is the story of the feeding of the five thousand people by Jesus. The narrative recalls the story of the food miraculously provided to the Israelites in the wilderness. The people declare Jesus to be the new prophet whom God had promised to raise up in Moses' place. But then they misunderstand Jesus' mission and want to make him a king because he has provided them with food. The story contains a number of other themes. The twelve baskets of fragments may signify the mission to the Gentile nations. Christians perceive in this meal a foretaste of the messianic banquet in heaven. It also prefigures the Eucharist. Jesus is the bread come down from heaven.

Prayers of the People

Presider: *Gracious God of abundance, you feed the hungry from your hand and visit us in our storms: Hear your people as we pray for the whole world,* saying: *May we know the love of Christ that surpasses knowledge, so that we may be filled with all the fullness of God.*

Litanist: Give to your Church, O God, the power to comprehend the breadth and length and height and depth of the love of Christ, that your power at work within us may accomplish abundantly far more than we can ask or imagine.

May we know the love of Christ that surpasses knowledge,

so that we may be filled with all the fullness of God.

Let our leaders and all in authority bow their knees before the Father from whom every family in heaven and on earth takes its name, that they may use their power justly, feed the hungry and share your abundance with all your children.

May we know the love of Christ that surpasses knowledge,

so that we may be filled with all the fullness of God.

In every place of hunger, bring food, O God; in every place of poverty, bring abundance; in every place of terror, bring comfort and security.

May we know the love of Christ that surpasses knowledge,

so that we may be filled with all the fullness of God.

Receive gifts from our children and from the poor in our community, and from their generosity create a plentitude which will satisfy the true needs of every person.

May we know the love of Christ that surpasses knowledge,

so that we may be filled with all the fullness of God.

Come to us in our stormy darkness and comfort us in our fears; with your generous touch, heal those for whom we pray, especially ___.

Hear our thankfulness for the abundance of your grace, especially for ___.

You gather up the lives of all your children, receive into your fullness those who have died, especially ___.

May we know the love of Christ that surpasses knowledge,

so that we may be filled with all the fullness of God.

Presider: *Your people look to you for nurture and healing, O Father: Fill our hungry lives with the abundance of your Spirit, that we may be fruitful disciples of the one whose compassion reaches across all boundaries, our Savior Jesus Christ.* **Amen.**

Images in the Readings

The most common biblical image for divine mercy is food. In Genesis 1, the plants and trees that God created are given to humans as food. Ancient narratives told of God providing food during famine. The Israelites' memories of their nomadic years recalled a miraculous food, manna, which God sent to keep them alive in the wilderness. Religious rules commanded the faithful to share their food with the hungry and to abstain from eating with the wicked. Disobedience was met with the punishment of famine. The people of Israel themselves were likened to food that God had planted. Food or fast was central to all the primary religious festivals of the Old Testament. Poems described the law of God as if it is nourishing food. Christ was born in Bethlehem, which means "house of bread." In John's metaphoric theology, Christ is the bread of life. We need food to live, and Christians have each week served out the word and the sacrament as the food that Christ continues to distribute to those of us who are hungry. Christians need not wonder whether the miracle of the feeding occurred back then; it occurs each week.

Barley was used to make the bread of the poor. Paradoxically, the great messianic banquet serves up barley. Despite this biblical reference, most Christians have used wheat for the bread of the Eucharist, and there is current debate about which other grains are appropriate for Sunday communion. The author of Ephesians might say that we are now like that barley, "rooted and grounded in love" and served up to feed the hungry.

A landed people, Jewish tradition spoke of the sea as a fearful place of chaos. Thus for Jesus to walk on the water shows him, like God, able to control the sea.

Ideas for the Day

+ A bishop once was talking up a trip to the Holy Land to a group of youth leaders. He told them about the chance to visit Jerusalem, to pray in the Church of the Holy Sepulcher, to visit Bethlehem. The bishop got quiet as he said to the youth leaders that his favorite place to visit was Galilee. "In the morning it is peaceful on the water," he said, "and you can swim in the footsteps of Jesus!" Isn't his joke an apt metaphor for the life of discipleship? Following Jesus is an inexact journey. Sometimes it requires swimming.

♦ Fill me with your love. Show me its breadth, length, height, and depth so that it can empower my inner being to live according to your will. Though others have turned away from you, I look to you to deepen my understanding in love. The Lord is our refuge from the society around us that continually tries to tear us down. Society loves destruction. Society loves some people to live in ignorance of spiritual power. Spiritual power is rooted in love. It is a love so deep that we don't understand it rationally, we simply feel its presence living in us.

♦ The feeding of the five thousand expresses the significance of the Holy Eucharist. This eucharistic theme will be carried out in Propers 13, 14, 15, and 16 this year. To accept the reality of Christ's presence in the bread of the sacrament is to be open to a whole new dimension of life. It is the Lord who is the source of our life and strength. It is he who quiets the waters and winds around us if we have the faith to perceive his presence. Our eyes become open to the events that happen around us as we see the Lord feeding us in the sacrament.

Making Connections

Miracles are always a bit confounding. Are they supernatural occurrences, like magic? Are they scientific processes we just don't understand yet? Are they a misunderstanding of what's happening? Who knows? I'm not sure there's much to be gained from getting caught up in the "how" of miracles. Far more interesting is the "why." Jesus chose to perform a miracle to feed hungry people; to take what had been generously shared and to make sure everyone had enough to eat. That tells us a lot about the priorities of God. God chooses to make sure that everyone has enough, by using what sometimes feel like the meager resources we offer.

Engaging all Ages

Jesus astonishes both the disciples and the gathered crowds. What must they have thought at the evidence of this kind of power? As we sing and pray together today, what do we see, hear, and feel as a gathered community? Are we open to signs and wonders? Do we hear Jesus say, "Where are we to buy bread for these people to eat?" Is there room for a solution offered by a child? In today's Prayers of the People, use Jesus' words for the congregational response, "It is I; do not be afraid." There is abundance and safety with Jesus. Celebrate this today.

Hymns for the Day

The Hymnal 1982
If thou but trust in God to guide thee 635
Before thy throne, O God, we kneel 574, 575 (SC)
As those of old their first fruits brought 705 (GR)
God, my King, thy might confessing 414 (GR)
We will extol you, ever-blessed Lord 404 (GR)
Awake, O sleeper, rise from death 547
Just as I am, without one plea 693
Not far beyond the sea, nor high 422
O love, how deep, how broad, how high 448, 449
O Love of God, how strong and true 455, 456
Bread of the world, in mercy broken 301
Hope of the world, thou Christ of great compassion 472
I come with joy to meet my Lord 304
My God, thy table now is spread 321
O Food to pilgrims given 308, 309
We the Lord's people, heart and voice uniting 51

Wonder, Love, and Praise
All who hunger, gather gladly 761
O wheat whose crushing was for bread 760

Lift Every Voice and Sing II
If I have wounded any soul today 176 (SC)
Just as I am, without one plea 137
Break thou the bread of life 146

Weekday Commemorations

Monday, July 30
William Wilberforce, 1833
Wilberforce dedicated his life to politics and Christianity. Born wealthy on August 14, 1759, he served in the House of Commons (1780–1825). He became an evangelical in 1784. He was convinced by friends not to abandon his outer work in politics for his inner life in religion; however, he refused to accept high office or a peerage. He dedicated himself to promoting overseas missions and popular education and to reforming public manners and morals. He fought unstintingly to abolish slavery (slave traffic ended in 1807); Wilberforce, an eloquent power for good, died

Pentecost

a month before Parliament ended slavery in the British dominions. He is buried in Westminster Abbey.

Tuesday, July 31
Joseph of Arimathaea

Little is known of the life of Joseph of Arimathaea beyond the stories of Jesus' burial in the gospels. John speaks of Joseph as a secret disciple and couples him with Nicodemus, also part of the Jewish Sanhedrin drawn to Jesus. Later legends describe them as leaders in the early church. One of the loveliest legends, which cannot be dated earlier than the 1200s, tells of Joseph's bringing the Holy Grail with him to the ancient Church of Glastonbury in Britain. More concrete, though, is Joseph's boldly stepping forward—unlike the cowering disciples—to do what Jewish piety demanded: to offer his own tomb to prevent further desecration of Jesus' crucified body.

The Eleventh Sunday after Pentecost: Proper 13

August 5, 2018

Jesus is the bread of heaven.

Color   Green

Preface   Of the Lord's Day

Collect

Let your continual mercy, O Lord, cleanse and defend your Church; and, because it cannot continue in safety without your help, protect and govern it always by your goodness; through Jesus Christ our Lord, who lives and reigns with you and the Holy Spirit, one God, for ever and ever. Amen.

Readings and Psalm

2 Samuel 11:26—12:13a (SEMI-CONTINUOUS) *or*

In our sequential reading from the Hebrew Bible, Nathan the prophet makes use of a parable to confront King David with his culpability in the murder of Uriah the Hittite. It is dangerous to speak words of judgment to persons in authority, and Nathan is shrewd in eliciting David's independent assessment before drawing the obvious parallels. David has broken the commandments against covetousness, adultery, and murder, and there will be consequences. Disaster will visit the house and lineage of David, says the Lord. David acknowledges his sin and submits to God's judgment.

Exodus 16:2-4, 9-15 (GOSPEL-RELATED)

From the Hebrew Bible, we hear the story of God's feeding of the people in the wilderness. The Israelites are full of complaints and now think they would prefer slavery and death in Egypt to their present difficulties. The Lord appears to them and promises sustenance, but also a test, for they will only be given food on a day-to-day basis. It is possible to explain the food in natural terms: the flock of quail provide flesh and the secretion of insects the bread-like substance. But the point of the narrative is that God provides.

The Israelites call the bread *manna* (perhaps from words meaning "What is this?").

Psalm 51:1-13 or

A confession of sin and guilt and a prayer for a clean heart.

Psalm 78:23-29

The psalm recalls Israel's trials and the Lord's sustaining grace in the wilderness after the escape from Egypt.

Ephesians 4:1-16

In this lesson, the new Christians in Ephesus are urged to lead lives of patient love, using their various gifts in the unity of the Spirit, while growing toward their maturity in Christ. There are many roles of service, but there is a oneness at the heart of the faith and in its goal. All the disciples' efforts are meant to build up the one body of Christ. While there remains a human perversity leading toward division, in the loving truth of the community Christians are to grow together toward their full humanity.

John 6:24-35

In our gospel, Jesus tells the crowd of the true bread of life, the bread from heaven. The people follow Jesus after he has fed the crowd of five thousand, but they come mostly to obtain more food for their stomachs. The bread which the Son of Man offers is more genuinely life-giving than the manna by which Israel was fed in the wilderness. In one sense this means that Jesus' teaching is greater than that of Moses. More significantly still, it is belief in Jesus himself that leads to eternal life.

Prayers of the People

Presider: *Gracious and generous God, in Christ you have given us the true bread from heaven which gives life to the world: Hear us as we call upon you, and give us all that we need to lead a life worthy of the calling*

Pentecost

to which we have been called, as we say: Create in us a clean heart, O God, and renew a right spirit within us.

Litanist: Benevolent and kind God, you have given the Church gifts as apostles, prophets, evangelists, pastors and teachers to equip the saints for the work of ministry: Build up the body of Christ until all of us come to maturity, to the measure of the full stature of Christ.

Create in us a clean heart, O God,

and renew a right spirit within us.

Just and compassionate One, raise up for us prophets like Nathan to speak truth to power when those in authority abuse the weak or act unjustly.

Create in us a clean heart, O God,

and renew a right spirit within us.

Merciful and powerful One, look upon all who suffer throughout the world and spread such humility, gentleness, and patience thoughtout humanity, that we may bear with one another in love, bringing food to the hungry and drink to the thirsty.

Create in us a clean heart, O God,

and renew a right spirit within us.

Amiable and bounteous One, open our eyes in this community to see the abundant gifts you give us, so that everyone may turn away from our efforts to gain those things that perish and work instead for the food that endures for eternal life.

Create in us a clean heart, O God,

and renew a right spirit within us.

Loving and healing God, we offer to your generous hand everyone for whom we pray, especially ___.

We bring our words of grateful thanksgiving, especially for ___.

May all who have died feast with Christ, the bread of life, at the banquet table of your eternal life. We remember especially ___.

Create in us a clean heart, O God,

and renew a right spirit within us.

Presider: In Christ you have called us to the one hope of our calling, one Lord, one faith, one baptism: Feed us with your Spirit, O Father, that we may build up your creation in love, and grow up in every way into him who is our head, Jesus Christ our Savior. **Amen.**

Planning for Rites and Rituals: Year B

Images in the Readings

For the image of food, see Pentecost 10.

The Pentateuch says that the Israelites were nomads in the wilderness for forty years, which, in the Bible's symbolic speech, means a very long time. These wilderness wanderings have also become a traditional way for Christians to talk about the difficulties of their life journey. In the Bible, God is praised for having miraculously fed the people a strange food, manna. To show to Christians the meaning of this manna for them, some depictions in medieval art show this manna as communion hosts that the Israelites are gathering up off the ground.

In the Bible, the wilderness is not a choice vacation spot or an adventure for the well-equipped backpacker, but rather a barren place, without ready food or available water, an area inhospitable to communal life. Biblical people want to get out of the wilderness into cultivated land, and in the book of Revelation, God's abode is in a city. Christians have used the imagery of wilderness to suggest that all human life is emptiness, unless it is transformed by God.

In describing the church, today's Ephesians reading uses the word "one" eight times and "unity" twice. This is a good week to pray for the unity of the church, because what we experience is, sad to say, not "the whole body joined and knit together."

Ideas for the Day

+ In the developed world, the discussions about bread in the gospel and in Exodus are often spiritualized. We are quick to move to the hidden meaning in bread given to people. People who are hungry don't hear the stories that way. Gandhi is often quoted for these words: "To the poor man God dare not appear except in the form of bread and the promise of work." How can the church move toward providing actual bread, not just symbolic wafers? Until the hungry are fed, do we have the luxury of asking "spiritual" questions?

+ That we may eat of spiritual food as we travel on our journey, the bread of life comes to us through Jesus that we might not hunger. We experience physical hunger everyday. If we have resources, we are able to satisfy that hunger. Food is energy. It gives us the strength to do what needs to be done in our daily lives. Spiritual food comes through our work in ministry. It is that work that gives us energy to continue growing in Spirit. Our journey requires a lot of us, and we must eat the bread of life so that we may continue on.

◆ We pray in our Collects as well as the proper preface during the Great Thanksgiving that we go out into the world spreading the Good News of God in Jesus Christ through the gift of the Holy Spirit. Our call is to be missionaries in our community as well as in the world. By bringing our prayers into action, we are called to think and respond in mission and ministry. The Season of Pentecost is a wonderful season to learn more, strengthen, or join an active partnership in global mission and ministries. Learn more at www.anglicancommunion.org/ministry/mission/companion.

Making Connections

The fourth gospel is obsessed with Moses. You can't see it unless you're looking for it, but like an optical illusion, once you notice it, it appears everywhere. This whole passage about Jesus and bread hearkens back to Moses providing the Israelites with manna in the wilderness. Just as Moses facilitated the survival of Israel by providing them with God's Torah (metaphorical sustenance) and with manna (literal sustenance) so, too, Jesus feeds the crowds. It's not that Jesus replaces Moses—it's more that he is following Moses' example and building on it. He is using a pattern that the crowd already recognizes to explain who he is and what he is doing. Jesus becomes a living metaphor so that the crowds may more easily understand.

Engaging all Ages

Jesus, as the bread that sustains life, is one of our most powerful images. This is the perfect day to use real bread for the Eucharist. Invite a family or a church school class to bring the bread for today's service and, if room allows, invite worshippers to gather at the altar for the powerful symbol of a loaf being broken and offered. Today we can all reflect on the hungers that are present in our own life and offer them to Jesus to be satisfied. Let the Prayers of the People reflect Jesus' promises . . . "whoever comes to me . . . whoever believes . . . will never be hungry . . . never thirst."

Hymns for the Day

The Hymnal 1982
Jesus, Lover of my soul 699 (SC)
Just as I am, without one plea 693 (SC)
Glorious things of thee are spoken 522, 523 (GR)
Guide me, O thou great Jehovah 690 (GR)
O Food to pilgrims given 308, 309 (GR)
O God of Bethel, by whose hand 709 (GR)

O God, unseen yet ever near 332 (GR)
Shepherd of souls, refresh and bless 343 (GR)
Awake, O sleeper, rise from death 547
Come, risen Lord, and deign to be our guest 305, 306
Eternal Ruler of the ceaseless round 617
Lord, you give the great commission 528
O Lord Most High, eternal King 220, 221
Put forth, O God, thy Spirit's might 521
Sing, ye faithful, sing with gladness 492
Singing songs of expectation 527
Bread of the world, in mercy broken 301
Deck thyself, my soul, with gladness 339
Father, we thank thee who hast planted 302, 303
I am the bread of life 335
Lord, enthroned in heavenly splendor 307
My God, thy table now is spread 321
O Food to pilgrims given 308, 309
We the Lord's people, heart and voice uniting 51

Wonder, Love, and Praise
Lord, you give the great commission 780
We are all one in mission 778
All who hunger, gather gladly 761
I am the bread of life 762
O wheat whose crushing was for bread 760

Lift Every Voice and Sing II
Jesus, Lover of my soul 79 (SC)
Just as I am, without one plea 137 (SC)
Break thou the bread of life 146
Come, ye disconsolate, where'er ye languish 147

Weekday Commemorations

Monday, August 6
The Transfiguration of Our Lord Jesus Christ
God authenticated Jesus as God's son in a series of supernatural manifestations. The Transfiguration is one of that series and, therefore, not to be taken only as a spiritual experience for Jesus, witnessed by Peter, James, and John. The Transfiguration fits with angels' appearing at Jesus' birth and resurrection and with the Spirit's descent at Jesus' baptism. In the Transfiguration, according to the Book of Matthew, the veil is drawn aside, and, again, a few witness Jesus as the earth-born son of Mary and as the eternal Son of God. In Luke's account, a cloud, a sign of divine presence, envelops the disciples, and a heavenly voice proclaims Jesus to be the Son of God.

Tuesday, August 7
John Mason Neale, Priest, 1866
Neale, born in London in 1818, is best known as a hymnodist, for a glance to the bottom of many pages

Pentecost

of *The Hymnal 1940* and *1982* finds his name as composer or translator. As scholar and poet, Neale composed hymns and transposed Latin and Greek hymns into English spoken syntax in such turns of phrase as "Good Christian men, rejoice" and "Come, ye faithful, raise the strain." He was also a priest of the Oxford Movement, which revived medieval liturgical forms, and a humanitarian; as such, he founded the Sisterhood of St. Margaret to relieve the suffering of women and girls. A gentle man of good humor and modesty, he lived "unbounded charity."

Wednesday, August 8
Dominic, Priest and Friar, 1221

Dominic, who was born in Spain around 1170, founded the Order of Preachers known as the Dominicans. In England, they were the Blackfriars, a reference to the black mantles worn over their white habits. Legend has Dominic, in searching for a life of apostolic poverty, selling all his possessions to help people hungry from the 1191 famine. He was ordained in 1196. In 1203, he began preaching tours in France, and in 1214, he manifested his idea for a preaching order, granted by Honorius III about 1216. The Dominicans' Constitutions, formulated in 1216, set a priority of intellectual rigor: "In the cells, they can write, read, pray . . . and stay awake at night . . . on account of study."

Friday, August 10
Laurence, Deacon, and Martyr at Rome, 258

The Emperor Valerian started persecuting upper-class clergy and laity in 257. Properties of the church were confiscated; Christian worship was forbidden. On August 4, 258, Pope Sixtus II and his seven deacons were apprehended in catacombs and executed, except for the archdeacon, Laurence, who was martyred on August 10, roasted alive on a gridiron. Legend has Laurence presenting the sick and poor to the prefect, who demanded to see the church's treasures. The Emperor Constantine erected a shrine and basilica over Laurence's tomb. For Laurence, to die for Christ was to live with Christ; a small, round, glass medallion, probably from the fourth century, now in New York's Metropolitan Museum, reads, "Live with Christ and Laurence."

Saturday, August 11
Clare, Abbess at Assisi, 1253

Clare, born to wealth, was inspired by the preachings of Francis, who established the mendicant order in 1212, gave her life to follow Christ's teaching. She begged Francis to become a member of the Franciscans; he placed her temporarily in a nearby Benedictine convent. Then, Francis escorted her to a poor dwelling beside the Church of St. Damian at Assisi, where several other women joined her. She became Mother Superior of the Poor Ladies of St. Damian, an austere order of absolute poverty. The nuns' days were spent begging and being merciful to the poor. She governed the convent for 40 years. She promised to do as Francis directed: "I am yours by having given my will to God."

The Twelfth Sunday after Pentecost: Proper 14

August 12, 2018

Jesus is the Bread of Life.

Color Green

Preface Of the Lord's Day

Collect

Grant to us, Lord, we pray, the spirit to think and do always those things that are right, that we, who cannot exist without you, may by you be enabled to live according to your will; through Jesus Christ our Lord, who lives and reigns with you and the Holy Spirit, one God, for ever and ever. Amen.

Readings and Psalm

2 Samuel 18:5-9, 15, 31-33
(SEMI-CONTINUOUS) or

In our opening lesson, David orders his most trusted military commanders to crush a coup led by Absalom, his son. He asks that "the young man, Absalom" be treated gently, expressing fatherly care even when dealing with that son's traitorous uprising. Those who followed Absalom in rebellion are defeated in a great slaughter, and Absalom is caught in the branches of an oak while seeking escape. In defiance of David's wishes, Joab and his men put Absalom to death. David, when told of Absalom's death, grieves deeply.

1 Kings 19:4-8 (GOSPEL-RELATED)

In our Hebrew scripture reading, Elijah seeks to escape the wrath of Jezebel after his successful contest with the priests of Baal. God miraculously intervenes on Elijah's behalf and gives him strength to journey forty days and nights to Mount Horeb, where Moses received the ten commandments. The number forty reminds us of other biblical journeys and experiences, such as the forty years in the wilderness, the forty days of Noah's flood, and, later, Jesus' temptation in the wilderness.

Psalm 130 or

The psalmist calls to the merciful Lord and waits upon God for forgiveness and redemption.

Psalm 34:1-8

A hymn of blessing and praise to the Lord for divine deliverance.

Ephesians 4:25—5:2

In this lesson, Christians are urged to conform to a new way of life which is pleasing to the Holy Spirit. They are to have a love like the love of Christ. All manner of evil is to be shunned. Especially are the new converts to put away spitefulness and other sins which harm the one body and grieve the Spirit with which they have been sealed in baptism. The model is none other than a God who is revealed in the Christ who sacrificed himself for us.

John 6:35, 41-51

In our gospel, Jesus continues to teach that he is the true bread who will bring all who have faith in him eternal life. The discussion is meant to recall the story of the Israelites protesting and murmuring against God in the wilderness because they had no bread. But even the manna that God gave them was only a temporary food. While Jesus seems very ordinary to the Jews (who represent a worldly lack of faith), he offers the world both his teaching and himself, a life-giving bread from heaven.

Prayers of the People

Presider: *God our Creator, you draw all humanity to yourself through your Son Jesus Christ, who gives the bread of life to all who are hungry: Hear our prayers for the whole human family, that we may be nourished and strengthened through your gracious care, as we say: We wait for you, O God; our souls wait for you; in your word is our hope.*

Litanist: Gracious One, the Church has been taught by God and drawn into your holy communion as members of one another: Feed us with the living bread of Christ, that we may be witnesses of his grace and ministers of his reconciliation.

We wait for you, O God; our souls wait for you;

in your word is our hope.

Almighty One, teach our leaders and all in authority in the nations of the world to put away all bitterness and wrath and anger and wrangling and slander, together with all malice, that they may be kind to one another, tenderhearted, forgiving one another, as God in Christ has forgiven.

We wait for you, O God; our souls wait for you;

in your word is our hope.

Compassionate One, look upon the needs of the world, and bring bread to the hungry, peace to the threatened, healing to the ill, hope to the despairing, and your continuing presence and vision to all.

We wait for you, O God; our souls wait for you;

in your word is our hope.

Loving One, grant us grace to put away falsehood and to speak the truth to our neighbors, that the relationships in our community may be useful for building up with words that give grace to those who hear, and that those who labor and work will do so honestly, so as to have something to share with the needy.

We wait for you, O God; our souls wait for you;

in your word is our hope.

Healing One, hear our prayers for those for whom we pray in intercession, especially ___.

We give you thanks and ask your blessing upon all teachers and students as they begin a new year of learning and exploration. Hear us as we express our gratitude for all of our blessings, especially for ___.

Mark all who have died with your seal for the day of redemption and grant them your gift of eternal life. We remember especially ___.

We wait for you, O God; our souls wait for you;

in your word is our hope.

Presider: Your beloved children come to you in trust, our Creator, opening our hands and mouths and hearts for your food and drink which alone satisfies our longings: Be present throughout your creation *to nourish life, that all the earth may wait upon you, O God, and receive your mercy and your plenteous redemption, through Jesus Christ our Savior, who with you and the Holy Spirit, lives and reigns, one God, for ever and ever.* **Amen.**

Images in the Readings

Sunday is truth-telling time. Today hunger and thirst are images for the essential human condition. We pray that, living in Christ, we will never be thirsty again.

In art, most angels are inadequate depictions of the identity as manifestations of the power and mercy of God. Angels are the way humans encounter God. Because angels surround God like a nimbus, they not only convey God's will but also perpetually praise God. Because angels are extensions of God, they protect, feed, guide, judge.

The author of Ephesians uses traditional religious categories to interpret Christ's crucifixion when he writes about "a fragrant offering and sacrifice." In Israelite religion until the destruction of the temple in 70 CE, and in many other world religions, animals are killed as symbols of the giving of oneself in repentance or praise to the deity. Countering the stink that accompanies such rituals, incense was also burned, thus symbolizing that one's worship of the divine was sweet and rendered the world sweet. Early Christians needed to find ways to understand the execution of the Messiah, and Christians are so accustomed to the description of Jesus' death as a sacrifice that we seldom meditate on the oddness of the image. Surely the destruction of the temple contributed to the acceptance of this imagery. Most profound religious imagery is odd.

In the Bible, God is praised for having miraculously fed the people a strange food, manna. To show to Christians the meaning of this manna for them, some depictions in medieval art show this manna as communion hosts that the Israelites are gathering up off the ground.

Ideas for the Day

◆ Sometimes we have to re-learn the same lesson again and again. We are now more than halfway through the "summer of bread." For five straight Sundays in Lectionary Year B, we read from the sixth chapter of the Gospel of John. The congregation (and the preachers) may be tired of bread, yet here we are again. Jesus says to us, again, "I am the bread of life." What lessons have we missed before? How can we learn and re-learn to be fed? After all, each Sunday we come looking for bread.

- We often have trouble seeing the godly in the ordinary. The people found themselves questioning Jesus, saying to themselves, "We know where this man grew up. Why does he think he comes from God?" We live in a day and age where we want to know the origins of everything. We feel this knowledge of origins gives us authority to speak and judge others. Some people find it very hard to believe things they have come in contact with through a Google search. God lives beyond all of that. We could read a thousand biographies and still know nothing about the Spirit within the people we are reading about. The Spirit of God cannot be captured in pixels, we must seek him out in the everyday contact we have with the people in our lives. We must seek him out in the ordinary, the people we take for granted. You never know where God might be living.

- The letter to the Ephesians reminds us that Christians are called to "live in love, as Christ loved us," to be kind and tenderhearted in our forgiveness of one another. Paul gives instruction about communal life in the church. How are your church and its members living this out in ministry and daily life?

Making Connections

Large groups never come across well in scriptures. The gospel writers seem to share Niebhur's suspicion of how moral crowds can be. The crowd—that amorphous character—does not ever seem to understand what Jesus is driving at in the gospels. At this moment, their problem seems to be a lack of imagination. When Jesus talks about being the bread of life, they scoff because they know his parents, and neither one is made of bread. It's funny—and very true. How often do we miss where God is pointing us because we cannot imagine such a future? So much of faith is an exercise in imagination, in the ability to envision a world radically different from what it currently is. When we lose touch with that creativity, we begin to lose touch with the vision of God.

Engaging all Ages

Today's gospel opens with the closing words from last week's gospel. In the call to worship, call attention to this and the importance that this particular promise has for our faith journey. Jesus' extraordinary words invite us into mystery. Living bread? Given for the life of the world? How amazing to explore these words today as we share worship time. Let each hymn or song, each prayer, each response and even the passing of the Peace reflect the glory of this promise. We live through Jesus' promise. We grow the kingdom through Jesus' words. Celebrate life itself in today's worship.

Hymns for the Day

The Hymnal 1982
From deepest woe I cry to thee 151 (SC)
Out of the depths I call 666 (SC)
Awake, O sleeper, rise from death 547
Baptized in water 294
God is love, and where true love is 576, 577
To thee, O Comforter divine 514
Where charity and love prevail 581
Where true charity and love dwell 606
Bread of the world, in mercy broken 301
Completed, Lord, the Holy Mysteries 346
Deck thyself, my soul, with gladness 339
Draw nigh and take the Body of the Lord 327, 328
Father, we thank thee who hast planted 302, 303
For the bread which you have broken 340, 341
I am the bread of life 335
Lord, enthroned in heavenly splendor 307
My God, thy table now is spread 321
O Food to pilgrims given 308, 309
We the Lord's people, heart and voice uniting 51

Wonder, Love, and Praise
All who hunger, gather gladly 761 (GR)
I will bless the Lord at all times 764 (GR)
Baptized in water 767
Ubi caritas et amor 831
All who hunger, gather gladly 761
I am the bread of life 762
O wheat whose crushing was for bread 760

Lift Every Voice and Sing II
I will bless the Lord at all times 154 (GR)
Baptized in water 121
Break thou the bread of life 146
I am the Bread that came down from heaven 150

Weekday Commemorations

Monday, August 13
Jeremy Taylor, Bishop of Down, Connor, and Dromore, 1667
Taylor, born August 15, 1613, in Cambridge, England, wrote his most influential works, *Holy Living* and *Holy Dying*, in 1651 during days of forced retirement.

He had served as chaplain to Charles I, but Oliver Cromwell's minions imprisoned Taylor and reduced him to retirement as a chaplain to a Welsh lord. Another work, *Liberty of Prophesying*, encouraged religious tolerance and appealed for freedom of thought. His work does not appear in the Prayer Book revision of 1662, but the first American Prayer Book included one of Taylor's prayers, and another appears in the current Book of Common Prayer. Later, he removed to Ireland, where he ended his days as vice-chancellor of Trinity College.

Wednesday, August 15
Saint Mary the Virgin, Mother of Our Lord Jesus Christ

Mary has been honored as the mother of Jesus Christ since the beginnings of the Church. Two gospels tell the story of Christ's birth to a virgin; Luke's gospel glimpses Christ's childhood in Nazareth under the care of his Mother and earthly father, Joseph. During Jesus' ministry in Galilee, Mary often traveled with the women who followed Jesus, ministering to him; at Calvary, she stood with the women who kept watch at the Cross. After the Resurrection, she accompanied the Twelve in the upper room. She was the person closest to Jesus, having humbly accepted God's divine will. Later devotions lay many claims for Mary that cannot be proved by Holy Scripture.

Saturday, August 18
William Porcher DuBose, Priest, 1918

Original thinker, professor, theologian, homebody, writer—DuBose well represented the American Episcopal Church of his era. Born in 1836 in South Carolina to a wealthy Huguenot family, he studied Greek at the University of Virginia, laying a foundation for his deep understanding of the New Testament. Ordained in 1861, he served as an officer and chaplain in the Confederate Army. Starting in 1892, he published books probing the inner meanings of the gospels, the epistles of Paul, and the Epistle to the Hebrews. He juxtaposed life with doctrine to create dramatic dialogue between personal and scriptural catholic theology and to reflect the renowned religious movements of the nineteenth century—from the Tractarians to the Germans.

The Thirteenth Sunday after Pentecost: Proper 15

August 19, 2018

God's Word (Logos, Wisdom) brings the life-giving knowledge of God. God's Word is the very bread of life.

Color   Green

Preface   Of the Lord's Day

Collect

Almighty God, you have given your only Son to be for us a sacrifice for sin, and also an example of godly life: Give us grace to receive thankfully the fruits of this redeeming work, and to follow daily in the blessed steps of his most holy life; through Jesus Christ your Son our Lord, who lives and reigns with you and the Holy Spirit, one God, now and for ever. Amen.

Readings and Psalm

1 Kings 2:10-12; 3:3-14 (SEMI-CONTINUOUS) or

In our Hebrew Bible lesson, Solomon assumes the throne of his father David and asks for an understanding and discerning mind to govern God's people. Because Solomon's request is not for riches and honor, God, in this dream vision, grants him a wise and discerning mind. God promises, if Solomon will walk in the ways of the Lord, to lengthen the days of his kingship.

Proverbs 9:1-6 (GOSPEL-RELATED)

In our opening lesson, Wisdom is pictured as a gracious hostess who invites the ignorant and foolish to her table. Several centuries before the time of Christ, Wisdom was understood to be an important characteristic of God and was often described as a judicious woman who spoke to human hearts and minds. In this way some of the feeling of distance between the people and the transcendent God was overcome. Those who heed Wisdom's counsels and do not follow the seduction of folly will be blessed.

Psalm 111 or

This psalm is an outpouring of praise for the majesty and graciousness of the Lord, who redeems the people of God.

Psalm 34:9-14

A hymn of blessing and praise to the Lord for God's deliverance.

Ephesians 5:15-20

In this reading, the new Christians at Ephesus are bid to live wisely and, glad with songs, to give thanks for everything to God. Instead of following drunken ways, symbolic of all kinds of foolish behavior, they are to be filled with the Holy Spirit. Because the time is in the grip of evil, opportunities to do the will of the Lord must be used to the full.

John 6:51-58

In the gospel lesson, Jesus speaks of the flesh and blood of the Son of Man as the bread from heaven which must be eaten in order to share in the life of the eternal age. Previously in this gospel, the bread of life had seemed to signify Jesus' teaching and his presence. Now it is given still more significance with the understanding that the believer may share deeply in the life of Jesus and his self-offering. This experience is enacted in the Holy Communion.

Prayers of the People

Presider: *Living Father, Holy Wisdom, you have come to us in Jesus as the living bread given for the life of the world: Accept our prayers on behalf of the whole human family, that all may abide in you, and live and walk in your ways, as we pray: Feed your creation with your eternal life; may Christ abide in us.*

Litanist: Nurture your Church, O God, with the food and drink of eternal life as we celebrate our Eucharist on this feast day of Christ's resurrection: Fill us with your Spirit as we sing psalms and hymns and spiritual songs, giving thanks to God the Father at all times and for everything in the name of our Lord Jesus Christ.

Feed your creation with your eternal life;

may Christ abide in us.

Guide the leaders of our nation and all who wield power and authority in the world, that they may have wisdom and understanding to discern between good and evil.

Feed your creation with your eternal life;

may Christ abide in us.

Be the bread of life for those who lack and suffer hunger throughout the world, that all who suffer may know the nourishment of your love.

Feed your creation with your eternal life;

may Christ abide in us.

Invite our community to the banquet of your divine life, where we may know the works of your hands, which are faithfulness and justice, full of majesty and splendor.

Feed your creation with your eternal life;

may Christ abide in us.

Let your nurturing life renew and strengthen those for whom we pray, especially ___.

We thank you for the living bread that came down from heaven; hear our prayers of gratitude, especially for ___.

May all who have died abide in you and rejoice at the banquet of your heavenly feast, especially ___.

Feed your creation with your eternal life;

may Christ abide in us.

Presider: Generous God, you call all people into your banquet to eat and drink of the true food and true drink that you give for the life of the world: Bless our celebration with the power of your presence, that we may grow in wisdom and faithfulness all our days, through Jesus Christ our Savior. **Amen.**

Images in the Readings

John's word "flesh" echoes the common Hebrew designation for humans as "bone and flesh," the hard and the soft of actual created matter. Adam recognizes Eve as his own bone and flesh. However, in descriptions of battle death, the Hebrew writes of "flesh and blood," so perhaps John meant to invoke the brutal death of Christ with his use of "flesh." In either case, "flesh" can recall the naturalism of Hebrew religion, as opposed to the more philosophically oriented Greek language and religion. The evangelist John was able to combine Greek categories such as Logos with a more Hebraic worldview indicated by "flesh." The more Greek usage of the term is found in Paul, for whom *sarx*, flesh, means inherent human sinfulness. Perhaps for us, calling the bread of communion the flesh of Christ means to hit us in the face with the reality of sacramental meaning. The use of genuine bread, for example, freshly baked pita or a large single flat bread, will enhance the experience of communing in the solidarity of Christ.

In a time that touts easy access to everything we want, we need to heed the biblical Wisdom. She comes from God, she is authoritative and mature, and she calls us walk uprightly. As a female biblical image for God, she complements the mother. No longer nursing an infant, Wisdom is constructing buildings and slaughtering animals for a massive feast.

Ideas for the Day

♦ "Abide" is a word you seldom hear outside of church, which is too bad. The Greek word we translate "abide" is important in scripture. You can also translate the Greek more literally as "hang in there." There's a big difference between "hanging in", and "hanging on." "Hanging on" is desperate. "Hanging in" is a longtime choice. When Solomon asks God not for power or strength but for wisdom, he signals his willingness to hang in there for the long haul, to govern God's people well. Ask the congregation: "where do you abide?"

♦ The symbols of life often confound us. I freely admit not to understand the world of emojis. It is not that I don't understand the symbols, for they are quite simplistic in nature, it is that I simply don't understand why someone would want to reduce the beauty and grace of language to something so basic. I was surprised to hear that there was recently a convention of emojis, a Comic-Con inspired event. I can relate to what people felt like when Jesus told them they must eat of his flesh and drink of his blood. Many could not extend their thinking to accept what they were being told, the symbol of Jesus being the bread of life. Yet, as I extend my own thinking to accept the teachings of Jesus Christ, I must also accept the symbols of life around me. Emojis are not here to annihilate language; they are simply here to provide a new way of communicating complex ideas in a way that can be understood. Let us be ready in our own lives for the different ways Jesus might choose to communicate with us.

♦ The wonderful heritage of hymnody is expressed in the reading from Ephesians.

♦ The writer of the Gospel of John sees Jesus as the incarnation of God's Wisdom, who came to humanity in the flesh to reveal God's Word by living it fully among people: In the beginning was the Word, and the Word was with God, and the Word was God . . . And the Word became flesh and lived among us (John 1:1, 14a).

Making Connections

The fourth gospel does not have a scene of the Last Supper. Instead, John describes the foot washing, and skips over any institution of the Eucharist. John does, however, gives us this lengthy passage in Chapter 6 about Jesus being the bread of life—which really does look a lot like some developed eucharistic theology. When we celebrate the Eucharist, we are not just remembering the sacrifice of Christ. We are also participating in a very real way in his life, so that we might be empowered to continue his ministry in the world. As Eucharistic Prayer C says, we try to avoid "the presumption of coming to this table for solace only, and not for strength, for pardon only, and not for renewal." The power of the Eucharist is meant to propel us back out into the world as the living Body of Christ, rather than to allow us to rest away in our own righteousness. We become what we eat.

Engaging all Ages

This is a very good day to offer an instructed Eucharist as part of the worship schedule. In today's gospel, Jesus is clearly teaching the truth of his life and ours. We have heard Jesus repeat some form of these words in our gospel readings for several weeks, and today is an excellent opportunity to invite worshippers into

an interactive experience to bring the words alive. You can choose to provide instruction for the whole service or for the Eucharist alone. There are a variety of choices, many suitable for children and youth. Here are a few: www.trinitycathedral.org/worship /instructed-eucharist, http://theadvocatechurch.org /worship-liturgy/an-instructed-eucharist/, and http: //bookofcommonprayer.blogspot.com/2009/04/ instructed-eucharist.html (all accessed 31 August 2017).

Hymns for the Day

The Hymnal 1982
All my hope on God is founded 665 (SC)
Be thou my vision 488
Creator of the earth and skies 148
Eternal light, shine in my heart 465, 466
God be in my head, and in my understanding 694 (SC)
God of grace and God of glory 594, 595 (SC)
God, you have given us power to sound 584 (SC)
Open your ears, O faithful people 536 (SC)
God, you have given us power to sound 584 (GR)
Open your ears, O faithful people 536 (GR)
Come, O come, our voices raise 430
Let all the world in every corner sing 402, 403
New songs of celebration render 413
O praise ye the Lord! Praise him in the height 432
Sing, ye faithful, sing with gladness 492
Singing songs of expectation 527
Songs of praise the angels sang 426
When in our music God is glorified 420
Bread of the world, in mercy broken 301
Completed, Lord, the Holy Mysteries 346
Deck thyself, my soul, with gladness 339
Draw nigh and take the Body of the Lord 327, 328
Father, we thank thee who hast planted 302, 303
For the bread which you have broken 340, 341
I am the bread of life 335
Lord, enthroned in heavenly splendor 307
My God, thy table now is spread 321
O Food to pilgrims given 308, 309
We the Lord's people, heart and voice uniting 51

Wonder, Love, and Praise
Even when young, I prayed for wisdom's grace 906
I will bless the Lord at all times 764 (GR)
Wisdom freed a holy people 905 (GR)
As newborn stars were stirred to song 788
All who hunger, gather gladly 761
I am the bread of life 762
O wheat whose crushing was for bread 760

Lift Every Voice and Sing II
I will bless the Lord at all times 154 (GR)
I'm goin'-a sing when the Spirit says sing 117
Break thou the bread of life 146
I am the Bread that came down from heaven 150

Weekday Commemorations

Monday, August 20
Bernard, Abbot of Clairvaux, 1153
In 1113, Bernard (born 1090 in Dijon, France) entered the Benedictine Abbey of Citeaux. His family was not best pleased with his monastic choice, but he persuaded four of his brothers and 26 friends to join him in establishing a monastery at Clairvaux in 1115. Bernard fiercely defended the church and preached love for God "without measure." He was absorbed and dedicated to God even to the dismissal of his own health. He refused sleep in order to write. His sermons were so persuasive, they led to the founding of 60 Cistercian abbeys affiliated with Clairvaux. By 1140, his writing made him a profound influence within Christendom. He supported mystery over reason and was canonized in 1174.

Thursday, August 24
Saint Bartholomew the Apostle
Bartholomew, though one of the Twelve Apostles, is known only by having been listed among them in the gospels of Matthew, Mark, and Luke. His name means "Son of Tolmai," and he is sometimes identified with Nathanael, the friend of Philip, the "Israelite without guile" in John's gospel, to whom Jesus promised the vision of angels ascending from and descending on the Son of Man. Nothing more is recorded. Some sources credit Bartholomew with having written a gospel, now lost but once known to Jerome and Bede. By tradition, Bartholomew traveled to India; another tradition has him flayed alive at Albanopolis in Armenia.

Friday, August 25
Louis, King of France, 1270
A saint and a king, Louis IX expressed purity of life and manners. Born at Poissy, on April 25, 1214, Louis was faithful and moral, couragous and fearless, impartial and just. Louis possessed integrity beyond measure. He ventured to the Middle East and in North Africa, following the trend of pilgrims of his times, but, unlike other people of his time, he seemed free of bigotry. He was intelligently curious about theological issues, and influenced by his mother, Blanche of Castile, he desired to practice Christian ethics in his life, personal and public. He led a life of Franciscan poverty, wearing a hair shirt under his royal dress.

The Fourteenth Sunday after Pentecost: Proper 16

August 26, 2018

The disciples respond to Jesus' pronouncement that he is the "bread of life."

Color   Green

Preface   Of the Lord's Day

Collect

Grant, O merciful God, that your Church, being gathered together in unity by your Holy Spirit, may show forth your power among all peoples, to the glory of your Name; through Jesus Christ our Lord, who lives and reigns with you and the Holy Spirit, one God, for ever and ever. Amen.

Readings and Psalm

1 Kings 8:(1, 6, 10-11) 22-30, 41-43
(SEMI-CONTINUOUS) *or*

In the Hebrew scripture lesson, Solomon offers praise to the Lord and prays that the newly built temple may be a house for the Lord's gracious presence. King Solomon and the elders have just given the ark of the covenant a home, placing it in the temple they are now dedicating. Solomon recognizes that God transcends all human buildings, but asks the Lord to be present to those who call upon God in this temple—not only the people of Israel, but also foreigners who come to worship in Jerusalem.

Joshua 24:1-2a, 14-18 (GOSPEL-RELATED)

In our first lesson, Joshua calls the people to renew their covenant with the Lord and to realize what it means to promise to worship the Lord as the only God. This takes place at Shechem after the journey through the wilderness to the promised land. Joshua's farewell speech is stern, for it is no easy matter to enter into relationship with such a holy Lord, who will not allow followers to reverence any other gods. (Historically it is possible that this ceremony was used to accept into the covenant peoples living in Palestine who were not themselves participants in the exodus.)

Psalm 84 *or*
A song of the pilgrims' happiness as they come to worship in the temple of the Lord.

Psalm 34:15-22
The Lord is gracious toward all who turn from evil and have reverence for God.

Ephesians 6:10-20
In this New Testament lesson, Christians are instructed to put on the whole armor of God in order to defend themselves from the powers of evil, which are beyond any human control. The passage recognizes that it is God who will take the active role against these superhuman forces. In this battle, it is the Christian's primary task to stand and resist. The language and imagery may once have been used in an address to newly baptized disciples. Finally, they are urged to be constant in prayer, remembering Paul, who is now in prison.

John 6:56-69
In the gospel, we hear of different responses to Jesus' claim that he is the heavenly bread that gives eternal life to those who eat it. His are words of spirit and life, but many can understand them only in a materialistic sense and are like the Israelites who did not trust God in the wilderness. Yet, if this saying is hard for them to believe, more difficult still will be Jesus' ascent into heaven as the Son of Man. As Jesus knew would happen, many disciples now turn away, but Peter confesses him to be God's holy one who has the words of eternal life.

Prayers of the People

Presider: *Your words are spirit and life, O God: Heed the cry and the prayer that your servants speak to you today as we stand before your altar in the presence of the assembly, saying: Happy are the people whose strength is in you; whose hearts are set on the pilgrims' way.*

Litanist:　Gracious One, your Church declares with boldness the mystery of the gospel as we put on the whole armor of God in the strength of your divine power: Gird your people with the belt of truth and the breastplate of righteousness, the shoes of the gospel of peace, the shield of faith, the helmet of salvation and the sword of the Spirit, that we may stand firm in Christ's Word of love and compassion.

Happy are the people whose strength is in you;

> *whose hearts are set on the pilgrims' way.*

Almighty One, let your word be confirmed before the rulers and authorities of the world, that they may walk before you with all their hearts and be instruments of your mercy and peace.

Happy are the people whose strength is in you;

> *whose hearts are set on the pilgrims' way.*

Compassionate One, though all creation cannot contain you, you come to abide with us and to hear the prayers of the foreigner as well as the prayers of your people.

Happy are the people whose strength is in you;

> *whose hearts are set on the pilgrims' way.*

Loving One, let your eyes be open night and day toward this house and this community that your name may dwell with us to bless all your creation.

Happy are the people whose strength is in you;

> *whose hearts are set on the pilgrims' way.*

Hear our prayer and supplication for all who are in need, especially ___. Those who go through the desolate valley will find it a place of springs.

Accept our grateful thanks for all the blessings of our life, especially ___. They will climb from height to height.

We remember before you today those who have died, especially ___. Our souls desire and long for your courts; happy are they who dwell in your house.

Happy are the people whose strength is in you;

> *whose hearts are set on the pilgrims' way.*

Presider:　Your Spirit, O God, gives life through Jesus, the bread that came down from heaven: Give us the words of eternal life, that we may believe and know

that Christ is the Holy One of God who brings us spirit and life, in your Holy Name. **Amen.**

Images in the Readings

Last week the image of flesh was discussed. This week, John finally throws up his hands and writes, "The flesh is useless." As Augustine said, the scriptures are "of mountainous difficulty and enveloped in mysteries."

Peter calls Jesus "the Holy One of God." In Psalm 106:16, this phrase describes the priest Aaron. In the Hebrew scriptures, "the Holy One" is a common circumlocution for God. John's high Christology allows him to call Jesus by this divine title. In one of the interesting parallels between Mark and John, in Mark 1:24, it is the madman who calls Jesus "the Holy One of God."

Each piece of armor is given a Christian parallel. God protects us with truth, righteousness, peace, faith, salvation, and the word of God.

Joshua calls us to choose the way of the Lord. When we hear "Joshua," we should think of one with this same name, Jesus.

Ideas for the Day

- ✦ When Solomon has finished building God's temple, a wonder of the world, he says that even this new glorious house cannot contain God. He also, surprisingly, asks God to hear the prayers of "foreigners" who pray toward the temple. Solomon has built his temple to be, in the words of Isaiah, "A house of prayer for all people." As our culture becomes more secular, how do we continue to recognize God beyond the walls of our buildings? Are our sanctuaries open for all people?
- ✦ Christians are called in baptism into an eternal covenant with God. The baptismal rite expresses the sense of call and the theme of choice ("Do you desire to be baptized?"). To be baptized is to enter into an eternal covenant with God.
- ✦ As my soul longs for the courts of the Lord, where one day there is better than a thousand elsewhere, I must be prepared to endure the journey set before me. I must put on the whole armor of God to ward off the powers of evil. The belt of truth, the breastplate of righteousness, the helmet of salvation and the sword of the Spirit will aid me in persevering against the onslaught of evil in my life. We must work in collaboration with our Lord and Savior to achieve the goal of everlasting peace.

Making Connections

Despite the best efforts of many in the twentieth century, Christianity has been offensive to many, even since the very beginning. The notion that God, the creator of the cosmos, became a human like us—with all the mess and grime that this entails, is not a particularly pleasant idea. We don't like to think of the perfect Almighty mixing with the imperfect, the limitless with the limited. It seems to tarnish and diminish the divine. Yet Jesus maintains that it is this paradox precisely that is so miraculous. We come to know God's power when God gives it away, and we only know God's vastness when God is limited. Perhaps the larger point, too, is that the most profound miracles are not the ones we would request. For us to enter into the mystery of God, we have to be challenged, stretched . . . and maybe a bit offended.

Engaging all Ages

Heads may be nodding in agreement during today's gospel as we hear the disciples complain, "This teaching is difficult." We have been hearing repeatedly Jesus' promises of who he is but we may still feel the sting as Jesus asks, "Do you, also, wish to go away?" We can all gather strength in worship and in our community today as we choose to say, with Simon Peter, "Lord, to whom can we go? You have the words of eternal life." Let the dismissal words be "We have come to believe and know that you are the Holy One of God."

Hymns for the Day

The Hymnal 1982
I come with joy to meet my Lord 304
Our Father, by whose Name 587
Praise the Lord, rise up rejoicing 334
Put forth, O God, thy Spirit's might 521
Thou, who at thy first Eucharist didst pray 315
How lovely is thy dwelling-place [Psalm 84] 517
I love thy kingdom, Lord 524
Only-begotten, Word of God eternal 360, 361
Spirit divine, attend our prayers 509
Ancient of Days, who sittest throned in glory 363
Guide me, O thou great Jehovah 690
Praise our great and gracious Lord 393
Sing praise to God who reigns above 408
Eternal Ruler of the ceaseless round 617
Go forward, Christian soldier 563
Soldiers of Christ, arise 548
Stand up, stand up, for Jesus 561

Alleluia! sing to Jesus! 460, 461
Blessed Jesus, at thy word 440
Bread of the world, in mercy broken 301
Help us, O Lord, to learn 628
I am the bread of life 335
I call on thee, Lord Jesus Christ 634
Lord, be thy word my rule 626
Lord, enthroned in heavenly splendor 307
O Christ, the Word Incarnate 632
Spread, O spread, thou mighty word 530
Word of God, come down on earth 633

Wonder, Love, and Praise
Come now, O Prince of peace 795
Unidos/Together 796
Wisdom freed a holy people 905
From the dawning of creation 748
I am the bread of life 762
O wheat whose crushing was for bread 760

Lift Every Voice and Sing II
I am the bread that came down from heaven 150

Weekday Commemorations

Monday, August 27
Thomas Gallaudet and Henry Winter Syle
Gallaudet is called "The Apostle to the Deaf," and Syle was his student. Gallaudet was born June 3, 1822; Syle, November 9, 1846. Gallaudet's mother's speech and hearing were impaired; his father founded a school for the deaf. When Gallaudet wanted to become an Episcopal priest, his father convinced him to teach in a New York school for the deaf instead. Gallaudet was ordained a priest in 1851; he founded St. Ann's Church for Deaf-mutes, thereby influencing the establishment of deaf missions in many cities. Syle, hearing impaired from scarlet fever, was determined to be educated. Mentored by Gallaudet although opposed by others, Syle was ordained in 1876—the first deaf person to receive Holy Orders.

Tuesday, August 28
Augustine, Bishop of Hippo, 430
Called "the greatest theologian in the history of Western Christianity," Augustine, born in 354 in North Africa, became a Christian in 386 under the guidance of his mother Monnica. He was baptized by Ambrose, Bishop of Milan, in 387. He returned to North Africa in 391, whereupon he was chosen by the people of Hippo to be a presbyter; four years later, he became bishop of Hippo. About 400, he wrote his spiritual

autobiography, *The Confessions*; the extended prayer became a classic. Augustine wrote reams of treatises, letters, and sermons, thereby providing a rich source of insights into Christian truth. In 410, he wrote his greatest work, *The City of God*.

Thursday, August 31
Aidan, Bishop of Lindisfarne, 651

After the see-sawing of Christianity and paganism in Northumbria in north England, Oswald regained the throne and restored the Christian mission begun in 627 when his uncle, Edwin, was converted by a mission from Canterbury. During his exile, Oswald had lived at the monastery of Iona, where he had been converted and baptized, so he sent to Iona for missionaries. Gentle Aidan, head of the new mission, set his work on the distant island of Lindisfarne. He and his monks and their trainees restored Christianity in Northumbria, extending the mission through midlands and as far south as London. According to the Venerable Bede, Aidan delighted in giving to the poor whatever kings gave to him.

Friday, September 1
David Pendleton Oakerhater, Deacon and Missionary, 1931

Oakerhater (O-kuh-ha-tuh), born about 1847, shifted from warrior to peacemaker, thanks, in part, to sponsors such as Deaconess Mary Douglass Burnham and philanthropist Alice Pendleton. Before the Civil War, he had fought with the Cheyenne Indians of Oklahoma against the U.S. government; in 1875 he and 27 other warrior leaders were imprisoned in Florida. There, they learned English and art, and, there, Oakerhater found Christ's path to peace. Under sponsorship from the Diocese of Central New York, Oakerhater went north to study for the ministry. He took Pendleton's name when he was baptized (1878). He returned to Oklahoma, where he founded schools and missions despite U.S. governmental resistance.

The Fifteenth Sunday after Pentecost: Proper 17

September 2, 2018

Put the love of God and neighbor above pious empty practices.

Color   Green

Preface   Of the Lord's Day

Collect

Lord of all power and might, the author and giver of all good things: Graft in our hearts the love of your Name; increase in us true religion; nourish us with all goodness; and bring forth in us the fruit of good works; through Jesus Christ our Lord, who lives and reigns with you and the Holy Spirit, one God, for ever and ever. Amen.

Readings and Psalm

Song of Solomon 2:8-13 (SEMI-CONTINUOUS) or
Our Hebrew Bible reading brings us a celebration of love in the springtime of the year. The lover bounds across mountains to peer through the lattice of his beloved's enclosure to summon her into the meadows. There was considerable discussion about the inclusion of the Song of Solomon in the Hebrew Bible, but many rabbis found here an allegory of God's love for Israel. Following this tradition, many Christian interpreters perceived in the Song of Solomon an allegory for the love between Christ and the church.

Deuteronomy 4:1-2, 6-9 (GOSPEL-RELATED)
In our first reading, Moses urges the people to keep the Lord's commandments in order that they and their children may live well in the promised land. The long journey through the wilderness is nearly over, and here Moses is presented speaking to the people shortly before his death. They are to observe the Lord's statutes and so become known as a great and wise people with a just law and a God close at hand.

Psalm 45:1-2, 7-10 or
A poem for a royal wedding celebrating the ruler's majesty.

Psalm 15
The psalm describes the virtues of one who is worthy to worship the Lord.

James 1:17-27
This lesson consists of a series of teachings on the meaning of true religion: doing God's word. Every good gift comes from the unchanging Father. By God's word of truth we are given birth and have a first place among all creatures. Purified from anger and all other bad conduct, we are not only to hear God's word but to put it into practice. So do we observe the perfect law that sets people free—the law as interpreted by Jesus.

Mark 7:1-8, 14-15, 21-23
In the gospel passage, Jesus denounces those who find ways to ignore the genuine commandments of God, and he calls people to the awareness that the only evil which can corrupt a person comes from within. His judgments are occasioned by an accusation against his disciples that they are not following the rules of ritual cleansing. On one level, Jesus' words warn against the human tendency to fashion traditions that become more important than the law itself. More significantly still, his teaching points to the dangers involved in making legalism the basis for one's life.

Prayers of the People

Presider: *Let the words of our mouths express the thoughts of our hearts, O God, as we offer to your divine compassion the needs of the world, praying: Let our hearts be conformed to your purpose; and grant us your blessing.*

Litanist: Gracious God, you have given birth to your Church by your word of truth and raised us as the first fruits of your creatures: Grant that we may be doers of your word and not merely hearers, effectively sharing in your reconciling work throughout the world.

Let our hearts be conformed to your purpose;

and grant us your blessing.

Almighty One, help our leaders to carry your scepter of righteousness in order to create justice and peace, care for orphans and widows, and remove the stains that pollute your creation.

Let our hearts be conformed to your purpose;

and grant us your blessing.

Ever-present God, you have so linked our lives one with another that all we do affects, for good or ill, all other lives: So guide us in the work we do, that we may do it not for self alone, but for the common good; and as we seek a proper return for our own labor, make us mindful of the rightful aspirations of other workers, and arouse our concern for those who are out of work.

Let our hearts be conformed to your purpose;

and grant us your blessing.

Compassionate God, let your generosity abound among all the peoples of the earth, that humanity may respond with empathy and grace toward all who suffer, especially orphans and widows and any who are vulnerable or poor.

Let our hearts be conformed to your purpose;

and grant us your blessing.

Loving God, our hearts and lips are close to you as we intercede for our community: Inspire us to resist following human traditions which divide rather than unite, that we may faithfully follow your perfect law of liberty.

Let our hearts be conformed to your purpose;

and grant us your blessing.

Healing God, empower our reconciling work to share your blessing with all for whom we intercede, especially ___.

We thank you for all that is good and true and gracious, especially for ___.

Welcome into your divine heart those who have died, especially ___.

Let our hearts be conformed to your purpose;

and grant us your blessing.

Presider: *Holy and Eternal One, you lead us through your Word Jesus Christ, who taught us to obey all of your commandments by loving you and by loving our neighbors as ourselves: Purify our hearts that we may be instruments of your reconciliation and peace, in the power of your Spirit, through Jesus Christ our Savior.* Amen.

Images in the Readings

In antiquity, the heart was described as the intangibility of human identity, the locus of personality, the location of thought, and the generator of emotion. In biblical poetics, even God has a heart. The metaphoric interpretation is clear when the Bible speaks of an uncircumcised heart. Still today, the heart functions as a primary synecdoche (a part that implies the whole) of the human being. Often connected with positive emotions such as pity and love, the heart is also a container of evil. Many churches in the nineteenth century worked to mitigate the traditional emphasis on evil from within.

James's image of the law as a mirror has been important for many Christian theologians. Daily we look at this mirror and there see our inadequacies.

James stresses the religious obligation to care for "orphans and widows." Repeatedly in the Bible, this phrase suggests everyone who fell outside the normal patriarchal social net: orphans and widows, in particular, lived without the protection and sustenance of a male. Early Christians debated whether widowed women might remarry, and the New Testament records special food supplies sent to widows. Because typically a marriage involved a husband much older than the wife, many women must have been widows for decades.

Ideas for the Day

♦ In the ancient monastic scriptoriums, the most often copied manuscripts were the gospels, followed immediately by the Song of Songs. The monks knew what was up. Today, our lectionary hardly touches the book. Maybe we are too censorious. Consider preaching and teaching about not just this selected passage, but the whole of the Song. What does it mean to use romantic imagery for God? Can our spirituality be described with words like "enraptured" or "carnal?" How can we see our sexuality not as a problem, but as an integral part of our pilgrimage?

♦ What happens when tradition no longer speaks the language of God? How many churches have died simply because they held onto a tradition that no longer had meaning in contemporary society? If a church ministers to only a select few, how does it reach others who may be in need. Jesus sets the example of breaking with traditions? The Pharisees were appalled to see some of the disciples eating with unwashed hands. Because of tradition, these disciples would have been shunned. Jesus shows that by living and working in the Holy Spirit, we are freed from the bonds of restrictive traditions.

♦ The history of liturgical change through the reform of the Book of Common Prayer has shown how the church has sought to be faithful to our theological and ethical convictions. In essence, liturgy is the work of the people. As Episcopalians, we use reason to connect scripture and tradition to culture, changing human experience, and new knowledge. From the first Book of Common Prayer of 1549 to our current 1979 book, as well as the *Book of Occasional Services* and supplemental texts, such as *Enriching Our Worship*, we continue to be cognizant of how we worship. What revisions do you believe need to be made in the future?

Making Connections

One of the knocks against a set liturgy is that it becomes repetitive. Say the same prayer so many times and you know it by heart—so how heartfelt could it be? Yet that is precisely the purpose. Liturgy is meant to be a sort of outside-in handwashing; something we engage in externally so that we are changed internally. Every time we gather and say the prayers of thanksgiving, and pass the peace, and act out our salvation, we are enacting the way God would have us behave in the world. The hope is for us to do it often enough so that the words we say become imprinted on our hearts and lives, not just on our lips. We will end up living out our liturgy outside the church, and not just inside.

Engaging all Ages

It might be illustrative, as we ponder the gospel together as a community, to consider where we impose "rules" for belonging, particularly as it pertains to children and youth. It may feel to newcomers that one has to be an insider to truly belong, to know the aerobics of worship and the order in which things happen. Tradition is a wonderful thing but if it is placed ahead of true inclusion, then we are all the poorer. It might be fun to appoint a few "observers" to take note of how all ages are made to feel welcome and included.

Hymns for the Day

The Hymnal 1982
Lord, dismiss us with thy blessing 344
Come away to the skies 213 (SC)
God, my King, thy might confessing 414 (GR)
Help us, O Lord, to learn 628 (GR)
Lord, be thy word my rule 626 (GR)
Praise to the living God! 372 (GR)
Surely it is God who saves me 678, 679 (GR)
Immortal, invisible, God only wise 423
Lord, whose love through humble service 610
O Master, let me walk with thee 659, 660
We plow the fields, and scatter 291
Before thy throne, O God, we kneel 574, 575
Blest are the pure in heart 656
God be in my head, and in my understanding 694
Lift up your heads, ye mighty gates 436
Lord Jesus, think on me 641
Rejoice, ye pure in heart! 556, 557
Take my life, and let it be 707

Wonder, Love, and Praise
Gracious Spirit, give your servants 782
The church of Christ in every age 779
We are all one in mission 778
Lord Jesus, think on me 798

Lift Every Voice and Sing II
Give me a clean heart so I may serve Thee 124
Lord, I want to be a Christian 138

The Sixteenth Sunday after Pentecost: Proper 18

September 9, 2018

Faith is shown by one's actions, especially in showing compassion. Jesus is a sign of the dawning of God's reign in this way.

Pentecost

Color Green

Preface Of the Lord's Day

Collect

Grant us, O Lord, to trust in you with all our hearts; for, as you always resist the proud who confide in their own strength, so you never forsake those who make their boast of your mercy; through Jesus Christ our Lord, who lives and reigns with you and the Holy Spirit, one God, now and for ever. Amen.

Readings and Psalm

Proverbs 22:1-2, 8-9, 22-23
(SEMI-CONTINUOUS) *or*

Our opening lesson offers instruction in the characteristics of a well-ordered and godly life drawn from wisdom literature. Both the rich and the poor have been created by God, and this awareness should lead those with power and privilege to act with justice. The generous will be blessed, and the unjust will be punished; the Lord is an advocate for the defenseless.

Isaiah 35:4-7a *(GOSPEL-RELATED)*

In this Hebrew Bible reading, God comes in judgment to save the exiled people, and the prophet foresees a time of healing. The blind will see; the deaf hear; the lame leap; and the dumb sing. Retribution will fall upon God's enemies, but Israel will be saved. Even in the wilderness, pools of water shall spring up for them. Oracles such as this became for Judaism visions of the Lord's final salvation. Christians believe the healing age to have begun with Jesus.

Psalm 125 *or*

An expression of confidence in the Lord, the defender of the righteous, and a plea for Israel.

Psalm 146

A hymn of praise to the Lord, who forms the world and rules in justice, who heals and cares for the needy.

James 2:1-10 (11-13) 14-17

In this New Testament lesson, practical matters of ethical behavior among Christians are inextricable from any expression of genuine faith. Believers are counseled against showing special treatment to the rich. God has chosen to honor the poor. The rich often trespass through oppressive conduct and, in any case, this way of treating people differently violates the royal commandment to love one's neighbor as one's self. Christians are reminded to live under the perfect law of liberty and to act with mercy.
If the shorter lesson is used, the final sentence may be omitted.

Mark 7:24-37

In our gospel reading, Jesus, traveling in Gentile territory, heals the daughter of a Gentile woman and then a deaf man with a speech impediment. The back-and-forth between Jesus and the Syrophoenician woman may seem playful or even harsh. It may be that through such a conversation Jesus saw how his mission was to include all peoples, as his followers came later to understand. The healing of the deaf man can be recognized as a fulfillment of prophecy as the new age of the kingdom draws near.

Prayers of the People

Presider: *Ever-present and compassionate God, you care for all persons with your unconditional divine love, and you extend your liberating grace to all peoples: Open our hearts to be strong and fearless in the pursuit of justice and relief, especially on behalf of the poor and the stranger, as we pray: You care for near and far alike; liberate your children from their oppression.*

Litanist: Gracious and loving God, you have called your Church to follow the royal law to love our neighbors as ourselves: Empower our witness of reconciliation that we may speak gracefully to those whose ears cannot yet hear the Good News of God's love and may serve generously those whose mouths cannot yet proclaim your grace.

You care for near and far alike;

> *liberate your children from their oppression.*

You guide the leaders of the nations to show mercy and to eschew partiality: Free from their bondage those whose lot is only the leftovers and crumbs, and empower those who struggle to live on what falls from their masters' tables.

You care for near and far alike;

> *liberate your children from their oppression.*

You embrace with your compassion, O God, those whom some call dogs and others who are poor or dishonored: Heal and comfort all who are in weakness or in need throughout the world.

You care for near and far alike;

> *liberate your children from their oppression.*

You have chosen the poor in the world to be rich in faith and heirs of the kingdom: Reconcile our community that we may be people of radical hospitality, welcoming native and foreigner, rich and poor, without distinction or partiality.

You care for near and far alike;

> *liberate your children from their oppression.*

You withhold your healing presence from no one: Honor our prayers for all who are in need, especially ___.

You call us to share in your work of reconciliation and freedom. We thank you for the many ministries of this congregation: our work of worship, outreach, education, service, and fellowship. Hear our joy as we give you thanks, especially for ___.

You keep your promise for ever; hear our prayers for those who have died, especially ___. You care for near and far alike;

> *liberate your children from their oppression.*

Presider: Gracious and living God, your loving care reaches to the ends of the earth, rescuing those who live in bondage and fear: Open our eyes and ears to your call of compassion, that we may joyfully share in your eternal life, and bring all humanity into the goodness of your Spirit, through Jesus Christ our Savior. Amen.

Images in the Readings

Most worshiping Christians are, like the Syrophoenician woman, Gentiles. The New Testament indicates the early church's debates as to whether non-Jews could be included in God's salvation. The question has been broadened in recent centuries: Who is the outsider? How ought Christian insiders relate to them?

Jesus responds to a needy woman. Most persons and cultures in most times and places, including those that are Christian, have been lousy at responding to needy women.

We are all deaf. Some Christians with the conditions cited in Isaiah—being blind, deaf, lame, mute—welcome metaphoric speech that likens all persons to them; however, other persons warn against using disabilities as symbols. Use your judgment as you apply the gospel narrative to everyone who gathers to hear the word of God.

Use of the term "the poor" raises similar concerns. We ought not easily categorize persons as "the poor," yet neither can we as Christians gloss over the radical disparity in most nations of the world between those with and those without the necessities of life.

Ideas for the Day

- Try to imagine what it would have been like if the healed man had done as Jesus had asked. Suddenly a man who has unable to speak is holding conversation with friends. Their jaws on the floor they ask "How did this happen?" The healed man replies, "never mind that." Couldn't have happened. Of course he was going to tell. We often hear the Episcopal Church doesn't know how to be "evangelists," but when gospel work is going on, it is hard to keep quiet. If our people aren't talking enough about faith, maybe we need to be about real healing.
- Lord, open my eyes, for I am blind. Open my ears, for I am deaf. Heal my lame legs, so that I might walk in your path. Lord, unloose my tongue, for I am mute. I have been blind to the suffering around me. I have been deaf to cries of people that I am in capacity to help. I am lame, sitting and waiting for others to do that which only I can do. I have been mute, silently watching the deeds of man

Pentecost

undermine the deeds of God. Lord, heal me so that I live in in the power of your glory.

♦ In response to Jesus' assertion that he came to give the good news to the Jewish people first (the children), the woman claims the scraps from God's table. Her rejoinder, full of humility and courage, reveals her as a woman of deep faith in a just and generous God. In rewarding her steadfast trust, Jesus declares her "clean," able to receive God's blessings, related to God in a way thought impossible by his Jewish opponents. Who are the "children" today? Who are the "dogs"? What does Jesus' example indicate about contemporary religious prejudices?

Making Connections

I find this gospel pericope to be disturbing. We can gloss over it if we choose, but all signs point to Jesus using an ethnic slur to respond to a woman who is seeking help for her daughter. (If you weren't shocked when he was talking about bread and wine, now would be the time to take some offense.) It's not clear why he does it—that's an argument for another time. What is remarkable is that when the woman stands her ground, Jesus allows his mind to be changed. Rather than claim divine knowledge or superiority, Jesus recognizes her claim to the truth after being challenged. His humility here is as wondrous as the healing itself.

Engaging all Ages

Using our words to ask for help is often daunting. Even though our prayers include "Thy will be done," it is okay to persist in our efforts. It is in our prayers of intercession and petition that we give voice to God's presence and power among us. What opportunities are being offered for all the generations to be bold with prayers, offering them to God in trusting and persistent ways? Today is a good day to offer guidance in these kinds of prayer, to learn the ways of petition and intercession, to persist in bringing all our concerns to God.

Hymns for the Day

The Hymnal 1982
I'll praise my Maker while I've breath 429
Immortal, invisible, God only wise 423 (SC)
On this day, the first of days 47 (SC)
Thou, whose Almighty word 371 (GR)
O for a thousand tongues to sing 493 (GR)
Father all loving, who rulest in majesty 568

Help us, O Lord, to learn 628
Jesu, Jesu, fill us with your love 602
Lord, whose love through humble service 610
When Christ was lifted from the earth 603, 604
From thee all skill and science flow 566
Give praise and glory unto God 375
Thine arm, O Lord, in days of old 567
Word of God, come down on earth 633

Wonder, Love, and Praise
The desert shall rejoice 722 (GR)
From miles around the sick ones came 774
Heal me, hands of Jesus 773
O Christ, the healer, we have come 772

Lift Every Voice and Sing II
Jesu, Jesu, fill us with your love 74

Weekday Commemorations

Wednesday, September 12
John Henry Hobart, Bishop of New York, 1830
Buried beneath the chancel of Trinity Church in New York City lies Hobart, a staunch, devoted leader in the revival of the Episcopal Church. Hobart, born September 14, 1775, graduated from Princeton in 1793 and was ordained a priest in 1801, having become an assistant minister at Trinity the year before. He was consecrated assistant bishop of New York in 1811; five years later, he became diocesan bishop and rector of Trinity. Within his first five years as bishop, Hobart doubled the number of clergy and quadrupled the number of missionaries. He planted a church in almost every major town of New York State and served as missionary among the Oneida Indians. He was a founder of General Theological Seminary.

Thursday, September 13
Cyprian, Bishop and Martyr of Carthage, 258
Cyprian so declared: "You cannot have God for your Father unless you have the Church for your Mother." Cyprian was born rich and lived an aristocratic and cultivated life in North Africa before converting to Christianity about 246. He was chosen bishop of Carthage two years later. His hiding in 249 during a persecution led to criticism; despite absence, he continued to lead the Church with compassion. After the persecution, Cyprian took the controversial position that those who had lapsed during the persecution could be reconciled to the Church after doing suitable penance. In the end, his moderate position prevailed. In another time of persecution under Emperor Valerian, Cyprian,

while under house arrest in Carthage, was beheaded. Many of his writings—on the Lord's Prayer, on unity in the Church—have been preserved.

Friday, September 14
Holy Cross Day

Supervision over the work of erecting a building complex in Jerusalem to mark the site of Christ's resurrection was entrusted to the empress Helena, mother of Emperor Constantine. Under Helena's direction, the excavation discovered a relic, believed to be of the "true cross." Calvary stood outside the city in Jesus' time; when *Aelia Capitolina* succeeded Jerusalem, the hill was buried. Constantine's magnificent shrine included two main buildings: a basilica and a round church known as "The Resurrection." The buildings were dedicated on September 14, 335, the seventh month of the Roman calendar; the date was suggested by the account in 2 Corinthians of the dedication of Solomon's temple hundreds of years before.

Pentecost

The Seventeenth Sunday after Pentecost: Proper 19

September 16, 2018

The cost of discipleship includes bearing the cross.

Color Green

Preface Of the Lord's Day

Collect

O God, because without you we are not able to please you, mercifully grant that your Holy Spirit may in all things direct and rule our hearts; through Jesus Christ our Lord, who lives and reigns with you and the Holy Spirit, one God, now and for ever. Amen.

Readings and Psalm

Proverbs 1:20-33 (SEMI-CONTINUOUS) or

Our opening lesson is an instructional poem in which Wisdom is personified as an attribute of God's character and a virtue to be sought and possessed. Lady Wisdom actively seeks out those as yet unformed in character and strives to gain their attention, for she offers to lead them into the way of life and goodness. Those who scoff or refuse her instruction court calamity, but those who listen will dwell secure.

Isaiah 50:4-9a (GOSPEL-RELATED)

Our first reading tells of the servant who speaks for the Lord and suffers persecution, but still trusts in God's help and vindication. This is the third of the "servant songs" which come from a period late in Israel's exile. The servant might be thought to be the faithful of Israel, the prophet himself, or another historical or idealized figure. The people are weary and tired of the Lord's calling, but the servant steadfastly continues. Christians have long perceived in these words a foretelling of Jesus' mission.

Psalm 19 or

A hymn which glorifies the Creator God, with special praise for God's law and a prayer for avoidance of sin.

Canticle: A Song in Praise of Wisdom or

Wisdom is extolled as an attribute of God of unsurpassed value.

Psalm 116:1-8

An offering of thanksgiving and praise by one who has been rescued from death.

James 3:1-12

In this New Testament lesson, the community is reminded that one who instructs others will be held to a high standard, and such a position should only be aspired to by those well-formed in faith. Of particular concern are habits of speech. The tongue is compared to a small rudder able to control a large ship at sea. There is great danger in an uncontrolled tongue, and many forms of careless speech are enumerated. The Christian must learn self-discipline in order that God may be glorified.

Mark 8:27-38

In the gospel, Peter recognizes that Jesus is the Christ, and Jesus then describes the true nature of the ministry of the Son of Man and what it means to follow in his way. The passage reminds us that during Jesus' lifetime and afterward there was speculation about his role. Some saw him as a kind of re-embodiment of John the Baptist or another prophet. Peter is called "Satan" because his words are a temptation to turn away from the suffering and death which come before resurrection. Disciples must also learn that the true self and true life are found by those who will let themselves be lost for the sake of Jesus and the gospel.

Prayers of the People

Presider: *Gracious God, you have saved us through your Son Jesus Christ and you call us to take up our cross and follow him: Incline your ear to us as we call upon you, saying: Let the words of our mouths and*

Pentecost

the meditations of our hearts be acceptable in your sight, O God, our strength and our redeemer.

Litanist: Holy God, you have promised life to your Church as we lose our lives for Jesus' sake and for the sake of the gospel: Inspire our witness to your Messiah, that we may share in his work of resurrection.

Let the words of our mouths and the meditations of our hearts be acceptable in your sight;

> **O God, our strength and our redeemer.**

Wise and Wonderful God, keep our leaders and all in authority from presumptuous sins and guide them, that they may set their minds upon divine things and not upon human things.

Let the words of our mouths and the meditations of our hearts be acceptable in your sight;

> **O God, our strength and our redeemer.**

Ever-present God, comfort all who undergo great suffering throughout the world and let your saving hand raise them to new life.

Let the words of our mouths and the meditations of our hearts be acceptable in your sight;

> **O God, our strength and our redeemer.**

Benevolent God, be near to us and sustain us in conflict and in prosperity, that our community may be whole and sound, and innocent of great offense.

Let the words of our mouths and the meditations of our hearts be acceptable in your sight;

> **O God, our strength and our redeemer.**

The heavens declare your glory, O God, and the firmament shows your handiwork. Hear our prayers for those for whom we intercede, especially ___.

We thank you for teachers and all who speak your good news to the world. Hear our gratefulness for our many blessings, especially for ___.

In Christ you have suffered, died, and risen. May Jesus, the Messiah, the Anointed One of God, bring all humanity into eternal life. Hear our prayers for those who have died, especially ___.

Let the words of our mouths and the meditations of our hearts be acceptable in your sight;

> **O God, our strength and our redeemer.**

Presider: Holy and Gracious One, through your Son, Jesus the Messiah, you have shown us how to save our lives by losing ourselves into the grace of your good news for all people: Fill us with the power of your Spirit, that we may live with faithful courage, sharing in Christ's sufferings so that we may share in his resurrection, who lives and reigns with you and the Holy Spirit, one God, now and for ever. **Amen.**

Images in the Readings

The most ancient depiction that has been found of Christ's cross is a carving on a late fourth-century ivory box. Not until Constantine forbade execution by crucifixion did the church draw, sculpt, and don the image of the cross. Today would be a good day to discuss all the crosses that are in on church property or are worn by members as identification or adornment.

Like Peter, sometimes we are mouthpieces for Satan, says James, spewing out evil. We need a bit in our teeth, a stronger rudder; we need to be a clean spring, a productive fig tree. Our baptismal water can put out the fires started by our speech.

Many generations construe their own sexual infractions as the worst ever, but even Mark has Jesus referring to first-century society as an adulterous generation. In another example of sexual imagery used to refer to other sin, the prophets condemned the Israelites for "lusting" after other gods.

Ideas for the Day

- ◆ "That's just my cross to bear," an all too common phrase that is pseudo-gospel, false. The words are often spoken by women facing abuse and others in reprehensible circumstances. Jesus does not counsel his followers to suffer in silence. Jesus himself suffered in public. His death brought God's light on systemic human injustice. How do we "lose our life?" How do we lose our sense of false comfort? How do we lose the blinders we all have to injustices in our world? Jesus didn't carry his cross silently. Crosses are about redemption, not silence.

- ◆ Stories of persons from *Lesser Feasts and Fasts* (or *A Great Cloud of Witnesses*) who have participated in the suffering of others to bring healing into their lives are part of our tradition. Stories of doctors, nurses, researchers in medical science who risked their lives, social workers among the poor and oppressed, political leaders and others who have attempted to enter the struggle of suffering would be appropriate to study and connect to today's readings.

◆ Fear can be one of the biggest deterrents in our lives. It often cripples us from taking action. Yet, so many before us faced persecution without fear. Isaiah says he gave his back those who struck him, his cheek to those who pulled out his beard and he did not hide his face from disgrace and spitting. He drew strength from his faith in the Lord. We must understand our role in the grand procession towards the kingdom of God. We must live fearlessly so that our story may be told in future generations.

Making Connections

When I was a child, it always confused me that we celebrated the Eucharist on Christmas Eve. The poor baby had just been born—couldn't we allow him even a day to enjoy it before we recalled his death? Similarly, no sooner has Jesus received recognition from the disciples as the messiah, than he announces his coming death. It's a bit of a downer, and Peter reacts accordingly. But Jesus' point is that to be the Messiah is inextricably linked with his crucifixion. To be the Son of God in this world does not earn you a celebration—it earns you death. When the Church fails to grapple with that reality, we lose sight of where Christ calls us.

Engaging all Ages

In identifying our first or our next steps in ministry, we may be helped by asking and answering questions. This process can help clarify where we feel called to serve. Jesus' question to his followers taps into both faith and imagination. In quiet moments during worship or formation time, we can ponder and wonder about our personal response to what Jesus asks. And it may be illustrative to turn the tables—to offer, in prayer, the same question to Jesus, "Who do you say I am?" What other questions might we ask Jesus? What can we learn from others' answers?

Hymns for the Day

The Hymnal 1982
The spacious firmament on high 409 (SC)
The stars declare his glory 431 (SC)
O sacred head, sore wounded 168, 169 (vs 1-3) (GR)
Before thy throne, O God, we kneel 574, 575
Strengthen for service, Lord, the hands 312
Day by day 654

From God Christ's deity came forth 443
Glorious things of thee are spoken 522, 523
New every morning is the love 10
Praise the Lord through every nation 484, 485
Take up your cross, the Savior said 675
The Church's one foundation 525
You are the Christ, O Lord 254

Wonder, Love, and Praise
Even when young, I prayed for wisdom's grace 906 (SC)
O sacred head, sore wounded 735 (vs 1-3) (GR)
Will you come and follow me 757
You laid aside your rightful reputation 734

Lift Every Voice and Sing II
O sacred head, sore wounded 36 (vs 1-3) (GR)
He never said a mumbalin' word 33 (GR)
I can hear my Savior calling 144
I have decided to follow Jesus 136
King of my life I crown thee now 31

Weekday Commemorations

Tuesday, September 18
Edward Bouverie Pusey, Priest, 1882
Pusey led the Oxford Movement, which revived High Church teachings and practices in the Anglican Communion. Pusey, born August 22, 1800, spent his scholarly life at Oxford as professor and as canon of Christ Church. With Keble and Newman, he produced Tracts for the Times in 1833 (thus, the movement is also known as Tractarianism). He proved most influential through sermons catholic in content and evangelical in zealotry, but dangerously innovative to some (Pusey was suspended from preaching for two years). Pusey influenced many from leaving the Anglican Church after Newman defected to the Church of Rome in 1845. With his money, he built churches for the poor; with his time, he established the first Anglican sisterhood since the Reformation.

Wednesday, September 19
Theodore of Tarsus, Archbishop of Canterbury, 690
Although Theodore was 66 when ordained Archbishop of Canterbury in 668, he provided strong leadership for a generation. He was a learned monk from the East who had been residing in Rome when he began his episcopate. The Church was riven between Celtic and Roman customs. When Theodore arrived in England, he set up a school excellent in all disciplines, and he unified Anglo-Saxon Christians, including regularizing

Pentecost

Chad's episcopal ordination. He defined boundaries of English dioceses, presided over reforming synods, and laid foundations of parochial organizations. According to Bede, Theodore was the first archbishop whom all English obeyed. He was buried in the monastic Church of Saints Peter and Paul at Canterbury.

Thursday, September 20
John Coleridge Patteson, Bishop of Melanesia, and his Companions, Martyrs, 1871

Patteson, who was stabbed five times in the breast, and his companions died at the hands of Melanesian islanders—the very people they had tried to protect from slave traders. As a result, the British government took serious measures to prevent pirates from hunting humans in the South Seas. Their martyrdom seeded the vigor of the Melanesian Church today. Patteson, born in London (1827), was ordained in 1853 after travel in Europe. While a curate in Devonshire, near his family home, he answered a call in 1855 for help in New Zealand, where he established a boys' school on Norfolk Island. He learned, some say, to speak 23 of the languages of the Melanesian people.

Friday, September 21
Saint Matthew, Apostle and Evangelist

A disciple of Jesus the Christ, Matthew left everything to follow the Master at his call. Matthew was identified with Levi, a tax collector, when tax collectors were seen as collaborators with the Roman State and, thus, spurned as traitors. Matthew was hardly the sort of person a devout Jew would associate with, yet Jesus noticed Matthew rather than someone else, such as a pious, proud, prayerful Pharisee. The disciple himself probably did not write the gospel of his name, given as author in homage. Through this gospel and its parables, Jesus speaks of faith and eternal life; of duty to neighbors, family, and enemies. Matthew is venerated as a martyr although circumstances of his death are unknown.

Pentecost

The Eighteenth Sunday after Pentecost: Proper 20

September 23, 2018

Jesus predicts his passion a second time and reminds his disciples that to be great in the kingdom of God is to be the servant of all.

Color Green

Preface Of the Lord's Day

Collect

Grant us, Lord, not to be anxious about earthly things, but to love things heavenly; and even now, while we are placed among things that are passing away, to hold fast to those that shall endure; through Jesus Christ our Lord, who lives and reigns with you and the Holy Spirit, one God, for ever and ever. Amen.

Readings and Psalm

Proverbs 31:10-31 (SEMI-CONTINUOUS) or

In this lesson from the Book of Proverbs, we find a poem to a woman of worth who embodies attributes beyond charm and beauty, all of which have their source in her allegiance to God. In an agrarian culture where the economic and social well-being of the household was primary, the industry and ability of ranking women were essential to the success of the extended family and its dependents. The virtues of the ideal woman described in this acrostic poem are substantially economic; she is an astute businesswoman, managing with excellence all that is in her charge. She is charitable to the poor and extends herself for the needy, displays wisdom, and teaches kindness.

Wisdom of Solomon 1:16—2:1, 12-22
(GOSPEL-RELATED) or

This first reading describes the philosophy of deluded sinners who find no purpose in life and persecute the one who is righteous. They wish not only to take advantage of the good person, but also to test and finally put to death anyone whose very goodness is a reproach to their way of life. They will make trial both

of those who perceive themselves to be among God's children, and of the God in whom they have placed their confidence. Christians have seen in these words a foreshadowing of Christ's sufferings and vindication.

Jeremiah 11:18-20

In this reading, the prophet Jeremiah offers the first of his laments to the Lord. Though he is innocent, there are those who seek to take his life because of his faithful outspokenness. Yet his confidence is placed firmly in God to whom he has committed his cause.

Psalm 1 or

The Lord makes fruitful those who choose the way of righteousness.

Psalm 54

A prayer of salvation by one who is persecuted.

James 3:13—4:3, 7-8a

In this New Testament epistle, believers are to cleave to wisdom that is pure, peaceable, gentle, and full of mercy and good fruits. The Christian community must recognize the results of worldly attitudes and desires: jealousy, disorder, quarrels, even murder. Prayers are too often offered for the wrong motives, but a harvest of righteousness is sown for those who sow in peace. The wise will refuse evil and draw near to God, and in doing so, they will find that God has also drawn near to them.

Mark 9:30-37

In the gospel, Jesus foretells his death and resurrection as the Son of Man, bidding his disciples to have a servant ministry and to learn to welcome him and God in a child. The several sayings are linked together by the theme of Jesus' lowliness and readiness to suffer for others. His followers' difficulty in understanding him and their discussion concerning which of them is greatest stand in sharp contrast to their Lord's teachings. Jesus' action and words with regard to the child remind us of another saying: whatever is done to the least member of the community is done to him.

Prayers of the People

Presider: *Wonderful and compassionate God, you have revealed yourself through your Son Jesus Christ as a God of gentle service, resisting the violence of the proud and confirming the goodness of the innocent: Hear the offering of our prayers on behalf of the little, the last, and the lost, as we say: Whoever wants to be first, must be last of all and servant of all.*

Litanist: You have called your Church to sacrificial service in the name of your Son Jesus: Grant us the wisdom from above which is first pure, then peaceable, gentle, willing to yield, full of mercy and good fruits, without a trace of partiality or hypocrisy, that your church may bring to you a harvest of righteousness.

Whoever wants to be first,

>   *must be last of all and servant of all.*

Confront the leaders of the world with your justice, and raise up courageous witnesses who will oppose wrong action and reprove the thoughts of the violent, that all who serve in positions of authority may join in your divine work to deliver the innocent and vulnerable from the hands of their adversaries.

Whoever wants to be first,

>   *must be last of all and servant of all.*

Be present with those who suffer throughout the world from war or violence or oppression, from poverty or hunger or sadness: Let your kind and gentle hand be with them to comfort and deliver them.

Whoever wants to be first,

>   *must be last of all and servant of all.*

Spread your teaching throughout our community to increase among us those who are wise and understanding, whose works are done with gentleness born of wisdom.

Whoever wants to be first,

>   *must be last of all and servant of all.*

We offer to your gracious protection our intercessions for those for whom we are called to pray, especially ___.

We thank you for the gift of children and for calm strength and patient wisdom to nurture them as they grow to love whatever is just and true and good. We bring you our gratefulness for our joys and blessings, especially for ___.

We entrust to your never failing care and love those who have died, especially ___.

Whoever wants to be first,

>   *must be last of all and servant of all.*

Presider: *God and Father of our Savior Jesus Christ, who has endured the path of betrayal and death and triumphed in humble resurrection: Help us to extend your gentle embrace to all your children, and thus welcome you into our lives through service and gratefulness, in the power of your Spirit and in the name of your risen and living Son.* **Amen.**

Images in the Readings

In our time, some little children are treasured, but we kid ourselves if we forget that the little child is still the most vulnerable, the most manipulated, the most readily discarded. We are to welcome those who are vulnerable, manipulated, discarded, as was Jesus himself.

To welcome others into our community is now a popular Christian understanding. Yet Christ welcomes us all to a community of suffering, of servanthood, of being the last. This message of the cross will influence how we think about how we welcome others and what we are welcoming them into.

Jeremiah uses the image of the helpless lamb led to slaughter. So in Christian iconography, Christ is the lamb, standing as if it had been slaughtered (Revelation 5:6). The one who models vulnerability for us is Jesus Christ.

James describes wisdom as the planting that grows into a harvest of righteousness.

Ideas for the Day

♦ Buddhist teachers often speak of the importance of the "beginner's mind." Rather than considering ourselves experts in the spiritual path, they say, it is important to remember we are all beginners. Get too assured of your own progress and you are sure to stumble. When Jesus hears his disciples arguing about greatness, he turns their expectations upside down. "Whoever would be first, must be last." Welcoming children helps us remember that in faith the basics are important, even crucial. We can never lose sight of the first steps of discipleship.

Pentecost

♦ We walk on, even in the midst of those who scoff at us. We walk on, even in the midst of those who devise schemes against us to do us harm. We walk on, even in the midst of those who seek to kill us. We then stand ourselves by the stream that gives us life, as a tree by the water, and when the wind blows, we are rooted. We will watch the others blow away like chaff. Our roots grow strong, being fed by love, peace, and faith. We then fully bear the fruits of the Spirit.

♦ Some questions to ponder: What kind of attitude is needed to receive a child? Who are the "children" in today's society? In what ways is your Christian community receiving these individuals? In what ways do you receive them?

♦ Compare Jesus' view of the kingdom of God with your own. Whom have you unconsciously wished to exclude from the kingdom? In what ways do these verses enable you to broaden your understanding of the kingdom?

Making Connections

As a general rule, one should not use children as props for object lessons, even if you are the Son of God. But Jesus' point lands—the reign of God is not based on greatness as the world sees it, but as God sees it, and God values especially the least of these. Children in our communities are an incredibly valuable presence, and yet they don't give us pledge income or volunteer hours in return for what we give them. The time and energy we put into empowering and teaching the youngest among us (and oldest, actually) is all sheer gift—yet it is a gift that proclaims the reign of God to all people.

Engaging all Ages

The gift of children, in addition to the delight and wonder they inspire in us, is often how they draw us into honest exchanges and sharing. Today is a fine opportunity to listen for their voices, to encourage the youth to lead the way in decision-making as well as in prayer. During worship, notice the ways we can proclaim to them, "You are welcome here." Name the young people in the prayers of thanksgiving and rejoice in their presence. Invite them to gather at the altar during the Eucharist and say aloud their names as you offer bread and wine.

Hymns for the Day

The Hymnal 1982
God moves in a mysterious way 677 (GR)
How firm a foundation 636, 637 (GR)
Praise to the Lord, the Almighty 390
Sing praise to God who reigns above 408
If thou but trust in God to guide thee 635 (GR)
Commit thou all that grieves thee 669
Before thy throne, O God, we kneel 574, 575
Eternal Spirit of the living Christ 698
Hope of the world, thou Christ of great compassion 472
Lord, for ever at thy side 670
All praise to thee, for thou, O King divine 477
God is Love, let heaven adore him 379
Lord of all hopefulness, Lord of all joy 482
O love, how deep, how broad, how high 448, 449
O Master, let me walk with thee 659, 660
Sing, ye faithful, sing with gladness 492
When Jesus left his Father's throne 480

Wonder, Love, and Praise
Peace among earth's peoples is like a star 789
These three are the treasures to strive for and prize 803

Lift Every Voice and Sing II
I am weak and I need thy strength and power 194 (GR)
I've been 'buked an' I've been scorned 195 (GR)
In God we trust 55 (GR)
When we walk with the Lord 205 (GR)

Weekday Commemorations

Tuesday, September 25
Sergius, Abbot of Holy Trinity, Moscow, 1392
Sergius' name is familiar to Anglicans from the Fellowship of St. Alban and St. Sergius, the society dedicated to promoting relationships between Anglican and Orthodox churches. To the people of Russia, Sergius serves as their patron saint. Born in 1314, he was 20 when his brother and he secluded themselves in a forest and developed the Monastery of the Holy Trinity, a center for reviving Russian Christianity. There, Sergius remained, a simple servant, mystical in temperament and eager to see his monks serve their neighbors. Sergius' support of Prince Dimitry Donskoi rallied Russians against Tartar overlords, thereby laying a foundation for independence. Pilgrims visit his shrine at the monastery of Zagorsk, which he founded in 1340.

Wednesday, September 26
Lancelot Andrewes, Bishop of Winchester, 1626
Andrewes' sermons, witty and grounded, made him King James I's favorite preacher. Andrewes (born 1555 in London) was also a fine biblical scholar, able in Hebrew and Greek, who served as a translator for the Authorized (King James) Version of the Bible. As Dean of Westminster and headmaster of its school, he influenced the education of many churchmen, including poet George Herbert. *Preces Privatae* illustrates his piety. He strongly defended the catholicity of the Church of England against Roman Catholic critics. He was a model bishop even when bishops were not esteemed. T.S. Eliot was inspired by Andrewes' Epiphany sermon for the opening stanza of "The Journey of the Magi."

Saturday, September 29
Saint Michael and All Angels
Christians have always felt attended by spiritual messengers, that is, angels: visible or not, human or not. These helpful spirits, powerful and enlightening, appear in Christian art in human form, their wings signifying swiftness and spaciousness, their swords attesting to their power, their dazzling raiment announcing their ability to enlighten. Many angels are mentioned in the Bible, but only four are named: Michael, Gabriel, Uriel, and Raphael. The Archangel Michael, a powerful agent of God, wards off evil from God's people and delivers God's peace. Michaelmas has been celebrated in many parts of the world. Michael is patron saint of many churches, including Mont-St.-Michel off Normandy and Coventry Cathedral in England.

Pentecost

The Nineteenth Sunday after Pentecost: Proper 21

September 30, 2018

Jesus' power breaks out in spontaneous acts of healing that cannot be confined to the church.

Color Green

Preface Of the Lord's Day

Collect

O God, you declare your almighty power chiefly in showing mercy and pity: Grant us the fullness of your grace, that we, running to obtain your promises, may become partakers of your heavenly treasure; through Jesus Christ our Lord, who lives and reigns with you and the Holy Spirit, one God, for ever and ever. Amen.

Readings and Psalm

Esther 7:1-6, 9-10; 9:20-22
(SEMI-CONTINUOUS) or

In this Hebrew Bible story, we hear how Queen Esther, by wisdom and providence, turns the tables and saves her people. Israel is in exile in Persia, where a Jewish woman is taken into the king's harem and is eventually made his queen. One of the king's advisors, Haman, makes a personal vendetta into a persecution of the entire Jewish people. This story of sorrow turned into gladness, set during the reign of Xerxes I (King Ahasuerus 486–465 BCE), is celebrated in the Jewish festival of Purim.

Numbers 11:4-6, 10-16, 24-29
(GOSPEL-RELATED)

In this Hebrew scripture story, the people weep and complain in the wilderness, and the Lord comes to Moses' help by sharing some of the prophet's spirit of leadership with seventy chosen elders and also with two others who were left behind in the camp. This spirit is manifested in temporary spells of ecstatic prophecy. The narrative has several interwoven themes. Once more, God turns away wrath at Israel's lack of trust. The story is meant to show that all leadership derives its authority from Moses' God-given power. That the Spirit falls on Eldad and Medad illustrates how it cannot be confined by human appointment.

Psalm 124 *or*
A hymn of thanksgiving for deliverance.

Psalm 19:7-14
A hymn which glorifies the Creator God, with special praise for God's law and a prayer for avoidance of sin.

James 5:13-20
This New Testament lesson is an affirmation of prayer and the power of forgiveness in all circumstances. Prayer should characterize the lives of the suffering and joyous alike, and those who are sick should seek the intercession of the church leaders. The community of believers is to strive for the restoration to faith of any who have strayed.

Mark 9:38-50
In the gospel, Jesus bids his disciples to accept all who seek to do good in his name and to deal ruthlessly with whatever part of themselves causes sin. Early Christians were doubtless faced with people outside their communities who said they were acting in Christ's name. The tolerant answer given here suggests that Jesus' followers must avoid arrogance and be open to God's divine actions. On the other hand, it is a serious matter to lead a believer astray. The counsel to destroy offending parts of the body is exaggerated to make clear the importance of avoiding various sins. The description of hell is drawn from the garbage dump outside Jerusalem.

Prayers of the People

Presider: *Ever-present God, you reveal yourself in the splendor and order of your creation: Heal our broken lives that we may join in the reconciling prayer and work of Christ, as we pray in faith: Our help is in the Name of God, the maker of heaven and earth.*

Litanist: Our Mighty God, you have taught us that whoever is not against us is for us, and you have promised a divine reward for all who befriend any of your children: Save your Church from whatever may cause us to stumble, that our hands may serve compassion, our feet walk in the ways of truth, and our eyes be set upon your unquenchable love.

Our help is in the Name of God,

the maker of heaven and earth.

Just and Compassionate One, you call us to defend the vulnerable and to resist the oppressor: Give our leaders vision and strength to be instruments of justice and servants of peace who will take up the burden of your people and serve them rightly. Our help is in the Name of God,

the maker of heaven and earth.

Kind and Gentle One, you uphold the little ones, the weak and the vulnerable: Raise up those who suffer or who are oppressed throughout the world, that they may know the comfort of your saving help.

Our help is in the Name of God,

the maker of heaven and earth.

Gracious and Loving One, you have surrounded us with neighbors from other traditions who do good in the name of Jesus, and you inspire others to serve you, though they follow not our beliefs: Bestow your reward upon any who act in kindness, and lead us to serve our community as ministers of the salt of peace.

Our help is in the Name of God,

the maker of heaven and earth.

Merciful and Healing One, you have taught us that the prayer of faith will save the sick and that you will raise them up: Hear us as we pray for all who suffer, especially ___.

You have told us to sing songs of praise with the cheerful: Hear our thankful hearts praising you, especially for ___.

You have overcome death in the resurrection of your Son Jesus Christ: Accept into your eternal love those who have died, especially ___.

Our help is in the Name of God,

the maker of heaven and earth.

Presider*: Send your Spirit into all the earth, O God, that every human being may know your love, grow*

in faith, and serve your creation in grateful humility, through Jesus Christ our Savior, who with you and the Holy Spirit, lives and reigns, one God, for ever and ever. **Amen.**

Images in the Readings

"Cut it off," in today's gospel and in Matthew 5, suggests the totality of ethical transformation that is expected of believers. However, when in the third century the biblical scholar Origen castrated himself in obedience to these passages, the church did not approve of such literal interpretation of these texts.

A cup of water, a great millstone, the undying worm, salt, and fire: Mark's passage includes powerful metaphors to describe the life in and away from Christ. In the Bible, salt is used as both a positive and a negative image, but here salt is good, a vital preservative in antiquity, with which newborns were rubbed. Some Christians have placed salt on the tongue of the baptized as part of the ritual. Christians are to flavor the world with righteousness and preserve it from rot by being the salt of the earth.

The unquenchable fire of eternal damnation was central to the Christianity of the Middle Ages and remains a significant doctrine for some Christians, although from the second century on, a minority of Christians maintained that a loving God will not condemn anyone to an existence without forgiveness. Contemporary systematic theologians debate the veracity and value of such passages that are translated with the noun "hell."

Ideas for the Day

♦ Rabbi Jonathan Sacks, speaking on a panel with Presiding Bishop Katharine Jefferts Schori and the Dalai Lama, said you could sum up almost all Jewish celebrations in three points: "They tried to kill us. We survived. Let's eat!" The book of Esther is read for Purim. While not a high holy day, Purim is a favorite among children (and the childlike), as noisemakers are used whenever the name "Haman" is read. The noise deafens ears from hearing the name a persecutor. Purim asks us: "How do we remember sacred history? Who are the victors? Who are the survivors?"

♦ Not everyone who works to the benefit of Jesus Christ and his church follow the teachings in the same way. Jesus instructs his disciples not to deter those people using his name to cast out demons. Jesus recognizes that though they were not followers, they were engaging in a power larger than themselves. The one who is not against us is for us. Help in building the kingdom of God on earth can come from anyone and anything. We must do our part to educate ourselves in the courses of action tailored to our talents. We must also not be a hindrance to those who work in ways different than our own

♦ The word fire in Mark 9:49 makes the transition from the punishment warned of in verse 48 to the counsel in verse 50. Fire both consumes the unrighteous and purifies the righteous. Only a consuming passion for God's will can make possible the sacrifice and discipline required to enter God's kingdom. What are some positive or neutral areas of contemporary life that may cause sin? What kind of sacrifice would it take to eliminate these areas from your life? Which of these do you find the most painful to contemplate sacrificing? Why?

♦ In first-century Israel, salt was invaluable as a preservative, as a healing agent, and as a seasoning. Its peculiar properties qualified it as a precious commodity, but when it lost its characteristics, either by diluting it or contaminating it with an excessive amount of another substance, it retained no value whatsoever. Suggest a spiritual equivalent for each of the qualities of salt. How salty is your faith community? Where has your spiritual life lost its saltiness? In what ways do the qualities of salt enable Christian brothers and sisters to "be at peace with one other"?

Making Connections

One of the oddities of the Elizabethan Settlement is the acknowledgement of the Anglican Church from its inception that we had no corner on the truth. Once the Church of England really got moving, there was no point at which it claimed to be the one, sole, arbiter of what Christianity was or could be—instead, it generally saw itself as the one part of the church that was rooted in England. (There were some notable exceptions to this—namely, the Puritans, but by and large, they were fewer in the Anglican Church than elsewhere.) From our tradition, then, Episcopalians are inclined to be kind to other churches. If they are not against us, they are for us! They might just express it in their own particular way. And while we do have much to learn from other traditions, we also have much to share from our own. We can rejoice in our own church, and the unique gifts God has given to us, without resorting to demeaning others.

Engaging all Ages

Life is full of temptations, and it is often feelings of inadequacy that we bring to God during worship. We know things we need to change, and so a brief silence following the Confession offers time to personally offer to God our regrets before we receive the wonderful words of forgiveness. Repeat Jesus' words, "have salt in yourselves and be at peace with one another" as worshippers are invited to carry the feeling of being loved and forgiven into the passing of the Peace. Place a small dish of salt on the altar as a reminder that "salt is good."

Hymns for the Day

The Hymnal 1982
Awake, my soul, stretch every nerve 546
Fight the good fight with all thy might 552, 553
Lo! what a cloud of witnesses 545
God moves in a mysterious way 677 (SC)
God of the prophets, bless the prophets' heirs 359 (GR)
O Food to pilgrims given 308, 309 (GR)
Shepherd of souls, refresh and bless 343 (GR)
The stars declare his glory 431 (GR)
Commit thou all that grieves thee 669
If thou but trust in God to guide thee 635
O God of Bethel, by whose hand 709
Spirit divine, attend our prayers 509
Before thy throne, O God, we kneel 574, 575
Go forth for God; go to the world in peace 347
Lord, dismiss us with thy blessing 344
Where cross the crowded ways of life 609

Wonder, Love, and Praise
Guide my feet, Lord, while I run this race 819
All who hunger, gather gladly 761 (GR)
It's me, O Lord, standin' in the need of prayer 797
Gracious Spirit, give your servants 782

Lift Every Voice and Sing II
It's me, O Lord, standin' in the need of prayer 177
Sweet hour of prayer 178
If I have wounded any soul today 176

Weekday Commemorations

Monday, October 1
Remigius, Bishop of Rheims, c. 530
"Remi," born about 438, was but 22 when he became Bishop of Rheims. As a patron saint of France, he is most noted for converting and baptizing King Clovis of the Franks on Christmas Day, 496. That changed the religious history of Europe. Most Germans were

Arians, but being Christian meant that Clovis could unite the Gallo-Roman population and its Christian leaders and also liberate Gaul from Roman domination. Clovis' conversion eased the Franks' cooperation with Pope Gregory the Great as he evangelized the English. The feast of Remigius is celebrated in Rheims on January 13, thought to be his death day; Ocotber 1 marks the translation of his relics to a church in 1049.

Thursday, October 4
Francis of Assisi, Friar, 1226

After a misspent youth as well as encounters with beggars and lepers, Francis embraced a life devoid of material goods. In 1210, Pope Innocent III confirmed The Rule for the Order of Friars Minor, the name chosen by Francis to underscore the "least" of God's servants. The order grew so large and lax that, by 1221, Francis had lost control of it. He remained joyful in his last years despite grievous suffering in body and spirit. Near his death, Frances received the *stigmata*, marks of Jesus' wounds, in his own hands and feet and side. Pope Gregory IX canonized Francis in 1228. Francis is admired for his bond with animals, if not imitated for voluntary poverty.

Saturday, October 6
William Tyndale, Author, 1536

Born about 1495 and educated at Oxford, Tyndale was ordained about 1521, then served as a domestic chaplain for two rich merchants. Determined to translate the scriptures into English but without official support, he removed from England to Germany in 1524. He was constantly hunted thereafter: King Henry VIII and Cardinal Wolsey and others wanted him dead and his work destroyed. Finally, a friend betrayed him: Tyndale was strangled at the stake and burned. Before his death, he had finished translating the New Testament, the Pentateuch, and Jonah but did not live to see them published. His work of translation, though often polemical, lives.

Pentecost

The Twentieth Sunday after Pentecost: Proper 22

October 7, 2018

The sanctity of human relationships.

Color   Green

Preface   Of the Lord's Day

Collect

Almighty and everlasting God, you are always more ready to hear than we to pray, and to give more than we either desire or deserve: Pour upon us the abundance of your mercy, forgiving us those things of which our conscience is afraid, and giving us those good things for which we are not worthy to ask, except through the merits and mediation of Jesus Christ our Savior; who lives and reigns with you and the Holy Spirit, one God, for ever and ever. Amen.

Readings and Psalm

Job 1:1; 2:1-10 (SEMI-CONTINUOUS) *or*

In our first lesson, we hear the beginning of the story of Job: the plight of a righteous man. Satan appears in God's heavenly court and charges that Job is upright only because of the many blessings that are his. God permits Satan to test Job greatly through terrible and tragic trials. Then, through dialogue and poetry, the Book of Job explores the problem of human suffering and faith in God's ways with unflinching honesty and feeling.

Genesis 2:18-24

Then the LORD God said, "It is not good that the man should be alone; I will make him a helper as his partner." So out of the ground the LORD God formed every animal of the field and every bird of the air, and brought them to the man to see what he would call them; and whatever the man called every living creature, that was its name. The man gave names to all cattle, and to the birds of the air, and to every animal of the field; but for the man there was not found a helper as his partner. So the LORD God caused a deep sleep to fall upon the man, and he slept; then he took one of his ribs and closed up its place with flesh. And the rib that the LORD God had taken from the man he made into a woman and brought her to the man. Then the man said, "This at last is bone of my bones and flesh of my flesh; this one shall be called Woman, for out of Man this one was taken." Therefore a man leaves his father and his mother and clings to his wife, and they become one flesh.

Psalm 26 *or*

A plea for justice by one who serves the Lord well.

Psalm 8

The psalmist glorifies the Lord, Sovereign of the earth and the magnificent heavens, who has made human life to have mastery over all other earthly creatures.

Hebrews 1:1-4; 2:5-12

The author of the Letter to the Hebrews teaches that Jesus, the exact imprint of God's being and the pioneer of our salvation made perfect through suffering, is superior to all the angelic order. God inspired the prophets but has now spoken through a Son, the heir of all things, and through whom the worlds were created. For a while made lower than angels, he now, through his death, sanctifies all whom he calls brothers and sisters.

Mark 10:2-16

In the gospel, Jesus, asked about divorce, reaches back to the creation story to set before his hearers the ideal of the marriage relationship and then blesses children. In Jesus' lifetime there were many views on divorce, some strict and some more lenient. In one sense, Jesus is the strictest of all: what through natural union God has made one cannot be separated by human action. Yet, in another sense, Jesus' answer refused to deal with the question in the way it is asked. Instead, he honors the solemnity and purpose of marriage. Anything less is sin, which cannot be dismissed by human regulations. His disciples seem surprised by this teaching and also by his embracing of children.

Prayers of the People

Presider: *Creator God, hear our prayers for the whole earth, that we may be loving companions, living responsibly within your covenant of creation, saying: We will proclaim your name to our brothers and sisters, in the midst of the congregation we will praise you.*

Litanist: You have made the Church to be the Body of Christ Jesus who is the reflection of your divine glory and the exact imprint of your divine being: Grant us grace to receive your kingdom as little children, knowing the comfort of your arms and the goodness of your blessing.

We will proclaim your name to our brothers and sisters,

in the midst of the congregation we will praise you.

You spoke to our ancestors in many and various ways by the prophets, and in these days you have spoken to us by a Son: Guide the leaders of our nation and all in authority to exercise wise stewardship of your creation and to protect the integrity of all people.

We will proclaim your name to our brothers and sisters,

in the midst of the congregation we will praise you.

You made Jesus perfect through sufferings, thus becoming the pioneer of our salvation: Uphold all who are in any need throughout the world and bring them your saving help.

We will proclaim your name to our brothers and sisters,

in the midst of the congregation we will praise you.

You reveal your divine being as a community of self-giving love, and you draw us together into families: Bless all couples in their commitments to be no longer two, but one flesh, that they may grow in grace, fidelity, and mutual affection all of their days.

We will proclaim your name to our brothers and sisters,

in the midst of the congregation we will praise you.

Hear our prayers for those for whom we pray in intercession, especially ___.

We thank you for the wonder of your creative power at work around us, especially for ___.

You crowned Jesus with glory and honor because of the suffering of death which he has tasted for everyone: Grant that all people may be raised with him in his resurrection, as we remember especially ___.

We will proclaim your name to our brothers and sisters,

in the midst of the congregation we will praise you.

Presider: *Let your children come to you, O God, that you may touch and bless us with your kindness and inspire our relationships with your love, which calls us to be faithful to our families and our communities, to the animals and birds that you have given to us as companions, and to all this glorious creation that you have made, through him, who is not ashamed to call us brothers and sisters, our Savior Jesus Christ.* **Amen.**

Images in the Readings

One flesh is the biblical language for the effect and goal of sexual intercourse. Some philosophers in antiquity proposed that the first human was androgynous. After male and female sexes split, the two sexes sought each other out to regain a primal wholeness.

In the biblical world, a child was the least and had no independent status. Under Roman law, the father had the right to discard any infant born to him or to his household.

The Hebrew noun *kenegdo*, traditionally translated in English as "helpmeet," is now usually translated "helper." In Psalm 121:1-2, the same noun is used for God.

The author of Hebrews sees the universe as a hierarchy, with God on top and then angels, humans, animals, and on down the created order to inanimate things. Philosophically this has been referred to as the Great Chain of Being. The letter to the Hebrews understands that in the incarnation Jesus Christ moved from a higher to a lower place—thus the discussion about the placement of angels. Jews adopted pagan language about angels from neighbors.

Ideas for the Day

♦ Almost no one plans their eventual divorce on their wedding day. People usually come to the altar with the best of intentions. But sometimes we can't keep even our best intentions. Sometimes marriages do not work. Marriage today is a different institution than in the times of the Bible. Jacob had to marry Leah first so that he could marry Rachel. Solomon had 700 wives. Jesus' words on divorce seem tough to us today because they are words for a different time. In some circumstances today divorce can be a blessing.

♦ A four-week, semi-continuous reading of the book of Job begins this Sunday. Take time to introduce Job and how it offers a sustained reflection on a single topic—God's governance of the world of human beings. Sit awhile with Job.

♦ Today also begins a seven-week, semi-continuous reading of the first ten chapters of Hebrews.

Providing an understanding of the temple priesthood and sacrificial system and connecting it our the Eucharistic prayers that reflect the sacrificial language of Hebrews: "You . . . sent Jesus Christ . . . to share our human nature, to live and die as one of us, to reconcile us to you, . . . and offered himself, in obedience to your will, a perfect sacrifice for the whole world" (BCP 362).

♦ Jesus is placed at the center above all of others. Through the centuries, God has spoken to us through prophets. God appointed his only begotten son to speak in a voice above all. "After making purification for sins," God placed Jesus at his right hand, even giving him superiority over angels. Jesus unifies the progress of time, putting a context to all of the prophets, saints, and martyrs. Our life in ministry must look ultimately to Jesus above all. He is the intermediary between ourselves and God. It is the Spirit than facilitates us doing the work that will glorify his name.

Making Connections

One of the founding myths of the Anglican Church is that King Henry VIII wanted a divorce, so he started his own church. That's not quite right. He wanted a lot of things: more money, land, control of his own local church, and a male heir. And then he became convinced that the reason things weren't going so well was because his wife used to be married to his brother, and God was angry at him for committing this sin. Things pretty much devolved from there, and by the end, Henry had broken loose from Rome, had won a divorce, and had upturned his entire kingdom. As Jesus points out, much of Henry's decision-making was led by "hardness of heart." He wanted certain things, and would not accept anything else. However, a similar hardness of heart has also caused the church to disallow divorce, even when it would be the best thing for all concerned. It is hardness of heart, ultimately, that destroys us, and not the legalities of marriage.

Engaging all Ages

It is tempting to focus attention on Jesus' blessing the children rather than the uncomfortable words concerning divorce. Are these words relevant today? Perhaps it is this very discomfort that we can address in the Prayers of the People. Notice today how it is possible to approach the altar knowing that you may not agree with your neighbor. And a question to ponder as we

return to the world, "To whom does the kingdom of God belong?"

Hymns for the Day

The Hymnal 1982
Eternal Spirit of the living Christ 698
Only-begotten, Word of God eternal 360, 361
Commit thou all that grieves thee 669 (SC)
If thou but trust in God to guide thee 635 (SC)
O worship the King, all glorious above 388 (SC)
Surely it is God who saves me 678, 679 (SC)
For the beauty of the earth 416 (GR)
Joyful, joyful, we adore thee 376 (GR)
Your love, O God, has called us here 353 (GR)
All hail the power of Jesus' Name 450, 451
From God Christ's deity came forth 443
Hail, thou once despised Jesus! 495
Lead us, heavenly Father , lead us 559
My song is love unknown 458 (1-2, 6-7)
O love, how deep, how broad, how high 448, 449
The head that once was crowned with thorns 483
Now thank we all our God 396, 397
O God of love, to thee we bow 350
O God, to those who here profess 352
When Jesus left his Father's throne 480

Lift Every Voice and Sing II
Oh Lord, how perfect is your name 57 (GR)
Children of the heavenly Father 213
Jesus loves me! this I know 218
There's not a friend like the lowly Jesus 90
Jesus loves the little children 222

Weekday Commemorations

Tuesday, October 9
Robert Grosseteste, Bishop of Lincoln, 1253
Distinguishing himself as a scholar in many disciplines, from law to science and languages, Grosseteste was appointed Master of the Oxford School. He was first teacher of theology to the Franciscans. He translated and commented on Aristotle's works from Greek as well as figuring a scientific method based on Augustine's theories. He influenced both Roger Bacon and John Wycliffe. In 1235, he was consecrated Bishop of Lincoln and executed his office efficiently and conscientiously, traveling to each rural deanery with alacrity to preach, confirm, convene, and answer doctrinal questions. Grosseteste opposed royal infringements on Church liberties and protested papal abuses of local prerogatives: "As an obedient son, I disobey, I contradict, I rebel. . . ."

The Twenty-First Sunday after Pentecost: Proper 23

October 14, 2018

The desire for wealth can lead to injustice, lack of compassion, and estrangement from God.

Color Green

Preface Of the Lord's Day

Collect

Lord, we pray that your grace may always precede and follow us, that we may continually be given to good works through Jesus Christ our Lord, who lives and reigns with you and the Holy Spirit, one God, now and for ever. Amen.

Readings and Psalm

Job 23:1-9, 16-17 (SEMI-CONTINUOUS)

In the continuing saga, the much-besieged Job longs for a divine court from which he might seek redress and justice. He casts about on every side for God, but is met with a devastating absence of God's presence. Though this reflection comes as a response to Job's accusatory "friend" Eliphaz, it is in the nature of an interior monologue as his distress mounts and he is subjected to a pervading sense of isolation. Job believes in God's justice, but is so bereft of any signs of its dawning that he thinks he would prefer entire darkness.

Amos 5:6-7, 10-15 (GOSPEL-RELATED)

In our opening reading, the prophet denounces corruption and injustice, but offers hope to the survivors of the impending destruction if they will seek the Lord and love good while hating evil. God's judgment will be like fire on all the iniquities of the people of the northern kingdom in Israel. They will not live to enjoy their ill-gotten luxury. The prudent individual will be shocked into silence.

Psalm 22:1-15 or

A psalm of lamentation and a plea for deliverance by one who feels deserted and pressed in on every side.

Psalm 90:12-17

The psalmist reflects on the passing character of human life in the face of the Lord's wrath and asks the everlasting God for wisdom to make use of the time.

Hebrews 4:12-16

The reading reminds us that the Lord's word is active, probing the human heart and all creation, while we can yet boldly approach God's throne because Jesus, our great high priest, has known our weaknesses and temptations. The first statement is a warning: God's word, which God has spoken at the creation, through the scriptures, and personally in Jesus, is everywhere and makes judgment. But we now have a heavenly high priest, our brother, who knows all about our life, and helps us to find God's mercy. The insistence that Jesus was without sin relies not on extensive knowledge of what he did not do, but on the memory of his positive dedication to God's will.

Mark 10:17-31

In the gospel, Jesus counsels a man to sell all for the benefit of the poor and follow him, and he then teaches how hard it is for those with riches to enter the kingdom. Disciples who now surrender much will receive back all manner of new relationships in the age to come. Jesus first refuses to let himself be called *good,* since that description belongs to God alone. He then finds that the man has tried to live out his duties toward his neighbors in response to divine love. But the decision for discipleship must go beyond this. If the heart is divided by desires for worldly security, there is no way one can enter into the kingdom's loving justice. Yet by the power of God, people can be converted and saved.

Prayers of the People

Presider: *Good Teacher, you look at us with love and teach us to trust our heavenly Father to give us the treasures of heaven: Open our hearts with divine*

Pentecost

generosity that we may share in your work of reconciliation, as we pray: Our forebears put their trust in you; they trusted, and you delivered them.

Litanist: Gracious God, you are one with Christ our great High Priest who has passed through the heavens: He sacrificed all things for the salvation of the world and called the Church to share in your generous work of resurrection and reconciliation.

Our forebears put their trust in you;

> ***they trusted, and you delivered them.***

Compassionate One, your Word is living and active, sharper than any two-edged sword and able to judge the intentions of the heart: Look upon our world and inspire the rich and powerful to generosity and justice.

Our forebears put their trust in you;

> ***they trusted, and you delivered them.***

Healing Physician, before you no creature is hidden: Reach out with your goodness and touch the lives of all who suffer throughout the world, that they may receive mercy and find grace to help in time of need.

Our forebears put their trust in you;

> ***they trusted, and you delivered them.***

Gracious Friend, show your compassion in this community, that we may be a city of graciousness and love.

Our forebears put their trust in you;

> ***they trusted, and you delivered them.***

Hear our intercession for those for whom we pray, especially ___.

You are gracious to your servants, and we give you thanks, especially for ___.

You have been tested in every respect as we are and have triumphed over death; let those who have died approach your throne of grace with boldness, especially ___.

Our forebears put their trust in you;

> ***they trusted, and you delivered them.***

Presider: Loving One, in Jesus you have taught us that for you all things are possible: Hear the prayers of your people, that we may persevere in generosity and continually be given to good works, through Jesus Christ our Savior, who is alive with you and the Holy Spirit, our One, Triune God, for ever and ever. **Amen.**

Images in the Readings

The church's adherence to the Ten Commandments, which Christian traditions have numbered in several different ways, relies in part on their Christian reinterpretation in the New Testament. This passage is one such Christian discussion of the historic Jewish law: here the law is understood as leading to Christ.

For centuries, Christians hung paintings in their churches that were referred to as the Throne of Grace: God the Father, shown as a loving old man, held in his arms Christ on the cross, and the Holy Spirit hovered nearby in the form of a dove. Grace is God's loving mercy.

The depiction of the word of God as like a sword that, nonetheless, conveys grace is picked up in Ephesians 6:17 and in Revelation 1:16. The word issues from the mouth of Jesus Christ, and with it believers can defend themselves from the evil one. This biblical image conveys the power of the word to slay evil and counters the temptation to tame the word of God into pleasant platitudes.

Ideas for the Day

♦ The letter to the Hebrews chooses "boldness" to describe our approach to faith. Jesus asks the same of the rich man. The writer David Foster Wallace once counseled the graduating class at Kenyon College to choose what they would worship. "Everyone worships," he said but the default settings are to worship money, things, beauty, power. Choosing to worship God, to put our faith ahead of our other pursuits, requires boldness. While Jesus may or may not require us to sell our possessions, our faith asks, boldly, what will you choose to worship?

♦ It is not easy to walk with God. Jesus tells the rich man to sell all of his possessions and give everything to the poor if he wants to follow the path of Christ. We would not find this an easy task. We are attached to so many of our material things. Yet, it is this attachment that pulls us away from doing the work of our spiritual journey. Our material possessions do not define us. It is our spirit of service and love that define us. Let us not allow earthly treasures distract us from our true spiritual purpose.

♦ The monastic tradition models a total dedication to God by requiring its members to live simply and hold all goods in common. Many Episcopalians are surprised to learn that there are religious orders in the Episcopal Church. Introduce your congregation to one of more of them, and learn their practices of prayer and community living. Among them are the Society of St. John the Evangelist (www.ssje.org), Order of the Holy Cross (www.holycrossmonastery.com), the Community of the Holy Spirit (www.chssisters.org), or the Society of St. Margaret (http://societyofstmargaret.org), accessed 1 September 2017.

Making Connections

A parishioner once remarked in Bible study that he wished we had more stories of Christians who were ordinary: people who believed in Christ and did quiet service for others in the midst of daily life. Instead, what we have are a litany of outrageous faithfulness—leaving house, livelihood, and possessions, risking death for the sake of the gospel. All of which, he pointed out, makes the average pew-sitter feel rather ineffective. Perhaps this is the dilemma shared by the disciples and the rich young man here. The gospel Jesus brings *is* hard; the command to love God and love one another is all-consuming, and how on earth are we supposed to even come close to achieving this in the midst of paying off student loans and worrying about who has walked the dog today? Yet, Jesus assures us that what seems impossible for us is possible for God. All that is required of us is that we try. And when we fail, to try yet again. God will help us with the rest.

Engaging all Ages

Like the rich man, we know how to live God's way and that we often fall short. What comfort in Mark's words, "Jesus, looking at him, loved him . . . " Let's examine together, as we repeat the well-known liturgy, what we are willing to leave behind in order to be a follower of Jesus. Echo Jesus' words in the Prayers, "for God all things are possible." Invite younger members of the congregation to offer a token such as a small cross to worshippers as they leave the service to serve as a reminder in the week ahead of the abundance Jesus offers.

Hymns for the Day

The Hymnal 1982
From deepest woe I cry to thee 151 (SC)
Out of the depths I call 666 (SC)
Father all loving, who rulest in majesty 568 (GR)
Give praise and glory unto God 375 (GR)

O day of God, draw nigh 600, 601 (GR)
O God, our help in ages past 680 (GR)
"Thy kingdom come!" on bended knee 615 (GR)
Alleluia! sing to Jesus! 460, 461
Before thy throne, O God, we kneel 574, 575
From God Christ's deity came forth 443
Completed, Lord, the Holy Mysteries 346
God himself is with us 475
Hope of the world, thou Christ of great compassion 472
Jesus, all my gladness 701
O for a closer walk with God 683, 684
O Jesus, I have promised 655
Sing praise to God who reigns above 408
Take my life, and let it be

Wonder, Love, and Praise
Gracious Spirit, give your servants 782

Lift Every Voice and Sing II
I have decided to follow Jesus 136
Thou my everlasting portion 122

Weekday Commemorations

Monday, October 15
Teresa of Avila, Nun, 1582
Even as a girl, Teresa studied saints' lives, delighting in contemplation and repeating, "For ever . . . they shall see God." She grew up to be one of two women declared a Doctor of the Church in 1970, primarily because of her two mystical contemplative works, *The Way of Perfection* and *Interior Castle*. To offset girlish worldliness following her mother's death, Teresa's father placed her in an Augustinian convent. After serious sickness ended her studies there, she chose the religious life in a Carmelite convent. She increasingly meditated, and she perceived visions—Godly or Satanic, she did not know. She traveled for 25 years through Spain, establishing 17 convents of Reformed Carmelites ("discalced," or unshod). Her letters provide insights to her heart.

Tuesday, October 16
Hugh Latimer and Nicholas Ridley, Bishops, 1555, and Thomas Cranmer, Archbishop of Canterbury, 1556
Cranmer (born 1489), the principal figure in the Reformation of the English Church, was primarily responsible for the first Book of Common Prayer of 1549. Compromising his political with his reformation ideals led to his death—despite his recanting. Ridley (born 1500) also adhered to reformation ideals as he served

as chaplain to King Henry VIII. Unwilling to recant his Protestant theology, Ridley died with Latimer at the stake. Latimer (born about 1490) was installed as Bishop of Worcester in 1535 under Henry VIII; he resigned his see in 1539 and refused to resume it after Edward VI was enthroned. Latimer was imprisoned and burned at the stake with Ridley under the crown of Mary on October 16, 1555.

Wednesday, October 17
Ignatius, Bishop of Antioch, and Martyr, c. 115

Ignatius' seven letters, written to Churches while he sojourned across Asia Minor, open insight to the early Church. In one, he cautioned against Gnostic teachings that underscored Jesus' divinity over his humanity; in another, he condemned biblical literalism, citing Jesus Christ as "the ancient document." Ignatius held that the Church's unity would rise from its liturgy by which all are initiated into Christ through baptism. Ignatius thought of the Church as God's holy order in the world; he was concerned, therefore, with ordered teaching and worship. In ecstasy, he saw his martyrdom as the just conclusion to a long episcopate as second Bishop of Antioch in Syria.

Thursday, October 18
Saint Luke the Evangelist

Luke's gospel serves, not as a biography, but as a history of salvation. Luke did not know Jesus, but he was inspired by those who had. He wrote the book that honors the name of the disciple and its sequel, the Acts of the Apostles. Luke wrote in Greek, allowing Gentiles to read his stories. Only Luke presents the familiar stories of the annunciation to Mary, of her visit to Elizabeth, of the child in the manger, and the angelic host's appearing to shepherds. He cites six miracles and 18 parables not recorded by the other gospellers. In Acts, Luke tells of the coming of the Holy Spirit and the struggles of the apostles.

Friday, October 19
Henry Martyn, Priest, and Missionary to India and Persia, 1822

Martyn translated the scriptures and prayer book into Hindi and Persian and served as an English missionary in India. Born in 1781 and educated at Cambridge, Martyn, influenced by Charles Simeon, Evangelical rector of Holy Trinity/Cambridge, changed his mind about becoming a lawyer and became a missionary. He traveled to India in 1806 as chaplain for the British East India Co. He was there but five years before dying at age 31; however, in that time, he organized private schools and founded churches in addition to translating the Bible. He also translated the New Testament into Persian. He died in Tokat, Turkey, where Armenians honored him by burying him like one of their own bishops.

The Twenty-Second Sunday after Pentecost: Proper 24

October 21, 2018

God calls the Christian into servant ministry, which means sharing in the suffering of others in order to bring life and healing.

Color   Green

Preface   Of the Lord's Day

Collect

Almighty and everlasting God, in Christ you have revealed your glory among the nations: Preserve the works of your mercy, that your Church throughout the world may persevere with steadfast faith in the confession of your Name; through Jesus Christ our Lord, who lives and reigns with you and the Holy Spirit, one God, for ever and ever. Amen.

Readings and Psalm

Job 38:1-7 (34-41) (SEMI-CONTINUOUS) or
Now God appears to Job out of the whirlwind and demands to know whether he is wise enough to question the Creator of the heavens and earth. The challenge seems almost brutal. Job, out of all his distress, had complained about the unfairness of life. He is now forced to recognize how little he understands the ways of the world and of God. More importantly for him, however, he at last has a direct relationship with the Lord.

Isaiah 53:4-12 (GOSPEL-RELATED)
Our opening lesson is the poem of the Lord's servant who suffers and bears the sins of many. The passage is part of the fourth and last of the "servant songs" which form a portion of the Book of Isaiah written when the exile was coming to an end. The servant is sometimes thought to be an historical individual or an idealization of the faithful of Israel. This "man of sorrows," "despised and rejected," "wounded for our transgressions," whom the Lord at last vindicates, is perceived by Christians to be a prefigurement of Jesus.

Psalm 104:1-9, 25, 37b or
The psalm describes the wonders of the world created and renewed by the Lord's Spirit.

Psalm 91:9-16
A hymn of trust in the Lord. God will guard and deliver the one who loves and seeks refuge with God.

Hebrews 5:1-10
In this New Testament lesson, we hear how through obedience and suffering Christ reached the perfection of his destiny and was designated by God to be the eternal high priest. The high priesthood of Jesus is the great theme of the Letter to the Hebrews. Like the high priests of the old covenant, Christ is chosen from among human beings and so has sympathy with human weakness. But he is the Son and has now been named high priest forever. He succeeds Melchizedek, a royal and priestly figure from antiquity, and has been made the source of salvation for all who trust in him.

Mark 10:35-45
In the gospel story, Jesus' followers still expect that his way will quickly lead to a state of glory in which they want special places. Jesus tells them of a different path of discipleship. First Jesus and then his disciples must experience the cup of sorrow and the baptism of death. They are not to live and act like worldly rulers. They must lead in servanthood. Their example is Jesus, who as the Son of Man serves and gives his life.

Prayers of the People

Presider: *Gracious God, you manifest your power primarily in the service of your compassion and love for all humanity, and you are clothed with majesty and splendor: Listen to us as we call upon you in prayer, saying: O God, how excellent is your greatness; the earth is full of your creatures. Alleluia!*

Pentecost

You have called your Church to be your humble community of service, having been baptized with the baptism of Jesus: Guide your people into such faithfulness, that we may serve the world in your name and make intercession on behalf of all.

O God, how excellent is your greatness;

the earth is full of your creatures. Alleluia!

In this fallen world, there are rulers who lord it over your children and great ones who are tyrants over others: Honor the sacrifice and sufferings of your lambs and take away these perversions of justice, so that the great among us will be servants, and those who wish to be first will become the slave of all.

O God, how excellent is your greatness;

the earth is full of your creatures. Alleluia!

Hear our prayers and supplications through our great high priest Jesus as we intercede for all who suffer throughout the world, especially those who live under the rule of tyrants or who face violence, oppression, or poverty.

O God, how excellent is your greatness;

the earth is full of your creatures. Alleluia!

You have bound us to you in love and called us to share in your ministry of service: Empower those in our community who give their lives as servants of others, that the will of the Lord may prosper.

O God, how excellent is your greatness;

the earth is full of your creatures. Alleluia!

We offer our prayers for those for whom we are called to pray, especially ___.

We offer our grateful thanks for your presence and deliverance, especially for ___.

Let those who have died sit with the triumphant Christ in glory, as we remember ___.

O God, how excellent is your greatness;

the earth is full of your creatures. Alleluia!

Presider: *Almighty God, through your servant Jesus Christ, the righteous one, you have made many righteous, raising him from suffering into glory: Let your resurrection power be present to all in need as you strengthen us for the leadership of service in your name, through Jesus Christ, who with you and the Holy Spirit, lives in unity and love, forever and ever.* **Amen.**

Images in the Readings

Both Paul and Mark, the two earliest writers of New Testament texts, describe Christ's crucifixion as a baptism. The Bible includes many narratives of people being swamped by water and so being washed clean of evil and renewed for life. For Christians, even death itself is like a baptism, a swimming away from sorrow and toward God.

Repeatedly in Mark, and especially in John on the day before his death, Jesus is described as a servant who wills all his people to join him in a life of service. Perhaps always, but certainly in our culture, being a servant is not an attractive role. We don't even like the noun *servant*, and we are repelled by the word *slave*, but use instead terms like *the help*.

In ancient throne rooms, monarchs were flanked on the right and the left by their most powerful assistants. In the New Testament, these positions are filled by the two bandits crucified with Jesus: thus, once again, a Christian reversal of the expected order.

Mark, Matthew (20:28), 1 Timothy, and 1 Peter used the imagery of ransom to explain why Jesus had to die. Later theologians elaborated on this metaphor, which was well known in a culture of warfare, capture, and prisoner exchanges, and many contemporary Christians know it best from C. S. Lewis's *The Lion, the Witch and the Wardrobe*, in which Aslan gives up his life as a ransom payment for Edward. The metaphor came to rely on the idea that God had to negotiate release of sinners from the devil, who through their complicity had achieved dominion over them.

The readings are filled with images, more than can be attended to in one service: diseases, wounds, sheep, offering, light, the spoil, to pour out, high priest, begotten, Melchizedek, cup.

Ideas for the Day

♦ The author of Hebrews throws a theological curveball giving Jesus the title: "a priest forever according to the order of Melchizedek." The shadowy character from the fourteenth chapter of Genesis is King of Salem and priest of the most high. He only appears for a few verses to receive Abraham's offering and bless the patriarch, offering bread and wine. Then he disappears again. Identifying Jesus with Melchizedek implies that God works beyond our usual human boundaries. God's story is bigger than ours. God's blessings can come from unexpected sources.

♦ We carry our griefs with us. We are assaulted by the stresses of everyday life. We feel loss. We feel the pain sometimes inflicted on us by other people. We feel like lashing out at those who may have power over, just as someone who may have had power over us has done. Yet, as Christians we must not give in to sadness. Our hope and trust is in the Lord who has borne our grief and our sorrow. We must live past our daily trials, so that we may fully minister and engage in the building of God's kingdom on earth.

♦ The role of deacon expresses the servant ministry of all the baptized. At ordination, the candidate hears these words from the bishop: "In the name of Jesus Christ, you are to serve all people, particularly the poor, the weak, the sick, and the lonely . . . You are to interpret to the Church the needs, concerns, and hopes of the world." (BCP 543). Many congregations do not have deacons serving in their midst. How can all members of the church be trained and encouraged to engage in servant ministry through their daily life and work in their community?

Making Connections

Notice how often the disciples try to get Jesus to promise them stuff? It's remarkable how often it happens. Jesus will be preaching about the ethics of divine love, or effecting another miraculous healing, and the disciples will pop in, and ask if *now* they can get a really plum seat in heaven. It's hard not to wonder if they're in this for the right reasons when they keep getting so distracted from the message. But distraction is a human failing, not just a problem for that group of twelve people long ago. We each have our own 'shiny object' that pulls our focus from Jesus and what he teaches us as we travel the spiritual path. For some of us, it's frustration at the failings of the institution. For others, it's the lingering hope that saying the right prayer will earn material prosperity forever. How much harder is it to keep our eyes focused on Christ, just for Christ's sake?

Engaging all Ages

A popular catchword in today's world is "empowerment." And we hear in today's gospel that this is exactly what Jesus offers. His extraordinary promise is that our transformation happens through servant-hood. This might be a good day to highlight particular ministries that require more help or to hear from volunteers who have been transformed through their personal ministry. Be sure to include the youth and any mission/outreach work in which they may be engaged. Incorporate the words "not to be served but to serve" in the congregational responses in the Prayers. Invite full participation in finding a meaningful personal ministry.

Hymns for the Day

The Hymnal 1982
God is Love, let heaven adore him 379 (SC)
Many and great, O God, are thy works 385 (SC)
Songs of praise the angels sang 426 (SC)
Ah, holy Jesus, how hast thou offended 158 (GR)
Hail, thou once despised Jesus! 495 (GR)
Jesus, our mighty Lord, our strength in sadness 478 (GR)
O sacred head, sore wounded 168, 169 (GR)
To mock your reign, O dearest Lord 170 (GR)
From God Christ's deity came forth 443
O Love of God, how strong and true 455, 456
All praise to thee, for thou, O King divine 477
By all your saints still striving 231, 232 [2: St. James]
For thy blest saints, a noble throng 276
Go forth for God; go to the world in peace 347
Jesu, Jesu, fill us with your love 602
Lord, we have come at your own invitation 348
O holy city, seen of John 582, 583
O Master, let me walk with thee 659, 660
Sing, ye faithful, sing with gladness 492

Wonder, Love, and Praise
As newborn stars were stirred to song 788 (SC)
O sacred head, sore wounded 735 (GR)
O wheat whose crushing was for bread 760 (GR)
Gracious Spirit, give your servants 782

Lift Every Voice and Sing II
He never said a mumbalin' word 33 (GR)
O sacred head, sore wounded 36 (GR)
Jesu, Jesu, fill us with your love 74

Weekday Commemorations

Tuesday, October 23
Saint James of Jerusalem, Brother of Our Lord Jesus Christ, and Martyr, c. 62
Saint James of Jerusalem is called the Lord's brother in the Gospel According to Matthew and

the Epistle to the Galatians. However, other writers, following Mark's path, thought James was Jesus' cousin; certain apocryphal writings name him as Joseph's son by his first wife. After Jesus' resurrection, James was converted and eventually became Bishop of Jerusalem. Paul's first letter to the Corinthians notes that James beheld a special appearance of the Lord before the Ascension; later, James was cordial to Paul at Jerusalem. At the Council of Jerusalem, it was James who would impose "no irksome restrictions" (circumcision) on Gentiles turning to God. His success at converting many to Jesus perturbed factions in Jerusalem, so he was cudgeled to death.

Friday, October 26
Alfred the Great, King of the West Saxons, 899
Alfred, born in 849, one of five sons of King Aethelwulf, lived during a time of murder as Vikings invaded and settled in Britain. At four, he was blessed by Pope Leo IV on a trip to Rome. Alfred became king in 871. He halted the invasions through heroic battles and stratagems, thus securing control of southern and parts of midland England. He persuaded his foe, the Dane Guthrum, to accept baptism after Alfred won the battle of Edington in 878. He sought to repair damage wrought by the Viking invasions, especially on culture and clergy. Because of his courage and virtue, Alfred is the only English ruler to be called "great."

The Twenty-Third Sunday after Pentecost: Proper 25

October 28, 2018

Jesus comes to proclaim God's new day where people who are physically and metaphorically blind to injustice will see clearly the way of God.

Color Green

Preface Of the Lord's Day

Collect

Almighty and everlasting God, increase in us the gifts of faith, hope, and charity; and, that we may obtain what you promise, make us love what you command; through Jesus Christ our Lord, who lives and reigns with you and the Holy Spirit, one God, for ever and ever. Amen.

Readings and Psalm

Job 42:1-6, 20-17 (SEMI-CONTINUOUS) or

In the conclusion of this saga, Job, who had demanded justice for his own life and was then encountered by the living and awesome God, now responds with great humility and finds restoration of his fortunes. Job recalls some of the earlier words of the Lord and realizes how far he has been from any true understanding. In the conclusion of the story, Job finds abundance far in excess of his previous state, and is fully restored to human community. An unusual feature of the story is that Job's three daughters are given equal inheritance and mentioned by name, though none of his sons. Job's tragic experience has given him an amplified view of the world and deepened empathy.

Jeremiah 31:7-9 (GOSPEL-RELATED)

This prophetic reading was originally composed as a vision of hope, full of joy, for the restoration of the northern tribes of Israel. The Lord will bring all back from exile, including the weak and the infirm. As a father God will comfort them and give them cause for great gladness.

Psalm 34:1-8 (19-22) or

A hymn of blessing and praise to the Lord for divine deliverance.

Psalm 126

A song of hope and joy sung to the Lord, who restores the fortunes of God's people.

Hebrews 7:23-28

In this New Testament lesson, the author demonstrates how Jesus is our perfect and everlasting high priest. He was appointed not by human beings according to the law, but by an oath of God. He had no need to offer sacrifices for his own sins, for he is holy and undefiled. Nor does he offer sacrifices repeatedly, but once for all he presented the perfect sacrifice of himself. His priesthood is forever and, as the Son, he now makes eternal intercession for us.

Mark 10:46-52

Our gospel is the story of the new vision of blind Bartimaeus. The evangelist has carefully prepared for this story by illustrating the inability of the religious officials to perceive who Jesus is and by describing the shortsightedness of the disciples. Now, with nothing but his great hope, this blind beggar calls out to Jesus. He uses the only title of honor he can think of: Son of David—dangerous words in the present political climate. But Jesus stops on his own profound journey, and Bartimaeus is healed through his faith. Then, as a model of a disciple who has received healing as a gift, he follows Jesus on the way.

Prayers of the People

Presider: *Gracious God, through your Son Jesus you call us to come to you, that we who have heard of you by the hearing of the ear may see you with our eyes and be healed, filled with the vision of your compassionate reign: Hear us as we cry out to you, saying: Taste and see that God is good; happy are they who trust in the Most High!*

Litanist: You have formed the Church to be the community of Jesus our eternal high priest, holy, blameless, undefiled, exalted above the heaven, able for all time to save those who approach you: Fill us with the faith that makes us well.

Taste and see that God is good;

> *happy are they who trust in the Most High!*

We know that you can do all things and that no purpose of yours can be thwarted, O God: Guide our leaders and all in authority that they may walk in your ways of compassion and peace.

Taste and see that God is good;

> *happy are they who trust in the Most High!*

Hear those who call to you in their affliction and save them from all their troubles.

Taste and see that God is good;

> *happy are they who trust in the Most High!*

You travel along the road of life's pilgrimage with us as our friend and guide: Reach out in our community to all who may sit on the side while life passes by, and give to them such hopeful hearts that they may rush to you and be healed.

Taste and see that God is good;

> *happy are they who trust in the Most High!*

Listen to our prayers of intercession as we come to you for help, praying especially for ___.

We proclaim the greatness of God and exalt God's Name together, offering our grateful thanks, especially for ___.

You save your people by drawing them into your eternal presence as our great high priest, let those who have died rejoice before you, especially ___. Taste and see that God is good;

> *happy are they who trust in the Most High!*

Presider: Gracious and loving God, we cry out to Jesus, Son of David, to have mercy on us your children who come to you in great need and hope: Restore our vision that we may see and embrace the faith that makes us well, and follow Christ on the way that leads

to eternal life, who with you and the Holy Spirit lives and loves, One God, forevermore. **Amen.**

Images in the Readings

The gospel's image of freedom presents a challenge to contemporary Americans, and perhaps to other Western societies as well, since popularly "freedom" is understood as the right of the individual to live out personal choices. John's gospel suggests instead that the freedom granted in Christ is the freedom of the son, who remains in the father's house and does the will of that father. Sixteenth-century Christians used this proclamation of freedom to leave behind regulations of the medieval church, but even Martin Luther wrote detailed interpretations of the Ten Commandments, understood as "law" for Christian use. We are free to be obedient children.

A covenant was a legal agreement in which the master promised protection because the participants met certain obligations. Ancient Israelites adopted this cultural category for their understanding of the relationship that God had offered the chosen people. Christians continued to use this language in articulating the renewed relationship with God that was effected through Christ. Particularly Methodists have kept this language alive in referring to the Baptismal Covenant and in their annual covenant renewal ceremonies. Lutherans understand the covenant as God's continuing mercy given in word and sacrament.

Ideas for the Day

♦ Today's reading from Job comes after a great deal of suffering. The text makes clear that Job has not earned punishment. Job's friends, seeing him in pain, want him to turn his back on God. His own wife tells him to "Curse God, and die." Bartimaeus' community tries to silence him when he calls out to Jesus. Neither one of these faithful characters can be persuaded. Their faith causes them to cry out for justice, for healing. Faith carries us through suffering, but God does not ask us to suffer silently.

♦ Arrogance sometimes carries us far in the eyes of people, but it is meaningless in the sight of God. Belief in our own abilities to solve all problems will lead us astray. Job grew to understand his limitations, so he goes to the Lord and repents of his attitude. He realizes that no one truly know the full majesty of God. We must humble ourselves in its presence. No one can look at the Grand Canyon and claim ownership, saying he built the rocks to be in exactly that shape. No one can look at seven seas and claim he filled them with water. Let us not glory so much in our work as people that we miss seeing the work of the Almighty God.

♦ A form of Bartimaeus' initial cry to Jesus has become known as the Jesus Prayer: "Jesus, have mercy on me, a sinner." What are the different elements of Bartimaeus' cry? What makes his cry an excellent model for prayer?

Making Connections

Putting on a fresh pair of glasses is one of the unparalleled joys of life. Everything that was blurry and fuzzy suddenly snaps into focus; parts of the world—leaves on trees, bricks on buildings, lettering on signs—that you had entirely forgotten existed suddenly appear before you. It's like being born all over again and meeting the world for the first time. Meeting Jesus is not unlike that. Finding faith does not immediately fix the world around you, so much as it changes the way you see the world. Growing in faith gives you new lenses through which to see the same reality. Now, as filtered through the reality of God, the first become last and the last become first, what was confusing now clarifies itself, and what was long unquestioned now becomes uncertain. A new way of seeing is born.

Engaging all Ages

Bartimaeus' persistence is such a great example for us, as is his clear statement about what he wants. It would be rare in today's world to encounter so straightforward a transaction. At the beginning of worship distribute paper slips and issue an invitation to worshippers to consider Jesus' question, "What do you want me to do for you?" Responses can be placed in the offering plate or in a special basket as folks approach the altar for communion. Let the words of dismissal include an invitation to consider, in the days ahead, the ways our faith can "make us well."

Hymns for the Day

The Hymnal 1982
God moves in a mysterious way 677 (SC)
New every morning is the love 10 (SC)
O bless the Lord, my soul! 411 (SC)
Praise, my soul, the King of heaven 410 (SC)
Father, we thank thee who hast planted 302, 303 (GR)

God is working his purpose out 534 (GR)
Lord, whose love through humble service 610 (GR)
O God of Bethel, by whose hand 709 (GR)
Sing, ye faithful, sing with gladness 492 (GR)
Surely it is God who saves me 678, 679 (GR)
The Lord will come and not be slow 462 (GR)
Ye servants of God, your Master proclaim 535 (GR)
Alleluia! sing to Jesus! 460, 461
From God Christ's deity came forth 443
Hail, thou once despised Jesus! 495
The Lord ascendeth up on high 219
Amazing grace! how sweet the sound 671
From thee all skill and science flow 566
Give praise and glory unto God 375
I'll praise my Maker while I've breath 429
Just as I am, without one plea 693
O for a thousand tongues to sing 493
Thine arm, O Lord, in days of old 567
Word of God, come down on earth 633

Wonder, Love, and Praise
I will bless the Lord at all times 764 (SC)
Through north and south and east and west 822 (GR)
Gracious Spirit, give your servants 782
Heal me, hands of Jesus 773
O Christ, the healer, we have come 772

Lift Every Voice and Sing II
I will bless the Lord at all times 154 (SC)
We are often tossed and driv'n on the restless sea of time 207 (SC)
He's got the whole world in his hand 217 (GR)
Amazing grace! how sweet the sound 181

Weekday Commemorations

Monday, October 29
James Hannington, Bishop of Eastern Equatorial Africa, and his Companions, Martyrs, 1885
Born in Sussex (1847), educated at Temple School, Hannington worked with his father in the family warehouse, and with his family joined the Church of England in 1867. He was ordained at Exeter. In 1882, he presented himself as a missionary to the Church Missionary Society for its mission in Victoria, Nyanza, Africa. He went home after an illness but returned to Africa in 1884 as Bishop of Eastern Equatorial Africa. From his mission field on the shores of Lake Victoria, Hannington and his party ventured toward Uganda; they were stopped by emissaries of King Mwanga, tortured and martyred. His last words were: ". . . I have purchased the road to Uganda with my blood."

Pentecost

Pentecost

Friday, November 2
Commemoration of All Faithful Departed
The New Testament uses the word "saints" to describe all members of the Christian community; in the Collect for All Saints' Day, the word "elect" is used similarly. From very early times, however, the word "saint" was applied primarily to people of heroic sanctity, their deeds recalled gratefully by succeeding generations. Beginning in the tenth century, the custom began to set aside another day on which the Church recognized the whole body of the faithful, unknown to the wide fellowship of the Church, a day to remember family and friends who have died. During the Reformation, observance of this day was abolished, but Episcopalians, redefining its meaning, include it as optional observance on their calendar.

Saturday, November 3
Richard Hooker, Priest, 1600
Standing high, perhaps first, on a list of Anglican theologians, Richard Hooker was born (1553) near Exeter and attended Oxford. Ordained in 1581, he served as Master of the Temple in London and, later, country parishes. His masterwork, *Laws of Ecclesiastical Polity*, based in Aristotelian thought, served as a comprehensive defense of the Reformation settlement under Elizabeth I. On this base, all positive laws of Church and State are grounded. Book V strongly defends the Book of Common Prayer against Puritan detractors by balancing powerful patristic learning with needs of contemporary worshippers. His style and his learning reveal a man of moderate, patient, and serene character. Hooker described the Church not as an "assembly, but a Society."

All Saints' Day

November 1, 2018

We remember the saints of God—all faithful servants and believers; a communion of saints who have died and of all Christian persons. We are always surrounded by a cloud of witnesses. (Hebrews 12:1)

Color   White

Preface   All Saints

Collect

Almighty God, you have knit together your elect in one communion and fellowship in the mystical body of your Son Christ our Lord: Give us grace so to follow your blessed saints in all virtuous and godly living, that we may come to those ineffable joys that you have prepared for those who truly love you; through Jesus Christ our Lord, who with you and the Holy Spirit lives and reigns, one God, in glory everlasting. Amen.

Readings and Psalm

Wisdom of Solomon 3:1-9 *or*

In our lesson from the Wisdom of Solomon, confidence in God extends beyond this world, and a hope in eternal life is expressed. The righteous are blessed and held fast by God despite the ravages of death and the trials of this earthly sojourn. Those who trust in God will abide with God in love and will shine forth because of God's grace and mercy.

Isaiah 25:6-9

In this Hebrew Scripture reading, we hear a prophetic hymn envisioning the day of the Lord's salvation. The prophet uses a rich banquet as an image for the time of festival. It takes place on the mountain of the Lord's temple, Mount Zion, where heaven and earth figuratively meet. This great feast will be for all people, and even the power of death will be overcome.

Psalm 24

As pilgrims go up to God's holy place for worship, they cleanse themselves and praise the just Lord, who has created all things.

Revelation 21:1-6a

In this apocalyptic vision of the world to come, God will indwell all creation, bringing transformation and renewal. Death and the first things have passed away, supplanted by the eternal order symbolized by the new Jerusalem, the church in culmination, coming down as from heaven. It is Christ, the Alpha and the Omega, who establishes this promise, and he will be as a spring of living and perpetual water to all who drink from him.

John 11:32-44

In our gospel lesson, Jesus raises Lazarus from the dead. Arriving in Bethany after the death of his friend Lazarus, Jesus encounters first Lazarus's sister Martha and then his sister Mary. Neither of the sisters fully comprehend Jesus' power over death. Deeply affected, Jesus weeps. So that they and others might believe more deeply in God, Jesus summons Lazarus to come forth from his tomb.

Prayers of the People

Presider: Almighty and Holy One, you have manifest yourself in Christ, the Alpha and the Omega, the beginning and the end: Grant us faith to see your glory, bringing life out of death, as we pray saying: You will dwell with us as our God, and we will be your people.

Litanist: The hope of your Church is full of immortality, O Holy One: Let your people trust in you and abide with you in love.

You will dwell with us as our God,

and we will be your people.

Almighty and Immortal One, the earth is yours and all that is in it: Let your power go forth throughout the earth to make all things new, guiding the rulers and authorities in this world to forsake falsehood and to live with clean hands and a pure heart.

You will dwell with us as our God,

and we will be your people.

Your home, O God, is among mortals, and you watch over your elect: Look upon all who suffer throughout the world, and wipe away every tear from their eyes.

You will dwell with us as our God,

and we will be your people.

Grant us faith to see your glory in this community, O God, that we may be people of compassion and new life.

You will dwell with us as our God,

and we will be your people.

We pray to you O Gracious One on behalf all for whom we intercede, especially ___.

We lift up our heads to thank you, O God, for all your blessings and grace, especially for ___.

The departed are in your hand, O God, where no torment will ever touch them for they are at peace: Bring into the heavenly Jerusalem all who have died, especially ___.

Presider: *O God of resurrection and new life, take away the stones that entomb us and darken our lives, and fill us with the power and peace of your eternal life, that we may see your glory and live in your light, through Jesus Christ the Risen One, in the power of the Holy Spirit, One God, for ever and ever.* **Amen.**

Images in the Readings

"Take away the stone," says Jesus. The stone recalls the rock that Moses struck so that saving water could flow forth (Exod. 17:6), the stone heart that God will replace with a heart of flesh (Ezek. 36:26), the rock rolled to cover the opening of Jesus' tomb.

Not surprisingly, when the Bible tries to describe the life of God, metaphors pile up: the mountain of God no longer a place of terror but of picnics; a communal feast; vats of good wine; a new earth; no more frightening and alien seas; a wedding; no more shrouds, no more tears. That life with God is not like a primordial garden, enjoyed by the few, but a city, is especially surprising, since much of the Bible, like many examples in world literature, describes cities as threatening places, filled with foreigners and immoral behavior. Thus even our metaphors are transformed by our hope in God. What is left at the end? What is the Omega? God.

Ideas for the Day

♦ Madeleine L'Engle canonized her own saints. She talked about "St. Johann Sebastian Bach," and "St. Albert [Einstein]." The Feast of All Saints invites us to remember lives well lived, people who taught great truths. Who are the figures, public and personal, that have shaped you, shaped your faith? How do you remember them?

♦ The day does not shy away from grief over the deaths of those we love. In the gospel Jesus weeps. He is "greatly disturbed" by his friend's death. We grieve those who have loved us well.

♦ I will sing to the Lord a new song. My song will honor those who have gone on before me. It will honor all of the saints and martyrs. It will honor all of the ancestors who have paved the way for a better life, those who sacrificed themselves for a future generation. May our lives today be lived in such a way that we might join the ranks of the saints who came before us. May we live not for ourselves, but our grandchildren's grandchildren. May the voice of spirit today sing through ages and touch the life of someone in a future generation. May our songs continue to be sung, our poems continue to be read, and stories continue to be told.

♦ Think about the many ways the people in any period of history (including our own) have expressed their love of God in service to others. Show the qualities of people's lives, whether famous or ordinary, in some visual form: a mural, a display, a mobile, an altar hanging, a collection of objects that symbolize loving acts, a parade of costumed persons show how they help or serve, or banners hung or carried in procession.

♦ Many groups, especially Asian Americans, use All Saints' Day as an opportunity to remember and respect family members who are elderly or who have lived in other generations. This might be the occasion for telling about where our families have come from and lived, what their lives were like, and what values we honor that they have passed on to us.

Making Connections

If we had patron saints of arguing, it would be Mary and Martha. While it's left out in this pericope, both sisters, when they meet Jesus after their brother's death, immediately confront him with the fact that he could have prevented this tragedy. And then, to top it off, Martha also pragmatically points out that if they open the tomb, there's going to be a stench. As much as we praise the saints for being lights of the world in their generations, and exemplars of what it means to live out the gospel, it is important to remember that the saints were also human. Part of their walk of faith involved the same struggles and frustrations that we know. Mary and Martha are both hailed as saints today, even as they argued with Jesus.

Engaging all Ages

Worship may look and feel different today according to your local custom. Many congregations include a "Roll Call" of those who have died in the past year. Opportunities to light candles for departed loved ones and to place names in a basket passed by the children enhance the theme of remembrance. Consider offering the powerful story of the raising of Lazarus as a dramatic reading with members or groups from the congregation reading the parts. Allow a short time of silence after the words, "Did I not tell you that if you believed, you would see the glory of God?"

Hymns for the Day

The Hymnal 1982
By all your saints still striving 231, 232
Christ the Victorious, give to your servants 358
For all the saints, who from their labors rest 287
For the bread which you have broken 340, 341
For thy dear saints, O Lord 279
From glory to glory advancing, we praise thee, O Lord 326
Give rest, O Christ 355
Give us the wings of faith to rise 253
Hark! the sound of holy voices 275
Let saints on earth in concert sing 526
Lift up your heads, ye mighty gates 436
Who are these like stars appearing 286
Ye watchers and ye holy ones 618
O what their joy and their glory must be 623
Ye holy angels bright 625
This is the feast of victory for our God 417, 418
This is the hour of banquet and of song 316, 317
Blessed city, heavenly Salem 519, 520
Christ is made the sure foundation 518
Glorious things of thee are spoken 522, 523
Jerusalem, my happy home 620
Jerusalem the golden 624
Light's abode, celestial Salem 621, 622
O holy city, seen of John 582, 583
O for a thousand tongues to sing 493
Thine arm, O Lord, in days of old 567
Thou art the Way, to thee alone 457
When Jesus wept 715
All who believe and are baptized 298
Baptized in water 294
Come away to the skies 213

Wonder, Love, and Praise
Give thanks for life 775
No saint on earth lives life to self alone 776
Baptized in water 767
I believe in God Almighty 768, 769
You're called by name, forever loved 766

Lift Every Voice and Sing II
Come, we that love the Lord 12
I want to be ready 7
Oh! What a beautiful city 10
Rockin' Jerusalem 17
Soon and very soon we are goin' to see the King 14
Baptized in water 121

Pentecost

The Twenty-Fourth Sunday after Pentecost: Proper 26

November 4, 2018

Loving God and neighbor are the greatest commandments.

Color   Green

Preface   Of the Lord's Day

Collect

Almighty and merciful God, it is only by your gift that your faithful people offer you true and laudable service: Grant that we may run without stumbling to obtain your heavenly promises; through Jesus Christ our Lord, who lives and reigns with you and the Holy Spirit, one God, now and for ever. Amen.

Readings and Psalm

Ruth 1:1-18 (SEMI-CONTINUOUS) *or*

Our opening lesson tells of Ruth's decision to leave her own country and return with her mother-in-law Naomi to Israel. Naomi's husband and two sons die while living in Moab. Ruth persists in her desire to go back to Bethlehem with Naomi and to accept Israel's God as her own. Later she will marry a relative of her father-in-law and, though a foreign woman, become the grandmother of King David. The narrative is both a touching lesson of loyalty and devotion and an illustration that God's ways of bringing about divine purposes often differ from human expectations.

Deuteronomy 6:1-9 (GOSPEL-RELATED)

In our opening reading, Moses tells the people that they must carefully keep the ten commandments he has just given them. This is the Lord's covenant, for, if Israel will observe these statutes, then all will go well with them in their new land. They shall teach them to their children and, as signs of their devotion, wear little boxes with passages of scripture in them. Central to Israel's faith is the *Shema,* which every Jew is to recite daily, and which begins: "Hear, O Israel: the Lord our God is one Lord." God shall be wholly loved. The Lord's claim upon Israel is total.

Psalm 146 *or*

A hymn to the Lord, who forms the world and rules in justice, who heals and cares for the orphan and widow.

Psalm 119:1-8

Happy are those who walk in the law of the Lord, who guide their ways by God's commandments.

Hebrews 9:11-14

In this New Testament lesson we are taught that Christ, our high priest, has fulfilled and surpassed the purposes of the earthly temple that served as an archetype of the heavenly reality. Through his faithful sacrifice, Jesus has entered the eternal holy of holies and obtained the everlasting redemption prefigured by the old rites of animal sacrifice. Believers may now worship the living God with a purified conscience, knowing themselves to be sanctified through Christ.

Mark 12:28-34

In the gospel, Jesus answers a question concerning the chief command of the law by reciting the double commandment to love God and one's neighbor. Jesus was not unique in bringing together these two great teachings from Israel's heritage, but the New Testament gives them special emphasis. They are closely linked, for in responding to God's love, we learn that we are lovable, and so begin to be able to love others as ourselves. In loving our neighbors we discover the mystery that we are also loving in them their Creator. The man who asked Jesus the question repeats the commandments in his own words. He is not far from the kingdom.

Prayers of the People

Presider: *Loving and gracious God, you have taught us to love you with all our heart and soul and mind and strength, and to love our neighbor as ourselves: Hear us as we express our love through prayer and intercession, saying: Alleluia! Sing to God a new song; sing praise in the congregation of the faithful.*

Litanist: Eternal and Majestic One, you have raised Christ our High Priest into the Holy Place, obtaining eternal redemption for your people: Guide the Church and purify our conscience from dead works to worship you, the living God.

Alleluia! Sing to God a new song;

> *sing praise in the congregation of the faithful.*

Almighty Ruler of All, guide all in authority to exercise their power with a commitment to compassion and justice, for you take pleasure in the people, and you adorn the poor with victory.

Alleluia! Sing to God a new song;

> *sing praise in the congregation of the faithful.*

Merciful and Compassionate One, look upon refugees and immigrants, widows and families who are poor and threatened, who leave their homes seeking hope and prosperity: Guide them into new places of security and hospitality.

Alleluia! Sing to God a new song;

> *sing praise in the congregation of the faithful.*

Creator and Sustainer, be with us in this community that we may be people who follow your law of love.

Alleluia! Sing to God a new song;

> *sing praise in the congregation of the faithful.*

Receive our prayers of intercession into your eternal heart of love, as we pray, especially for ___.

Your faithful people rejoice in our Maker and Monarch, hear our prayers of thanksgiving, especially for ___.

Christ the high priest of the good things that have come has entered into heaven; bring all who have died into your eternal presence, especially ___.

Alleluia! Sing to God a new song;

> *sing praise in the congregation of the faithful.*

Presider: *Holy and gracious One, your eternal and unqualified love exceeds all we can desire or imagine: Guide us in your way, that we may love you, our neighbors, and ourselves with such singleness of heart, that your kingdom may come quickly among us, through Jesus Christ our great High Priest, in union with the Holy Spirit, One God, for ever and ever.* **Amen.**

Images in the Readings

In Judaism, the commandments are understood as a gift from God to guide the faithful people in how to live. Paul taught Christians a more critical attitude toward commandments, seeing the gospel as having trumped the law. Jesus is remembered as having honored especially the principle of love that stands behind the commandments. In Deuteronomy 6:8-9, the directives to bind, to fix, and to write the commandments have led to Orthodox Jews literalizing these verbs by their use of phylacteries on their arms and forehead and of mezuzahs on their doorposts.

Milk and honey is a phrase used repeatedly in the Old Testament to convey the wholesomeness of the promised land. Milk was a staple in Israelite diet, and honey adds the sweetness. It is interesting that human breast milk is sweeter than cows' or goats' milk. Some early Christians gave a drink of milk and honey to the newly baptized as part of the baptismal ritual, seeing the water of baptism, like the Red Sea, as having brought the candidates into the promised land. Currently Christians need to be aware of the political debates in which some Jews and some Israelis understand a specific geography to be part of the Jewish state by right of God. Many biblical scholars judge the story of a mass exodus from Egypt and a subsequent takeover of Canaan as more mythic identity than historical fact.

The tent that the author of Hebrews cites was the tabernacle used by Israelites during their time as nomads before the construction of Solomon's temple. In antiquity, many religious traditions practiced animal sacrifice, and there is considerable debate among anthropologists, historians, and psychologists as to the several meanings of this practice. The Latinate term *sacrifice* suggests one meaning: that burning up something of value rendered the suppliant holy. Christians have used this idea as one interpretation of the crucifixion.

Ideas for the Day

+ After tragic death of their husbands, Naomi tries to send Ruth back to the Moabites. Though she faces potential persecution, Ruth rebels against her mother-in-law. Her words "Your people will be my people, and your God my God" are spoken in defiance. God works through Ruth's defiance. Not only is Naomi saved when Ruth marries another Israelite, but Ruth's marriage to Boaz sets more in motion. Ruth and Boaz are

David's great-grandparents. God sometimes works through rebellious women.

♦ We must learn to love ourselves in order to love our neighbor. So often, when we feel poorly about ourselves, we make others feel poorly as well. This self-absorption pulls us away from the love of Christ. We get caught up in our own inadequacies and insecurities, not realizing Christ loves us as we are. He knows we are not perfect. We don't have to be perfect to minister in the name of the Lord, we simply have to be willing to give of ourselves. It is through this giving that we can see ourselves in a different light. We can learn to love who we are and not judge ourselves by what other people think. Our only judgment comes from God through Jesus Christ. He guides us on how we should live our lives through his word. When we learn to live into the life of the Lord's words, we can accept ourselves for who we are, confident that are doing and giving our all in everything we do.

♦ The commandments to love God and neighbor serve as a way of measuring a congregation's faithfulness to the gospel. It is part of the optional penitential order before the Eucharist (BCP 319, 351) and is also reflected in the Baptismal Covenant: "Will you seek to serve Christ in all persons, loving your neighbor as yourself?" (BCP 305).

Making Connections

No one dares ask Jesus any more questions after this, because, as he points out, he effectively sums up everything he's been saying. Two neat commandments: Love God and love your neighbor. In Rite I, we read these at the start of each service, as a reminder of what our job is as Christians. The problem is, these are the hardest to keep, because they are so encompassing. Loving God, loving the people around us takes all that we are, and includes everything that we do. These commands touch on every aspect of our lives. We can never hope to perfect the way of love, only to get better at it.

Engaging all Ages

The great story of Ruth begins today in the Hebrew scripture reading—God's surprising work in the lives of ordinary people. In worship today, let us think about how we, too, can choose similar responses based on love, a concept echoed in Jesus' words in Mark's gospel, "you shall love . . ." As this theme is echoed in prayers and music today, do we accept the challenge?

Send worshippers home with a reminder that Jesus' words are even more important today and a question to ponder, "Who do you see as your neighbor? How do you love with heart, soul, mind, and strength?"

Hymns for the Day

The Hymnal 1982
Awake, my soul, stretch every nerve 546
Fight the good fight with all thy might 552, 553
Lo! what a cloud of witnesses 545
Help us, O Lord, to learn 628 (GR)
Open your ears, O faithful people 536 (GR)
Praise to the living God 372 (GR)
Alleluia! sing to Jesus! 460, 461
Draw nigh and take the Body of the Lord 327, 328
From God Christ's deity came forth 443
Glory be to Jesus 479
Hail, thou once despised Jesus! 495
Let thy Blood in mercy poured 313
The Lord ascendeth up on high 219
For the fruit of all creation 424
Jesu, Jesu, fill us with your love 602
King of glory, King of peace 382
Rise up, ye saints of God 551
Where charity and love prevail 581

Wonder, Love, and Praise
Guide my feet, Lord, while I run this race 819
Sh'ma Yisrael, Adonai Eloheinu 818 (GR)
Gracious Spirit, give your servants 782
Jesus said: The first commandment is this 815

Lift Every Voice and Sing II
There is a fountain filled with blood 39
Jesu, Jesu, fill us with your love 74

Weekday Commemorations

Wednesday, November 7
Willibrord, Archbishop of Utrecht, Missionary to Frisia, 739
While studying in Ireland for a dozen years (678-690), Willibrord heard a call to missionary work. Born in Northumbria (about 658), he was educated at Bishop Wilfrid's monastery at Ripon. In 690, he set out with 12 companions for Frisia (Holland); the area, though pagan, was increasingly being dominated by Christian Franks. Bishop Wilfrid and a few English people had delved in this mission field unsuccessfully; but, aided by the Frankish rulers, Willibrord established a base at Utrecht. Thus, Willibrord prepared the way for

Boniface's greater achievements. Pope Sergius ordained him a bishop in 695. Three years later, Willibrord founded the monastery of Echternach, near Trier, where he died.

Saturday, November 10
Leo the Great, Bishop of Rome, 461

Leo was born (about 400) to an empire in shambles; still, he received a good education. He was ordained deacon, responsible for administering church finances, for which he won admiration. In 440, while on a mission in Gaul, he was unanimously elected Pope *in absentia*. He was an able preacher, as shown by his 96 extant sermons: he expounded doctrine, encouraged almsgiving, and handled heresies. He presided with a strong hand over Gaul, Africa, and Spain; similarly, he negotiated with Attila, whose Huns were ready to sack Rome, and with Vandals against Rome. Thereafter, he worked to repair damaged and broken vessels—to restore the morale of the Romans.

Pentecost

The Twenty-Fifth Sunday after Pentecost: Proper 27

November 11, 2018

The offering of several women is a witness to the true faith of God. (Note: The themes of the season of Advent begin to be expressed this week, offering an opportunity to explore the rich heritage of Advent; this week's focus is on the coming of Christ in glory and on the last judgment.)

Color   Green

Preface   Of the Lord's Day

Collect

O God, whose blessed Son came into the world that he might destroy the works of the devil and make us children of God and heirs of eternal life: Grant that, having this hope, we may purify ourselves as he is pure; that, when he comes again with power and great glory, we may be made like him in his eternal and glorious kingdom; where he lives and reigns with you and the Holy Spirit, one God, for ever and ever. Amen.

Readings and Psalm

Ruth 3:1-5; 4:13-17 *(SEMI-CONTINUOUS) or*

In our continuing Hebrew scripture reading, we hear how Naomi helps Ruth to secure her future as she gives instruction as to how she may make herself attractive and available to her rich and well-connected kinsman Boaz. The success of Naomi's intercession comes in Ruth's marriage to Boaz, and in her subsequent delivery of a son. God's providential intercession is seen in this conception and in the birth of a male, who will one day become the grandfather of the future king David. Ruth the foreigner is now in every way incorporated into the people and community of Israel.

1 Kings 17:8-16 *(GOSPEL-RELATED)*

From the Hebrew scriptures, we hear the story of the food which God miraculously provided for the prophet Elijah and the widow of Zarephath and her family. There is famine throughout the land, which Elijah has prophesied because of the sinfulness of King Ahab. The story shows that God is present to care for his prophet and also for this woman who, though a foreigner, has shared with Elijah what little she has. The word of the Lord is powerful to fulfill its promise even beyond the borders of Israel.

Psalm 127 *or*

The Lord is the source and foundation for all successful human endeavor, and a growing family is a blessing from the Lord.

Psalm 146

A hymn to the Lord, who forms the world and rules in justice, who heals and cares for the orphan and widow.

Hebrews 9:24-28

This reading tells how Christ, the eternal high priest, has entered into the heavenly sanctuary to present the ultimate and perfect sacrifice of himself for sins. It is the author's theme that Jesus has superseded the need for all other priestly offerings such as were made annually on the Day of Atonement. These were never more than foreshadowings of what Christ was to accomplish. The earthly temple, which was but a copy of the true sanctuary in heaven, is no longer of significance. As the end of the ages draws near, our brother Jesus, who died as we must, appears before God on our behalf and will appear once more to save those who wait for him.

Mark 12:38-44

In the gospel lesson, Jesus warns against religious officials who love honors and flattery, and he then points out a poor widow who makes an offering of what little she possesses. Together the two stories stress a theme found often in the gospels: those who think themselves religious are in great danger of living a life of hypocrisy, while genuine trust in God may be found among the least obvious. The religious officials take advantage of people like widows, and wealthy persons make a show of giving large sums of money, but the woman herself is an example of the greatest generosity. Her gift of all she has points forward to Jesus' self-offering.

Prayers of the People

Presider: *Generous God, you raise up the humble and poor, and you inspire us to generosity and love: Hear us as we offer our intercessions on behalf of your creation, saying: Christ our High Priest makes intercession for us, in the presence of God on our behalf.*

Litanist: You have purified your Church as Christ is pure, for Jesus has entered into heaven itself as our high priest who removes sin from the earth: Fill us with generosity and faith, that we may reflect your loving compassion and grace throughout creation.

Christ our High Priest makes intercession for us,

in the presence of God on our behalf.

Watch over the city and build our house, O God: Enlighten our leaders and all in authority to forego the appearance of piety, the abuse of privilege, and the selfishness of power; that they may lift up those who are bowed down, sustain the orphan and widow, and lead generously on behalf of the humble.

Christ our High Priest makes intercession for us,

in the presence of God on our behalf.

You see when the poor and humble give generously out of their poverty and when the privileged and wealthy contribute out of their abundance: Be present in your mercy as a restorer of life and a nourisher in our old age.

Christ our High Priest makes intercession for us,

in the presence of God on our behalf.

You call all in our community to the responsibilities of stewardship and mutual care: Grant us everything necessary for our common life and lead us to share so freely that none may be alone or in want.

Christ our High Priest makes intercession for us,

in the presence of God on our behalf.

You love the humble and needy: Be with all for whom we pray, especially ___.

You bless us with children and honor us with age: Hear our grateful thanks, especially for ___.

You have promised to save those who are eagerly waiting for you: Receive into your eternal and glorious kingdom those who have died, especially ___.

Christ our High Priest makes intercession for us,

in the presence of God on our behalf.

Presider: *Almighty and gracious God, you care for all whom you have made and you invite us into your life of abundant charity: Give us generous and compassionate hearts, that we may live in unity with one another in the Spirit of Jesus Christ our Savior, to whom we give glory, forever and ever.* **Amen.**

Images in the Readings

On many Sundays, the lectionary readings include the widow as an image of those who are financially poor and socially helpless. In the culture of the emerging Christian churches, most wives were far younger than their husbands, which meant many widows were around. The New Testament writings indicate early Christian methods for maintaining widows, as well as disagreement as to whether remarriage was advisable. However, for centuries a wealthy widow was seen as a social anomaly, because she was independent from the authority of a male, and thus the community welcomed a second marriage. A poor widow, especially if childless, was a drain on the community.

Medieval Christian art presented a parallel between the woman carrying sticks and anticipating the death of her son and Christ carrying the wood of the cross for his death. Is this kind of biblical parallelism useful in our time?

The small portions of meal and oil are like the small portions of bread and wine that God continuously provides. The meager amount is enough for life.

Ideas for the Day

♦ "Money is a powerful tool. If you can give away your money, at least some of it, you have power over the tool. If you can't give any away, Money has power over you." The Rev. Luis Leon, rector of St. John's Church in Washington, D.C., says these words at the start of every annual giving season. The poor woman and the wealthy people in today's gospel have very different relationships with money. While annual giving is important for

Pentecost

Pentecost

keeping church doors open, how can giving also be taught as a spiritual practice?

♦ It is so easy to walk around disconnected from the Spirit. We follow the routine of our daily lives, getting up early, going to bed late, "eating the bread of anxious toil" and making ourselves sick with exhaustion. We buy nice clothes. We vie for positions of power within and outside of work. We seek to be recognized for our good deeds by other people. It is written that the Lord gives rest to his beloved. When one works for the Lord, one needs no recognition. We take refuge in the blessings that we have, and whatever we have more than what we need, we give away. We learn to live into the work we have, instead letting work dictate who we are. The work of Christ is the work of Christ no matter what profession we happen to be in.

♦ The offertory at the Eucharist expresses the theme of self-offering in today's lections. The call for total self-offering is reflected in the eucharistic prayers: "And here we offer and present unto thee, O Lord, our selves, our souls and bodies, to be a reasonable, holy, and living sacrifice unto thee." (BCP 336). For many congregations, this is the time of year for stewardship programs. How can you connect today's theme with how your congregation pledges to the mission and ministry of the church, and ultimately, to God?

Making Connections

Remember Admiral Ackbar from Star Wars, looking at the secretly-fully-operational Death Star? Imagine Jesus here doing something similar regarding the widow giving her last two coins to the upkeep of the Temple. "It's a trap!" It is tempting to romanticize this story, especially from what historically has been our tradition's place of upper-middle-class privilege. However, because Mark slides it in between Jesus' critique of the Pharisees' extortion of the poor, and his critique of the extravagant nature of the Temple— in context—it's hard to think he means to praise what is happening when the widow gives her last coin to the Temple. He's lamenting. There's nothing just about a poor woman turning over the last of what she has to live on to support a system that already has more than enough. The act of selfless giving is to be commended, but that act can be exploited and perverted by greedy people and institutions. God wants us to be generous; not to take advantage of generosity.

Engaging all Ages

A warning about ego in today's gospel: It is a good opportunity for us to reflect on when we have walked around in fine clothes, expecting the best seat or place of honor, making our offering public and a matter of pride. Yet the widow teaches us a profound way to approach God in worship—humbly, with an open and generous heart. During the offertory invite everyone to think honestly about what they offer. Distribute some sort of token to the children that they can hold while they consider how it represents what they would like to offer to God.

Hymns for the Day

The Hymnal 1982
O heavenly Word, eternal Light 63, 64
God moves in a mysterious way 677 (SC)
Praise, my soul, the King of heaven 410 (SC)
I'll praise my Maker while I've breath 429 (GR)
Sometimes a light surprises 667 (GR)
Come, thou fount of every blessing 686
Cross of Jesus, cross of sorrow 160
Jesus came, adored by angels 454
Lo! he comes with clouds descending 57, 58
Lord, enthroned in heavenly splendor 307
Once he came in blessing 53
As those of old their first fruits brought 705
Blest are the pure in heart 656
God of grace and God of glory 594, 595
Lord, make us servants of your peace 593
Not here for high and holy things 9
Take my life, and let it be 707

Lift Every Voice and Sing II
Come, thou fount of every blessing 111

Weekday Commemorations

Monday, November 12
Charles Simeon, Priest, 1836
Simeon's influence on Christian life was greater "than any primate," according to historian Thomas Macaulay. Simeon converted in 1779 while a student. His first communion depressed him, based as it was on a devotional tract, "The Whole Duty of Man." While preparing for communion before Easter, he read Bishop Thomas Wilson's *Instructions for the Lord's Supper*, wherein he recognized a truth: the law cannot make one righteous; only faith can enable a worthy communication. He experienced communion as the marriage of peace and exhilaration. That led to his

becoming leader of the evangelical movement in the Church of England and his founding of the Church Missionary Society. His sermons were consistently biblical, simple, and passionate.

Wednesday, November 14
Consecration of Samuel Seabury, First American Bishop, 1784

Seabury could not—would not—swear allegiance to the English crown. After the American revolution he had sailed for England in 1783 to seek episcopal consecration in England, but as an American citizen, he refused to swear. He turned to the Non-Juring bishops of the Episcopal Church in Scotland: he was consecrated on November 14, 1784, as the first American Bishop of the Episcopal Church. When he returned to these shores, he was recognized as Bishop of Connecticut, and, with Bishop William White, he helped organize the Episcopal Church at the General Convention of 1789. He kept his promise to persuade the American Church to adopt the Scottish form for the celebration of Holy Eucharist.

Friday, November 16
Margaret, Queen of Scotland, 1093

Scotland's most beloved saint was an English princess when King Malcolm married her about 1070. She devoted her queenly life to country, church, and family (this conscientious wife bore eight children). She considered practices among Scottish clergy to be old-fashioned and sloppy: Lent should start on Ash Wednesday not on the following Monday; the Lord's Day was for applying "ourselves only to prayers." She encouraged the founding of schools, hospitals, and orphanages, and she provided opportunity for her servants to worship. She influenced Malcolm, who trusted her political judgment, to reach out to isolated clans, although she was not successful in ending their bloody warfare. Malcom and Margaret rebuilt the monastery of Iona.

Saturday, November 17
Hugh, Bishop of Lincoln, 1200

Hugh, born about 1140 to a noble family in France, was a bishop of humility and tact. His lack of self-regard and his cheerful disposition made it difficult to oppose him in matters of Christian principle. About 1160, he joined the strict contemplative order of the Church, the Carthusians, and became procurator. Reluctantly, he accepted King Henry II's invitation to travel to England as prior of a new Carthusian foundation in Somerset; just as reluctantly, he accepted the King's appointment to the See of Lincoln in 1186. His people loved him because he championed the poor, the oppressed, the outcast (lepers and Jews). Even as bishop, Hugh lived by the strict discipline of his order.

Pentecost

The Twenty-Sixth Sunday after Pentecost: Proper 28

November 18, 2018

The coming day of glory and judgment is ushered in by a time of frightening upheaval and persecution.

Color Green

Preface Of the Lord's Day

Collect

Blessed Lord, who caused all holy scriptures to be written for our learning: Grant us so to hear them, read, mark, learn, and inwardly digest them, that we may embrace and ever hold fast the blessed hope of everlasting life, which you have given us in our Savior Jesus Christ; who lives and reigns with you and the Holy Spirit, one God, for ever and ever. Amen.

Readings and Psalm

1 Samuel 1:4-20 (SEMI-CONTINUOUS) or

In this Hebrew Bible reading, we hear the story of the birth of the prophet Samuel, on whom the guidance and direction of Israel waits. In distress because of her barrenness, Hannah makes fervent intercession before the Lord, pleading for a male child and promising that, should her hope be granted, the child will be set aside for the Lord's service. The priest Eli at first thinks Hannah is drunk, but when he perceives her faithfulness, prophesies that the Lord will fulfill her petition. Against all expectation Hannah becomes pregnant and delivers Samuel, who will become a nazarite, a prophet, and a great judge over Israel.

Daniel 12:1-3 (GOSPEL-RELATED)

In our Hebrew scripture lesson, Daniel is given a vision of the end of human history: after a period of great distress, some will be brought to their salvation and others to eternal disgrace. This was a time of persecution for Israel which took place two centuries before the life of Christ. This oracle of hope makes use of imagery common to apocalyptic visions. Evil will

mount up in a last desperate effort before Michael, Israel's patron angel, intervenes to bring justice. The names of all who will be saved are written in the book of life, which must for now remain sealed. In what is a new idea for Judaism, even the faithful dead will be raised to receive their reward.

Canticle: The Song of Hannah (1Sam. 2:1-10) or

The Song of Hannah portrays the mother of the prophet Samuel rejoicing in the Lord's provision.

Psalm 16

Contentment, refuge, and joy are found in the presence of the Lord. To the faithful one, God will show the path of life.

Hebrews 10:11-14 (15-18) 19-25

In this New Testament lesson, we learn that Christ's sacrifice, supplanting those of the early offerings of the people, is the effective provision for all time and all people, and he has become a new and living way offering access to God, who may now be freely approached. The Holy Spirit confirms within all disciples that what was promised by the prophets has now been fulfilled; God's eternal law is now inscribed on human hearts and minds. Believers who have been washed in baptism must continue in the faithful way, encouraging each other to love, good deeds, and frequent assembly.

Mark 13:1-8

In our gospel lesson, Jesus predicts the destruction of the temple, and tells of what is to come. One of the disciples expresses awe at the grandeur of the temple built by Herod. Then, while viewing the temple complex from the Mount of Olives, four of the disciples privately inquire as to when Jesus' prophecy might come to pass. Jesus responds that wars and imposters, political upheaval and natural disaster will come, but they are but birth pangs of the end.

Prayers of the People

Presider: *Holy God, our hearts exult in you as we present ourselves in your Temple to perform our vows and pour out our prayers in earnest supplication: Hear the petitions of your servants that we may find favor in your sight as we pray: Our heart exults in you, O God; our triumph song is lifted in you.*

Litanist: You have given your people the confidence to come before you through the new and living way that Jesus Christ has opened for us. Grant your Church grace to provoke one another to love and good deeds, not neglecting to meet together but encouraging one another in Christ.

My heart exults in you, O God;

> *my triumph song is lifted in you.*

Illumine the minds of the leaders of the world with the wisdom that does not heap up prideful words or speak in arrogance. Help us to remember that the future is in your hands and hidden from human view, so that we might place our faith less in our clouded understanding than in your divine guidance.

My heart exults in you, O God;

> *my triumph song is lifted in you.*

In this time of wars and rumors of war, earthquake and famine, and of nation rising against nation, we pray for the welfare of the world and for the faith to see that these troubles are but the birthpangs of your coming kingdom of peace.

My heart exults in you, O God;

> *my triumph song is lifted in you.*

Put your laws in the hearts of this community and write them on our minds, that we may approach one another with true hearts in full assurance of faith.

My heart exults in you, O God;

> *my triumph song is lifted in you.*

You raise the poor from the dust and lift the needy from the ash heap: Hear our prayers for those who call to you, especially ___.

With a glad heart we give thanks for ___.

We commend to you those who have departed before us, especially ___. Help us to remember that in your love, all of us, those here and those gone before us, rest in hope. My heart exults in you, O God;

> *my triumph song is lifted in you.*

Presider: *Loving God, you have inscribed your holy will upon our hearts and minds: Grant us grace to hold fast to the confession of our hope, without wavering, in the assurance of your faithfulness, through Jesus Christ our Savior, who lives and reigns with you and the Holy Spirit, one God, for ever and ever.* **Amen.**

Images in the Readings

The Bible occasionally uses labor pains as an image for the suffering that can be endured since it births new life. Although some world religions, such as Buddhism, offer advice in light of perpetually recurrent suffering, Christianity, like biblical Judaism, trusts that God will finally bring an end to suffering. Labor will be over, and a newborn will live.

Although many contemporary Christians believe in the immortality of the soul, the New Testament instead inherits from late biblical Judaism the doctrine of the resurrection of the body. Christ is the first to experience this bodily resurrection, but at the end of time all the dead will receive new life to experience everlasting joy or everlasting contempt. The emphasis on a renewed body reflects the Jewish idea that a human person is a body, rather than the Greek worldview, according to which a soul inhabits a body for a time. For Judaism and Christianity, the body God created is so good that God will recreate it when all death is over.

In the several centuries before Christ, Judaism had been influenced by Zoroastrianism, which speculated about many types of supernatural beings. In Jewish angelology, God had four primary angelic assistants, who, according to some of the pseudopigraphal writings, held up the throne of God: Gabriel, who was to announce the end of the world; Michael, who was the conqueror of Satan; Raphael, who healed the sick and protected travelers; and Uriel, who punished evildoers. Many medieval artists depicted the Archangel Michael as victorious over the monster Satan or tumultuous battle scenes.

Ideas for the Day

- ♦ We often avoid the Book of Hebrews, in part because it is bloody. In North America, we tend to shy away from texts about blood. Not all of the church has that luxury. Jon Sobrino, a theologian in El Salvador, survived the assassination of his bishop and his theological colleagues in the

Pentecost

Salvadoran Civil War. He describes his friends as "Jesus martyrs" because they lived lives committed to Jesus' liberating way and, for their witness, died bloody deaths like Jesus did. How does our own experience of faithful suffering change how we read the bloody texts?

♦ Apocalyptic literature is heard during this pre-Advent and the Advent season. This style of literature uses poetry and rich imagery to emphasize that suffering and struggle lead to God's final intervention at the end of the present age. God will come to usher in the kingdom of God, a time when God's full sovereignty is known as "on earth as in heaven." Apocalyptic literature gives hope to a church under persecution, for the struggles of the present moment are a sign that God's reign is indeed coming. Persecution and suffering are not the end, but the beginning. God's kingdom brigns the promise of judgment and salvation. It may arrive at any time, so the church must always be ready. See *An Outline of the Faith*, "The Christian Hope" section (BCP 861-862).

♦ May I continue to follow the path you have made known to me. May I not be deterred by the events of my time. My journey can not be defined by a political system or form of government. I will not be lead astray by those who are confused and by those whose spirits are dead within them. The kingdom of God will rise above and beyond that which people build. Not skyscrapers, space stations, nor underground cities can capture the majesty of God.

Making Connections

In the aftermath of Hurricane Sandy, the pictures that affected me the strongest were not of washed out homes or crying children. They were of flooded subway tunnels and stalled trains. In the three years I lived in New York City, the subway system seemed to me to be the most permanent, inexorable aspect of the greatest city I knew. To suddenly see it devastated was disorienting in a particular way. We humans like the illusion of permanence. We love to construct things that we believe will endure the test of time and outlive our mortal lives—whether it be a transportation system, buildings, or the Episcopal liturgy we adore so much. However, Jesus reminds us that in fact, nothing we construct will endure forever. Only God is forever; everything else changes, regardless of our desires. And yet, in God, we are held steady in the divine eternal changelessness, even as the world around us moves.

Engaging all Ages

Mark offers profound words in today's gospel, "This is but the beginning of the birth pangs." So much is changing in our world and in the church. Maybe you have recently introduced changes in your worship style or formation programs. We may long for a "sign," as did the disciples, so we can be prepared. Today, encourage worshippers to find comfort in the familiar and look eagerly to the new. Our "sign" may be that we change together as we embrace a transformed community. Embrace the leadership of youth in today's worship. They lead us fearlessly into imagination and change.

Hymns for the Day

The Hymnal 1982
Help us, O Lord, to learn 628
Lord, be thy word my rule 626
O Christ, the Word Incarnate 632
Word of God, come down on earth 633
Christ, the fair glory of the holy angels 282, 283 (GR)
Judge eternal, throned in splendor 596 (GR)
O day of God, draw nigh 600, 601
The Lord will come and not be slow 462 (GR)
Come, thou fount of every blessing 686
Help us, O Lord, to learn 628
Lord, enthroned in heavenly splendor 307
O day of radiant gladness 48
We the Lord's people, heart and voice uniting 51
All my hope on God is founded 665
All who love and serve your city 570, 571
Lord Christ, when first thou cam'st to earth 598
O God of every nation 607
Thy kingdom come, O God! 613

Wonder, Love, and Praise
Signs of endings all around us 721 (GR)

Lift Every Voice and Sing II
My Lord, what a morning 13 (GR)
Steal away 103 (GR)
Come, thou fount of every blessing 111
Jesus, we want to meet 81
We have come into His house 245

Weekday Commemorations

Monday, November 19
Elizabeth, Princess of Hungary, 1231
Born in 1207 in Bratislava, the daughter of King Andrew II of Hungary married Louis IV in 1221, then bore three children. Elizabeth, who had always been concerned with the poor and ill, was attracted

to the Franciscans, who arrived in the Wartburg in 1223 and directed her spiritually. Louis allowed her to spend her dowry for almsgiving. In 1226, during a famine and epidemic, she sold her jewels to establish a hospital, which she supplied by opening the royal granaries. When Louis died in 1227, the court opposed her "extravagances," forcing her to leave. She eventually donned the habit of the Franciscans. With Louis of France, she shares the title of patron of the Third Order of St. Francis.

Tuesday, November 20
Edmund, King of East Anglia, 870

At 15, Edmund ascended the throne of East Anglia and ruled as a Christian for 15 years before Danish armies invaded England in 870. The Danes burned monasteries and churches, among other murderous atrocities. The leaders confronted Edmund and demanded he acknowledge their supremacy and forbid the practice of Christianity. Edmund refused. His army fought bravely against the Danes, but King Edmund was eventually captured; according to the account by Dunstan, Archbishop of Canterbury 90 years later, Edmund was tortured, beaten, shot with arrows, and beheaded. His remains were enshrined in a Benedictine monastery now called Bury St. Edmunds; this place of pilgrimage honors a saint steadfast in faith and to his people.

Friday, November 23
Clement, Bishop of Rome, c. 100

Little is known of the life of Clement and what is known is contested. He is said to be the third bishop of Rome, after Peter and Linus, or the fourth after Jerome. Clement, it is also said, was consecrated by Peter himself. Clement ruled from 88 to about 100. As a disciple of the apostles, he was active in the early church. He is generally regarded as having written a letter about 96 from the Church in Rome to the Church in Corinth. A younger group at Corinth had deposed the elder clergy, jeopardizing the Church. In response, Clement organized a hierarchical structure of Church authority, interchanging the terms "bishop" and "presbyter." This letter was rediscovered in 1628.

Pentecost

Thanksgiving Day

November 22, 2018

The church recognizes the traditional Thanksgiving holiday as a holy day for our land, life, and heritage.

Color   White

Preface   Trinity Sunday

Collect

Almighty and gracious Father, we give you thanks for the fruits of the earth in their season and for the labors of those who harvest them. Make us, we pray, faithful stewards of your great bounty, for the provision of our necessities and the relief of all who are in need, to the glory of your Name; through Jesus Christ our Lord, who lives and reigns with you and the Holy Spirit, one God, now and for ever. Amen.

Readings and Psalm

Joel 2:21-27

In our lesson from Hebrew scripture, the prophet speaks words of reassurance to the people. God will address the earth and its creatures, the orchards and the harvest, making certain a time of great abundance and gladness. All plague and famine are in the past. The Lord will be present to the people of God, and they will never again be put to shame.

Psalm 126

A song of hope and joy sung to the Lord, who restores the fortunes of God's people.

1 Timothy 2:1-7

In this lesson, disciples are called upon to pray for all, including political rulers, so that Christians may lead peaceable and moral lives. It is God's will that everyone should find salvation. Jesus is the mediator between the one God and humanity; he has sacrificed himself for the freedom of all. Paul has been appointed an apostle to make his saving work known to the Gentiles. During this period, the newborn Christian

movement was a tiny part of society, and Christians felt that they needed peaceful conditions to spread the gospel. They usually took a positive view of the functions of the state in maintaining peace and justice.

Matthew 6:25-33

In our gospel, Jesus urges his followers to give their allegiance to God alone and not to be anxious about life's necessities. There are no two ways; a fundamental decision must be made between worshiping God or Mammon, the god of money. Individuals who trust in God need have no anxious worry about the material goods of life. Those who put their faith in God's reign will find they have all they need.

Prayers of the People

Presider: *We give thanks to you, our Gracious God, for the abundance of creation, for the gifts of the earth, and for your benevolent care for all life: Hear our grateful prayers as we come to you, saying: "God has done great things for us, and we are glad indeed."*

Litanist: Our good and generous God, you have given yourself to the Church through your Son, Jesus Christ our Savior: Free us from worry or anxiety that we may be your thankful and eucharistic people, sharing your abundant love for all creation.

God has done great thing for us,

and we are glad indeed.

Wise and Wonderful One, hear our supplications, prayers, intercessions, and thankgivings for all who are in high positions: Guide them with your wisdom, that we may lead quiet and peaceable lives in all goodness and dignity.

God has done great thing for us,

and we are glad indeed.

Compassionate One, listen to those throughout the world who sow with tears or who live with any form of anxiety or threat: Comfort them with your gracious generosity, restore their fortunes, and establish them securely so they may never again be put to shame.

God has done great things for us,

and we are glad indeed.

Loving One, bless this community: Feed us with your abundance like the birds of the air and clothe us in beauty like the grass of the field.

God has done great thing for us,

and we are glad indeed.

Gracious One, we bring to your loving presence all who suffer or who need our intercession, especially ___.

On this day of thanksgiving and praise, we offer our prayers of deep gratitude, especially for ___.

Bring into the feast of your heavenly banquet all who have died, especially ___.

God has done great things for us,

and we are glad indeed.

Presider: *With thankful hearts we offer our prayers to you, O God, the source of all that is: Grant us grace to strive first for your kingdom and your righteousness, and give us all things necessary for our flourishing and service, through your Son Jesus Christ, who with you and the Holy Spirit, lives and reigns, for ever and ever.* **Amen.**

Images in the Readings

The birds of the air and the lilies of the field are images of nature for which God continually cares. In traditional Christian doctrine, "creation" was not a single action in the distant past but is an ongoing daily activity of the Creator. The Joel reading includes a welcome word from God to even the soil and animals, which receive their life from the Creator. The fruit trees and rain are seen, not as natural phenomena, but as gifts from God. These images help move our gratitude away from merely personal conditions and possessions toward the created earth itself.

Accustomed as we are to the idea of the benevolence of the Creator, we may miss what would have been heard in the first century as surprising language, that God is a heavenly Father. Both ancient paganism and contemporary capitalism have little room for God as the one who provides all that is good.

Perhaps Joel was referring to an actual locust plague, and perhaps an enemy army was likened to locusts that destroy everything in their path. In either case, Joel includes the biblical claim that even harmful things have come from God, who is the single power in the universe.

According to the Bible, humans do not merit any goodness from God on their own. Rather, we need Jesus Christ as a mediator through whose intercession we receive blessings from God. This biblical idea balances, or even conflicts, with that of God as a universally available father of all, an understanding that undergirds much of America's civil religion.

Ideas for the Day

- Thanksgiving can take a great deal of diplomacy. A few years ago Saturday Night Live aired a sketch where a family was bitterly divided by politics, attitudes about race, and sexual orientation. But everyone comes together to lip-synch a song by the pop star Adele. Politics and religion often divide us. When they don't, small family disputes can still erupt around the table. In our Baptismal Covenant we promise to "seek and serve Christ in all persons." This even includes those family members we struggle with. If all else fails, maybe your family needs a lip sync battle . . .
- Simple living, with respect for each other and the earth's resources, is a way to be thankful stewards of our blessings so that all may share them. God's creation has been given to us as a sacred trust.
- The meaning of Eucharist is Thanksgiving.
- We must give thanks and praise to the Lord for all of the blessings that have been bestowed on us. It is also important that we not be blind to those blessings. Let us not take for granted the resources we have access to. Whether they be physical, emotional, or material resources, let us recognize what we have been given and be grateful. It is easy to think that we have been given certain resources because we are well liked and favored. However, the reality is we have been given these resources not solely for our benefit. When we live fully in ministry, we learn to live with only what we need and to share any additional resources with others.

Pentecost

Making Connections

If you've been an Episcopalian for any length of time, then you've heard small children sing "Seek Ye First" at some point. It is one of the modern classics that we teach to children at an early age. And what better idea to pass on to the youngest churchgoers than the idea that God provides for us when we pursue the will of God? Jesus does not tell the disciples that they will always be rich, or comfortable, or even secure. What he tells them is that when they prioritize doing the will of God and seeking the kingdom, then God will ensure that they have enough. Once we get our priorities in the right order, then God takes care of the rest.

Engaging all Ages

Invite members of the congregation to bring one of their serving dishes (either empty or containing food to be served) and place it on the altar to receive a blessing during worship. Also invite worshippers to bring an offering of food that can be given to a local shelter, food pantry, or soup kitchen after Thanksgiving, when their shelves may be empty following the holiday.

Hymns for the Day

The Hymnal 1982
All people that on earth do dwell 377, 378
As those of old their first fruits brought 705
Come, ye thankful people, come 290
For the beauty of the earth 416
From all that dwell below the skies 380
Glory, love, and praise, and honor 300
Now thank we all our God 396, 397
Praise to God, immortal praise 288
We gather together to ask the Lord's blessing 433
We plow the fields, and scatter 291
When all thy mercies, O my God 415
For the fruit of all creation 424
I sing the almighty power of God 398
Let us, with a gladsome mind 389
O all ye works of God, now come 428
Seek ye first the kingdom of God 711
Sometimes a light surprises 667
Holy Father, great Creator 368
To God with gladness sing 399
By gracious powers so wonderfully sheltered 695, 696
Commit thou all that grieves thee 669
Jesus, all my gladness 701
Joyful, joyful, we adore thee 376

Wonder, Love, and Praise
Let all creation bless the Lord 885
O all ye works of God, now come 884

Lift Every Voice and Sing II
Give thanks to the Lord for he is good 93
God is so good 214

The Last Sunday after Pentecost: Christ the King

November 25, 2018

This day is often referred to as the Sunday of Christ the King or Reign of Christ. "Jesus is Lord" (the earliest Christian creed) means that Jesus stands above all other earthly power and authority.

Color   White

Preface   Of the Lord's Day

Collect

Almighty and everlasting God, whose will it is to restore all things in your well-beloved Son, the King of kings and Lord of lords: Mercifully grant that the peoples of the earth, divided and enslaved by sin, may be freed and brought together under his most gracious rule; who lives and reigns with you and the Holy Spirit, one God, now and for ever. Amen.

Readings and Psalm

2 Samuel 23:1–7 (SEMI-CONTINUOUS) or

From the Hebrew scriptures, we hear a lyric poem that celebrates the Davidic monarchy. God has established David's throne. David is in turn to make himself a blessing to the people, ruling justly and in the fear of the Lord. The godless will be overturned, and the faithful ruler, it is implied, will be the tool for their unseating. God's covenant with the just ruler, David, is an everlasting covenant.

Daniel 7:9-10, 13-14 (GOSPEL-RELATED)

With striking imagery, this reading presents a scene of judgment in heaven and a vision of one like a son of man coming to rule in an everlasting kingdom. The ancient figure is God, and the one who appears like a human seems to be symbolic of the future people of Israel. The imagery derives from pre-Israelitic mythology and once was used to picture the beginning of a reign of a new ruler. Christians later understood the vision to be a prefiguration of Jesus' exaltation and role in judgment as the divine Son of Man.

Psalm 132:1–13 (14–19) or

A petition to the Lord to remember the promise to David of a son to reign after him and for a lasting kingdom.

Psalm 93

God reigns, the Lord of all creation. God has established the earth and subdued the great waters.

Revelation 1:4b-8

In this lesson, the revelation made known to a disciple named John begins with a greeting from the everlasting God, from the seven spirits which worship God, and from Jesus Christ, the firstborn from the dead. Jesus, who continues to love his disciples, is praised as the faithful witness whose sacrifice has formed a royal household, a new priestly people to serve God. Soon he will come, like the one foreseen by the prophet Daniel, on the clouds of heaven. He now rules over all earthly kings, and God, the Alpha and Omega, the first and the last, is sovereign over all.

John 18:33-37

In the gospel, as his passion draws near, Jesus comes face to face with the Roman governor and seeks to explain the nature of his kingship. It has been suggested to Pilate that Jesus pretends to be some form of political ruler. But Jesus' kingship does not use the force of this world's weapons. Pilate then realizes that Jesus' kingship must be of a different order. The sovereignty of Jesus is found in his witness to divine truth. He reveals God's purpose and character, and those who share in this truth hear his voice.

Prayers of the People

Presider: *Almighty One, the source and giver of life, the Alpha and Omega, who is and who was and who is to come: You have poured out your divine life into humanity through Christ, to whom is given dominion and glory and authority; let our prayers come into your holy presence with reconciling and healing power, as we pray: To Christ who loves us and freed us; to Christ be glory and dominion forever.*

Litanist: You have united us to your Son Jesus Christ, the faithful witness, the firstborn of the dead, and the ruler of the kings of the earth: Let your priests be clothed with righteousness and your faithful people sing with joy, that your Church may belong to the truth and listen to Christ's voice.

To Christ who loves us and freed us;

> ***to Christ be glory and dominion forever.***

You reign in transcendent splendor over all rulers and authorities, all powers and principalities: Let your dream and hope for your creation give vision to our nation, its leaders, and to all who hold authority in the world, that all the earth may be reconciled under your reign of love.

To Christ who loves us and freed us;

> ***to Christ be glory and dominion forever.***

The kingdom of our Christ is without boundary or limitation: We pray for everyone throughout the world who looks for help from above, relief from suffering, liberation from oppression, and hope for the future.

To Christ who loves us and freed us;

> ***to Christ be glory and dominion forever.***

Your reign, O God, is like the sun rising in a cloudless sky, a morning gleaming after rain on the grassy land: Bless this community with your grace and peace, that we may be a kingdom of priests who serve each other in your name.

To Christ who loves us and freed us;

> ***to Christ be glory and dominion forever.***

The spirit of the Lord speaks and the Rock of Israel is our hope: Be present in the lives of those who need you, as we intercede on behalf of ___.

We praise and thank you for the manifestation of your presence and power among us, especially for ___.

Jesus Christ is the firstborn of the dead. Bring all humanity into your divine life; and welcome those who come to you, especially ___.

To Christ who loves us and freed us;

> ***to Christ be glory and dominion forever.***

Presider: Almighty and transcendent God, your glory fills all creation and your authority extends beyond time and forever: Let your Spirit open our lives to your grace and truth, that we may always see your Christ at his coming, to whom be glory and dominion forever and ever. **Amen.**

Images in the Readings

Calling this Sunday Christ the King may elevate that image above all others. Currently on the world scene, some nations have rejected monarchies, some maintain figurehead monarchs, and some, while not using the term *king*, maintain heads of state with absolute, even ruthless, power over the people. The Bible promises that God's power and majesty differ radically from the reign of human monarchs. Thus we need to use the image of king as correcting the image of king. Several hymns do a splendid job of playing the image against itself. As an example of how God's reign differs from that of human monarchs, the baptized saints receive riches and power from God. Some churches prefer the phrase "the Reign of Christ" as stressing Christ's activity rather than status: unfortunately, English has the problem of the homonym "rain." A welcome alternative is "the Sovereign Christ."

It might be interesting were Christian art to depict God as a king with Daniel's imagery: not an old European man but rather one with white clothing and hair, a mouth issuing forth fire, the throne a flaming chariot, attended by a hundred thousand worshipers.

Religions use the word priests to designate those who are authorized to appear before God in order to plead divine blessing for everyone else. We are an entire kingdom of priests, serving God and our neighbor.

Ideas for the Day

+ Christ the King is a relatively new feast day. Pope Pius the XI instituted the observance in 1925, and only since 1970 has it been celebrated on the last day of the liturgical year. The feast was instituted because the pope was worried about growing secularism. The pope couldn't stop the trend. Secularization has accelerated through the twentieth and into the twenty-first century. As our world grows less churched, saying "Jesus is Lord" may become again, as it was in the early church, a radical and political statement.

- We build on, even in the midst of those who destroy and tear down. When we build empowered by the Holy Spirit, no one can tear it down. Though our body be persecuted our spirit will live on. Our spirit will join with those who have gone on before. We will create one long procession, marching through the passages of time, raising our voices in praise. No person can kill the spirit that lives within us. No person can destroy the legacy of love and peace established by our Lord and Savior, Jesus Christ. Our story will be told and retold for generations to come.

- Some of the traditions associated with worship in the Episcopal Church have their origins in the royal court: for example, purple, the color for Advent (in some congregations) and Lent, was the color associated with royalty and became linked to the coming of Christ as king.

- "Jesus is Lord," means that Jesus stands above all other earthly power and authority. All through history and into the present moment, choosing God above earthly authority has caused persecution and conflict in the life of the Church. The congregation and wider church must witness always to the authority of Jesus Christ, realizing that there will be times when conflict will be the direct result of such witness.

Making Connections

It is a fitting contradiction that on the Sunday we recall the kingship of Christ, we also read a text about his trial and sentencing. Ironically, the feast of Christ the King came into being as the Roman Catholic Church started to worry about a decline in its secular might. As the Holy Roman Empire's fortunes decreased, the pope wanted to reemphasize who was really in charge, so he began the feast of Christ the King. Today, we don't worry so much about whether the church maintains a large enough standing army. However, the lingering concern over our place in the world persists. And it is only fitting that as we move into the frenetic Christmas season, Christ reminds us that the kingdom he calls us to is not one that this world can measure, but one where earthly glory doesn't matter, and a crucified criminal reigns from on high.

Engaging all Ages

The liturgical year and Ordinary Time conclude. Green is put aside, and we prepare for a new year with the purity of white. Jesus reaffirms who he is; we reaffirm the truth of the king in whom we believe. Children may need help with this image of a crownless king. As they understand that Jesus always tells the truth, we follow their example of trust. Affirm that all ages are included in Jesus' invitation to belong to the truth and listen to his voice. Together, bid farewell to the year that has passed as you express gratitude for community life.

Hymns for the Day

The Hymnal 1982
Alleluia! sing to Jesus! 460, 461 (vs 1, 3-5)
All praise to thee, for thou, O King divine 477
Christ is the King! O friends upraise 614
Jesus shall reign where'er the sun 544
King of glory, King of peace 382
Lead on, O King eternal 555
Ye servants of God, your Master proclaim 535
All hail the power of Jesus' Name 450, 451 (SC)
Hail to the Lord's Anointed 616 (SC)
O God of Bethel, by whose hand 709 (SC)
Ancient of Days, who sittest throned in glory 363 (GR)
Come, thou almighty King 365 (GR)
Immortal, invisible, God only wise 423 (GR)
Jesus came, adored by angels 454 (GR)
Lo! he comes with clouds descending 57, 58 (GR)
The God of Abraham praise 401 (GR)
At the Name of Jesus 435
Crown him with many crowns 494
Draw nigh and take the Body of the Lord 327, 328
Jesus came, adored by angels 454
Let all mortal flesh keep silence 324
Lo! he comes with clouds descending 57, 58
Lord, enthroned in heavenly splendor 307
Rejoice, the Lord is King! 481
The head that once was crowned with thorns 483
Hail, thou once despised Jesus! 495
Lord Christ, when first thou cam'st to earth 598
My song is love unknown 458

Lift Every Voice and Sing II
He is King of kings, he is Lord of lords 96
Ride on, King Jesus 97

Pentecost

Weekday Commemorations

Wednesday, November 28
*James Otis Sargent Huntington, Priest
and Monk, 1935*

Huntington, committed to active ministry, based in the
spiritual life, founded the first permanent Episcopal
monastic community for men in the United States on
those commissions. He was born in Boston (1854),
graduated from Harvard, and studied theology in Syracuse, New York. He was ordained deacon and priest
by his father, the first Bishop of Central New York.
Upon receiving a call to religious life, he resolved to
found an indigenous American community. Beginning
his common life at Holy Cross Mission on New York's
Lower East Side, Huntington made his life vow on
November 25, 1884. He increased his social witness to
the Church by working with immigrants and for the
single-tax and labor union movements.

Friday, November 30
*Kamehameha and Emma, King and Queen
of Hawai'i, 1864, 1885*

Within a year of ascending the throne in 1855, King
Kamehameha IV and Queen Emma (each 20 years
old) solicited funds to build a hospital in response to
a smallpox epidemic. The people of Hawai'i, more
accustomed to pomp than to humility in royalty,
came to revere Emma and Kamehameha. In 1860,
the king and queen petitioned the Bishop of Oxford
to send missionaries to establish the Anglican
Church in Hawai'i; the priests arrived in 1862 to
confirm the queen and king. Kamehameha translated
the Book of Common Prayer and the Hymnal. He
died a year after his little boy. Emma declined to
rule alone but chose to end her days in a life of good
works.

INDEX OF SEASONAL RITES

Index of Seasonal Rites

CPSIA information can be obtained
at www.ICGtesting.com
Printed in the USA
LVOW06s2115181017
552864LV00035B/524/P